Critical Theory in Political Practice

Critical Theory in Political Practice

Stephen T. Leonard

PRINCETON UNIVERSITY PRESS

PRINCETON, NEW JERSEY

Copyright © 1990 by Princeton University Press
Published by Princeton University Press, 41 William Street,
Princeton, New Jersey 08540
In the United Kingdom: Princeton University Press, Oxford

Library of Congress Cataloging-in-Publication Data

Leonard, Stephen T., 1954–
Critical theory in political practice / Stephen T. Leonard.
Includes bibliographical references.
1. Critical theory. 2. Political sociology. I. Title.
HM24.L447   1991   306.2—dc20   90-33736

ISBN 0-691-07840-8

This book has been composed in Linotron Primer

Princeton University Press books are printed on acid-free paper,
and meet the guidelines for permanence and durability of the
Committee on Production Guidelines for Book Longevity of the
Council on Library Resources

Printed in the United States of America by Princeton University Press,
Princeton, New Jersey

10 9 8 7 6 5 4 3 2 1

FOR OUR CHILDREN

A fronte praecipitium a tergo lupi

Contents

Preface and Acknowledgments

THIS BOOK is about critical social theory. So much has been written about critical theory in recent years that it might seem little remains to be said. But I hope this book provides something in the way of novel and useful insights into what critical theory is, and what it should be. These are high, perhaps even inflated, expectations, and I have no illusions about what I will be able to accomplish here.

Whatever readers may find novel and useful in these pages will be, I think, less a function of any original insights I have to offer than a feature of the way I have brought together a diverse body of extant arguments. I began this project with the conviction critical social theory is a viable and necessary idea, and an equally strong conviction that the idea had not yet been realized. I was also convinced there was a kernel of insight in much of the contemporary discourse of critical theory, whether "modernist" or "postmodernist," that might be recovered so that the idea of a critical theory might be realized. The first part of the book documents these convictions. In the course of my intellectual travels, I was also exposed to a number of social theories that seemed to realize—and enrich—these insights. These theories are seldom cast as "critical theories," and they are more often treated in the context of discussions of the social and political movements with which they are associated. But I found that by exploring the theoretical and philosophical foundations of these theories, they could be plausibly reconstructed as examples of critical theory—examples that showed how critical theory might make good its political intentions. The second part of this book documents these explorations.

What emerges from all of these discussions is, I hope, a way of rethinking critical theory. Some readers, like some of those who have read prepublication drafts of this work, may ask who it is I hope will engage in this "rethinking of critical theory," and how I understand my own role in this. These are important questions, if only because two of the central conclusions I draw in this book are that (1) all social discourse is historically and contextually specific, which in essence means that it originates in and is addressed (even if only implicitly) to a specific set of social and political interests; and (2) that any potentially effective critique must be self-conscious about *whose* interests it serves (in part) by being attentive to the idiom in which it is cast.

If one thing is clear about this book, it is that it is an academic discourse first and foremost—a fact that appears to fly in the face of my plea that critical social theory must be more than an esoteric and purely academic ideal. I have recognized this tension ever since I began this project—indeed, since I began my academic career. My political inclinations are the result of a variety of factors: I came to know the limits and complexities of "dominant discourse" from regular dinnertime "critiques" with my parents, from four sisters who never let me forget the privileges I enjoyed as a male, from being a white, Anglo-Saxon Protestant in a community in which most of my contact was with blacks, Jews, and Catholics, and in a short but eye-opening stint as an auto assembly-line worker. But college, graduate school, and now professorial status meant a significant change in my context, and with this change has come a shift in my own discourse.

I now see that these experiences (and a host of others) are what led me to this project. In "critical theory" I saw the possibility of reconciling my political commitments and my position as a member of the (white, male, "first-world") academic community. What motivated me to criticize "modernist" and "postmodernist" critical theory, and seek out examples of "critical theories in practice," is that I saw the former as a limited, and the latter as a more promising, way of understanding not only the relationship between theory and practice, but between theorist and audience. (The autobiographical thread should be obvious.)

Making clear these relationships occupies much of my attention here, and it also defines two potential audiences for this book. By discussing the metatheoretical problems of critical social theory my aim is to (1) clarify for my students and colleagues who know little about critical theory what this form of inquiry is and what it should be, and (2) invite proponents and students of critical theory to reflect on their self-understandings and arguments.

I have no doubt that these are the two audiences who will comprise most of my readership. But there is a third audience I hope to reach as well. However abstract and esoteric my discussions may often appear, they are informed by a desire to reach out to those who are engaged in the kind of day-to-day empowerment struggles in which "critical theories in practice" purport to be embedded. By critically reconstructing what I believe to be the shared philosophical foundations of these several discourses, I hope to show that these practical political struggles are, or can be, informed by a coherent, defensible understanding of knowledge and human identity. This understanding, moreover, is one that both preserves the specificity of these struggles while identifying the extent to which their political aims overlap.

Thus, I hope to promote political solidarity while preserving plurality, even if I do so almost exclusively in terms of grand philosophical issues.

I have no illusions that most of those who comprise this third audience will probably never read this book. The very nature of my project makes it so. That it is concerned more with theory—or theories about theory—than with practice is something I cannot deny. I have tried to make this discourse more accessible to a wider audience, perhaps with only partial success, if any at all. Maybe my best hope is that I have explicated some analytical insights that might allow some—even if they are "only" theorists—to begin to bridge the gap between critical theory and concrete, historically contingent political struggles. But even if this were the case, then I would have made some step, however small, however indirect, toward reaching out to those who now suffer damaged lives.

. . .

My confessions aside, I want to thank those whose support, guidance, and criticism, made this undertaking possible. I owe a special debt to my teacher and friend, Terry Ball, who encouraged me when I was a fledgling theorist, and who read and re-read what now seems like endless drafts of this manuscript when it was still a dissertation. Richard Leppert and Naomi Scheman also provided much needed guidance throughout the dissertation phase. Mary Dietz taught, and continues to teach me about what it means to be a feminist. Jim Farr renewed my energy when it was flagging with his intellectual and personal support. Mike Lienesch carefully read, edited, and criticized the manuscript, and pushed me to bring it to fruition. Jonathan Hartlyn provide helpful suggestions for the chapter on dependency theory. Issac Balbus, David Held, and Daniel Levine all helped me rethink my arguments in their role as readers for Princeton University Press. Sandy Thatcher, Margaret Case, and Marylyn Marshall guided the manuscript through the editorial and publishing process. The shortcomings and deficiencies of this book are, of course, my responsibility.

Finally, special thanks to my wife, Kristin, for her love and friendship, and to my children, Braden and Kendal, for constantly reminding me of the wonders and joys that life can hold. This book is dedicated to them, and to all children. I hope they may live to see the day when critical theory is no longer needed.

General Introduction

IN THE social sciences and humanities it has become fashionable to speak the language of "critical theory." In most instances, the idea of a critical theory has been advanced in opposition to prevailing disciplinary orthodoxies. Orthodoxy in many of these disciplines has meant a commitment to "the advancement of knowledge," which is usually understood as the articulation of timeless truths, objective facts, unmediated readings of texts, causal explanation and prediction, and the like—in short, a commitment to simply understanding the world as it really is. Critical theory, by contrast, has usually meant showing that the notion of understanding the world as it really is is a philosophically incoherent, theoretically deficient, and politically pernicious ideal. The social disciplines, according to advocates of critical theory, must play a role in changing the world—and changing it in ways that can help "emancipate" those on the margins of society by providing them with insights and intellectual tools they can use to empower themselves.

The figure who looms large in the background of this conception of social and political inquiry is Karl Marx. With his proclamation that "The philosophers have only *interpreted* the world, in various ways; the point, however, is to *change* it" (Marx 1978: 145),[1] Marx not only gave impetus to an intellectual self-understanding that finds its expression today in the idea of critical theory, but did so in the context of a philosophical and theoretical project charged with—and informed by—radical political concerns. Indeed, it would not be farfetched to argue that any sort of social inquiry that claims to be, or can be characterized as, a critical theory, owes its title to Marx.

This debt notwithstanding, contemporary critical theory cannot be unproblematically called "Marxist." Marx may have served as the most important founding figure of critical theory, but the development of the idea of a critical theory did not end with him. For Marx's critical theory was not entirely free from potential difficulties, and in the intervening years since he lived, these difficulties have themselves become sources of philosophical, theoretical, and political dispute.

One trajectory of development made Marxism over into a kind of social theory that appeared to be at odds with his emancipatory inten-

---

[1] All italics in quoted passages throughout this book originate in the cited texts unless otherwise noted.

tions. Indeed, Marxism itself became a form of dogmatic orthodoxy in many regimes that claimed to embody the practical realization of his arguments. This tradition is usually identified with the appellation of "Marxism," and the kind of ossified dogmatism characteristic of this tradition is one reason why critical theory today is not easily described as Marxist.

Another trajectory of development was guided by an interest in preserving Marx's useful insights in a way that could render them relevant in the changed historical conditions of twentieth century bureaucratic capitalism, but without falling prey to the ossification of Marxist orthodoxy. "Western Marxism" is the umbrella term often used in referring to this alternative; the "critical theory" of the Frankfurt School with its heir apparent, Jürgen Habermas, is often cited as the most influential school in this tradition. This form of critical theory has also become known as "modernist." It shared with Marx a commitment to the idea that modern society contained within it the possibility of overcoming domination and oppression in all its forms, even while it distanced itself from Marx's (and orthodox Marxism's) tendency to equate this possibility with the revolution of the working class.

"Modernist" critical theory had long dominated discussions of what critical theory was and should be. It no longer does. In fact, it is only in reference to a third trajectory of development in critical theory that calling the critical theory of the Frankfurt School and Habermas "modernist" even makes sense. This third movement, "postmodernist" critical theory, is like modernist critical theory in its commitment to a conception of social theory as politically engaged. It also shares with modernist critical theory an opposition to disciplinary orthodoxies and orthodox Marxism. But it indicts, sometimes explicitly, more often implicitly, the idea that modernity contains within itself the potential for human emancipation, hence its title. The most influential figures in this tradition have been French, and it was Michel Foucault who emerged as its most prominent proponent.

The extent to which these figures, and the "modernist" and "postmodernist" movements they represent, have shaped the contemporary discourse of intellectuals committed to critical theory is difficult to overstate. No discussion of social inquiry today can ignore the insights that critical theory has articulated in its criticisms of prevailing disciplinary orthodoxies. It may even be argued, as I shall do in this book, that critical theory embodies the most perspicacious extant understanding of what social inquiry is and must be. But no discussion of critical theory itself can ignore the ways in which its modernist and postmodernist versions have failed to realize their own stated aims. For while modernist and postmodernist critical theory may have established good reasons for seeing that social and political theory must be committed to social and political emancipation, neither has been able to make good this commitment.

This last point is not one that has come from outside critical theory. Rather, it is a criticism common to many scholars who are sympathetic to the idea of critical theory. Sometimes these criticisms are lodged by advocates of modernist critical theory against postmodernism, sometimes the reverse has been the case, and sometimes they have been internal to each tradition.

When taken together, however, these criticisms suggest that there is a curious tension in much of the contemporary discourse of critical theory. On the one hand, advocates of critical theory insist that social and political theory must be politically engaged and emancipatory in intent. On the other hand, the discourse of critical theory has simply failed to make clear its own political implications and how it is to be related to concrete political practices. In short, the idea of a critical theory, whether modernist or postmodernist has remained just that— an idea.

· · ·

My aim in this book is to try to move beyond what I think is an increasingly sterile debate between modernist and postmodernist critical theorists by exploring how the gap between the political intentions and political implications of critical theory might be closed. Three related themes guide this exploration. The first I have already intimated: The contemporary discourse of critical theory, both modernist and postmodernist, has done much to show why social and political inquiry must be politically engaged and emancipatory in intent. The second is that modernist and postmodernist critical theory both contain insights that are useful for seeing how this project might be carried out, but they also contain arguments that are at odds with these insights. The third theme is that it is possible to move beyond the modernist/postmodernist impasse by turning the insights they offer against their own arguments, and that there are examples of what I call "critical theory in practice" that are able to make good the aims of critical theory without falling prey to the debilitating difficulties that seems to have characterized much of the debate about critical theory.

I develop these themes as follows:

In the first part of the book I offer an historical and analytical reconstruction of the idea of a critical theory as it is found in Marx, the Frankfurt School, Habermas and Foucault. In chapters 1 and 2 I critically examine the themes and development of the conception of critical theory that stretches from Marx through the Frankfurt School to Habermas. As I shall argue, the movement of this tradition is characterized by a steady turn away from considerations of practice to questions of normative foundations. In part, this movement can be understood as an attempt to preserve the useful philosophical insights Marx offered while articulating a conception of critical theory better suited to the changed historical circumstances of the twentieth century. This "metatheoretical turn," attending issues with which Marx was only occasionally, and then only unsystematically, concerned, is not in itself responsible for opening the gap between the political intentions and implications of modernist critical theory. But the same cannot be said of the particular form of argument in which this concern was expressed. And in this respect Marx may have done more damage than is at first sight apparent. For the Frankfurt School and Habermas may well have distanced themselves from some of the more problematic features of Marx's work, but the one questionable assumption they did not abandon was Marx's particular understanding of the way in which critical theory's "emancipatory interest" was to be conceptualized.

For Marx, the unity of theoretical enlightenment and political emancipation was possible only if this unity embodied universalizable implications. Thus, Marx identified the proletariat as the subject, or bearer, of an interest in emancipation of "mankind as such." At the hands of the Frankfurt School and Habermas, this assumption is revised, but its core remains intact. Habermas's comments are particularly instructive in this matter. On the one hand, he argues,

> What separates us from Marx are evident historical truths, for example that in the developed capitalist countries there is no single identifiable class, no clearly circumscribed social group which could be singled out as the representative of a general interest that has been violated. (Habermas 1982: 222)

But, on the other hand, he also insists that failing to ground the emancipatory interest of critical theory in universal terms leads to the error of commitment "to fortuitous historical constellations" which would "relativistically deprive self-reflection of the possibility of a justificatory basis of its claims to validity" (Habermas 1973a: 14–15). Thus, modernist critical theory from Marx through Habermas held that an emancipatory interest must be universal, or it has no claim to validity. The fact that the Frankfurt School and Habermas criticized Marx for having mistakenly identified this interest in the life experiences of the proletariat did nothing to diminish this view. And the main problem is that it is just this view which makes modernist critical theory a problematic political theory.

This is, however, only the negative side of the story. I also try to show that there is much in their work which points to an alternative model of critical theory, one that can bridge the gap between the idea and its practical realization. What one finds in modernist critical theory is a persistent emphasis on the historicity and contextuality—and hence nonuniversalizability—of social knowledge. These arguments are obviously at odds with the principle of universalizability to which they also subscribe, and which is dominant in their work. But as I shall argue, this contextualist alternative is a more perspicacious position; it not only grounds a critique of universalism itself, but provides intimations of the philosophical grounds for a critical theory that is historically and contextually situated—and rationally defensible.

That critical theory is contextually bound, and that its norms and values are not "relativistic" or arbitrary, is a crucial point for my argument. But its defensibility does not depend only on working through the tensions and contradictions of modernist critical theory. It is a lesson implicit as much in Foucault's postmodernist critical theory. What's more, this lesson is no less at odds with postmodernist celebrations of normative skepticism than it is with modernist normative universalism. In chapter 3, then, I take up Foucault in order to continue developing the reconstruction of critical theory.

Asked in an interview some years ago to characterize the goal of his many works, Foucault answered by saying

> What I am trying to do is grasp the implicit systems of thought which determine our most familiar behavior without our knowing it. I am trying to find their origin, to show their formation, the constraint they impose upon us; I am therefore trying to place myself at a distance from them and show how one could escape. (In Simon 1971: 201)

The need for such a self-description may seem odd, but in Foucault's case the proliferation of interpretations and misinterpretations of his work demands nothing less. In this respect, Foucault seems to have suffered a fate similar to that of Habermas; both range so widely that they often appear to be engaged in undertakings far removed from their professed political intentions.

But Foucault himself (also like Habermas) is at least partially to blame for the difficulties encountered by his readers. He wants to provide a politically engaged theory, but his understanding of rationality seems to undercut the grounding that might justify such efforts. Emphasizing the historical discontinuities in both scientific and social knowledge, Foucault argues that a "rational" grounding for knowledge claims is but a myth of the Enlightenment, and a particularly pernicious myth. His own inquiry, which he calls "archaeological" in its earliest expressions, and "genealogical" later on, suggests that appeals to rational knowledge—whatever their source—are necessarily "disciplinary."

The dilemma here is that Foucault wants to help us loosen the binds of "discipline"—including the discipline of "reason"—yet the viability of his intentions depends in large part on their rational warrants. This tension should not, however, lead to a speedy dismissal of Foucault's work. For one thing Foucault has shown, perhaps as well as anyone, that the kind of universalistic claims characteristic of modernist critical theory cannot be defended. More positively, there are aspects of his work which suggest that something like a contextualist conception of critique might provide the rational warrants his own discourse requires. But the predominant themes in Foucault's work, like the predominant themes in modernist critical theory, implicate him in the same kinds of political difficulties the modernists suffer.

Both models of critical theory share a common frame of reference in the assumption that political choices must be grounded in universally applicable normative claims, or, failing this, that all normative claims rest on ultimately arbitrary preferences. Of course the difference between them is that modernists seem unwilling to give up the ghost of universal rationality in favor of the kind of contextualized rationality toward which aspects of their own work point, and postmodernists are unwilling to recognize that from the failures of universal rationality the abandonment of rationality does not follow. In essence, then, modernist and postmodernist critical theory both anticipate, but do not themselves pursue, an understanding of critical theory that can help bridge the gap between what critical theory says it seeks—enlightenment and emancipation—and what, in its received versions, it actually does—undermine its political intentions. And so one lesson of my discussions in Part I is that we ought to move beyond modernist and postmodernist critical theory.

In Part II, I offer reconstructions of four social theories that seem to do just that. These examples of "critical theory in practice"—dependency theory, Paulo Freire's pedagogy of the oppressed, liberation theology, and (some forms of) feminist theory—are self-consciously tied to particular historical circumstances and practical contexts. Moreover, all share a commitment to the idea of empowerment and emancipation one finds in the received view of critical theory, but each in its own way provides resources that can be used for rethinking the relation between theory and practice generally, and critical theory and political practice specifically.

Of the examples I consider, dependency theory (chapter 4) is perhaps closest to the interests of many practicing social scientists. While focused specifically on socioeconomic development in Latin America, dependency theory has nonetheless been influential in shaping much of the current debate among scholars interested in general issues of development. One side effect of this growing influence has been the appropriation of dependency theory by social scientists working within a naturalistic (positivist) conception of social inquiry, and by those working within a mechanistic Marxist framework. But these appropriations, according to Henrique Fernando Cardoso—who has been called the "grandfather of dependency theory"—distort the intentions of the dependency theorists. By fleshing out these distortions, a clearer account of how dependency theory is a critical theory in practice begins to emerge.

Dependency theory, Cardoso argues, is not a scientific theory in the sense its positivist or Marxist consumers want it to be, but a "radically critical" theory because it seeks to provide social agents with the theoretical tools for understanding and changing their oppressed condition (1977: 16). While criticizing commonly accepted interpretations of underdevelopment, dependency theory also grounds a perspective in which oppression in Latin America is seen not as natural, necessary, or inevitable, but a feature of the place of Latin America on the periphery of the global capitalist system. This theoretical criticism, and the reinterpretation of social and political processes in Latin America is, of course, subject to standards of theoretical coherence and empirical adequacy—it purports to be rationally defensible. But its "verification" is not to be understood as having been completed only when these standards have been met. Rather—and this is what defines dependency theory as a critical theory—the "verification" of dependency theory "depends on the capacity of social movements to implement what are perceived as structural possibilities" and thus "on its own ability to show socio-political actors the possible solutions to contradictory situations" (Cardoso and Faletto 1979: xiv).

Despite its influence, dependency theory has not been without its critics. But as we shall see, these critics have been no better able to adequately interpret dependency theory than have its sympathetic "consumers." Indeed, one of the real ironies in this play of misinterpretations is that the critics (when they are not themselves "consumers") have often criticized the "consumers" interpretations rather than those of the dependency theorists themselves. Debunking the critics claims is, then, another element in my attempt to clarify how dependency theory is a critical theory.

Finally, some scholars have argued more recently that dependency theory is anachronistic given the changed conditions in many Latin American states, in particular because of the movement toward "democratization" (sometimes "redemocratization") in many of these countries. It may be true that dependency theory took shape against the background of authoritarianism, but against these assertions I shall try to show that dependency theory is not anachronistic; that it still has much to offer. Conditions have perhaps changed, but not so radically that oppression has ended. If my reconstruction of dependency theory is correct, then the commitment to contextually sensitive critique it embodies should enable the dependency theorists to accommodate changed conditions. And as we shall see, it has.

The second example of a critical theory in political practice I cite, Paulo Freire's "pedagogy of the oppressed" (chapter 5), is perhaps more familiar to educators than to practicing social scientists. The core of Freire's pedagogy derives primarily from his distinction between traditional pedagogical thought and his own. This traditional thought Freire characterizes as the "banking" model of education, an understanding that presupposes not only a conception of the student as an empty vessel into which information is to be poured, but also a conception of the teacher-as-expert. This banking model views knowledge as "a gift bestowed by those who consider themselves knowledgable upon those whom they consider to know nothing" (Freire 1983a: 58). Demonstrating that this self-understanding is not unrelated to broader socioeconomic concerns, Freire argues that the basic presuppositions of the banking model also "mirror(s) oppressive society as a whole." Because they involve viewing human beings "as adaptable, manageable beings," the assumptions of banking education are indicted as examples of "the effort to turn men into automatons—the very negation of their ontological vocation to be more fully human" (Freire 1983a: 59–61 passim).

Against the banking model Freire articulates his "pedagogy of the oppressed," an educational model which has as its goal the development of *conscientização*, or the raising of critical consciousness. The primary aim of *conscientização* is to help those in situations of domination see that their condition is often the result of distorted accounts of social reality, which often lead them to "fatalistically 'accept' their exploitation" (Freire 1983a: 51). Such a recognition is not simply a matter of the teacher telling the student of his/her plight, however; a truly liberating pedagogy is "a pedagogy which must be forged *with*, not *for*, the oppressed (whether individuals or peoples) in the incessant struggle to gain their humanity" (Freire 1983a: 33). Nor is this pedagogy simply a theory of enlightenment and emancipation, for the theory-practice relationship is inseparable: "Reflection—true reflection—leads to action" and "that action will constitute an authentic praxis only if its consequences become the object of critical reflection" (Freire 1983a: 52–53). Hence, Freire provides useful insights into the way that theoretical enlightenment and practical emancipation may be linked.

My third example of a critical theory in practice is liberation theology (chapter 6). While there is a widespread belief (particularly among those who are committed to political liberation) that religious faith is antithetical to critical, rational, reflection and action, liberation theology clearly shows this to be an unwarranted prejudice. Rather than being a theology shaped by reflections in the cloister, liberation theology is intimately tied to, and dependent upon, actual social practices for its inspiration. As Gustavo Gutierrez (1973a) explains, liberation theology is "a theological reflection born of the experience of shared efforts to abolish the current unjust situation and to build a different society, freer and more human."

Throughout the writings of the liberation theologians there is recurrent reference to this connection between social (and theological) theory and political practice. This in turn issues calls for both a "critical analysis" of the historically situated conditions of the oppressed, and for a Christian commitment to political, not just spiritual, transformation. For the Christian committed to liberation, liberation theology is supposed to help show "that his faith does not imply the acceptance of a world that is already made, or of a predetermined history, but rather that the very living of this faith involves the creation of a new and solidary world and leads to historical initiatives fertilized by Christian hopes" (Bonino 1975: xxvii).

Obviously such hopes require nothing less than the "liberation of theology" itself. This liberation, and the liberation of faith it underwrites is not, however, grounded strictly in biblical or church authority; it derives as much from "an analysis that will highlight the mechanisms that really drive society" as it does from "vague denounciations and good will" ("Documento Final" of the 1972 meeting of Christians for Socialism, quoted in Bonino 1975: xxvi). Against the fidelity to purely "religious" doctrine characteristic of orthodox theology, the liberation theologians assert their commitment to "orthopraxis," and in this the "truth" of the theology of liberation lies in "its ability to liberate . . . forces for the reconstruction of a more human society" (Kirk 1979: 35).

Liberation theology, as I shall try to show, is truly a form of critical theory in practice, albeit one in theological guise. Along with dependency theory and Freire's critical pedagogy, liberation theology provides a number of analytical insights that can be deployed in the re-thinking of the idea of a critical theory. In bringing them together I mean to emphasize the deeper philosophical presuppositions they share in order to show that they all may be understood as having a common purpose. The fact that all are products of the Latin American context suggests a high degree of cross-fertilization and a common intellectual and practical milieu, and this in part explains their deep similarities. Indeed, each makes reference, implicit and explicit, to the others. But as my last example of a critical theory in practice demon-strates, these shared presuppositions and common purposes are not confined to Latin America.

Of all the examples of critical theory in practice I cite in this book, feminist theory (chapter 7) is that which is lacking in any central fig-ures or texts to which one may appeal for grounding. On the one hand this may appear as a difficulty for my argument, for it presupposes that there are many different kinds of feminist theory and a diversity of specific issues to which feminists address themselves. On the other, this may be seen as the basis for a stronger case of feminism-as-criti-cal-theory, for it presupposes, as Habermas suggests, that "in a pro-cess of enlightenment there can be only participants" (1973a: 40). As Mary Dietz puts it, "If internal conflict, dissent and persistent contro-versy are the stuff of political movements which struggle toward self-consciousness, take nothing as 'given,' think and rethink their aims, then there can be no doubt that the women's movement . . . is such a struggle" (Dietz 1983: 2).

I argue that it is precisely this ongoing critical self-examination and consciousness-raising project that makes feminist theory a genuinely critical theory. With respect to many issues concerning the theory-practice relationship, feminists appear to have worked through in great detail many of the most problematic features of a theory which has practical intent. Much of this is the result of taking on what may initially appear rather abstract concerns regarding the nature of hu-man identity and social knowledge. Here I attend feminist critiques of liberal, Marxist, and scientistic accounts of identity and knowledge in order to illuminate the alternative account they imply. But while the grounding of feminist political practice stems from such abstract con-cerns, it is clear that feminists themselves have been guided first and foremost by the need to articulate these issues in terms that are emi-nently practical.

This is an important consideration for anything that can legiti-mately claim the title of a critical theory. But there is more. For as Brian Fay suggests, in distinguishing between a truly critical and a manipulative, instrumentalist social theory what matters "is not only the fact that people come to have a particular self-understanding, and that this new self-understanding provides the basis for altering social arrangements, but also the manner in which they come to adopt this new 'guiding idea.' In fact, rational discourse must be the cause of the oppressed's change in basic self-conception" (Fay 1977: 224–25). As we shall see, the meaning of "rational discourse" undergoes a radical transformation at the hands of feminist critical theory, and in a way that dovetails with the other critical theories in practice I cite. However, we shall also see that some feminists posit a basis for feminist practice that is antithetical to the idea of a rationally compelling, contextually specific critical theory. Thus, by examining the differences between these feminist theories and a critical feminist theory, the emancipatory possibilities and practical implications of feminism should become clearer.

This last chapter of Part II serves to bring together the issues introduced at the close of Part I and developed in my discussions of dependency theory, Freire, and liberation theology. In these first two parts of this book I consider in some detail the problem of grounding critical theory in specific historical-contextual circumstances. In Part III I address the constellation of issues involved in this problem by analyzing in greater detail the differences between modernist and postmodernist critical theory, and "critical theory in practice." After summarizing the need for making questions of practice central to the philosophical foundations of critical social theory (or what I call putting practice back into theory), in my concluding chapter (chapter 8) I argue that the more questionable features of the "critical theory" of Marx, the Frankfurt School, Habermas, and Foucault, must be abandoned in favor of the kind of "critical theory in practice" one finds in dependency theory, Freire, liberation theology, and feminist theory. I also go on to argue that the idea of a critical theory is one we ignore at our own intellectual and political peril.

· · ·

I hope this book will help to identify the difficulties a critical theory may encounter in attaining its political objectives, as well as the prospective lines of argument that would overcome these difficulties. The achievement of Marx, the Frankfurt School, Habermas, and Foucault is that they point us in the right direction, but the achievement of the dependency theorists, Freire, the liberation theologians, and feminists, is that they show us how the difficult task of critical theory might be made good. These otherwise disparate inquiries provide evidence that critical theory need not remain an esoteric and purely academic ideal. Derived from particular and highly specific contexts, these critical theories remain committed to changing those contexts. This specificity may appear as a weakness to many, but my point here is that without it the promise of a truly emancipatory social theory will remain hopelessly utopian.

This would be an unfortunate condition, and it is one that the dominant discourse of critical theory often seems to approach. By getting beyond this dominant discourse, perhaps we will be in a better position to realize the ideals it embraces. The continued fact of human suffering speaks volumes to this need. If we are to avoid the mistakes of Marx, the Frankfurt School, Habermas and Foucault, we should recognize, with John O'Neill, that "critical theory must begin work wherever the opportunity affords itself" before we speculate at "the ascending heights of theory" (O'Neill 1976: 10). As I hope to show here, this work has already begun, and if we seek a model of social theory that can be emancipating, we would be well advised to look to those theories that are self-consciously part of struggles where people are emancipating themselves.

PART I

Critical Theory

A CRITICAL theory of society is defined as a theory having practical intent. As its name suggests, it is critical of existing social and political institutions and practices, but the criticisms it levels are not intended simply to show how present society is unjust, only to leave everything as it is. A critical theory of society is understood by its advocates as playing a crucial role in changing society. In this, the link between social theory and political practice is perhaps the defining characteristic of critical theory, for a critical theory without a practical dimension would be bankrupt on its own terms.

Forging a link between social theory and political practice is, however, no mean task. Today it is commonly understood that theory may explain social processes, but it is nevertheless quite independent of political practice. Because its task is merely explanation, social theory—at least when it is done according to the canons of scientific inquiry—purports to tell us nothing about how the world ought to be, but only how it actually is. Describing and explaining the "facts" of social life are its concern, and if social theory has any effect on political practice, it is only a contingent, and not a necessary, effect. So goes the received view.[1]

[1] By "the received view" of social scientific inquiry I mean that methodological self-understanding to which most Anglo-American (and to a lesser extent, continental) social scientists adhere. According to this view, the proper methodology for the study of social phenomena is some version of methodological naturalism or positivism, which is constituted by a particular philosophical reconstruction of the methods of the natural sciences. Later in this chapter I discuss the critique of methodological naturalism offered by the members of the Frankfurt School and Habermas. In those pages I attend to the understanding of the theory-practice presupposed in the tenets of methodological naturalism. At this point I simply offer the account of positivism articulated by G. H. von Wright (1971). According to von Wright, the central tenets of positivism are:

a. *Methodological monism*, or the idea that all sciences (social and natural) must be unified with respect to their methods.

b. This methodological ideal or standard is set by the exact natural sciences, in particular mathematical physics, against which the sophistication of all scientific inquiry is to be judged.

c. On this account, all scientific explanation is "causal," consisting of the subsumption of individual cases under hypothetically assumed general laws of nature, including, for the social sciences, an unchanging "human nature."

Taken together, the tenets of this methodological self-understanding are reflected in the arguments advanced by numerous social scientists who insist that social inquiry be "value free," and therefore neutral with respect to questions of political practice. A more complete account of methodological naturalism will emerge as this chapter progresses.

A critical theory, by contrast, presupposes a radically different view of the relationship between theory and practice. On this view, a social theory is not true or false simply by virtue of its ability to give an accurate account of the "facts" of the world, but rather by virtue of its ability to show social agents how their beliefs and self-understandings partially constitute those "facts." More than this, a critical theory strives to show how unrealized hopes for social justice may be the result of social practices the oppressed are fully capable of changing through their own critically informed actions. Critical theory thus finds its final "verification" in the practice of social agents who act, in their own interests, to free themselves of what Jürgen Habermas has called "ideologically frozen relations of dependence that can in principle be transformed" (1971: 310).

The task of a critical theory of society is thus bringing about this self-liberating practice. And success in this task in turn requires three crucial undertakings. First, critical theory must provide a coherent account of how present circumstances and the systemic self-(mis)understandings of social agents are in large part responsible for the unfreedom many of them suffer. Second, critical theory must provide an alternative vision of social relations that those who are oppressed can embrace as their own. But these two theoretical moments can be realized only if a critical theory embodies a philosophical self-understanding that can underwrite a translation of its theoretical claims into an idiom that is intelligible to the communities of sufferers to whom it is directed.

These, then, are the requirements of a critical theory that can inform an emancipatory political practice: it must locate the sources of domination in actual social practices; it must project an alternative vision (or at least the outline) of a life free from such domination; and it must craft these tasks in the idiom, so to speak, of its addressees—or risk seeing the practical-emancipatory project recede ever further into the distance of abstract philosophical speculation far removed from the concerns of daily life.

In the three chapters that constitute this first part of my book I examine several influential attempts to articulate a critical theory. In these examples we shall see why the features of a critical theory I enumerated are necessary, how they might be articulated, and how critical theory might fail to realize them.

One of these examples is the work of Karl Marx, arguably the "founding father" of critical theory. Marx's contributions to shaping the idea of a critical theory are important indeed, but his own version of a critical theory is not without difficulties. One such difficulty is that Marx's critique of nineteenth-century capitalism no longer seems applicable in the changed conditions of the twentieth century. As a result—and this is another difficulty—Marxism has been reinterpreted, and the most influential of these reinterpretations has come in the form of the "orthodox" Marxism underpinning the authoritarian political institutions and social structures of many modern "Socialist" states. This orthodoxy appears quite at odds with Marx's own emancipatory intentions, although the distortions it embodies may be attributed to some of Marx's own philosophical and theoretical formulations.

But Marxism has not been abandoned to its orthodox proponents, and a number of individuals have tried to preserve Marxism's emancipatory, antiauthoritarian intentions by recasting his ideas in ways that might better fit changed historical conditions. The most prominent of these efforts has been the "Critical Theory" of the Frankfurt School (especially Max Horkheimer, Theodor Adorno, and Herbert Marcuse) and its heir apparent, Jürgen Habermas.[2]

The work of Marx, the Frankfurt School, and Habermas are, then, central to this first part of my book. The vision of critical theory these thinkers hold can be understood as "modernist." That is, all hold that the promise of a critical theory can be realized through the recovery of a critical, reflective form of thought and action whose possibilities are present in modern social and political practices. The notion of recovering these possibilities is crucial to this project, for it is also the case that these thinkers believe that the dominant forms of thought and action in modernity are both uncritical and unreflective. As Marx once put it, "Reason has always existed, only not always in reasonable form" (Marx 1978: 14). And so the task for these theorists is to recover

[2] On the history of the origins and development of the Frankfurt School, see Jay (1973). David Held's (1980) "introductory" text on critical theory provides a useful analytical/critical overview of the work of specific Frankfurt School members and the continuities and discontinuities between Habermas and the several Frankfurt thinkers. Benhabib's (1986) work reaches back to Marx and Hegel in a thematically rich treatment of the development of critical theory. Her conclusions, and Schroyer's (1973) approach, are in many ways complementary to the thesis I pursue here.

On Adorno's work see Jay (1984), Rose (1978) and Buck-Morss (1977).

On Horkheimer, Jay (1973) and Held (1980) are still the best sustained overviews available in English.

On Marcuse, see Schoolman (1980).

In addition to the Schroyer (1973), Held (1980) and Benhabib (1986) treatments of Habermas, the best single text addressed specifically to the thought of Habermas remains McCarthy (1978). A useful collection of articles on Habermas, complete with a response by Habermas, is Thompson and Held (1982). A more self-consciously metaphilosophical work is Kortian (1980). Each of these texts contains useful bibliographies on both primary and secondary literature.

that "reason" in modern life which has been subverted by the "unreasonable forms" that have been predominant.

But my examination of the idea of a critical theory does not end with Marx, the Frankfurt School, and Habermas. For in the last few years a "postmodernist" understanding of critical theory has also gained prominence. This understanding, best exemplified in the work of Michel Foucault,[3] shares with its modernist counterpart a commitment to an emancipatory politics and a principled opposition to the domination engendered in much of modern life. Yet Foucault does not see the recovery of critical reason as the means of realizing these aims, and in this he mounts a challenge to the modernist conception of critical theory.

United by a common opposition to domination in all of its forms and a common commitment to an emancipatory politics, Marx, the Frankfurt School, Habermas, and Foucault all have had a profound influence in shaping contemporary discussions of the nature of critical theory. Indeed, in a sense they have together defined what critical theory is all about. Despite those themes they all share, there has not been any easy rapproachment between modernists and postmodernists, and as a result much of the character of contemporary discourse about critical theory has centered on the differences and antitheses between these thinkers. Such disputes, I argue, may well be what critical theory is all about, but they are certainly not what critical theory should be about.

What has been lost in the contemporary discourse of critical theory is the emancipatory, practical goals that informed its development. The irony of this is that Marx, the Frankfurt School, Habermas, and Foucault are in large part responsible for shunting practical questions to secondary status. As a result of an ever growing preoccupation with what might be called a radical "metacritique of modernity," critical theory has come to look more like a form of academic, intellectual introspection than a form of politically engaged, emancipatory critique.

In trying to show why this is the case, I do not mean to imply that the metacritique of modernity is without merit. Metacritique, as Garbais Kortian (1980: 28) argues, calls into question the initial presuppositions which sustain the critical enterprise. In doing so, the metacritique of modernity undergirding critical theory offers an insightful critique of the received view of social theory. Against the common as-

---

[3] Extended, exclusive treatments of Foucault's work can be found in Sheridan (1980), Dreyfus and Rabinow (1982), Lemert and Gillan (1982), Major-Poetzl (1983), Cousins and Hussain (1984) and Rajchman (1985).

The bibliographies in these works are useful for those seeking to become more familiar with the literature by and about Foucault.

sumptions that social knowledge is "objective" and that human beings have an immutable "nature" that can be objectively known—and manipulated—the critical theorists have shown that these assumptions are neither philosophically defensible nor politically desirable. And in this respect, the critical theorists all seem to share a position Kortian (1980: 30) describes as involving the recognition that "knowledge . . . cannot be absolute," but only that which "man, a contingent being, has of himself and of the historical conditions of his being."[4]

The historicity and contextuality of our knowledge and being: these are the lessons of the metacritique of modernity—at least in its deconstructive moment. But when the deconstructive moment gives way to the reconstructive task—the task of articulating the foundations on which social and political emancipation might be realized—the metacritique of modernity falters. Rather than taking seriously the fact that critical theory must be, because all theory is necessarily, historically and contextually specific, the critical theorists seem to be committed to the task of articulating a conception of emancipation without careful consideration of the historical and contextual practices of which it is supposed to be the expression. Thus, while the metacritique of modernity provides useful philosophical insights that would enable the linking of critical theory and political practice, the contemporary discourse of critical theory fails to heed these insights because of its particular metatheoretical preoccupations. And the result has been that the practical, emancipatory project has receded almost irretrievably into the background.

And so my engagement of Marx, the Frankfurt School, Habermas, and Foucault takes the form of a kind of "immanent critique."[5] I take as the defining feature of critical theory the same political intentions they profess, and I try to show that the critical theory they advance involves a radical discrepancy between these political aims and the actual political implications of their work. At the same time, I want to

---

[4] Throughout this text I have retained the gendered language of the theorists I consider. I think it is important to be clear about the fact that this is the way most of these thinkers have written, a fact which often reflects the historical contexts of their work. I leave it to the reader to determine whether the many references to "man," and in liberation theology references to God as "him," are necessarily androcentric.

[5] In his "immanent critique" of Herbert Marcuse, Richard Bernstein suggests that he uses a method which "judges [Marcuse's] work by the guiding principle he enunciated" (1971b: 97). My intention in the first three chapters of this book is, like Bernstein, to judge the critical theory of Marx, the Frankfurt School, Habermas, and Foucault according to what I take to be the central concern of a critical theory: to assist its addressees in engaging in an "enlightening and emancipatory" political practice. By showing how the critical theorists *fail* to produce such a theory, I hope to identify the deficiencies in their work as well as suggest ways these deficiencies may be overcome.

recognize their achievement in having identified those insights that might close this gap.

All of this perhaps begs the question, why critical theory? The Frankfurt School and Habermas provide an answer that is anticipated in Marx, and one that also anticipates Foucault's postmodern alternative. It is with this answer that I begin.

CHAPTER 1

The Metatheoretical Turn

> If by enlightenment and intellectual progress we mean the
> freeing of man from superstitious belief in evil forces, in de-
> mons and fairies—in short, the emancipation from fear—
> then denunciation of what is currently called reason is the
> greatest service reason can render.
>
> —Max Horkheimer

THE DIALECTIC OF REASON AND ENLIGHTENMENT

Perhaps the most important central theme espoused by the Frankfurt
School and Habermas is the role of reason in emancipating human
beings from all forms of domination. But these critical theorists understand the concept in a way that is different from and critical of
most contemporary meanings. The critical theorist therefore faces the
dilemma of criticizing reason in the name of reason.

On the one hand, reason is said to serve as the guiding principle,
the "critical tribunal" (Marcuse 1968: 136) of a critical theory. This
particular form of reason "takes up a partisan position between critique and dogmatism, and with each new stage of emancipation it
wins a further victory" (Habermas 1973a: 254). On the other hand,
we live in a time when critical reason has been "eclipsed" (Horkheimer 1947).

Today, reason is a purely "subjective" and "instrumentalist" concept, having no bearing on the choice of the ends of life, nor can it
provide, as it once did, a justification of the role of knowledge in social
progress and freedom. In the dominant discourse of modern societies,
reason is "assigned to the level of subjective consciousness" (Habermas 1973: 262) where

> It is essentially concerned with [the relationship between] means and ends,
> with the adequacy of procedures for purposes more or less taken for granted
> and supposedly self-explanatory. If it concerns itself at all with ends, it takes
> for granted that they too are reasonable in the subjective sense. . . . The
> idea that an aim can be reasonable for its own sake—on the basis of virtues
> that insight reveals it to have in itself—without reference to some kind of
> subjective gain or advantage, is utterly alien to subjective reason. . . .
> (Horkheimer 1947: 3–4)

But the "critical reason" and "subjective reason" of which the critical theorists speak should not be thought of as having two distinct philosophical heritages. They are not simply in a relation of opposition, although they may initially appear to be (Horkheimer 1947: 174). They are instead two distinct aspects of the proper sense of reason understood as *logos* or *ratio*:

> This concept of reason never precluded subjective reason, but regarded [it] as only a partial, limited expression of a universal rationality from which criteria for all things and beings were derived. The emphasis was on ends rather than means. (Horkheimer, 1947: 4–5)

Reason thus understood incorporated both critical and subjective aspects, and the proper ordering of these aspects meant putting subjective reason in the service of critical reason. In this sense, the guiding principle of reason was that in it "insight and the explicit interest in liberation converge":

> The higher level of reflection coincides with a step forward in the progress toward the autonomy of the individual, with the elimination of suffering and the furthering of concrete happiness. Reason involved in the argument against dogmatism has definitely taken up this interest as its own—it does not define the moment of decision as external to its sphere (Habermas 1973a: 254).

But ours is an age in which this proper ordering of reason has been inverted. Hence Horkheimer's (1947: 187) claim that "the denunciation of what is currently called reason is the greatest service reason can render." Paradoxically, the critical theorists do not mean that this denunciation involves a return to a philosophical self-understanding that was dominant before the advent of modernity. For while the Enlightenment, that crucial age in which modernity begins to take shape, made possible the inversion of critical and instrumental reason, it also marked a significant moment in the development of human society in which reason—properly understood—became a guiding ideal.

"The Enlightenment" is not merely a convenient phrase we have coined to identify the years of the late seventeenth and eighteenth centuries in the West. It is rather a way of understanding the hopes and desires of those who thought a new era of civilization and progress was emerging, one in human reason that would replace superstition and dogma as the basis of social and political life. In this, the critical theorists argued, the Enlightenment embodied the ideal that "Ignorance coincides with suffering and happiness denied, uncertainty with slavery and the incapacity to act correctly" (Habermas 1973a: 257).

Abstractly stated, the Enlightenment commitment to reason seems a laudable notion. In practice, however, its pursuit had precisely the opposite of its intended effect. In the first place, the dominant philosophical concerns of the Enlightenment may have been guided by practical considerations, but the immediate issue was one of gaining insight into the laws of nature, which were "believed to be capable of providing . . . instruction for the just life" (Habermas 1973a: 258). It was but a short step from this understanding to one in which all of the sciences, natural and moral, were conceptualized as having the same foundations. This step was clearly anticipated in Descartes, who argued that it was mistaken to distinquish the sciences on the basis of their objects:

> Distinguishing the sciences, one from another, according to the diversity of their objects, [men] have come to think that they ought to be studied separately, each science independently of all the others. In this they are indeed deceived. (Descartes 1958: 2)

But the difficulty here was that this also led to an erasure of the differences between the kind of knowledge provided by the natural sciences, and that provided by the moral sciences. For "as soon as nature is objectivated in empirical science, the hope of at the same time drawing from the knowledge of causal laws any certainty with respect to normative laws must be abandoned" (Habermas 1973a: 258). As a consequence, questions of what is good for human beings as such were progressively sundered from questions amenable to "objective," empirically verifiable knowledge. And in this, what began as the pursuit of knowledge for the sake of human emancipation was soon transformed into the pursuit of knowledge for its own sake. Again, Descartes anticipated what would become a widely accepted view:

> Nothing is so likely to divert us from adopting the true path in our pursuit of truth as the directing of our studies not to [the] comprehensive end [of knowledge for its own sake] but to particular topics. . . . I am speaking of pursuits which are in themselves honorable and praiseworthy. For often the manner in which these influence us is the more subtly misleading. Consider, for instance, those sciences which contribute to the conveniences of life, or which yield the pleasure found in the contemplation of truth, almost the only one of our earthly delights that is blameless and free from all vexations. These legitimate fruits the sciences carry in their train, and we can count on them; but if, in the midst of our studies, we allow ourselves to think of them, the effect of our doing so is that we are then apt to omit many matters which may well seem to be of little utility and of no particular interest. (Descartes 1958: 2–3).

Between the conflation of the natural and moral sciences, the constriction of all valid knowledge claims to those provided by objective, empirical verification, and the concommitant sundering of the pursuit of knowledge and an interest in human emancipation, we have a few of the core features of the dialectic of Enlightenment reason. But these are merely anticipatory developments, for the full constriction of reason to its purely "subjective" or "instrumental" aspect is only realized with "the reduction of science to a productive force in industrial society" (Habermas 1973: 262). With this, science, indeed "reason" itself, becomes defined by the "demand of an industrially advanced society that it look after its survival on the escalating scale of a continually expanded technical control over nature and a continually refined administration of human beings" (Habermas 1973a: 254).

Now considering that it is the natural sciences that provide the most successful examples of technical control, the conflation of the natural and moral sciences turns out to be the restriction of legitimate knowledge claims to those most closely resembling "natural laws." Thus, the demand for objective, empirically verifiable knowledge, and the dismissal of normative concerns, is reinforced. And perhaps most importantly, the assumption that knowledge is pursued for its own sake becomes a kind of dogmatism in itself: When "knowledge" is equated with successful control of nature and other human beings, it is not disinterested, but actually presupposes a particular kind of interest—an interest in manipulation.

In subsequent sections of this chapter we shall have occasion to flesh out these developments in greater detail. But from what has been said thus far, the answer to the question "why critical theory?" should be clear. A critical theory is needed because what was once the hopeful promise of the Enlightenment—human emancipation—has turned out to be a new form of enslavement. Thus, the members of the Frankfurt School, and their heir apparent, Habermas, understood the primary task of a critical theory of society as coming to grips with the "dialectic of the Enlightenment" and the "eclipse" of reason it engendered:

> The dilemma that faced us in our work proved to be the first phenomena for investigation: the self-destruction of the Enlightenment. We are wholly convinced—and therein lies our *petitio principii*—that social freedom is inseparable from enlightened thought. (Horkheimer and Adorno 1972: xiii)

How the "self-destruction" of the Enlightenment was to be overcome, and how a critical theory would articulate the relationship of "social freedom" and "enlightened thought" are of course important questions to be addressed as well. In doing so, however, critical theory cannot fall back behind the Enlightenment; it must embrace the Enlightenment ideal that knowledge and commitment cannot be separated even while it turns this ideal in a critique of Enlightenment ideology. Thus Habermas:

> In the concept of reason active as critique of ideology, knowledge and commitment are related dialectically: on the one hand, it is only possible to see through the dogmatism of a congealed society to the degree to which knowledge has committed itself to being guided by the anticipation of an emancipated society and actualized adult autonomy for all human beings; at the same time, on the other hand, this interest demands that insight into the processes of social development already be attained, because only in these processes can such insight be constituted as objective. (Habermas 1973a: 262).

As we shall see, the unity of knowledge and commitment implied by this claim may indeed be difficult to attain in modern society, but neither is critical theory without historical and philosophical resources in this regard. For the Frankfurt School and Habermas, it was Marx who provided the most promising example of how this unity of knowledge and commitment—how a critical theory—might be realized. For "On the level of the historical self-reflection of a science with critical intent, Marx for the last time identifies reason with a commitment to rationality in its thrust against dogmatism" (Habermas 1973a: 262).

So it is to Marx that I turn.

MARX AND THE GROUNDING OF CRITICAL THEORY

Marx's intentions are clearly revealed in the titles of many of his works: *Critique of Hegel's Philosophy of Right*; *The Holy Family*, subtitled "A Critique of Critical Criticism"; *A Contribution to the Critique of Political Economy*; *Capital: A Critical Analysis of Capitalist Production*; and the *Critique of the Gotha Program*, among others. But what Marx meant by "critique" was first and foremost a project having practical intent: "to overthrow all those conditions in which man is an abased, enslaved, abandoned, contemptable being" (*MER*: 60).[1] And while it was only through a "ruthless criticism of everything existing" that a new world could be found (*MER*: 13), an adequate understanding of Marx's critical theory must begin with the recognition

---

[1] All abbreviated references in this chapter are to Marx's work, found in the following texts (full citations in the Bibliography):

MER: *The Marx-Engels Reader*
PP: *The Poverty of Philosophy*
EPM: *Economic and Philosophical Manuscripts*
GI: *German Ideology*
SC: *Selected Correspondence*

that it is the lived experience of suffering and misery which provokes the "emancipatory interest" of any critical theory (Wellmer 1971: 48). Without the recognition of a class of persons who suffer oppression, conditions from which they must be freed, critical theory is nothing more than an empty intellectual exercise. For Marx, that class of persons was the proletariat; in proletarian life he found the suffering and misery which provided for him the lived experience that stands most in need of changing.

But the interest in emancipation is a problematic "prejudice" for critical theory. In order for critical theory to realize its practical aims, it must become a "material force" for the oppressed:

> It is clear that the arm of criticism cannot replace the criticism of arms. Material force can only be overthrown by material force, but theory itself becomes a material force when it has seized the masses. (MER: 60)

Moreover, for critical theory to become part of the "material force" of revolutionary change, it must be rendered in ways that are intelligible to its addressees. As Marx put it, "Theory is only realized in a people so far as it fulfills the needs of the people" (MER: 61).

By these standards, it would appear that Marx's critical theory was in important respects deficient. After all, the proletarian revolution Marx thought his criticisms would help bring about never materialized. This is not to say that Marx's work has had no effect on political practice. Half the world today lives within political systems that claim Marx as their philosophical spokesman. But the revolutions that brought these regimes to power were not proletarian in character. Marx's intended audience may have been the wrong one, or he may have simply failed to make his critique accessible to them. I shall return to these issues later. For the moment, however, I want to emphasize a crucial feature of Marx's self-understanding: Marx did have a particular addressee in mind when he took up his critique, and he made this a defining feature of a critical theory. Thus did Marx establish what might be called the "practical dimension" of critical theory: such a theory is precipitated by oppression, and it seeks to help end that oppression by becoming a part of the critical consciousness of the oppressed, who would then emancipate themselves.

How a critical theory might realize these aims is yet another important question, and Marx had little to say about this matter. But in another respect, the way in which Marx actually carried out his work itself provides a model of how a critical theory can be "enlightening." Most of Marx's corpus consists not of practical strategies for overcoming the dehumanizing conditions of the proletariat, but of criticisms of those forms of thought he believed perpetuated the proletariat's oppression. Habermas has suggested that "with this unpretentious title, [Marx's] 'critique' to begin with, claims that term's meaning of a critical examination of the extant literature; but beyond this it also claims the associated meaning of a theory developed with the practical intention of overcoming the crisis [of ideological mystification]" (Habermas 1973a: 219). Indeed, there is much in Marx to suggest that he saw this criticism of various philosophical systems of his day as a necessary prolegomenon to an emancipatory practice. In a letter to Arnold Ruge, for instance, Marx suggested that "we do not attempt dogmatically to prefigure the future, but want to find the new world through criticism of the old" in which "We have to concern ourselves just as much with the other side [of reality], the theoretical existence of man, in other words to make religion, science, etc., the objects of our criticism" (*MER*: 13).[2]

The point I want to make here is that Marx understood that a critical theory could become part of the consciousness of its intended audience through a confrontation with belief systems that "legitimated" domination. But there is more here as well, for these systems made domination possible because of the particular ways in which they had characterized social life and human identity. This can be readily seen in Marx's criticisms of the philosophical presuppositions of Hegelian idealism and bourgeois political economy, arguably the most important theories Marx attacked.[3] Both, Marx argued, could be read as apologies for the social relations of capitalist production. In the case of Hegel, the "civil society" of capitalism, in which "The whole society exists only in order to guarantee for each of its members the preser-

[2] It is interesting to note that when Marx wrote this letter to Ruge, he suggested that the question of how critique was to be approached had "two circumstances": the criticism of religion and the criticism of politics. But these were only a "starting point." Marx equated religion with the "theoretical struggles of mankind" and politics with the "practical struggles." In numerous places in his work, he charges Hegel and the Young Hegelians with being concerned only with "religion," or strictly theoretical matters (see, for example, his critique of Hegel in *EPM*: 124–46). As I shall discuss shortly in this section, it was precisely Hegel's "religious" (read purely theoretical) philosophy that Marx thought was necessarily conservative. This was an assumption Marx held regarding all religious thought. But in this, Marx also failed to see that a *critical* religious orientation could be potentially emancipatory, as my chapter on Liberation Theology shows.

[3] Marx's charges against Hegelianism and the materialism of the political economists in many ways reflect the criticisms Hegel leveled at romanticism and "logicalism" (see Taylor 1975). In this, Marx's conception of critical theory can be understood as itself having historical and philosophical predecessors. Nonetheless, it is he who is most often cited as the "founding father" of critical theory, for reasons that should become obvious shortly.

vation of his person, his rights and his property" (*MER*: 43), was understood to be the *telos* of history, "the state of need and reason" (*MER*: 43). But Marx found this sort of conception to be one "which justifies the infamy of today by that of yesterday" (*MER*: 55):

> The exponents of this conception of history have consequently only been able to see in history the political actions of princes and States, religious and all sorts of theoretical struggles, and in each particular epoch have had to *share the illusion of that epoch*. (*MER*: 165)

And Marx thought that the political economists had similarly fallen into an uncritical acceptance of the present by virtue of their philosophical assumptions:

> There are only two kinds of institutions for them, artificial and natural. The institutions of feudalism are artificial institutions, those of the bourgeoisie are natural institutions. (*PP*: 105)

Thus, both Hegelian idealism and bourgeois political economy made the mistake of assuming that the abstract categories they articulated were derived from "the *absolute method*, which not only explains all things, but also implies the movement of things" (*PP*: 93), when the reality was that "These ideas, these categories, are as little eternal as the relations they express. They are *historical and transitory products*" (*PP*: 95–96). Both systems of thought, then, served to legitimate present realities by abstracting their concepts and categories from those realities, then restating them as resting on the eternal facts of nature (as with the political economists) or on a belief in the present as the embodiment of reason (as with Hegel). Marx therefore found in Hegelianism an "uncritical positivism and equally uncritical idealism" that involved a "philosophical dissolution and restoration of the empirical world" (*EPM*: 130); and in the political economists a "singular method of procedure" in which "present day relations—the relations of bourgeois production—are [considered] natural," implying "that these are the relations in which wealth is created and productive forces developed in conformity with the laws of nature" (*PP*: 105). In light of the kind of suffering and misery Marx saw in the condition of the proletariat, it is not surprising that he objected to those philosophical systems that justified the present—in whatever terms—and undermined the possibility of criticism that might help change it.

Yet while Marx was critical of both these forms of thought, he nonetheless found in them some useful insights for critical theory. In fact, he even went so far as to define his own method as "the unifying truth of both" (*EPM*: 135). According to Marx, Hegel correctly "grasps *labor* as the *essence* of man," but his understanding of this self-formative process was limited by the fact that "the only labor which Hegel knows and recognizes is *abstractly mental* labor" (*EPM*: 131). Hegel's idealism therefore presupposed what Marx considered to be a peculiar account of human identity. "For Hegel, the *human* being—man— equals self-consciousness," an assumption which led inevitably to an ontological model of "man as abstract egoist—egoism raised in its pure abstraction to the levels of thought" (*EPM*: 132). While Hegelianism *did* develop "the *active* side" (*GI*: 121) of human life by recognizing "the self-creation of man as a process" (*EPM*: 131), it was nonetheless burdened by an emancipatory promise limited only to the level of thought alone. Such an "idealism" could hardly inform a political practice intended to relieve the real material sufferings of those who lived in the squalor, poverty, and meanness of the proletarian existence. This much Marx makes clear in his attack on the Young Hegelians who, while far more radical in their criticisms of current conditions than many other Hegelians, were still unable to break with idealist assumptions:

> Since the Young Hegelians consider conceptions, thoughts, ideas, in fact all the products of consciousness, to which they attribute an independent existence, as the real chains of men (just as the old Hegelians declared them the true bonds of human society) it is evident that the Young Hegelians have to fight only against these illusions of consciousness. Since, according to their fantasy, the relationships of men, all their doings, their chains and their limitations are the products of their consciousness, the Young Hegelians logically put to men the moral postulate of exchanging their present circumstances for human, critical or egoistic consciousness, and thus removing their limitations. . . . The most recent of them have found the correct expression for their activity when they declare that they are only fighting against 'phrases.' They forget, however, that they are in no way combatting the existing world when they are combatting it merely with the phrases of this world. (*MER*: 149)

The "naturalism" of the political economists, even while hampered by some philosophical confusions, served as an important corrective to Hegelian idealism. For Marx, their work showed how it was possible to examine "the categories of bourgeois economy," those "forms of thought expressing with social validity the conditions and relations of a definite, historically determined mode of production" (*MER*: 324). In fact, they had even "discovered what lies beneath these forms" (*MER*: 327). By emphasizing the need to begin one's inquiry with the actual social practices of social agents, thus avoiding "the kind of consciousness—and this is characteristic of philosophical [that is, Hegelian] consciousness—for which conceptual thinking is the real human being, and for which the conceptual world as such is thus the only reality" (*MER*: 238), bourgeois political economy championed a method of analysis which had as its most basic point of departure the actual social practices of human beings. But it was here that the political economists remained; in assuming that these social relations, and their own categories, represented what was natural or inevitable, they neglected the *historical* character of capitalist society and theory. For example, speaking of the category of labor, Marx argues that it "seems a quite simple category . . . when economically conceived," but is nonetheless "as modern a category as are the relations which create this simple abstraction" (*MER*: 239–40):

> This example of labor shows strikingly how even the most abstract categories, despite their validity—precisely because of their abstractness—for all epochs, are nevertheless, in the specific character of this abstraction, themselves likewise a product of historical relations, and possess their full validity only for and within these relations. (*MER*: 241)

From this brief discussion, I think it is now possible to see what Marx meant when he suggested that

> Social life is essentially *practical.* All mysteries which mislead theory into mysticism find their rational solution in human practice and the comprehension of this practice. (*MER*: 145)

It should also be evident that when he insisted that "The philosophers have only *interpreted* the world, in various ways; the point, however, is to *change* it" (*MER*: 145), he was at once indicting those forms of thought that "mislead theory"—and practice—"into mysticism," and proclaiming the ground from which a critical theory should build. Provoked by the experience of human suffering, a critical theory demonstrates the intimate link between this suffering and those forms of thought that justify it, and it turns this link between theory and practice to emancipatory ends by providing a *critical* theory that would show the oppressed that their freedom "is a question of revolutionising [*sic*] the existing world, of practically attacking and changing existing things" (*MER*: 169). Most, importantly, such a theory would be informed by the recognition that "*Every* emancipation is a *restoration* of the human world and of human relationships to *man himself*" (*MER*: 46).

These were the aims and foundations of Marx's "materialist conception of history." But they were not those realized by many who took up revolution in Marx's name.

THE HISTORICAL DISTORTION OF HISTORICAL MATERIALISM

When Marx spoke of the need for a "ruthless criticism of all that exists," he staked out an understanding that critical theory was not only to be "ruthless" in its "conflict with the powers that be," but it was also to be "ruthless" with respect to itself. For if critical theory is not to "be afraid of its own conclusions" (*MER*: 13), it must be "ruthlessly" reflexive on its own arguments and assumptions. This need for a critical reflection on the character of one's criticisms Marx recognized as central to the project of emancipation, although he also realized that "The inner difficulties" of engaging in critical theorizing "seem to be almost greater than the external obstacles" (*MER*: 13). Nonetheless, critical theory cannot avoid the demand for self-reflection if it is to avoid the "attempt to dogmatically prefigure the future" (*MER*: 13).

History has proven Marx prescient in recognizing that critical theory was a difficult undertaking. Little did he know that in the intervening years since he wrote these words, a number of movements would arise in which his own theory would be transformed into exactly the kind of dogmatism that Marx sought to avoid. David McLellan offers what I think is a good account of the rise and effect of this transformation:

> Marx urged his followers not to interpret the world, but to change it. But the more successful they were in this the more Marxism tended to become the doctrine of a mass movement. . . . [W]hat distinguished Marxism in this context was its rare ability to link revolutionary fervor and a desire for change with a historical perspective and a claim to be scientific. Almost inevitably, therefore, the inherited ideas were simplified, rigidified, ossified. Marxism became a matter of simple faith for its millions of adherents, to whom it gave the certainty of final victory. But this entailed an ever-growing distance from the original ideas of Marx and their transformation into a dogmatic ideology with the correlative concept of heresy—or revisionism as it was often called. (1979: 2)

It has been suggested that this ossification of Marxism (and the loss of critical self-examination that it entailed) may be attributed to the success of the Russian Revolution, and the institutionalization of the Soviet political system (Habermas 1973a: 197; Milliband 1977: 2–4; McCarthy 1978: 18). But Marx himself is not completely absolved of some responsibility for these developments. Even sympathetic students have charged that the transformation of Marxism into a kind of absolute knowledge which could be used to justify the "legal terror of Party dictatorship" (Habermas 1973a: 197) can be traced directly back to the "latent positivism" or scientism Marx himself sometimes seemed to tender (Habermas 1971: esp. chaps 2–3; Wellmer 1971: 67–119; Schroyer 1973: 92–97).

Suffice it to say that Marx did in fact leave open the door to an interpretation of historical materialism (the term itself is Engels', not Marx's) as a "scientific" method which "scientifically" guaranteed the inevitable revolutionary overthrow of capitalism. But whether one attributes this interpretation to a correct or mistaken reading of Marx misses the point that Marx's theory was first and foremost a theory having emancipatory intent. And it is quite clear that the kind of society one sees in many modern states is far from the kind of emancipation Marx had in mind. At any rate, ignoring the centrality of this emancipatory intent runs the risk of presenting a one-sided, and distorting reading of Marx:

> For unless we make Marx's own notion of critique thematic in the treatment of his work we shall risk reducing its unity and development to the contingencies of world politics and bibliographical discoveries which make of Marx an intellectual dope and of Marxism nothing but a series of historical and political pitfalls. (O'Neill 1972: 237)

My claim then, boils down to this: the historical distortion of historical materialism consists in the loss of the understanding Marx had of critical theory as "the ruthless criticism of everything existing" wherever human suffering and misery were to be found, and regardless of the forms that suffering might take. Changed historical circumstances may require that critical theory take different forms. But when Marx's critical theory of capitalism, situated as it was in a specific set of social relations, is transformed into the orthodoxy of a "scientific" world view that justifies domination, then the understanding of critique which informed Marx's work is distorted, if not lost. Such a possibility Marx seemed to anticipate, and it was not without good reason that he took as his own watchwords "Doubt all things" (quoted in Milliband 1977: 5).

There still remains, however, the need to give an account which would explain how Marx has been read as offering a scientific account of the necessary fall of capitalism and rise of communism. The Second International may well have secured the interpretation of Marxism, in the form of Dialectical Materialism (Diamat), as a general orientation to nature, history and thought that enabled its adherents to discover the "laws" that justified, in purportedly scientific terms, elitist politics and technocratic social management (McCarthy 1978: 18). But none of this might have occurred were it not for the fact that the downfall of capitalism Marx had predicted never took place.

When Marx undertook the task of criticizing capitalist relations of production, his critique was provoked by the suffering and misery of the proletariat Marx saw around him. For the most part the suffering he regarded as most insidious was that of the material emiseration of the working class. To be sure, Marx recognized that the causes of this material emiseration also had other effects on human beings, such as the estrangement (or alienation) of human beings from the products of their labor, the process of labor, their own self-identities, and their relations with each other (see especially *EPM*: 61–74). Nonetheless, the proletariat's material deprivations remained central to Marx's critique, and in fact Marx insisted that it would be the increasing emiseration of the proletariat, which would result from the periodic and ever more serious crises of overproduction inherent in the economic logic of capitalism (see *MER*: 443–65), that would be an important impetus for their self-reflection on the causes of their situation:

> Since the fully developed proletariat represents, practically speaking, the complete abstraction from everything human, even the *appearance* of being human; since all the living conditions of contemporary society have reached the acme of inhumanity in the living conditions of the proletariat; since in the proletariat man has lost himself, although at the same time he has both acquired a theoretical consciousness of this loss and has been directly forced into indignation against this humanity by virtue of an inexorable, utterly unembellishable, absolutely imperious *need*, that practical expression of *necessity*—because of all this the proletariat can and must liberate itself. (*MER*: 134)

But capitalism has subsequently shown itself to be much more resilient than Marx had anticipated, and the proletariat, rather than becoming increasingly emiserated within the relations of capitalism, enjoyed an ever-growing standard of living and relief from the insecurity of the proletarian existence Marx had portrayed.[4] It should therefore come as no surprise that Marx's revolution of the proletariat never materialized.

Perhaps, as Marcuse (1958: 24–25) has suggested, Marx's concepts were not intelligible to the proletariat in his time, and Marxian political theory and its goals were as a consequence alien to the existence and interests of the proletariat in the mid-nineteenth century. But whether this is true or not, the fact of the matter is that the capitalism that Marx knew, and the capitalism that the proletariat came to know in the years after Marx's death were in many respects altogether dif-

---

[4] For an account that attempts to treat these issues as a basis for reconsidering the central theses in Marx's work, see Wolin, 1983.

ferent modes of production.[5] The apparent autonomy of society and state, which was characteristic of Marx's understanding of capitalism, has been dissolved in advanced capitalism as the state has become increasingly active in intervening in the economic process in order to stave off crises that resulted from the anarchic conditions of an unregulated market (Habermas 1975: esp. 33–41).[6] The result has been an unprecedented growth in the wealth of the industrial-capitalist states, growth that has also raised the standard of living of the proletariat.

With the possibility of waiting on events in the industrialized countries diminishing, and in light of continued pressure from capitalist states, it should come as no surprise that Marxism was revised in order to accommodate the needs of what would come to be called "socialism in one country." Viewing itself as the most important bearer of the Marxist tradition, the Soviet Union, for example, was faced with the challenge of matching the capitalist states in material production if its revolution was not to be viewed as a failure, or overthrown by force. Thus the Soviets aimed "*to outstrip the economic level of the chief capitalist countries*" (Stalin, quoted in Marcuse 1958: 75). But the imperatives of economic development also had profound effects on the interpretation of Marxism.

It is here that my argument takes a turn towards the topic of the next section of this chapter, the attempted recovery of critique by the Frankfurt School and Habermas. For the historical distortion of historical materialism in part results from the same configuration of socioeconomic imperatives that have accompanied the rise of instrumental rationality in the capitalist societies. And as we have seen, it is this instrumental rationality that the Frankfurt School and Habermas

---

[5] It appears that Marx himself would have had no trouble accepting the need for a changed critical theory in the face of changed historical circumstances. See, for example, his attack on "*doctrinaire socialism*" as an "application of systems" (*MER*: 592). His comments on the interpretations of his theory in the Afterword to the Second German Edition of *Capital* (*MER*: 299–302), and his letter to the editorial board of the *Otechestvenniye Zapiski* (*SC*: 291–94), are also instructive in this regard.

[6] It is curious that Habermas fails to treat the effects of the exportation of exploitation to the Third World in his account of advanced capitalism. In this, he may well have overlooked the regions in which critical theory might be most effective. In fact, three of my chapters (on dependency theory, liberation theology and Paulo Freire) treat what we might call Third World critical theories. Larry Biskowski (1984), in his treatment of Sandinismo as a kind of critical theory, also appears to find the Western ethnocentrism of critical theory inadequate for situations in which oppression is most blatant—and where the need for a critical theory is most obvious. David Held (1980: 399–400) reaches similar conclusions when he notes that "critical theory loses sight of a range of important social and political struggles both within the West and beyond it—struggles which have changed and are continuing to change the face of politics."

argue constitutes the modern threat to critical reason as a guiding principle of social life.

I do not mean to argue that the scientization of Marxism began with Stalin's call for socialism in one country any more than I mean to suggest that the rise of instrumental rationality in the capitalist states began with advanced industrial capitalism. As we have seen earlier in this chapter, instrumental (or subjective) reason had its roots in the Enlightenment, but only became ascendent within the context of a particular set of social relations embodying its tenets. Much the same is true of Soviet Marxism:

> While not a single [one] of [Marx's] basic dialectical concepts has been revised in Soviet Marxism, the function of the dialectic itself has undergone a significant change: it has been transformed from a mode of critical thought into a universal method with rigidly fixed rules and regulations. . . . The change corresponds to that of Marxism itself from theory to ideology; dialectic is vested with the magical qualities of official thought and communication. As Marxian theory ceases to be the organon of revolutionary consciousness and practice and enters the superstructure of an established system of domination, the movement of dialectical thought is codified into a philosophical system. (Marcuse 1958: 137)

In the context of "socialism in one country" and the immediate goal of material advancement, these philosophical presuppositions were deployed in a form of Marxism that embodied a "new rationality." In this, the Soviet system and the Western capitalist systems came to share features common to late industrial society: centralization and regimentation over individual enterprise and autonomy, the organization and "rationalization" of economic competition, the joint rule of economic and political bureaucracies, and the coordination of activities through mass media (Marcuse 1958: 81).[7] It is a very small distance between the establishment of these practices and their justification in purportedly "scientific" terms. Thus, "The dialectic is petrified into a universal system in which the historical process appears as a 'natural' process and in which objective laws over and above the individuals govern not only the capitalist but the socialist society" (Marcuse 1958: 149), and in Soviet Marxism "historical materialism becomes one particular branch of the general scientific and philosoph-

---

[7] It is beyond the scope of my book to explore the ways that these features of the Soviet system represent a "convergence" between East and West. The differences between East and West are no less important than the similarities. My intention is only to suggest that a "scientized" interpretation of Marxism can be used to justify an instrumentalist political practice.

ical system of Marxism which, codified by the officials of the Party, justifies policy and practice" (Marcuse 1958: 145).

The historical distortion of historical materialism is therefore symptomatic of a changed historical situation in which two apparently opposed social forms take on increasingly similar tendencies. Joined in the general trend of technical progress and a "civilization of productivity" (Connolly 1981), both the self-proclaimed Marxist states and the advanced industrial-capitalist states raise to the level of principle the idea of "rationalization." In the modern period, says Marcuse, "The fusion between economic, cultural and political controls is an international phenomenon, cutting across differences in economic, cultural and political institutions" (Marcuse 1958: 187).

The scientization of politics and the rise of instrumental reason is, then, a peculiarly "modern" phenomenon. Faced with the rise of Soviet Marxism and a concomitant "insuperable barrier to any theoretical acceptance of Marxism" (Habermas 1973a: 198), the idea of a critical theory must be recovered against the various attempts that have been made to discredit it. This recovery entails the reconstruction of Marx's philosophical grounding of critical theory in light of changed historical circumstances that have rendered several tenets of his substantive theory anachronistic [i.e., the condition in which "the designated executor of a future socialist revolution, the proletariat *as* proletariat, has been dissolved" (Habermas 1973a: 196)]. Such a reconstruction cannot however merely return uncritically to Marx for its concepts and categories. For it must also detail a metatheoretical framework that can transcend the limitations of classical Marxism in light of new problems, new ways of thinking, and new forms of unfreedom.

This reconstruction is the task that the members of the Frankfurt School and Habermas undertake with their attempts to formulate a "critical theory of society."

THE FRANKFURT SCHOOL, HABERMAS, AND THE CHALLENGE OF INSTRUMENTAL REASON

> In what counter-tongue can reason be articulated?
> —Herbert Marcuse

With this probing question, Marcuse defines the task that the members of the Frankfurt School and Habermas take up in their attempts to formulate a "critical theory of society." Faced by a situation in which there is apparently "no mode of thought . . . which may criticize the conceptual forms and the structural patterns of science"

(Horkheimer 1982: 145), finding the "counter-tongue" of critical reason now requires a direct confrontation with scientism and instrumental reason.

It is in this project that the themes I have addressed in previous pages converge. We have seen that the need for a critical theory arises primarily from a situation in which social theory and practice are increasingly carried out in the terms set by "scientism," which is "the conviction that we can no longer understand science as *one* form of possible knowledge, but rather must identify knowledge with science" (Habermas 1971: 4). The political effect of this conviction is that questions regarding the ends of human existence are relegated, by philosophical injunction, to the realm of mere personal preference. We have also seen that it was Marx who stood as the last major figure whose work expressed the possibility of realizing the Enlightenment ideal of a unity of critical reason and political commitment. Against the uncritical defense of the status quo in both Hegelian idealism and bourgeois political economy, Marx attempted to hold open the possibility of rationally guided social change. But whatever the virtues of Marx's ideals, the fact that Marxism became "scientized," providing the ideological justification for the domination of human beings by an "enlightened" avant garde party, made the project of reconstructing critical theory that much more difficult.

The term "critical theory" was first coined by Max Horkheimer in his essay "Traditional and Critical Theory" (Horkheimer 1982: 188–243). In this essay, which came to serve as the general statement for the self-understandings of the members of the Frankfurt School and Habermas, Horkheimer says that he was interested in showing that there were "two ways of knowing: one based on [Descartes'] *Discourse on Method*, the other on Marx's critique of political economy" (Horkheimer 1982: 244), and that Marx's approach was the more perspicacious. With this particular claim, Horkheimer established a continuity between contemporary critical theory and Marx's understanding of critical theory, while at the same time defining the new context in which critique was to be carried out.

In their *Dialectic of Enlightenment* (1972) Horkheimer and Adorno characterized this context as one in which there was an intimate connection between "the enigmatic readiness of the technologically educated masses to fall under the sway of any despotism" (Horkheimer and Adorno, 1972: xiii) and the rise of a philosophy in which "the rational domination of nature comes increasingly to win the day" (Horkheimer and Adorno 1972: 223). This philosophy of domination is, of course, the same "scientism" of which Habermas often speaks; it provides the metatheoretical underpinnings of Horkheimer's "traditional" theory; and it entails the embodiment of "instrumental" reason. In its most sophisticated form, this philosophy was "positivism,"[8] which, Habermas argues, has "strengthen[ed] science's belief in its exclusive validity . . . with remarkable subtlety and indisputable success" (Habermas 1971: 4–5). And although we shall later see that there are some important differences between the critical theory of the Frankfurt School and that which Habermas envisions, all nonetheless agree that the function of contemporary critical theory is first and foremost to "reflect upon and give expression to . . . the socially conditioned tendency toward neopositivism or the instrumentalization of thought" (Horkheimer 1974: viii). In fact, it has even been suggested that contemporary critical theory is defined by an opposition to positivism (Wellmer 1971: 11–12; McCarthy 1978: 20), an interpretation apparently confirmed in Habermas's claim that "Every discussion of the conditions of possible knowledge *today* . . . must begin from the position worked out by analytical philosophy of science" (Habermas 1971: 5).

The importance of this emphasis cannot be overstated. But the critique of scientism also marks something of a radical departure from the immediate, practical issues critical theory is supposed to address. For the critique of scientism takes place primarily at a metatheoretical, rather than a specifically practical, level.[9]

Marx himself was seldom explicitly concerned with such metatheoretical questions, and whatever he did have to say about them often has to be extracted from texts attending other matters. To some extent this lack of metatheoretical concern may be explained by the fact that the threat posed by Hegelian idealism and bourgeois political economy was that they assumed the present to be the realization of human emancipation from dogmatism, and in this they did not deny

---

[8] "Positivism" is used rather loosely here—and in the work of the critical theorists. I use the term to denote the understanding of the critical theorists who, according to David Held, use "positivism" to mean any philosophy that adheres to the following five tenets (note the overlap with von Wright's account in note 1, Part I):

1. All (synthetic) knowledge is founded in sensory data.
2. Meaning is grounded in observation.
3. Concepts and generalizations represent only the particulars from which they have been abstracted. Conceptual entities don't exist in themselves—they are mere names; positivism is (normally) associated with nominalism.
4. All sciences are unified according to the methodology of the natural sciences.
5. Values are not facts and hence cannot be accorded the status of knowledge claims. (Held 1980: 163–64).

[9] As I suggested earlier this "metatheoretical turn" is not in itself problematic for critical theory. But the critical theorists fail to heed the lessons they learn from the critique of scientism, thereby relegating questions of political practice to secondary status.

the value of critical reason as positivism later would. Marx's concern was therefore not so much one of defending the place of critical reason as much as it was showing that "the idea of a reasonable organization of society that will meet the needs of the whole community" (Horkheimer 1982: 213) had not yet been met.

Whatever explanation we may have for Marx not treating systematically the metatheoretical foundations of critique, any attempt to recover the practical and emancipatory intent of Marx's social theory must now fill this gap. Moreover, any attempt to recover Marx's conception of critical theory must do so in a way that can separate its less obvious metatheoretical features from its more prominent theoretical claims. By this I mean that one must distinguish between Marx's theoretical (and historically contingent) claims and the philosophical grounding on which they are constructed. As a result, the concern for the realization of a truly emancipated society which Marx thought "was necessarily generated in the proletariat" (Horkheimer 1982: 213) cannot now serve to define the practical aim of critical theory. For in the changed historical circumstances of modern industrial society, "even the situation of the proletariat . . . is no guarantee of correct knowledge" (Horkheimer 1982: 213). Habermas puts the matter this way:

> Under these conditions [of modern industrial life], the designated executor of the socialist revolution, the proletariat as proletariat, has been dissolved. To be sure, the mass of the population, judging by their objective role in the process of production, is "proletarian"; they have no actual powers of control over the means of production. . . . But on the other hand, the exclusion from control over the means of production is no longer bound up to such an extent with deprivation of social rewards (income security, education, and so forth) that this objective situation would still in any way be experienced subjectively as proletarian. And any class consciousness, especially a revolutionary class consciousness, is not to be found in the main strata of the working class today. Every revolutionary theory, under these circumstances, lacks those to whom it is addressed; therefore arguments can no longer be translated into slogans. Even if there were still the critical mind, its heart is lacking; and thus today Marx would have to abandon his hope that theory can become a material force, once it has taken hold of the masses. (Habermas 1973a: 196–97)

Yet none of this should be taken to imply that Marxism's "truth is thereby contradicted" (Marcuse 1968: 142). On the contrary, such changes indicate the need to show that Marx's critique of capitalist political economy is *more* than an account of the inefficiencies and latent contradictions of capitalist production (Marcuse 1968: 144).

Critical theory still begins, says Horkheimer, as Marx did: "with the characterization of an economy based on exchange"; but it goes on to demonstrate

> that the basic form of the historically given commodity economy on which modern history rests contains in itself the internal and external tensions of the modern era; it generates these tensions over and over again in increasingly heightened form; and after a period of progress, development of human powers, and emancipation for the individual, after an enormous extension of human control over nature, it finally hinders further development and drives humanity into a new barbarism. (Horkheimer 1982: 227)

Thus "The new situation expressed in the authoritarian state could be easily comprehended and predicted by means of the concepts worked out by [Marx's] theory" (Marcuse 1968: 144).

For all their emphasis upon the continuities between Marx's critical theory and their own, it is nonetheless clear that for the Frankfurt School and Habermas, the "new situation" has in fact resulted in some substantial revisions. In the first place, Marx's theoretical concepts and categories were cast in a form specific to the anarchic competition of nineteenth-century capitalism, an "uncontrolled economy [which] controlled all human relations." This has since been replaced by "the rational organization of society . . . which is more than a new form of economic control" (Marcuse 1968: 144). This "rationalization" of society, in the interest of the increasingly "efficient" economic production *and* social control, Max Weber clearly "revealed as *technical* reason, as the production and transformation of material (things and men) through the methodical-scientific apparatus" (Marcuse 1968: 205). Thus, "Bureaucratic control is inseparable from increasing industrialization; it extends the maximally intensified efficiency of industrial organization to society as a whole" (Marcuse 1968: 216). Or as Habermas describes it:

> The laws of self-reproduction demand of an industrially advanced society that it look after its survival on the escalating scale of a continually expanded technical control over nature and a continually refined administration of human beings and their relations to each other by means of social organization. In this system, science, technology, industry, and administration interlock in a circular process. (Habermas 1973a: 254)

Claims of continuity notwithstanding, then, contemporary critical theory has done more than simply extend Marx's concepts and categories. Moreover, faced with a situation where "Emancipation by means of enlightenment is replaced by instruction in control over objective *or objectified* processes" (Habermas 1973a: 254–55), contemporary critical theory cannot assume that it shares with its opposition a similar aim. Marx may have been able to do so, for his intellectual opponents were at least committed to the idea of critical reason. But contemporary scientism is not the same beast he faced in Hegelian idealism and bourgeois political economy. Contemporary scientism and contemporary critical theory are, by contrast, at odds on issues that run deep, right down to the basic presuppositions of human knowledge and human identity.

The Critique of Scientism

In light of the interlocking relationship between positivist philosophy of science, technology, industry, and bureaucratic social organization, the critique of scientism is supposed to provide the means of bringing down the edifice of instrumental reason while simultaneously clearing ground for the reconstruction of critical reason. As I suggested earlier, these inquiries may appear distant from practical issues of day to day life, but for the critical theorists they are not. As Albrecht Wellmer argues,

> critical theory recognizes the meta-theory of method as one of its constituent parts. This union of theory and meta-theory is only another expression of the unity of theory and practice (*praxis*), which critical theory has made its own. In the controversy about method the actual political struggle is reproduced as a battle of minds: accordingly, critical theory treats the expectation of a resolution of this conflict in the pure medium of the mind as a bourgeois illusion. (1971: 15)

The claim in this passage, that social theory and social practice are but two aspects of the same activity, may have been unproblematic in an earlier time. Since the rise of "traditional" theory, however, the practical and emancipatory interest of critical theory appears "subjective and speculative, one-sided and useless. Since it runs counter to prevailing habits of thought . . . it appears to be biased and unjust" (Horkheimer 1982: 218).

Against this view, the critical theorists argue that scientism ignores such normative issues at the risk of undermining the legitimacy of science itself. This is clearly evident in the case of the positivist presuppositions that inform scientism. On the one hand, positivists must "rely on the successes of science as a justification of their own method" (Horkheimer 1947: 78), but in doing so they beg the question of why science should be taken as the only means by which useful knowledge may be attained. Thus Horkheimer:

The same vicious circle is involved in any justification of scientific method by the observation of science: How is the principle of observation itself to be justified? When a justification is requested, when someone asks why observation is the proper guarantee of truth, the positivists simply appeal to observation again. But their eyes are closed. Instead of interrupting the machine-like functioning of research, the mechanisms of fact-finding, verification, classification, et cetera, and reflecting on their meaning and relation to truth, the positivists reiterate that science proceeds by observation and describe circumstantially how it functions. . . . In other words, in refusing to verify their own principle—that no statement is meaningful unless verified—they are guilty of *petitio principii*, begging the question. (Horkheimer 1947: 76)

The point here is that committed positivists cannot provide an explanation of why scientific knowledge is accepted as rational. What's more, the positivist cannot treat his or her acceptance of scientism in scientistic terms. Thus positivism is unable to "justify any reflection that goes beyond science, including itself" (Habermas 1971: 87). By virtue of its philosophical injunctions, then, positivism establishes a definition of "knowledge" in which *The meaning of knowledge itself becomes irrational*—in the name of rigorous knowledge" (Habermas 1971: 68–69).

Some readers may interpret the criticisms of positivism advanced by the critical theorists as attacks on science itself. But this is to misunderstand their intent. The fact of the matter is that the critical theorists recognize the enormous success of scientific inquiry carried out within the framework of "traditional" theory—at least in the case of the natural sciences. As a model for these disciplines, "traditional" theory has proven enormously useful. As sciences that aim to causally explain the workings of natural processes, the natural sciences have made themselves the cornerstone of technological progress which has offered human beings the objective prerequisites for their emancipation from material wants:

The technological advances of the bourgeois period are inseparably linked to . . . the pursuit of science. On the one hand, [traditional theory] made the facts fruitful for the kind of scientific knowledge that would have practical application in the circumstances, and, on the other hand, it made possible the application of knowledge already possessed. Beyond doubt, such work is a moment in the continuous transformation and development of the material foundations of that society. (Horkheimer 1982: 194)

Thus, the critical theorists find no fault in the "demystification" of the world that Enlightenment thinkers sought, and which scientism has made possible.[10] But as we saw earlier in this chapter, the Enlightenment also opened up more pernicious possibilities which scientism has all too effectively realized. "Reason" had indeed objectified nature, thereby making possible the control of natural processes for human ends; but it had also gone beyond this kind of knowledge, and was "turned against the thinking subject" (Horkheimer and Adorno 1972: 12). And so for the critical theorists the real problem with instrumental reason is not that it is inherently mistaken, but that it had been expanded "to the proportions of a life form, of the 'historical totality' of a life world" (Habermas 1970: 90).

Positivism in this sense embodies a principled refusal to distinguish between the subject who creates knowledge and the objects of that knowledge. Collapsing the distinction, however, leads to what Karl-Otto Apel has called "methodical solipsism"; "the tacit assumption that *objective* knowledge should be possible without *intersubjective* understanding by communication being presupposed" (Apel 1972: 10). By this, Apel means that positivism assumes that the "rationality" of knowledge claims can be asserted without recognizing that the procedures, norms and standards for making such claims are the result of intersubjective, communicatively attained agreement. Positivists must therefore either ignore the intersubjective, communicative foundations of science itself, or they must treat the social basis of science as a field of inquiry coextensive with those of the natural sciences. The first solution, while ignoring important questions about the foundations of scientific activity, may be effective in producing knowledge that allows human beings to control natural processes.[11] But when the second line of argument is pursued, the result is a misrepresentation of social reality and human subjectivity, a misrepresentation that in turn underwrites instrumentalism in social relations.

The misrepresentation of social phenomena occurs because of the "objectivist" assumptions of positivism. Simply put, objectivism assumes that the world exists independently of what human beings may think of it. "Knowledge" of the world therefore requires empirically

[10] The exception here appears to be Marcuse, who seems to indict both technology and (natural) science as a form of "ideology" in his *One Dimensional Man* (1964). Habermas takes issue with Marcuse on this matter, however. See Habermas 1970: 81–122.

[11] In subsequent chapters I occasionally return to these issues. As we shall also see in the case of feminist critiques of scientism, the problem of scientism is not that it makes it impossible for natural scientists to achieve rationally justified accounts of the features and causal relationships between natural phenomena; rather, the problem is that scientism fails to explain how these achievements have been gained. And when scientism is taken to be a model for knowledge *simpliciter*, the social and political consequences of its philosophical commitments and self-understandings are pernicious.

verifiable claims; no others may be admitted as legitimate. On these assumptions,

> The real validity of the theory depends on [its] derived propositions being consonant with the actual facts. If experience and theory contradict each other, one of the two must be reexamined. Either the scientist has failed to observe correctly or something is wrong with the principles of the theory. (Horkheimer 1982: 188)

Because these assumptions also issue in a strict separation of "knower" from that which is "known," they also underwrite a separation of theory and practice:

> The object with which the scientific specialist deals is not affected at all by his own theory. Subject and object are kept strictly apart. Even if it turns out that at a later point in time the objective event is influenced by human intervention, to science this is just another fact. The objective occurrence is independent of the theory, and this independence is part of its necessity: the observer as such can effect no change in the object. (Horkheimer 1982: 229)

Thus, the objectivism of positivism supports a view of an empirical world independent of theoretical considerations and theorists' constructions, one which "correlates theoretical propositions with matters of fact" (Habermas 1971: 307). But it is precisely in this that positivism precludes any consideration of how the findings of science might be used; indeed, it renders as mere "opinion" any consideration of these uses, for "the genesis of particular objective facts, the practical application of the conceptual systems by which it grasps the facts, and the role of such systems in action, are all taken to be external to the theoretical thinking itself (Horkheimer 1982: 208).

For the critical theorists, this apparent neutrality is illusory. In fact, the kind of practical applications to which scientific knowledge may be put are dictated by its analytical presuppositions. As Habermas argues,

> In the *empirical-analytical sciences* the frame of reference that prejudges the meaning of possible statements establishes rules both for the construction of theories and for their critical testing. Theories comprise hypothetical-deductive connections of propositions, which permit the deduction of lawlike hypotheses with empirical content. The latter can be interpreted as statements about the covariance of observable events; given a set of initial conditions, they make predictions possible. Empirical analytical knowledge is thus possible predictive knowledge. (Habermas 1971: 308)

To repeat, the objectivist assumptions of positivism may not be problematic in the natural sciences. Our ability to predict and control the course of natural events and processes in fact depends in large part on our ability to formulate law-like hypotheses. But when the methodological tenets of positivism are deployed in the explanation of social events, social processes, and actions of social agents—such as those of science as a social activity, and scientists as agents of that activity—the "objectivist illusion" of positivism becomes obvious.

What positivism fails to recognize is that in their objectification of the world, scientists cannot objectify themselves lest they leave unexamined and unaccounted the basis of their objectification. Positivism ignores the fact that something is an object only for a subject capable of objectification. As Marcuse argues, "Scientific experience as well as pre-scientific experience are false, incomplete insofar as they experience as *objective* (material or ideational) what in reality is subject-object, objectivation of subjectivity" (Marcuse 1974: 234).

To be sure, this is a rather sweeping indictment. The history of the philosophy of science, after all, has been characterized by a progressive refinement of the arguments in defense of scientism. The crude "subjective realism" of early (Humean) empiricism, in which the world simply became known to the subject through unmediated sense perception, has been superseded by the more sophisticated physicalism of the Vienna Circle, and more recently the "critical rationalism" of Popper. But while the difference between these schools is important, and while it may confuse matters somewhat to call all of them positivist, as the critical theorists do, they all nonetheless exhibit an important central assumption that justifies treating them as a whole. Because all assume that human subjects can be validly known as objects of science, all deny the intersubjectivity of human experience; scientism assumes "that the knowing subject can, in principle, win objective knowledge of the world without at the same time presupposing knowledge by sign interpretation or intersubjective understanding, . . . that one solitary subject of knowledge could objectify the whole world, including his fellow men" (Apel 1972: 5). Science, in other words, becomes unintelligible as a human social activity in which socially created rules, norms and conventions define what can and cannot be counted as "science." Science becomes reified, its origins in communicative activity forgotten, and its methodology comes to dictate the structure of its objects rather than the reverse. "But by making a dogma of the sciences' belief in themselves, positivism assumes the prohibitive function of protecting scientific inquiry from epistemological self-reflection" (Habermas 1971: 67). Thus the social foundations of science recede into the background as the philosophy of science renounces inquiry into the knowing subject. It orients itself directly toward the sciences, which are given as systems of propositions and procedures, that is, as a complex of rules according to which theories are constructed and corroborated. For an epistemology restricted to methodology, the subjects who proceed according to these rules lose their significance. Their deeds and destinies belong at best to the psychology of the empirical persons to whom the subjects of knowledge have been reduced. (Habermas 1971: 68)

As the community of scientists is reified, so too is the social world generally. When social theory becomes subsumed under the methodological rubric of positivism, society becomes conceptualized as a "second nature" (Adorno 1976: 243). And when this "naturalization" of society and human beings is linked with positivism's methodological exclusion of all forms of knowledge that are not matters of "fact," it leads to a misdescription of social relations. Positivism blinds human beings from recognizing that society and social beliefs, "the given, the facts which, according to its methodology, it encounters as ultimate, are themselves not ultimate but conditional" (Adorno 1976: 225).

With the rise of positivism as the dominant philosophical understanding of what can be called legitimate knowledge, the dialectic of the Enlightenment reaches its zenith. Indeed, in a civilization which defines itself by the ever more efficient and ever more productive harnessing of nature and humanity, positivism provides the measure of all knowledge. What cannot contribute to a more "efficient" realization of the aims of that society cannot be counted as valid, real, or rationally defensible knowledge. Morality, ethics, politics: if the arguments for proper conduct in these specifically human spheres of action cannot be given the kind of rigorous theoretical grounding demanded by the methodological structures of "science," then they are dismissed as value-laden and their proponents as ideologues and dogmatists. Yet to treat moral, ethical, and political questions as if they can be answered in the same way as questions about nature is to establish a philosophical justification for the objectification and instrumental treatment of human beings themselves. Buttressed by its purported elimination of subjectivity in favor of an "objective" and therefore "value free" knowledge, positivism merely champions a particular value orientation—instrumental rationality.

In a passage that still seems to speak to us across the years, Marx characterized the then incipient spirit of objectification and its effects in these words:

There is one great fact, characteristic of this our nineteenth century, a fact which no party dares deny. On the one hand, there have started into life industrial and scientific forces, which no epoch of the former human history had ever suspected. On the other hand, there exist symptoms of decay, far surpassing the horrors recorded of the latter times of the Roman empire. In our days everything seems pregnant with its contrary. Machinery, gifted with the wonderful power of shortening and fructifying human labor, we behold starving and overworking it. The new-fangled sources of wealth, by some strange weird spell, are turned into sources of want. The victories of art seem bought by the loss of character. At the same pace that mankind masters nature, man seems to become enslaved to other men or to his own infamy. Even the pure light of science seems unable to shine but on the dark background of ignorance. All our invention and progress seem to result in endowing material forces with intellectual life, and in stultifying human life into a material force. (*MER*: 577–78)

Marx wrote these words when the objectifying spirit of modern industrial society was a looming specter whose contours were yet to clearly take shape. He thought the fact that "everything seems pregnant with its contrary" implied not only domination of human beings by those same material forces which seemed to promise freedom from want, but also the imminent birth of a revolutionary fervor that would restore control of their lives to human beings. His prognosis was only half right. The objectifying spirit did not give way to a proletarian revolutionary fervor. It has merely become a "new barbarism" far more subtle and complex than he could have imagined.

But it is not enough to attack positivism and instrumental reason. If critical theory is to restore the proper relationship of critical and instrumental reason, and thereby ground a commitment to enlightenment and emancipation, it can do so only by providing a philosophically perspicacious reconstruction capable of showing what possibilities are open to human beings. The next chapter examines how Marx, the Frankfurt School, and Habermas pursue this project.

CHAPTER 2

The Nature of Modernist Critical Theory

MY DISCUSSION to this point has primarily addressed the background against which the critical theory of Marx, the Frankfurt School, and Habermas take their shape. Two themes are central to that discussion. The first is that these critical theorists may be understood as seeking to realize the promise of the Enlightenment ideal of emancipation through reason. The second is that the character of unreason has changed and transformed, and in many respects it has done so in terms that were also set by the Enlightenment. It would now seem that in both East and West, the "Iron Cage" Weber thought was the consequence of "rationalization" is nearly closed. Human beings and society, now conceptualized as "objects," are manipulated by those who lay claim to specialized—often "scientific"—knowledge. But perhaps the greatest tragedy is that those being manipulated often accept the same discourse of instrumental reason that undergirds their oppression. For the critical theorists, then, the task of an enlightening and emancipatory critical theory is to break the grip of objectification. Indeed, in this context, a critical theory must seek the means that would realize Marx's call that *"Every* emancipation" be "a *restoration* of the human world and of human relationships to *man himself"* (*MER*: 46).

From his reading of the critical theorists, Raymond Geuss (1981) has culled three central metatheoretical features that serve to define how a critical theory might realize this project. These are its *goals, logical or cognitive structure,* and *standards of confirmation* (1981: 55). The goal or aim of a critical theory, as I have emphasized, is enlightenment and emancipation; in short, "a form of life free from unnecessary domination in all its forms" (McCarthy 1978: 273). The logical or cognitive structure of a critical theory is what Geuss calls "self-referential" or "reflective." Where objectifying theories (as we have seen) assume the strict separation of the theorist and theory from the theoretical object, "a critical theory is itself always a part of its object domain" (Geuss 1981: 55). Or as Habermas puts it, "The theory occupies itself with reflection on the interrelationships of its origin and with anticipation of those of its application" (1973a: 2). And this cognitive structure in turn helps define the standards of confirmation which apply to critical theory. As Habermas says,

By anticipating the context of its own application, critique differs from what Horkheimer has called "traditional theory." Critique understands that its claims to validity can be verified only in the successful process of enlightenment, and that means: in the practical discourse of those concerned. (Habermas 1973a: 2)

When we consider what holds together, the goals, structure, and standards of verification of critical theory, what makes them complementary parts of a coherent conceptual whole, one particular precondition is crucial: the presence of an addressee. Without a specific audience who "with its aid can gain enlightenment about their emancipatory role in the process of history," in whose social life it can be anticipated "as a necessary catalytic moment," and in whose *practice* "its claims to validity can be verified" (Habermas 1973a: 2), the goal, structure and confirmation of a critical theory are incoherent ideals. Without an addressee, a critical theory is bankrupt on its own terms.

In this chapter I try to show that in spite of their expressed commitment to these methodological principles, Marx, the Frankfurt School, and Habermas are unable to realize them. I should note at the outset that there are important differences among the critical theorists on these matters. My intention, however, is to emphasize the similarities in their positions, for I believe it is in attending to the shared themes in their work that we can best see why the critical theory of the Frankfurt School and Habermas has thus far remained primarily an academic preserve, and also why Marx's critical theory contributed to this development. But I also suggest that there are intimations in all their work of how a critical theory might in fact realize its promise.

My plan is to develop these themes in four parts. I first return briefly to Marx in order to illustrate how he managed to present a consistent, albeit problematic, critical theory. I then point out how the members of the Frankfurt School and Habermas share with Marx a commitment to the unity of theory and practice, even while they go beyond Marx in developing the basis of this relationship via their critique of scientism. In the third section I consider the Frankfurt School's and Habermas's criticisms and consequent abandonment of some of the central assumptions in Marx's work—particularly the abandonment of the proletariat as the audience of critical theory—and how this creates a tension between the practical aims and political implications of their own work. Finally, in the last section I offer a tentative resolution of these tensions. Here I suggest that just as the critical theorists used Marx to move beyond Marx in order to keep alive the idea of a critical theory of society, so too can we use the Frankfurt School and Habermas to move beyond the current impasse of modernist critical theory.

MARX'S CRITICAL THEORY

For Marx, critical theory was inextricably bound up in the proletariat. As we saw in chapter 1, it was in the proletariat that Marx found the experience of suffering and oppression that served to ground the emancipatory interest of critique. As we shall see here, it was in the historical development of the proletariat that Marx located the origin of his theory, in their future development that he anticipated its application, and on their revolutionary practice that he made the confirmation of his theory depend.

Thus did Marx's theory embody the characteristic goals, logical structure, and standards of verification of a critical theory outlined above. Indeed, it may even be said that Marx set the terms by which these would come to be recognized as defining features of a critical theory. But as I shall argue, the problem with Marx's critical theory is that it is not a very good one. Not only did it not issue in a proletarian revolution, but its many ambiguous claims and problematic assertions actually became the source of the instrumentalist practices I discussed in chapter 1.

We can begin sorting out these difficulties by turning first to Marx's understanding of the unique character of the proletariat. For him, the proletariat embodied the potential for realizing a universal human interest in emancipation and freedom because of its particular place in history. The extent to which Marx believed this reconciliation of the abstract and the specific, the universal and the particular, was located in the proletariat is best captured in the introduction to his *Contribution to the Critique of Hegel's Philosophy of Right*. Speaking to the specific problem of "a *real* emancipation in Germany" Marx clearly delineates what he believes is the universal character of the proletariat's real interests:

> *This is our reply* [to the question of German emancipation]. A class must be formed which has *radical chains*, a class in civil society which is not a class of civil society. A class which is the dissolution of all classes, a sphere of society which has a universal character because its sufferings are universal, and which does not claim a *particular redress* because the wrong which is done to it is not a *particular wrong* but *wrong in general*. There must be formed a sphere of society which claims no *traditional* status but only a *human* status, a sphere which is not opposed to particular consequences but is totally opposed to the assumptions of the German political

system; a sphere, finally, which cannot emancipate itself without emancipating itself from all the other spheres of society, without, therefore, emancipating all the other spheres, which is, in short, a *total loss* of humanity and which can only redeem itself by a *total redemption of humanity*. This dissolution of society, as a particular class, is the *proletariat*. (*MER*: 64)

It was thus in the emancipation of the proletariat that Marx believed the future freedom of all humanity could be realized. In this respect, the proletariat was for Marx the "universal class"; within the particular philosophy of history to which Marx subscribed the proletariat was unquestionably the historically specific embodiment of a universal interest in emancipation. This reconciliation of the universal and the particular may also be seen as an aspect of Marx's understanding of how his theory was "self-referential." Thus Marx: "Philosophy finds its *material* weapons in the proletariat, [and] the proletariat finds its *intellectual* weapons in philosophy. . . . *Philosophy* is the *head* of this emancipation and the *proletariat* its *heart*" (*MER*: 65). And it also undergirded his understanding that the emancipation of the proletariat would "confirm" his theory: "Philosophy can only be realized by the abolition of the proletariat, and the proletariat can only be abolished by the realization of philosophy" (*MER*: 65).

Now whether Marx was right in his account of the proletariat's position as the "universal class," and whether the anticipated appropriation of his theory by the proletariat would take place is an important question. But we should not lose sight of the essential practical implications of Marx's understanding of critical theory. Maintaining that "Theory is only realized in a people so far as it fills the needs of the people" (*MER*: 61), Marx laid down methodological principles that anticipated the Frankfurt School's and Habermas's later accounts of the differences between "traditional" and "critical" theory:

> The question whether objective truth can be attributed to human thinking is not a question of theory but is a *practical* question. Man must prove the truth, that is, the reality and power, the this-sidedness of his thinking in practice. The dispute over the reality or non-reality of thinking which is isolated from practice is a purely *scholastic* question. (*MER*: 144)

Given the ascendency of "traditional" theory, Marx's claims may appear (in Horkheimer's words) "subjective and speculative . . . biased and unjust" (1982: 218). These claims are not, however, mere bias or speculative assertion for Marx. They are rather based upon a rigorous analysis of the teleological claims of Hegelian idealism and the naturalistic claims of the political economists. Marx's criticisms of these two systems of thought are grounded in a critical analysis of the origins of social beliefs, values and practices. For Hegel, these origins were attributable to the movement of Spirit; for the political economists they were the natural outcome of an aquisitive, self-interested human "nature." But neither was correct. As Marx argued, "Men make their own history," and while they may not "make it under circumstances chosen by themselves" (*MER*: 595), it was precisely in recognizing their capacity for making their own history that human beings could overcome the dead weight of the past:

> Communism differs from all previous movements in that it overturns the basis of all earlier relations of production and intercourse, and for the first time consciously treats all natural premises as the creatures of hitherto existing men, strips them of their natural characteristics and subjugates them to the power of the united individuals. . . . The difference between the individual as a person and what is accidental to him is not a conceptual difference but a historical fact. (*MER*: 193–94)

So for Marx, the necessary relationship between a critical theory and political practice is the logical conclusion of an analysis which shows that human beings make their own history, yet fail to realize this fact because of beliefs that obscure it. A critical theory would thus be confirmed when it assisted its addressees in recognizing their ability to make their own history—a recognition that is verified only when the theory's addressees actually begin to exercise that ability. But this is why I suggested that Marx's critical theory was not a very good one. By the same standards to which Marx subscribes, it may be safely said that his theory was a failure. There has been no proletarian revolution. Marx was able to articulate reasons why the proletariat had to be emancipated. He was also able to spell out the historical origins of his theory and anticipate the conditions of its application. But the apparent "falsification" of his theory means that we must ask whether the particular form it took was in part responsible for its failure.

One important point in this regard is the tension between Marx's criticisms of Hegelian idealism and bourgeois political economy, and the substantive content of Marx's reconstruction of the proletariat's situation. These other theories, Marx insisted, had misdescribed social relations and practices; they described historically contingent, mutable conditions as natural and/or inevitable. Yet at the same time, Marx appeared to suggest that the emancipatory interest of the proletariat was not merely contingent and specific, but universal. This universality went beyond the proletariat sharing with human beings generally an interest in emancipation and freedom, for the proletariat's freedom was made the precondition of freedom for all. This, then, is the tension in Marx's critical theory: on the one hand he insists on the historical and contextual character of all theory, and on the other his work appears to be haunted by the ghost of a transhistorical assumption of the sort he so effectively criticizes in other theories.

This tension can be resolved only by jettisoning the theoretical self-certainty of Marx's account of the proletariat as the "universal class" in favor of the metatheoretical claims that emerge from the critique of Hegelianism and bourgeois political economy. The reasons should be obvious enough, especially in light of available historical evidence. Theoretical self-certainty too easily slides off into an instrumentalist practice—it in effect reifies the proletariat. And the historical distortion of historical materialism stands as proof of the effects of this reification and instrumentalism.

This much the members of the Frankfurt School and Habermas appear to have recognized. Indeed, their critique of scientism can be understood as in part turning on an effort to preserve Marx's metatheoretical insights while distancing themselves from the destructive features of Marxism. As we shall see, however, there is an intricate dialect in this preservation and distancing, the consequence of which is an increasing separation between modernist critical theory and its practical intentions.

CRITICAL THEORY AFTER MARX

The extent to which the Frankfurt School and Habermas maintain the centrality of the theory-practice relationship is evident throughout their work. Marcuse captures this basic presupposition best in his claim that "Marxism comes to life in the inseparable unity of theory and practice; and every Marxist analysis must retain this unity as its most important guiding principle" (Marcuse 1969: 3). This principle takes shape through an immanent critique of the dominant self-understandings of particular historical contexts—for Marx, Hegelian idealism and the naturalism of the political economists; for the critical theorists, scientism and instrumental reason. But the principle involved is more than just a negation of particular, historically specific theories; it establishes metatheoretical foundations for critiques that may be taken up in contexts quite different from those in which it was initially formulated. In other words, Marx's immanent critique of Hegelian idealism and bourgeois political economy, and the Frankfurt School's and Habermas's critique of instrumental reason, serve as examples of more general philosophical foundations:

> By criticism, we mean that intellectual, and eventually practical, effort which is not satisfied to accept the prevailing ideas, actions, and social con-

ditions unthinkingly and from mere habit; effort which aims to coordinate the individual sides of social life with each other and with the general ideas and aims of the epoch, to deduce them genetically, to distinguish the appearance from the essence, to examine the foundations of things, in short, really to know them. (Horkheimer 1982: 270)

What are these "foundations of things," and in what sense do they provide the essential underpinning for an understanding which makes political practice an essential moment in a critical theory? Two related themes, both of which may be found in Marx, are important here. The first is that of the belief-constituted character of social relations; the argument that social institutions and practices are constituted by the beliefs, values, norms, concepts, in short, the language of social agents. The second is the historicity of our social knowledge. And for the Frankfurt School and Habermas, these same themes issue from the critique of scientism.

We have already seen how scientism obscures these insights. To briefly recapitulate, a scientistic account of the origins of scientism cannot be given, for only when the intersubjective, communicative foundations of science are recognized are we able to understand and account for those origins. And one can readily extend the insights here by pointing out the fact that science is merely one among many social practices; thus it may be said that all social practices are in large part constituted by the belief-informed actions of social agents.

More than this, however, is implied in recognizing the belief-constituted character of social institutions and practices:

> On the one hand, neither the direction and methods of theory nor its object, reality itself, are independent of man, and, on the other hand, science is a factor in the historical process. (Horkheimer 1982: 4)

In fact, even "the separation of theory and action is itself an historical phenomenon" (Horkheimer 1982: 4), the result of a particular, historically contingent constellation of beliefs that comprises the ascendent modern conception of social knowledge. As Marx said, social institutions—and the systems of thought that purport to describe them—are "historical and transitory products" (*PP*: 95–96). Knowledge must be understood as part and parcel of specific social practices; not by "describing in advance the cognitive achievement in accordance with a logical or scientific knowledge to which, in truth, productive knowledge in no way corresponds" (Adorno 1969: 111).

All of this of course also implies that any theory which purports to be "emancipatory and enlightening" recognizes its own practical and contextual grounding. Such a theory would be "practical" by enlightening its addressess regarding the contingency of the oppression they suffer, and it would be "contextual" by being attentive to "the constitutive historical complex of the constellation of self-interests, to which the theory still belongs across and beyond its acts of insight" (Habermas 1973a: 2). Only with this can a critical theory intervene in that constellation of interests. Thus, a critical theory is understood "as a theory of society conceived with practical intent" (Habermas 1973a: 3), because "in regard to the essential kind of change at which the critical theory aims, there can be no corresponding concrete perception of it until it actually comes about. If the proof of the pudding is in the eating, the eating here is still in the future" (Horkheimer 1982: 220–21).

We can see in this brief discussion the same constitutive connections between the goal, logical structure and conception of verification in critical theory we found in Marx. In a dense, but nonetheless illuminating passage, Habermas describes these connections this way:

> The theory serves primarily to enlighten those to whom it is addressed about the position they occupy in an antagonistic social system and about the interests of which they must become conscious in this situation as being objectively theirs. Only to the degree that organized enlightenment and consultation lead those groups toward which this is directed actually recognizing themselves in the interpretations offered, do the analytically proposed interpretations actually become consciousness, and does the objectively attributed situation of interests actually become the real interest of a group capable of action. (Habermas 1973a: 32).

In other words, "the theory legitimizes the work of enlightenment, as well as providing its own refutation when communication fails" (Habermas 1973a: 33). Its goal is to enlighten its addressees so that their self-emancipatory action can begin; its logical structure is such that it strives to be part of their self-understandings in terms of both origins and application; and the success of the goal and the verification of the argument depend in the final analysis on the actual self-emancipating practices of those addressees. This is the basis of my earlier claim that a critical theory without this practical dimension is bankrupt on its own terms.

To whom, then, is the critical theory of the Frankfurt School and Habermas addressed? In whose life experiences does the emancipatory interest of modernist critical theory find its grounding? In whose emancipatory practices can the theory be embodied and therefore verified? These are straightforward questions demanded by the claims of critical theory itself. The answers we find, however, are not so straightforward.

CRITICAL THEORY FOR WHOM?

In the accounts of many scholars, one of the most problematic features of the work of the Frankfurt School and Habermas is the surprising underdevelopment of its practical dimension. The comments of Thomas McCarthy, Martin Jay, David Held and Richard Bernstein, all of whom are sympathetic to the idea of a critical theory, are typical. What follows is an array of passages from these scholars on the work of Horkheimer, Adorno, Marcuse and Habermas.

> For critical theorists it became a central issue—some might say, their Achilles heel—to determine who is or will become [the] revolutionary class; who are the subjects to whom critical theory is addressed. Indeed, what is the function of critical theory, if no such class seems to exist? (Bernstein 1976: 183)

> It is striking that critical theory acknowledges no central revolutionary agent, while its proponents seek to develop Marxism. They present a revolutionary theory in an age which, on their account, is nonrevolutionary. In doing so, their work exhibits a paradox, particularly embarrassing since they maintain that the potentialities for human and social change must be historically based: they offer a theory of the importance of fundamental social transformation which has little basis in social struggle. (Held 1980: 399)

> Paradoxically, Adorno's "reflections on damaged life," which contain insights full of practical implications, tied him to a position which prevents recognition of the relation of these reflections to concrete historical problems. (Held 1980: 385)

> [Adorno] continued to defend the importance of critical thinking as "bottles thrown into the sea" for future addressees, whose identity was still unknown. (Jay 1984: 54)

> Horkheimer's argument about how in a capitalist mode of production the needs of the members of the community as a whole remain unfulfilled is an interesting step. . . . But the connections, in actual social movements, between needs, interests and the universal principles of equality and liberty, remain unexplored. (Held 1980: 386)

> Marcuse's central concern has been to establish for our own time "the inseparable unity of theory and practice," and yet it is precisely in this project that he most dramatically fails. . . . With all his talk of the need for critical theory to become historically relevant, to analyze the tendencies within existing society that can lead to radical change, and to be concrete and spe-

cific, Marcuse has never fulfilled the demands of his own basic conception of critical theory. (Bernstein 1971: 97, 106)

There is little approaching a revolutionary subject in Habermas's argument; and this despite the fact that he recognizes the need for a theory such as his to be able to identify the subject of emancipation. Processes of actual transformation remain unthematized: we remain very much in the dark as to the nature of political processes and events. As a consequence, it is difficult to draw any political conclusions from [his legitimation] crises argument. The practical implications of the theory are undeveloped. (Held 1980: 376)

[C]ritical theory finds itself in a familiar embarrassment; there is no organized social movement whose interests it might seek to articulate. It is this, I believe, that is ultimately behind the generality of Habermas's crisis argument. . . . His critique retains an anonymous character, addressed to "mankind as such" and thus to no group in particular. (McCarthy 1978: 385–86)

The very self understanding of the nature of a theory with practical intent by critical theorists requires the existence of a group or class of individuals to whom it is primarily addressed, and who will be the agents of revolution. . . . No critical theorist, including Habermas, has been absolutely clear on this point in the way that Marx was. . . . Despite the lip service paid to Marx, are not the critical theorists betraying what even *they* take to be the vital core of Marxism—the development of a theory with genuine practical intent? (Bernstein 1976: 206)

My intention in providing this long list of criticisms is to document what appears to be endemic to critical theory as we know it, namely, the lack of a practical dimension in the work of the Frankfurt School and Habermas. Accounting for the ways in which the critical theorists have managed to displace the practical dimension in their work is a task of some magnitude, well beyond the scope of this book.[1] Nonetheless, I think some useful lessons may be realized if we pursue the genesis of this displacement.

I shall argue that the critical theory of the Frankfurt School and Habermas has no practical dimension because it is too close to Marx's Marxism and some of its most questionable formulations, and that this continuity with Marxism has made it difficult for the Frankfurt School and Habermas to recognize, or adequately conceptualize, the emancipatory potential of many contemporary struggles for empowerment.

[1] For more exhaustive treatments of the Frankfurt School and Habermas, see the works cited in notes 2 and 3 of chapter 1.

Bluntly stated, I shall contend that modernist critical theory is unable to break from the "universalist" assumptions that have plagued attempts to realize "critical reason" since, perhaps, the Enlightenment itself.

We can begin by noting the potential for "relativism" which follows from both Marx's critique of Hegelian idealism and bourgeois political economy, and the Frankfurt School's and Habermas's critique of scientism. This goes directly to the contextualist theses that emerge from these critiques. David Held poses the issues this way:

> How can the possibility of critique be sustained, if the contextuality of knowledge is recognized? Or, to put the question differently, how can critical theory at once acknowledge its historicality and yet be critical? How can critical theory be part of the movement of history and a means of enlightenment? (1980: 398)

That these matters are a source of worry for modernist critical theorists is clearly revealed in Habermas's claim that admitting the historical contingency of critical reason itself would come "at the cost of a historicism which would, at the very least, tie the emancipatory interest of knowledge to fortuitous historical constellations and would thus relativistically deprive self-reflection of the possibility of a justificatory basis of its claims to validity" (Habermas 1973a: 14–15).

For Marx, the potential problem of relativism was easily resolved by vesting the proletariat with a "universal" interest. The proletariat was at once an oppressed and exploited class, and the class whose objective position in capitalist society made its particular interests universal. The formula was apparently coherent enough that it remained central even to "nonorthodox" Western Marxism for some time. Georg Lukács, who was arguably the most important figure in the early development of Western Marxism, and who had important influence on the critical theorists (see Arato and Breines 1979), continued to accept the traditional Marxian identification of the industrial working class with a universal emancipatory interest. Thus Lukács continued to insist, with Marx, that "only the proletariat is capable of historical subjectivity in the positive, constructive sense of overcoming all reified objectivity" (Arato and Breines 1979: 147). And even the members of the Frankfurt School continued to accept the formula well into the 1930s (Held 1980: 195).

All of this was to change, however. The twin specters of fascism and Stalinism probably served, as much as anything else, to erode the critical theorists' willingness to identify critical theory with the interests of the proletariat. Or so it would seem in light of Habermas's assertion that

What today separates us from Marx are evident historical truths, for example that in the developed capitalist societies there is no identifiable class, no clearly circumscribed social group which could be singled out as the representative of a general interest that has been violated. This insight already separated the older generation of Frankfurt theorists, who had both fascism and Stalinism before their eyes, from their great predecessor, Georg Lukács. (Habermas 1982: 221–22)

As a consequence, we find claims like the following appearing regularly in the work of the critical theorists: "Even the situation of the proletariat is, in this society, no guarantee of correct knowledge" (Horkheimer 1982: 213); "Nor is there a social class by whose acceptance of the theory one could be guided" (Horkheimer, 1982: 242); that "any class consciousness, especially a revolutionary class consciousness, is not to be found in the main strata of the working class today . . . , and thus today Marx would have to abandon his hope that theory can become a material force, once it has taken hold of the masses" (Habermas 1973a: 196–97); and that "the proletariat is *neither* the blind agent of historical necessity *nor*, as self-conscious suffering, the direct consciousness of what is historically necessary (Wellmer 1971: 56).

Abandoning the proletariat as the universal class did not, however, lead the critical theorists to abandon the notion of a universal interest in emancipation that is a feature of the historical development of human society. At the same time, they were unwilling to ground this interest in the historical situation—the suffering—of any other identifiable class or group. The effect of this, however, was to strip critical theory of any explicit identification with specific political practices.[2] Practically or politically speaking, it does not seem to make much difference whether an "emancipatory intent" is grounded in an appeal to immanent critique (Horkheimer), negative dialectics and nonidentity thinking (Adorno), a theory of human instincts (Marcuse), or a theory of transcendental interests and a counterfactual ideal speech situation (Habermas). The result in each and every one of these attempts was the same: the critical theorists fell "back on a concept of critique which they, themselves, in other contexts, rejected: an ahistorical es-

---

[2] By suggesting that modernist critical theory was not explicitly identified with any particular political practices does not mean that it is thereby apolitical. As we shall see in Part II, there is a sense in which all social theory has more or less readily identifiable political implications, and modernist critical theory is no different in this regard. In the chapter on feminist theory, and in my concluding chapter, the political implications of modernist critical theory should become clear.

sence becomes the criterion for the evaluation of the present" (Held 1980: 371).

With the recognized loss of the proletariat as the universal class, critical theory began to travel "the last leg of its long march away from orthodox Marxism" (Jay 1973: 256). In the rise of both fascism and Stalinism, the members of the Frankfurt School seemed to believe that instrumental reason had become a "new barbarism" whose effects were so widely distributed that critical theory could no longer find the grounding required to maintain the relationship of theory and practice. As Marcuse suggested in his *One Dimensional Man*, "There is no ground on which theory and practice, thought and action meet" (1964: xiii). In trying to explain why the revolution envisaged by Marx had failed to occur, they pointed to the all-embracing, "one-dimensional" character of modern civilization:

> Confronted with the total character of the achievements of advanced industrial society, critical theory is left without the rationale for transcending this society. The vacuum empties the theoretical structure itself, because the categories of a critical theory were developed during the period in which the need for refusal and subversion was embodied in the action of effective social forces. (Marcuse 1964: xiv)

It is here, however, that Habermas departs radically from the Frankfurt School. While the members of the Frankfurt School had for so long embraced a commitment to the unity of critical theory and political practice, by 1940 it appeared that questions of practice were receiving less and less emphasis (Jay 1973: 253). Seeing only the "total character" of modern civilization, they even began to rethink the idea that the aims of critical theory could be realized in practice. What began, then, as a movement that increasingly downplayed practical questions ended up in a jettisoning of the unity of theory and practice (Jay 1973: 296). Theory alone, they seem to be saying, was the only kind of practice still available to the social critic (Jay 1973: 280). Without the proletariat, indeed without anything resembling an addressee, Horkheimer, Adorno and Marcuse conceived critical theory

> as a protest, but a protest impotent in practice, against an apocalyptically self-obturating system of alienation and reification; and as the spark whose preservation in a self-darkening world will keep alive the memory of something quite different. (Wellmer 1971: 52)

For Horkheimer, this memory was a "hope for the wholly other" (1982: xviii); with Adorno, Horkheimer sought to preserve this hope for an "imaginary witness—lest it perish with us" (1947); for Marcuse, it was a matter of trying to "remain loyal to those who, without hope, have given their life to the Great Refusal" (Marcuse 1964: 257). In the final analysis, the members of the Frankfurt School had given up on the practical intent of critical theory; they had, in the apt words of Georg Lukács, "taken up residence in the 'Grand Hotel Abyss' " (quoted in Jay 1984: 18).

But while Habermas may have shared much in common with the Frankfurt School, he also tried to distance himself from the "politics of despair" into which its members had fallen. From the failure of revolutionary movements he arrives not at despair, but at the need to rethink the relationship between theory and practice (Wellmer 1971:53). As Habermas sees it,

> Of course *today* we have good reasons that might keep us from blindly following Marx in his value-theoretic reflections, or the older Frankfurt School in its philosophy of history, or Adorno and Marcuse in their desperate attempts to find a way out of the dead end of totalized critique. (1982: 232)

"My own efforts," he says, "can be undertood in connection with the undertaking critical theory broke off at the start of the 1940s" (1982: 232). But Habermas's account of this project replicates, rather than moving beyond, the tension between the search for a universally applicable foundation for critical theory and the historical and contextual constraints that any theory necessarily reflects:

> My intention is to renew a critical social theory that secures its normative foundations . . . [by] explicating a concept of reason that falls prey neither to historicism nor to the sociology of knowledge, and that does not stand abstractly over against history and the complex of social life. (1982: 232)

The defense of such an ideal, Habermas himself admits, "increases the distance between theory and practice" (1982: 223). Yet he is unwilling to give up the project because, he believes, there can be no other way of finding a justified ground for critical theory.

> Even Marx set out his theory in such a way that he could perceive and take up the trial of reason in the deformations of class society. Had he not found in proletarian forms of life the distortion of a communicative form of life as such, had he not seen in them an abuse of a universal interest reaching beyond the particular, his analysis would have been robbed of the force of *justified* critique. His critique . . . would have been reduced to a lament or to a sheer agitation. (Habermas 1982: 221)

In a stance not entirely unlike that taken up by the members of the Frankfurt School, Habermas seems to be saying that critical theory cannot find its grounding *in practice*; its animating interest—reason—"is not to be reconciled with the particularity which must adhere to every interest, even that which aims at self-reflection (Habermas 1973a: 15).

. . .

We are left at an impasse, or perhaps a crisis, in modernist critical theory. There is near unanimous agreement among critics that neither the Frankfurt School nor Habermas succeed in giving critical theory a grounding that would preserve its practical intentions. It would appear then, that the idea of a critical theory remains just that—an idea. Perhaps we might even agree with Richard Bernstein that "in the final analysis we must honestly confront the gap that has always existed—and still exists—between the idea of such a critical theory of society and its concrete practical realization" (Bernstein 1976: 225). But the lessons to be learned from modernist critical theory are not merely negative; they are not exhausted by its self-imposed impasse.

Out of Impasse

To equate the idea of a critical theory with the work of Marx, the Frankfurt School, and Habermas is to overlook the ways in which that work points beyond itself. In this respect, two things are clear.

First, the attempt to ground critical theory without reference to a practical context—an addressee—makes critical theory bankrupt in its own terms. Without the identification of historically situated individuals to whom it is addressed, and for whom it might serve as a means of "enlightenment and emancipation," a critical theory becomes nearly indistinguishable from those forms of theory which, in Marx's words, "have only *interpreted* the world" when "the point" should be "to *change* it" (*MER*: 145). Without a practical dimension, critical theory cannot achieve its own stated aim of helping those who suffer from domination and unfreedom to understand the sources of their oppression, and emancipate themselves from that oppression. It is not enough to claim that one is committed to the emancipation of those who suffer from unwarranted and unnecessary domination. For such a theory must also be committed to understanding its own origin in specific, historically situated struggles, and it must be committed to understanding its verification as being tied to the self-emancipating actions of those to whom it is addressed. As Habermas once put it, "in a process of enlightenment there can be only participants" (Habermas 1973a: 40), an insight no less true when we ask of what struggle this process is a part.

Here we see once again how a critical theory is defined in terms of the constitutive connections between its goals, logical or cognitive structure, and conception of verification. It is the achievement of Marx, the Frankfurt School, and Habermas to have demonstrated that if social theory is not understood in these terms, it may perpetuate unfreedom. Through their metatheoretical critiques of theories that purport to be absolute, objectivist, transhistorically and noncontextually bound, they have identified the ways in which all social theories are necessarily bound by their historical context. Moreover, they have also shown that when a social theory misdescribes the nature of social reality by virtue of mistaken metatheoretical claims, the consequence is the reification of domination as a natural or inevitable feature of social relations. By unmasking the historicity and contextuality of all forms of social knowledge, a critical theory thereby lays bare the conceptual relationship between metatheoretical commitment, theoretical claims, and the practical relations between individuals. But if other theories are so bound, then a critical theory must be as well.

Showing human beings that they have made their own history, albeit in ways that have been unreflective, is the reason a critical theory cannot proceed without first unmasking those forms of thought that inform this lack of reflection. In this, a critical theory moves from the critique of practice, to theory, to metatheory. Turning this unmasking into what Marx calls "a material force" is a matter of showing human beings that they perhaps can make their own history in ways that treat domination and inequalities as merely contingent and, in principle, transformable. But to note this is to once again raise the issue of a critical theory's need for a practical dimension, for if social theory is logically and conceptually related to a particular historically situated practice, critical theory is no exception. It, too, must be cognizant of the practice(s) of which it is supposed to be the expression and critical reflection. Critical theory is not unpremised, unsituated or absolved from practical implications—and if it is to make good its aims, it must take these assumptions with the utmost seriousness.

All of this brings me to the second insight intimated in Marx, the Frankfurt School, and Habermas. This feature is in an important sense related to the first. It can be approached by asking what kind of transformation, what kind of emancipation, human beings are capable of achieving given the metatheoretical insights already enumerated. In this regard, what Marx, the Frankfurt School, and Habermas have made clear is that any account of emancipation will be limited by its own historically specific and contextually limited origins. To note this is to take seriously the lesson of Marx's critique of Hegelianism and bourgeois political economy, a lesson repeated in the Frankfurt School and Habermas's critique of instrumental reason and scientism. It is also to recognize that Marx, the Frankfurt School, and Habermas have failed to come to grips with an apparent tension in their own critical theories. On the one hand, their metatheoretical criticisms of the discourses they oppose, and the metatheoretical standards for critical theory these criticisms establish, point toward a historically specific and contextually situated model of critical theory. On the other, all continue to subscribe to the belief that criticism requires some form of "universal reason." To once again repeat David Held's apt characterization, the critical theorists "often fall back on a concept of critique which they, themselves, in other contexts, rejected: an ahistorical essence becomes the criterion for the evaluation of the present" (Held 1980: 371).

The question of whether critical theory can be embodied in political practice still remains unanswered. And whether it can be answered now appears to turn on the resolution of a highly complex set of deeper issues: Can the imperatives of critical reason find their expression among the plurality of histories and contexts that shape our knowledge and our identities? Or, to put the matter another way, can critical theory be justified without appeal to "universal" standards of reason? If we uncritically follow Marx, the Frankfurt School, and Habermas, the possibilities are not very promising. But if we follow through the implications of their rejection of transhistorical, transcendental, and naturalistic social "truth," then the possibility of a critical theory remains open. This is what I meant when I said that the work of Marx, the Frankfurt School, and Habermas points beyond itself.

Thus, Marx, the Frankfurt School, and Habermas themselves provide a possible way out of the impasse of modernist critical theory. Ironically enough, there are even occasional intimations in some of their work of how this might be done. Adorno (1973), for example, argued that we must avoid the kind of "logic of identity" which assumes that a universal interest can be readily vested in any particular interests. And Marcuse emphasizes the need to articulate concepts and categories of emancipatory discourse that are "forms and determinations of actual existence" located in "concrete, living foundations" (Marcuse 1969: 19). But it is Habermas, the heir apparent to the tradition of modernist critical theory, who most clearly helps us see the way out:

> The destruction of the historico-philosophical certainty that the industrial working class and the European labor movement were targets for possible, theoretically induced processes of enlightenment and bearers of a politically pursued, revolutionary transformation is not, in my view, entirely a disad-

vantage. Today the place of very general theoretical assertions, to which organizational efforts were supposed to be directly linked, must be taken by an empirical analysis that is sensitive to contemporary history and is social-scientifically well informed—an analysis that differentiates its object not only according to stage of development, mode of production, class structure and political order, but according to national traditions, regions, subcultures and according to contingent historical constellations. (1982: 222)

What Habermas appears to be suggesting is that the idea of a critical theory must be cast in terms that clears a philosophical space for a plurality of critical theories. Such a space, moreover, can be made good only by sound epistemological and ontological insights, a metatheoretical self-understanding, that can accommodate plurality and difference while cultivating solidarity. At the same time, the historical and contextual specificity of such theories cannot give up the claim to "reason" if they are to avoid being cast as merely arbitrary assertions of particularistic interests.

Later I shall argue that such theories exist, theories that are faithful to both the defensible metatheoretical insights, and the emancipatory intentions of Marx, the Frankfurt School, and Habermas. But before considering these, we must examine the "postmodernist" critical theory of Michel Foucault. For his represents yet another influential example of how the pursuit of an enlightening and emancipating theory can subvert its own aims.

CHAPTER 3

Postmodernist Critical Theory: Michel Foucault

> What I am trying to do is grasp the implicit systems of
> thought which determine our most familiar behavior without
> our knowing it. I am trying to find their origin, to show their
> formation, the constraint they impose upon us; I am there-
> fore trying to place myself at a distance from them and show
> how one could escape.
>
> It is not a matter of emancipating truth from every system of
> power (which would be a chimera, for truth is already power)
> but of detaching the power of truth from the forms of hege-
> mony, social, economic and cultural, within which it operates
> at the present time.
>
> —Michel Foucault

IT WOULD be difficult to overstate the influence that Marx, the Frankfurt School, and Habermas have had on scholars committed to the
idea of a critical social theory. But a quick perusal of recent issues of
academic journals dealing with social theory, as well as quasi-aca-
demic journals dedicated to "critical" political discourse, indicates the
emergence of a rival perspective on critical social theory.[1] The tradition of critical theory running from Marx through the Frankfurt
School to Habermas seeks to recover the promise of "modernity" reflected in the Enlightenment ideal of critical reason, an ideal subverted by the progressive collapsing of reason into its purely instrumental moment. The rival perspective, however, belongs to "a
tradition of rejectionist criticism of modernity, one which includes
Nietzsche, Heidegger, and the French poststructuralists," the central
aspiration of which is "a total break with the Enlightenment" (Fraser
1985a: 165–66). With the rise of this perspective, now commonly
characterized as "postmodernism," the lines of dispute have been
drawn up, and it would appear that the major issues in critical theory
now turn on settling the significant differences between the modernist and postmodernist traditions.

In this chapter I consider the work of Michel Foucault, arguably the
most influential contemporary figure in this postmodernist movement.

---

[1] See, for example, recent (post–1980) issues of *Political Theory, Praxis International, New German Critique, Telos, New Left Review, Social Text.*

Just as with Marx, the Frankfurt School, and Habermas, it is difficult to overstate the extent to which Foucault's work has influenced those sympathetic to the idea of a critical theory. The reason for this influence is that Foucault provides a compelling critique of many of the concepts and categories central to modernist critical theory, even while he describes his as a theory having emancipatory intent.[2] But my aim is not to defend modernist against postmodernist critical theory, nor vice versa. There may be significant tensions between the political intentions and political implications of the work of Marx, the Frankfurt School, and Habermas, but as I see it, Foucault's postmodernist critical theory fares no better in this regard. In this, Foucault and the modernists are perhaps more alike than either they, or their respective sympathizers, would care to admit. For the one thing both traditions share is an inability to follow through the implications of their criticisms of other social theories, and as a result they undercut the practical aims to which they subscribe.

But there is more. In my discussion of Marx, the Frankfurt School, and Habermas, I also suggested that there are elements in their arguments that point beyond their work, insights that promise the possibility of closing the gap between the ideal and the reality of critical theory. I aim to show that this possibility is also present in Foucault's work. By leading us to question and reexamine the metatheoretical presuppositions of critique, Foucault challenges us to develop those arguments in ways that can avoid the pitfalls he identifies. Still, Foucault did not seem able to see his way clear in attending to such issues; indeed, much of what he said appears to cut off their consideration. Nonetheless, if he shares more in the way of problematic positions with the modernists than is at first sight apparent, he also shares with them a number of insights that help us to recognize not only what a critical theory cannot look like, but more importantly, what it must look like if it is to be more than a wistful ideal.

[2] For most students of the Marx-Frankfurt School-Habermas tradition, differences within the tradition are often given extensive treatment, but this tradition *qua* tradition is usually said to be constituted by its common identification with what Seyla Benhabib (1986) has called "the philosophy of the subject," or the idea that there is a single perspective from which justifiable norms of action can be determined. The members of the tradition, of course, differ on the substantive content of such a perspective, but nonetheless continue to subscribe to this ideal.

By contrast, Foucault (and the "postmodernism" he is said to represent), specifically repudiates the philosophy of the subject as an illusion, the effects of which (according to Foucault) are oppressive.

These opposed stances have been juxtaposed as antithetical and incommensurable (see, for example, White [1986]; Dreyfus and Rabinow [1982: 129–31]; Lemert and Gillan [1982: 106–9]; Fraser [1985a]). The thesis I am pursuing here regarding the gap between the practical aims and practical implications of both modernist and postmodernist critical theory is similar to that found in Fraser (1985a: 181–83).

Foucault, then, occupies a crucial place in my dicussion as a whole. Between the failures—and achievements—of the modernist and post-modernist projects there is much to be learned. I hope to have made some of these lessons clear; here I hope to advance the discussion to the point where it is possible to see in sketch outline what form a practically effective critical theory might take.

SITUATING POSTMODERNISM

In France, the developmental history of critical theory parallels in many ways the history of the tradition that would culminate in the work of the Frankfurt School and, later, Habermas. But there are also notable dissimilarities, particularly after the Second World War, and it is in part out of these that postmodernism would take shape. It is beyond the scope of this work to detail these developments, but a few crucial junctures should be noted.[3]

A useful point of departure is the assimilation of Marxism in France. Before the First World War, this assimilation progressed rather slowly (Hirsh 1981: 8; Poster, 1975: 36). The French had a rich variety of revolutionary and Socialist traditions that had been worked out more or less independently of Marxist thought, a fact which in essence made Marxism philosophically, intellectually, and politically superfluous for many French thinkers. Even in those circles where Marxism had been assimilated, this assimilation was at best partial, and perhaps even a bit eclectic (Hirsh 1981: 8–9). All of this was to change with the advent of World War I and the Bolshevik Revolution in Russia, after which many French radicals endorsed the Soviet experiment as the best hope in the struggle against capitalism. The result was a kind of "Manichean political context" which translated into an intellectual battle where "philosophy was viewed as an instrumental weapon to be used by one side or the other," and for many French intellectuals the Communist movement became "the only hope of human salvation in a capitalist world threatened by war, depression, and fascism" (Hirsh 1981: 9; see also Poster 1975: 36–42).

In this context Marxism was rather uncritically appropriated directly via the scientistic and positivistic reading imposed by the Second International, an appropriation no doubt facilitated by the fact that much of Marx's early work, so influential in shaping the anti-scientistic "critical" interpretations of many Western Marxists, was virtually ignored by French intellectuals (Hirsh 1981: 9; Poster 1975: 37). However, a rift soon opened between those committed to this sci-

[3] Three good introductions to the social and intellectual context from which Foucault worked are Poster (1975), Descombes (1980) and Gorz (1981). The (arguably thin) intellectual history I provide in this section draws heavily on these works.

entistic reading of Marx and those who opposed scientism and "positivism," whether bourgeois or Marxist. In part, this rift resulted from a "Hegel renaissance" that began in the 1930s, and the gap was widened when Marx's "early" work became more widely read (Hirsh 1981: 13–17; Descombes 1980: 9–16; Poster 1975: 3–71). Many French intellectuals discovered that they were perhaps philosophically closer to the "critical" Marxism that would later be most clearly associated with the Frankfurt School (Poster 1975: 42–43). But these sympathies were complicated, for there was another ascending intellectual tradition that soon reshaped the contours of French social thought. That tradition was existentialism, and its most important figure was Jean Paul Sartre.

Existentialism's concept of freedom, which emphasized a radical notion of individual autonomy, was at first understood even by Sarte himself as antithetical to Marxism. But as Marxism itself became "Hegelianized," these antitheses dissolved. As Mark Poster (1975: 104) argued, both critical Marxism and existentialism minimized the idealist elements in Hegel, focusing instead on Hegel's attempts to articulate the historicity of society and human identity. Other themes readily followed: a similarly shared emphasis on the primacy of life over thought; the interdependence of thought and action; a concept of freedom that made theory and practice two related moments in an emancipatory process (Poster 1975: 104–5). After some two decades of antagonism, by the mid-1960s a rapproachment was effected in the form of an "existential Marxism," the substance of which

> conceptualizes advanced industrial society in a way that points toward the possible elimination of its alienating structures; that looks to all the relations of daily life, not simply to relations of production, to make society intelligible; that picks up from existentialism the effort to capture human beings in the moment of their active creation of their world, in their subjectivity; and finally, that rejects the attempt to have a closed theory complete within itself. (Poster 1975: ix)

Thus did Sartre claim for the existentialist movement that "we were convinced *at one and the same time* that historical materialism furnished the only valid interpretation of history and that existentialism remained the only concrete approach to reality" (Sartre 1963: 21).

We are now in a position to begin to situate the postmodernist assault on the modernist conception of critical theory. Existentialism, critical Marxism, and later "existential Marxism," shared an opposition to scientism and the objectification of social relations, and a concomitant emphasis on the importance of critical reason. But in France it was the question of "humanism," in particular the idea of an active subject, associated with these movements that became a focal point of dispute. Like the modernist critical theory of the Frankfurt School and Habermas, they all held firm to the notion that a human capacity for critical self-reflection and political self-transformation was crucial to emancipation. And it was the "structuralist" school, which came into prominence nearly simultaneously with existential Marxism in the early 1960s, that mounted the most serious challenge to this view (Hirsh 1981: 149; Descombes 1980: 75–77; Poster 1975: 306).

Structuralism was never a consistent, fully articulated system of thought, but its many diverse forms did share something like a common body of themes that served to give it a more or less coherent philosophical identity (Descombes 1980: 77; Poster 1975: 306). In their reaction to existential Marxism, the structuralists attacked what they took to be "the most insidious form of the 'logic of identity' " as "the supreme philosophical illusion" (Descombes 1980: 75). As Vincent Descombes describes it, this "logic of identity" involves the

> principle of the *subject* . . . the name given to a be-ing whose *identity* is sufficiently stable for it to bear, in every sense of the word (sustain, serve as a foundation for, withstand), change or modification. The subject [in other words] is [that feature of human existence which] remains the same, while accidental qualities are altered. (1980: 76)

In short course, this attack on the logic of identity embodied in existentialism became "conducted under the banner of a single crusade against the *subject in general*" (Descombes 1980: 76).

This crusade against "the subject in general," then, is one of the defining marks of structuralism. For our purposes, perhaps the most interesting feature of this crusade against the subject was that it recapitulated what the Frankfurt School and Habermas identified as the objectivist illusion in modern positivism and scientistic Marxism (see chapter 1). Indeed, because structuralism often conceptualized social and political practices as the result of forces over which individuals (as "subjects") have no control, and knowledge of those structures and relations as knowable only in a scientific way, it has often been characterized as a kind of "positivism" (Hirsh 1981: 149; Descombes 1980: 87ff, Poster 1975: 314). Thus did structuralism face off against existential Marxism as yet "another classical confrontation between subjectivist and objectivist conceptions of social theory" (Hirsh 1981: 150).

Again, we must note that there are divergent schools within the structuralist camp. One commentator, Alan Sheridan, has even gone so far as to suggest that "structuralism" was nothing more than a "fad" (1980: 89), a "journalist's invention" (1980: 205), and another intellectual movement that "the French, as we know, are very good at concocting" (1980: 89).[4] Sheridan is, I think, only half right on this score, for Levi-Strauss, Lacan, Althusser, and a host of other prominent thinkers, were not at all reticent to claim the title of "structuralism" for their works. And whether fad, journalist's invention, or profound philosophical movement, it would be a mistake to underestimate the way structuralist themes shaped French social theory after they appeared. For if there is anything structuralism did, it was to lay the thematic foundations for the kind of postmodernist conception of critical theory that Michel Foucault has come to represent in recent years.

Foucault's relationship to the existentialist and structuralist movements has been the subject of wide-ranging interpretations. On the one hand, Foucault has been called the "enfant terrible" (Poster 1975: 334) and "the" philosopher of the French structuralist movement (White 1973: 23). On the other hand, he has been "read out of the structuralist establishment" (White 1973: 23), or he has "defined the limits of structural Marxism and prepared for its possible integration with existential Marxism" (Poster 1975: 334–35). These characterizations, disparate and contradictory though they may be, should not be attributed only to uncomprehending readers. For Foucault himself said that he did not see "who could be more of an anti-structuralist than myself" (PK: 114),[5] even while admitting that some of the themes he employs "may, if one so wishes, be labelled structuralism" (AK: 11; see also AK: 234).[6]

---

[4] In defense of Foucault, Sheridan attacks those who have attempted to brand Foucault a "structuralist" by arguing that the label is often carelessly applied, and "accompanied by much fudging of issues, blurring of distinctions, and yoking by violence together of heterogeneous ideas" (1980: 89). Pages 200–205 of Sheridan's *Will to Truth* contain his account of the philosophical foundations of "structuralism" and its adherents. For those unfamiliar with the movement, these pages provide a fair—if terse—representation of structuralist themes.

[5] Abbreviated references are to Foucault's work. Full citations may be found in the Bibliography.

AK: *The Archaeology of Knowledge*
BC: *Birth of the Clinic*
DP: *Discipline and Punish*
FR: *The Foucault Reader*
HS: *The History of Sexuality*
LCP: *Language, Countermemory, Practice: Selected Essays and Interviews*
MC: *Madness and Civilization*
OT: *The Order of Things*
PK: *Power/Knowledge: Selected Interviews and Other Writings, 1972–1977*
SP: *The Subject and Power*

[6] In the introduction of *The Order of Things*, Foucault gives an abbreviated account of the themes that inform this particular work. He concludes the introduction with "a

When Foucault is read as a structuralist, it is usually because of his questioning of the status and role of human subjectivity in the constitution of social knowledge and power. Until the mid-1970s, Foucault rejected any sort of philosophy of the subject, and in this he seemed to share the structuralists' "antihumanism" and "antisubjectivism." But he also differed from the structuralists in that they had rejected the concept of the subject only to fall back into a kind of scientism inextricably bound to concepts of truth and objectivity, which, Foucault argued, were also problematic notions. Thus Foucault appeared to take up a position that was antithetical to both objectivist and subjectivist conceptions of social theory. Foucault would later begin to advocate "new forms of subjectivity" (*SP*: 216), but even this did not put him in the camp of those subjectivist philosophies, including modernist critical theory, that most scholars usually think of, for he refused to truck with the idea that these forms might be characterized in terms of "reason."

What I shall argue is that Foucault's attempt to articulate an alternative to both objectivist and subjectivist conceptions of social theory is not always conducive to his intention of producing "a project that is historical and critical" (*BC*: xix), and capable of showing "how one could escape" from the forms of thought and practice that "determine our . . . behavior without our knowing it" (Foucault, in Simon 1971: 201). As we shall see, even the various transformations through which Foucault's work moved, from its characterization as an "archaeology of knowledge" in its early form, through its later phase as a "genealogy of power," to its final expression as a search for "new forms of subjectivity," do not alter the force of my indictment. Yet I also insist that Foucault has much to teach us. But if we are to accept his insights as evidence of constraints imposed upon us from which escape is indeed possible, as he says we should, we cannot fully accept most of the philosophical presuppositions that inform them. In other words, if the lessons of postmodernist critical theory are to be realized, Foucault needs to be salvaged from Foucault.

FOUCAULT, OBJECTIVISM, AND SUBJECTIVISM

Foucault articulated the ground on which his critical theory was shaped in terms similar to those found in Marx, the Frankfurt School,

request to the English-speaking reader" which pleads his case against those who have called him a structuralist (1970: xiv). Most interesting, however, is the conclusion of the *Archaeology of Knowledge*. Here Foucault engages in a dialogue with an imaginary interlocutor, the central theme of which is the question of structuralism in Foucault's work. In this chapter, I make heavy use of the dialogue as a means of illuminating the tensions in Foucault's social ontology and his desire to formulate a "critical" theory.

and Habermas. Just as the modernist critical theorists initially proceeded by way of a critique of extant philosophical discourses they thought undergirded and informed relations of domination, so too did Foucault. In his context, as we have seen, the predominant philosophies in question were those of structuralism and existentialism. But these were in a sense only expressions of two more basic perspectives: "objectivism" on the one hand, and "subjectivism" on the other.

If we think of this dispute in terms of how the object of the social sciences—the social object—is conceptualized, the radical differences between the two frameworks become clearer. For objectivists, "man" is considered a "natural" object whose behavior, and the practices and institutions that arise from that behavior, can ultimately be attributed to "causal" factors. According to this account, the presence of intentions, beliefs, choice, and deliberation cannot serve to demarcate the natural from the social sciences, since they are nothing more than "caused" states amenable to explanation by reference to certain natural "laws."

Against this view, subjectivist philosophers have often argued that this conception of the social object is based upon a set of philosophical/methodological assumptions and strictures which ignore or obscure the unique character of human action, practices and institutions. This unique character derives in no small part from the problematic of language: human action is not merely described through language, it is performed in and through language (Fay and Moon 1977: 210–15). Human actions and practices are intentional and subjectively meaningful, and the social object emerges as being in part constituted by the belief-informed actions of social agents. And this means that any claims about what agents believe, or should believe, are going to involve interpretations aimed at clarifying for those agents the meanings of action, and perhaps the possibility for change open to these agents.

Foucault opted for neither of these antinomies. He found the "positivism" of objectivism and the "interpretivism" of subjectivism methodologically and philosophically inadequate. On his understanding, "positivism," with "its myths of scientific objectivity" (*MC*: 276) is engaged in a project which attempts to demarcate what can and cannot be called knowledge by trying "to lay down the law of each and every science" (*PK*: 64–65). This objection would seem to vindicate the antipositivist claims of interpretivism, but for Foucault it did not. While he did maintain that he was "not at all the sort of philosopher who conducts or wants a discourse of truth on some science or other" (*PK*: 64), he also argued that he had "no great liking for interpretation" (*AK*: 202). Interpretation, it seems, consists of nothing more than "the violent or surreptitious appropriation of a system of rules, which in itself has no meaning, in order to impose a direction, to bend it to a new will, to force its participation in a different game, and to subject it to secondary rules." Indeed, the whole development of humanity, according to Foucault, consists of "a series of interpretations" that perform this insidious appropriation of meaningless systems of rules (*LCP*: 151–52).

Professing neither positivist nor interpretivist sympathies, Foucault attempted to distance himself from these approaches to social inquiry by subsuming his projects under the rubric of an "archaeology" of knowledge and a "genealogy" of the will to power. Together these were intended to "reveal that all knowledge rests upon injustice (that there is no right, not even in the act of knowing, to truth or a foundation for truth) and that the instinct for knowledge is malicious (something murderous, opposed to the happiness of mankind)" (*LCP*: 163).

Foucault read both positivism and interpretivism as part of this will to achieve knowledge, and ultimately power, over human beings. In this respect he argued that even the disputes between these two schools were "wearisome not only because they are hackneyed, but because they lack relevance" (*OT*: 349). His claims here are perhaps best understood in the context of his account of the rise of the social sciences. The study of human beings, which was for centuries limited by the character of human discourse, required that "The old Aristotelean law, which prohibited the application of scientific discourse to the individual" (*BC*: 170) be eliminated. The positivist-interpretivist dispute, then, could be articulated only after the ushering in of a new "episteme"[7] that authorized conceptualizing "man" as either subject or object of knowledge.

---

[7] The *episteme*, as Foucault sees it, is

> the total set of relations that unite, at a given period, the discursive practices that give rise to epistemological figures, sciences, and possibly formalized systems; the way in which, in each of these discursive formations, the transitions of epistemologization, scientificity, and formalizations are situated and operate; the distribution of these thresholds, which may coincide, be subordinated to one another, or be separated by shifts in time; the lateral relations that may exist between epistemological figures or sciences in so far as they belong to neighboring, but distinct, discursive practices . . . it is the totality of relations that can be discovered, for a given period, between the sciences when one analyses them at the level of discursive regularities. (*AK*: 191)

The "episteme" for Foucault is functionally equivalent to the kinds of knowledge claims accepted as legitimate in a particular sociocultural milieau. Foucault used the term for only a short time, but the idea of the link between knowledge and power which runs through all of Foucault's work can be seen as presupposing the idea of an episteme. For Aristotle, *episteme* was associated with rigorous science, and separated from *phronesis*, which was associated with practical knowledge. Foucault's use of the term grasps at

Prior to this new episteme, philosophical discussions about human beings as objects of knowledge was impossible within the then-current conceptual universe. For example, while "Renaissance 'humanism' and Classical 'rationalism' were indeed able to allot human beings a privileged position in the order of the world" (*OT*: 318), there nonetheless existed "no epistemological consciousness of man as such" (*OT*: 309). When this consciousness did develop, philosophical speculation about man-as-object emerged. But the dispute over how this newly emergent object was to be understood and studied, a dispute so often expressed in the apparently irreconcilable positions of positivism and interpretivism, was not for Foucault an example of opposing philosophical frameworks. The irreconcilability of positivism and interpretivism is that of appearance only; it "does not necessarily mean that their development occurs within the element of pure contradiction; their existence, and their untiring repetition for more than a century, do not indicate the permanence of an ever-open question: they refer back to a precise and extremely well determined epistemological arrangement in history" (*OT*: 346).

Given Foucault's emphasis on the central place of language in the shaping of an episteme, it is hardly surprising that he located the modern episteme in the development of a radically new set of discursive practices. More than simply a change in language, the modern episteme was characterized by a change in the language we use to talk *about* language. As the Classical age came to a close, and as the nature of language began to come under increasing scrutiny, a new set of perceptions about the origins, historical development and function of language in social relations took shape. This new set of perceptions meant that "language began to fold in upon itself, to aquire its own particular density, to deploy a history, an objectivity and laws of its own. It became one object of knowledge among others" (*OT*: 296). In the classical period, by contrast, language had served a simple representational function:

> In the seventeenth and eighteenth centuries it was the immediate and spontaneous unfolding of representations; . . . Thus, language occupied a fundamental situation in relation to all knowledge: it was only through the medium of language that the things of the world could be known. (*OT*: 295–96)

In this respect the status of language was unproblematic, and the status it reflected for classical thinkers implied that language was con-

---

this meaning in that he wants to characterize modern forms of knowledge—whether objectifying or subjectifying—as claims to absolute knowledge.

sidered transparent and capable of representing the world to thought. Thus, "Classical knowledge," Foucault argued, "was profoundly nominalist" (*OT*: 296).

With the growing awareness that language no longer served a transparent representative function, it was in a sense demoted from its privileged status and became simply one object among others. Its study was now authorized within the same methodological frameworks applied to other objects of knowledge. While language "may possess its own concepts, . . . the analyses that bear upon it have their roots at the same level as those that deal with other empirical forms of knowledge. . . . To know language is no longer to come as close as possible to knowledge; it is merely to apply the methods of understanding in general to a particular domain of objectivity" (*OT*: 296). No longer transparent, language in our time has been subject to a "critical elevation" (*OT*: 299), and its study developed into a crucial aspect of modern philosophical thinking:

> The threshold between Classicism and modernity (though the terms themselves have no importance—let us say between our prehistory and what is still contemporary) had been definitively crossed when words ceased to intersect with representations and to provide a spontaneous grid for the knowledge of things. . . . Once detached from representation, language has existed, right up to our own day, in only a dispersed way: for philologists, words are like so many objects formed and deposited by history; for those who wish to achieve a formalization, language must strip itself of its concrete content and leave nothing visible but those forms of discourse that are universally valid; if one's intent is to interpret, then words become a text to be broken down, so as to allow that other meaning hidden in them to emerge and become clearly visible: lastly language may sometimes arise for its own sake in an act of writing that designates nothing other than itself. This dispersion imposes upon language, if not a privileged position, at least a destiny that seems singular when compared with that of labour or of life . . . when the unity of general grammar—discourse—was broken up, language appeared in a multiplicity of modes of being, whose unity was probably irrecoverable. (*OT*: 303–4)

For those interested in imposing a scientistically conceived regime of truth, language had to be reconstructed in terms of the methodological requirements of the scientific enterprise; where language could not be fitted within this framework, it had to be rendered "meaningless." Since scientific knowledge had to be expressed in language, the task became one of overcoming the problems inherent in the fact that language "cannot be arranged, deployed and analysed beneath the gaze of a science because it always reemerges on the side of the knowing subject—as soon as that subject expresses what he knows" (*OT*: 296). The solution was the "positivist dream of keeping strictly to the level of what is known" through the "neutralizing," "polishing," or purging of all of the potentially subjective elements in language, "of all of its accidents and alien elements—as though they did not belong to its essence" (*OT*: 296).

Against this scientistically conceived regime of truth the techniques of interpretation and the critical study of language were arrayed:

> Having become a dense and consistent historical reality language forms the locus of tradition, of the unspoken habits of thought, of what lies hidden in a people's mind; it accumulates an ineluctable memory which does not even know itself as memory. . . . Hence the need to work one's way back from opinions, philosophies and perhaps even from sciences, to the words that made them possible, and beyond that, to a thought whose essential life has not yet been caught in the network of any grammar. (*OT*: 297–98)

To know language in the context of the modern episteme is thus to be that much closer to knowing human beings, their true nature, historical development, and place in "the order of things"—or so we might be tempted to think. Yet Foucault is not similarly tempted; he sees the matter quite differently:

> Strangely enough, man—the study of whom is supposed by the naive to be the oldest investigation since Socrates—is probably no more than a kind of rift in the order of things, or, in any case, a configuration whose outlines are determined by the new position he has so recently taken up in the field of knowledge. Whence all the chimeras of the new humanisms, all the facile solutions of an "anthropology" understood as a universal reflection on man, half-empirical, half-philosophical. It is comforting, however, and a source of profound relief to think that man is only a recent invention, a figure not yet two centuries old, a new wrinkle in our knowledge, and that he will disappear again as soon as that knowledge has discovered a new form. (*OT*: xxiii)

Thus did Foucault reconstruct the "historical *a priori*" of the social sciences (*OT*: xxii; *AK*: 127). As integral elements of the modern "will to knowledge" about himself, the social sciences—and the "humanism" and "anthropology" in which they are grounded—now "calls [man] to the sacrifice of the subject of knowledge" (*LCP*: 163). Yet for Foucault, to try to develop any kind of knowledge about human beings was an exercise in "injustice," something "malicious." Rather than realizing the possibilities of human freedom, the modern episteme merely introduced new ways in which human beings might be subjected to "discipline," not only at the hands of others, but, perhaps more perniciously, at their own hands.

And so to help discover that "new form" of knowledge that might displace the modern episteme, Foucault proposed "a method of historical analysis freed from the anthropological theme" and "an enterprise by which one tries to throw off the last anthropological constraints; an enterprise that wishes, in return, to reveal how these constraints could come about" (*AK*: 15–16 passim).

ARCHAEOLOGY, GENEALOGY, AND THE SOCIAL OBJECT

In *The Archaeology of Knowledge*, Foucault first attempted to give a systematic elucidation of what his method entails and how it differs from the "humanism" and "anthropology" of the modern social sciences. His intention in writing the *Archaeology* was "to try to reveal the specificity of a method that is neither formalizing nor interpretive" (*AK*: 135).

Foucault's *Archaeology* was not, however, the first of his works that he had characterized as "archaeology." Even as early as his *Madness and Civilization* he called his project "archaeological," and although most of his early writings contained only "a very imperfect sketch" of Foucault's method, they nonethless offered some glimpse of the methodology informing them (*AK*: 15–16).[8] But this self-understanding would change. In his later works Foucault appears to take a new and important turn in the development of his thought, a turn marking a transformation of previous concerns, interests, and focuses. This has given rise to a "two Foucaults" thesis.[9] The first is said to have centered on the archaeological theme; the second involved a "new realization of the role of power in discourse," a realization of such import that he "never again uses the term archaeology, or any of the 'panoply of terms' so laboriously elaborated in *L'archaeologie du savoir*" (Sheridan 1980: 116). This new emphasis Foucault described as turning on a form of inquiry he called "genealogy."[10]

[8] The "early" works are *Madness and Civilization*, *Birth of the Clinic*, *The Order of Things*, and *The Archaeology of Knowledge*.

[9] See, for example Sheridan (1980) and Major-Poetzl (1983).

[10] The turn toward the political implications of discourse—and power—begins with Foucault's "Discourse on Language," which appears as an Appendix in the American edition of the *Archaeology* (*AK*: 215–37). After the *Archaeology*, Foucault begins to call his project "genealogical" to reflect Nietzsche's concern with "power."

The (commonly held) characterization of Foucault as Nietzschean or neo-Nietzschean is in large part a consequence of Foucault's own characterization of his work as a kind of "genealogy" in which the "will to truth" and the "will to power" are intimately linked. For Foucault's understanding of genealogy, see "The Discourse on Language" (*AK*: 215–37). Dreyfus and Rabinow (1982: 104–17) provide a particularly insightful discussion of Foucault's notion of genealogy and its relation to Nietzschean themes.

There is indeed a shift of major significance in this turn from archaeology to genealogy, and I shall have occasion to address this shift shortly. But at this point, I want to emphasize that, *contra* the two Foucaults thesis, for Foucault himself the shift was a matter of bringing to light what had always been implicit: power. Speaking in an interview first published in 1977, Foucault claimed that, in retrospect, the question of power was in fact what he had been talking about all along (*PK*: 113, 115).

With this, it can be argued that in its archaeological form, Foucault's project involved conceptualizing the power relations implicit in language as part of language's status as an "event," an "object which men produce, manipulate, use, transform, exchange, combine, decompose and recompose, and possibly destroy" (*AK*: 105). The core of this event was the statement, "the atom of discourse" (*AK*: 80), which seemed to allow that human beings were in some sense the authors of their own lives. But for Foucault, the statement was an event that "from the moment of its existence (and not only in its 'practical applications'), poses the question of power, an asset that is, by nature, the object of a struggle, a political struggle" (*AK*: 120). And it was thus something that pointed to a fundamental relation not exhausted by its "meaning" (*AK*: 28).

Neither positivism, nor interpretivism, nor for that matter any type of philosophy of history was capable of recognizing the "event" or "object" of language. Positivism made the "logical error" of confusing the event of language as "a material process" and a "physicalism" (*LCP*: 175); it tried to subsume the event of language by conceptualizing language as "the exact reflection, the perfect double, the unmisted mirror of a non-verbal knowledge" and "nature's perfect portrait" (*OT*: 296–97). Interpretivism (Foucault speaks here of phenomenology as interpretive) "reoriented the event," assuming that the event of language was a domain of "primal significations, which always existed as a disposition of the world around the self" (*LCP*: 175). And the philosophy of history made the "grammatical" error of treating "the present as framed by the past and future: the present is a former future where its form was prepared and the past, which will occur again in the future, preserves the identity of its content" (*LCP*: 176).

The problem with all of these approaches is that they presuppose a kind of "continuous history" providing a "privileged shelter for the sovereignty of conciousness" (*AK*: 12). Either this continuous history "sees the historical analysis of discourse as the quest for and the repetition of an origin that eludes all historical determination" (as with positivism), or it sees discourse "as the interpretation of 'hearing' an 'already said' that is at the same time a 'not said' " (*AK*: 25) (as with interpretivism and philosophies of history). As Foucault saw it, these approaches thereby avoided the "difference" between present and past, and analysis of practices authorized by the modern episteme (*AK*: 204), because they "deny in the historical analyses themselves the use of discontinuity, the definition of levels and limits, the description of specific series, the uncovering of the whole interplay of differences" (*AK*: 13):

> Western thought has seen to it that discourse be permitted as little room as possible between thought and words. It would appear to have ensured that *to discourse* should appear merely as a certain interjection between speaking and thinking; that it should constitute thought, clad in its signs and rendered visible by words, or, conversely, that the structures of language themselves should be brought into play, producing a certain effect of meaning. (*AK*: 227)

The reasons why Foucault indicted the modern episteme should now be coming into clearer focus. Modern thought does not, he seemed to be saying, show that the study of human beings began when some hitherto ignored object of inquiry was finally discovered. Rather, it shows that this object was constituted by the new episteme and those discursive practices authorized by it. For like all discourses, modern discourses "systematically form the objects of which they speak" (*AK*: 49). Thus, it is in an effort to demonstrate this that Foucault's archaeological method seeks out "discourses in their specificity [and] to show in what way the set of rules that they put into operation is irreducible to any other" (*AK*: 139).

Foucault's preoccupation with trying to separate himself from traditional social-scientific methodology led him to make quite radical claims for the status of his philosophical presuppositions. As the object of social inquiry, human beings, practices, and institutions were in a sense created by the modern episteme. The rules of discourse which "objectified" and "subjectified" human beings could not be reduced to the assumption that "things murmur meanings our language has simply to extract" (as with positivism), nor could they be read as if "the task of the founding subject is to animate the empty forms of language with his objectives" (*AK*: 227) (as with interpretivism). As Foucault sees it, the choice here is between two, and only two, methods of social inquiry. One is the method common to positivism and interpretivism, which leads us to search for the origin of language in human beings, whether conceived as physiological objects or as reflective social agents whose "subjectivity" is crucial to the constitution of the social world. The other method is the archaeological and genealogical: archaeology demonstrating that "the rules of formation [are shown to have] operated not only in the mind or consciousness of individuals, but in discourse itself; they operate, therefore, according to a sort of uniform anonymity, on all individuals who undertake to speak in this discursive field" (*AK*: 63). And genealogy provides "a form of history which can account for the constitution of knowledges, discourses, domains of objects etc., without having to make reference to a subject which is either transcendental in relation to the field of events or runs in the same empty sameness throughout the course of history" (*PK*: 117).

But while discourse is the locus of power and political struggle, or as the "later" Foucault might put it, the creation and creator of power and political struggle, neither power nor discourse are things that can be simply grasped by an active subject and used to serve his or her own interests. As an "anonymous" constraint on practice "at once controlled, selected, organized and redistributed according to a certain number of procedures, whose role it is to avert its powers and its dangers, to cope with chance events, to evade its awsome materiality" (*AK*: 216), discourse enables "the various statuses, the various sites, the various positions that (the subject) can occupy or be given" (*AK*: 54). But to grasp at power as a means of shaping discourse is equally futile, for "The individual is an effect of power," and "individuals are the vehicles of power, not its points of application" (*PK*: 98).

By turning from the archaeological analysis of discourse and the "will to truth" to the genealogical unmasking of the "will to power," Foucault's critical theory finds its footing. As he put it, "there is no power relation without the correlative constitution of a field of knowledge, nor any knowledge that does not presuppose and constitute at the same time power relations" (*DP*: 27). Most important for our concerns, however, is Foucault's assertion that this power/knowledge relation is not constituted by "a" subject, but is rather constitutive of subjects, and must therefore "be analyzed" on the basis of "the subject who knows, the objects to be known and the modalities of knowledge [which] must be regarded as so many effects of these fundamental implications of power/knowledge and their historical transformations" (*DP*: 27–28; see also *PK*: 117). And because the modern form of this power/knowledge constellation "reaches into the very grain of individuals, touches their bodies and inserts itself into their actions and attitudes, their discourses, learning processes and everyday lives" (*PK*: 39), a critical theory cannot deploy the concepts and categories of modernity, whatever their form, if it is to be emancipating.

To be sure, there are some important differences between the archaeological and genealogical projects. For example, in its archaeological moment, Foucault's methodology is understood to be a "pure description of discursive events" (*AK*: 27) which reveals that human beings are given, and do not create, "their history, their economics, their social practices, the language (langue) that they speak, the mythology of their ancestors, even the stories that they were told in their childhood" because these are "governed by rules that are not all given to consciousness" (*AK*: 211). In his genealogical reformulation, however, Foucault said that what was missing was the "problem of the 'discursive regime,' of the effects of power peculiar to the play of statements. I confused this," he says, "too much with systematicity, the theoretical form, or something like a paradigm" (*PK*: 113).

The shift from archaeology to genealogy, then, entails Foucault's abandonment of an assumption that discourse is autonomous from practice. The effect was not to abandon archaeological inquiry, but to resituate it as an analysis of discursive practices within a genealogical critique of power relations that discursive practices presuppose and reinforce (Dreyfus and Rabinow 1982: 103). But whether it is knowledge and discourse, or practice and power, that was given priority in analysis, some crucial underlying philosophical assumptions remained constant. One of these was that acting on the basis of characteristically "modern" knowledge claims was to operate within a field of discourse that is "linked in a circular relation with systems of power which produce and sustain it, and to effects of power which it induces and which extend it" (*PK*: 133). And to be a "subject" who seeks knowledge and truth is to recapitulate the power/knowledge grid that defines what it means to be a subject; it is to conceptualize oneself in a way that is the product of, and the means of reproducing, those "sites" and "statuses" the power/knowledge grid issues.

The striking feature of these assumptions is that they appear to leave no philosophical space for grounding an oppositional discourse and practice. To seek "knowledge" about social relations was to perpetuate the "malicious" will to truth; and to seek to be the author of one's own life was to be an active participant in the "will to power." Foucault did come to realize that he had to give a fuller account of the bases of opposition and potential emancipation, and in these attempts he provided intimations and insights useful for understanding how modern forms of domination might be overcome. But however useful, these attempts were not unambiguous, and it is to explicating these ambiguities—and their positive potential—that I now turn.

FOUCAULT AND CRITIQUE

If Foucault is on the mark in his account of the rise of modern thought, and if his description of these developments as issuing in circular, self-referential and closed systems of discourse and power is right, perhaps the question that should be asked is this: What is the status of the discourse from which Foucault himself speaks, and how does this discourse enable social agents to become aware of and possibly escape from the constraints that the modern power/knowledge grid establishes? How Foucault answered this question—and his answers changed significantly over time—makes for an interesting narrative about the development of his thought, for it recapitulates a progressive recognition on his part that the requirements of a politically motivated critical theory could be met without substantial revision of some of his positions.

At the heart of the various answers Foucault provided there is a single theme that repeatedly resurfaces, and that theme is "the subject." Indeed, in one of his last essays Foucault retrospectively reinterpreted his work precisely in terms of this theme. If power was always implicit in the archaeological unmasking of "the will to truth," and made central to the genealogical unmasking of the "will to power," both were (now) understood as serving "to create a history of the different modes by which, in our culture, human beings are made subjects." "Thus," he claimed, "it is not power, but the subject, which is the general theme of my research" (SP: 208).

Foucault's self-conscious reinterpretation of his corpus may be viewed in light of the brief history of French social theory I provided earlier in this chapter. It might be said that Foucault progressively moved away from a wholesale (and "structuralist" inspired) attack on the subject and a "logic of identity," toward the advocacy of a project in which "we have to promote new forms of subjectivity" (SP: 216). In a sense, this should not be surprising. For if Foucault was to sustain his practical intentions, he could not easily dispose of some account of subjectivity, if only because his "critical" project required at least some kind of philosophical account of the ways that social agents could change their practices.

The problem of subjectivity, then, is conceptually related to broader issues of the status of Foucault's critical, political intentions. What I would like to suggest is that if there is any meaningful sense in which there might be said to be a "break" in Foucault's corpus, this break is not (contra most interpretations) marked by the shift from archaeology and discourse analysis to genealogy and power analysis. Rather, it is a break between his attacks on the notion of subjectivity itself, and his advocacy of new forms of subjectivity. This break also entails a radical transformation in Foucault's understanding of the relationship between the archaeological/genealogical project and political practice (or critical theory and practice), as well as his understanding of the relationship between theorist and audience. I do not mean to imply that this break was a sudden one; it develops over time, with fits and starts. But it is a break nonetheless.

The narrative tracing the development of this break begins with the events of May 1968 in France. During the May events, "the most radical domestic upheaval since 1945 in Western Europe" (Poster 1975: 370), students and workers brought French society to a virtual standstill. The effects of this movement were also felt in the otherwise abstract realm of social theory; "walls became theorists" (Poster 1975: 381), and it was the existential Marxism inspired by Sartre that was the social theory written on those walls (Poster 1975: 383). It was in this context that many of those associated with structuralism sought to identify themselves with the May movement (Hirsh 1981: 153), a response no doubt facilitated by the fact that many of the students had declared the "structuralist" school, of which Foucault was considered a part, "dead," and instead embraced the "humanism" and "anthropology" of Sartre's existentialist Marxism (Gardner 1981: 213–15).

It was this situation that served as a catalyst for Foucault's characterization of his work as a project that aimed to show how one could "escape" from the systems of thought "which determine our most familiar behavior without our knowing it" (in Simon 1971: 201). More than one observer has noted that Foucault's restatement of his intentions was perhaps precipitated by the May events (Poster 1975: 340; Dreyfus and Rabinow 1982: 104; Habermas 1987: 249). Foucault's philosophical and theoretical claims, it seems, were now informed by the same political aims as those of the May rebels. In this respect Foucault perhaps suffered the fate of many social theorists who, in the face of questions regarding the political significance of their work, must reconsider their position on what would be, in periods free of obvious crisis, more "esoteric" philosophical matters.

These tensions were not, however, immediately disposed. For example, in the conclusion of *The Archaeology of Knowledge*, Foucault took up these practical matters in a somewhat strange, though intriguing, dialogue with an imaginary interlocutor. "[W]hat then is the title of your discourse?" the interlocutor asks; "Where does it come from and from where does it derive its right to speak? How could it be legitimated? . . . And how could your enterprise prevail against the question of origin, and the necessary recourse to a constituent subject?" (*AK*: 205). In response, Foucault admitted that he found the questions "embarrassing" because, he said, "my discourse, far from determining the locus in which it speaks, is avoiding the ground on which it could find support. It is a discourse about discourses" (*AK*: 205).

Rather than providing an account of what the interlocutor calls "the curious use of freedom that you question in others" (AK: 208) Foucault at this point tries to skirt the issue completely, and his remarks serve only to further undermine whatever attractions his inquiries might otherwise have had for his more skeptical readers. It was, as the interlocutor says, a situation in which Foucault's discourse either "does not reach us, or we claim it" (AK: 205).

Now given his philosophical formulations to this point in his work, the only way in which Foucault might sustain his practical intentions is by admitting that he speaks from within the modern episteme, in which case we have good reason to reject his characterization of modernity as exhausted by a "rancorous will to knowledge" that is necessarily "malicious" and "unjust." For if the archaeologist can create a discourse within that episteme that is not malicious, not unjust, then surely others can as well.

As Alasdair MacIntyre has argued, every moral philosophy offers an implicit conception of the relationship between social agents and their reasons, motives, intentions and actions (1981: 22). And Foucault's is no exception. But his conception of this relationship was that we are in an important sense "determined" by the language we speak and the positions we occupy in the power/knowledge grid. Yet Foucault also had to admit, given his emancipatory intentions, that our roles, statuses, and the "sites" we occupy are not determined in a strong sense. If we cannot also make our own roles, our "selves," then any talk of "escape" is conceptually contradictory and practically impossible.

There is a "thin," as well as a more complex "thick," sense in which Foucault must admit a conception of subjectivity into his discourse. The first is grounded in the fact that his discourse has meaning *only for a subject*. Foucault's discourse, if we are to understand it at all, cannot take place outside, as it were, the language we share with him; it has meaning only in the sense that it can be understood by "subjects" for whom it would be intelligible. Foucault himself provides an argument to this effect when he maintains that positivism has failed in its attempts to elude the problematic of language because language "always re-emerges on the side of the knowing subject—as soon as that subject expresses what he knows" (OT: 296). Every such attempt to understand human beings without reference to the language they speak must, according to Foucault, fail: when man "attempts to define his essence as a constitutive subject, prior to any effectively constituted language, all he ever finds is the previous unfolded possibility of language, and not the stumbling sound, the first word upon the basis of which all languages and even language itself became possible" (OT: 330). This, we might say, is Foucault's argument for the recognition of the "hermeneutic circle": the fact that we cannot escape an appeal to a common understanding of language we use (Taylor 1977: 103). It is in this "thin" sense that Foucault must have some notion of a subject in his discourse. For if he cannot recognize that the intelligibility of his own work requires (as the interlocutor in the *Archaeology* says) that we can "claim it," then there is a sense in which it could "not reach us."

Thus, Foucault's political intentions require some notion of subjectivity, even if only in the "thin" sense of recognizing that any discourse is necessarily bound up in the web of interpretations that make social life meaningful. But even this thin conception of subjectivity cannot carry the weight of Foucault's political aims. Intelligibility is not enough; some standards of judgment are needed if social agents are to critically engage the various models of "freedom" to which they are exposed. Foucault clearly ruled out any appeal to "universal" norms, such as those common to modernist critical theory. As he put it, one of his aims was to expose the "crisis that concerns that transcendental reflection which philosophy since Kant has identified" (*AK*: 204). This "essential task" was to be the means of freeing "the history of thought from its subjection to transcendence" (*AK*: 202).

This would not be particularly problematic; as I argued in my discussion of modernist critical theory, we have good reasons for rejecting the search for "universal" norms. Still, it is difficult to follow Foucault past this particular claim. For while he insisted that he had "not denied—far from it—the possibility of changing discourse," he nonetheless held to the assumption that he had "deprived the sovereignty of the subject of the exclusive and instantaneous right to it" (*AK*: 209). But if "subjects" cannot claim the "right" to change discourse, who can? Indeed, where are emancipatory values and norms to come from if not from "subjects?"

These questions speak directly to the second, and more complex, conception of subjectivity Foucault's project requires. If the partners in his critical project are to be considered capable of recognizing the constraints that their language and practices impose, then they cannot be conceptualized as mere objects upon whom these constraints operate. They must in some sense be capable of seeing themselves as agents who are not exhaustively "defined" by dominant discourse. In other words, they must be capable of articulating counter-discourses; as those who can exercise the "curious use of freedom that you [Foucault] question" (*AK*: 208). If social agents, like Foucault himself, possess at least the potential for seeing previously unexamined and unarticulated presuppositions of language and practice as constraining where they need not be, then there must be some sense in which they can be the authors of their own actions.

We need not suppose, as Foucault did, that a claim to self-determination necessarily implies an appeal to transcendentalist "logic of identity." But certainly the fact that Foucault wants us to, and was himself able, to unmask the pernicious effects of modern discourse means that human beings must have some capacity for self-transformation. He is perhaps right to have criticized the modernist impulse to seek a universal human identity. But if there is to be any meaningful content to the claim that human beings can escape from the impositions of power/knowledge, there must also be a sense in which that grid of impositions, so long as we are aware of its density and difficulties, does not leave us as we have always been. Only as potentially reflective social agents are we capable of seeing that Foucault may be right about the limitations of our discourse, and only as reflective social agents are we capable of *acting* upon that knowledge.

Perhaps we can now better understand why, in his "archaeological" moment, Foucault found his imaginary interlocutor's questions "embarrassing." Yet even in the transition to his geneaological inquiries, the practical goals of Foucault's project appeared foreclosed. For if the will to knowledge is "unjust," so too is "the will to power," even the power of opposition, at least when it is conceptualized as "the endlessly repeated play of dominations" (*LCP*: 150), and when human history is seen as nothing more than proceeding "from domination to domination" (*LCP*: 151).

There are, however, some useful insights to be gleaned from Foucault's genealogical inquiries, and these help us see through the illusion of "universal" solutions to situations of domination. One of these is that the origins and effects of power are not centralized, but are "situated at a quite different level" (*DP*: 26). Whatever power "apparatuses and institutions operate is, in a sense, a micro-physics of power," and this power is "exercised rather than possessed" by those in dominant positions, "an effect that is manifested and sometimes extended by the position of those who are dominated" (*DP*: 26–7). Another useful insight, related to the first, is that the localized character of power "define[s] innumerable points of confrontation, focuses of instability, each of which has its own risks of conflict, of struggles, and of at least temporary inversion of the power relations" (*DP*: 27). In other words, the power/knowledge grid was understood as producing relations of inequality, domination, and subordination differently in different localities, and different for different persons. Moreover, the localized character of power gives rise to localized, contextually specific forms of resistance. (Interestingly enough, even with respect to this set of issues the May events may be seen as playing a crucial role in Foucault's development. As he sees it, the task of analyzing "the mechanics of power . . . could only begin after 1968, that is to say on the basis of daily struggles at grass roots level, among those whose fight was located in the fine meshes of the web of power" [*PK*: 116].)

The philosophical and practical implications of these insights (first published in 1975) were soon to be cast in terms of the political intentions Foucault had professed some years earlier. Whereas genealogy was once (in 1970) understood as being concerned with "how series of discourse are formed, through, in spite of, or with the aid of . . . systems of constraint" (*AK*: 232), it was later (in 1976) understood as "the union of erudite knowledge and local memories which allows us to establish a historical knowledge of struggles and to make use of this knowledge tactically today" (*PK*: 83). Thus was genealogy wrested from its early association with archaeology, and rather than "avoiding the ground on which it could find support" (*AK*: 205), Foucault now saw his work as facilitating "an *insurrection of subjugated knowledges*," those "blocs of historical knowledge" that have been "disqualified as inadequate," and which "were concerned with *a historical knowledge of struggles*" (*PK*: 81-83 passim).

But a crucial question still remained: in what sense did these "subjugated knowledges" bear on the possibility of emancipation? Surely such knowledges did not necessarily entail elimination of relations one could, in good conscience, identify as emancipating. It does not take a great deal of imagination to see many forms of "subjugated knowledge" as just the opposite of what Foucault has in mind. We need not appeal to "subjugated knowledges" such as those that justify the infamy of slavery, monarchical rule, the oppression of women, and the exclusion of vast majorities of persons from the determination of their own lives, in order to see the thin veneer of Foucault's claims. Even one of Foucault's most ardent defenders, William Connolly, saw his sweeping support of "subjugated knowledges" as politically irresponsible (Connolly 1983: 332). In light of this, one might even ask, as Nancy Fraser (1981: 283) has, why struggle would be preferable to submission, and why domination ought to be resisted, for it is only "with the introduction of normative notions" that would enable us to distinguish "emancipating" from "dominating" subjugated knowledges that Foucault could "begin to tell us what is wrong with the modern power/knowledge regime and why we ought to oppose it."

It is at this point that we can begin to situate Foucault's transition to the advocacy of "new forms of subjectivity," and its implications for his practical political goals. One element of this entailed doing away with the subject as a "problem," and turning the subject into a "presupposition" of critique. Foucault now admitted that if "one defines the exercise of power as a mode of action upon the actions of others

... one includes an important element: freedom." For freedom is a condition for the exercise of power over others and a precondition of the power to resist: it is "exercised only over free subjects, and only insofar as they are free," and "freedom must exist for power to be exerted." With this admission, Foucault perhaps repudiated his earlier claim that he denied the subject's "right" to change discourse and practice (see *AK*: 209), because it is only in our capacity as active agents who are "free" to constitute and reconstitute relations of power that domination and resistance exist at all. In short, Foucault now seemed to have conceded that human beings *are* in some sense constitutive subjects, for "[t]he relationship between power and freedom's refusal to submit cannot therefore be separated" (*SP*: 221).

But if subjects are going to be "free" in a normative sense, and not merely "free" in the descriptive sense of possessing a constitutive capacity, they must also exercise this capacity in highly specific ways. Foucault began to supply this normative criteria when he argued that the struggle against the pernicious effects of modern thought and practice were not to be understood as "a matter of emancipating truth from power (which would be a chimera, for truth is already power) but of detaching the power of truth from the forms of hegemony, social, economic and cultural, within which it operates at the present time" (*PK*: 133). What this required, he believed, was that subjects must resist the temptation to use that "form of power which makes individuals subjects" in the sense of making others "subject to someone else by control and dependence," or in the sense of making someone "tied to his own identity by a conscience or self-knowledge," for "Both meanings suggest a form of power which subjugates and makes subject to" (*SP*: 212).

It was the "objectivizing of the subject in what I shall call 'dividing practices' " (*SP*: 210), best captured in his *Discipline and Punish*, that made others subject to control and dependence. And it was in those forms of power/knowledge in which "a human being turns him- or herself into a subject" (*SP*: 210), best captured in his *History of Sexuality*, that made one subject to one's conscience or self-knowledge. Together, these constituted the basis of "a new political form" that was "both an individualizing and totalizing form of power" (*SP*: 213), at once objectifying subjects through "carceral" practices (*DP*: 293ff.) and subjecting them to "a knowledge of the conscience and an ability to direct it" through "pastoral" practices (*SP*: 213ff.). It is "the modern Western state" that embodies this new political form (*SP*: 213). And an "embodiment" it was indeed. For as Foucault saw it, the break that was initiated with the modern episteme, "what might be called a society's 'threshold of modernity,' " was a new power/knowledge grid that "reaches into the very grain of individuals, touches their bodies and inserts itself into their actions" (PK: 39), thereby making "the body . . . directly involved in a political field" marked by "the proliferation of political technologies that ensued, investing the body, health, modes of subsistance and habitation, living conditions, the whole space of existence" (HS: 143–44).

Useful insights? Yes. But Foucault's attempts to flesh them out merely served to raise further questions about his political intentions. To be free of the political "investment" of the body, an emancipatory subjectivity could be realized, Foucault argued, only if we recognize that "the political, ethical, social, philosophical problem of our days is not to try to liberate the individual from the state, and from the state's institutions, but to liberate us both from the state and from the type of individualization which is linked to the state." Such resistance must embody "a non-disciplinary form of power . . . liberated from the principle of sovereignty" (PK: 108) because "sovereignty and disciplinary mechanisms are two absolutely integral constituents of the general mechanisms of power in our society" (PK: 108). In fact, as Foucault viewed them, the same "subjugated knowledges" he aimed to recover were directed against the political technologies of the body:

> The "right" to life, to one's body, to health, to happiness, to the satisfaction of needs, and beyond all the oppressions and "alienations," the "right" to rediscover what one is and all that one can be, this "right"—which the classical juridical system was utterly incapable of comprehending—was the political response to all these new forms of power which did not derive, either, from the traditional right of sovereignty. (HS: 145)

It follows from all this that Foucault's emancipatory subjectivity, the severing of truth from its contemporary hegemonic forms, and the form of power that does not recapitulate "the power of normalization and the formation of knowledge in modern society" (DP: 308) must "counter the grips of power with the claims of bodies, pleasures, and knowledges, in their multiplicity and the possibility of resistance." The "rallying point" against the deployment of political technologies of the body ought, then, to be "bodies and pleasures" (HS: 157).

In a number of interviews before his untimely death (in 1984), Foucault seemed to characterize this form of nonnormalizing, nonsovereign subjectivity as involving "politics as an ethics" (FR: 375). This ethics, best represented by the ancient Greeks, was understood as having as its "principal target . . . an aesthetic one" (FR: 341); it "centered on a problem of personal choice, of aesthetics of existence" (FR: 348). It was an ethics "without any relation with the juridical per se, with an authoritarian system, with a disciplinary structure," nor did this kind of ethics involve "an attempt to normalize the population" (FR: 348, 341). Rather, it was informed by "the will to live a beautiful life, and to leave to others memories of a beautiful existence" (FR: 341).

As John Rajchman (1986: 178) argues, Foucault's politics-as-ethics "advances a liberty of 'choosing' or 'inventing' oneself within a kind of experience not fixed through the dictates of religion, state or law." According to Rajchman (1986: 166–167), "It is the philosophy for a practice in which what one is capable of being is not rooted in a prior knowledge of who one is. Its principle is freedom, but a freedom which does not follow from any postulation of our nature or essence."

This interpretation is, I think, on the mark—but it is also the source of profound difficulties. Even if one reads Foucault as offering a conception of freedom and subjectivity that is not tied to a prior knowledge of what one is, it is nonetheless the case that Foucault does appear to assume that there is "nature" or "essence" to human beings— an essence that lies in the distinctively human capacity for self-transformation, an ability to "make" one's identity (and thus history itself). This is not an arbitrary assumption; it follows not only from Foucault's critique of modern discourse and power, but also from his various reinterpretations of his own thought. Indeed, it is a presupposition shared as well with the modernist critical theorists, and it is one that no critical theory can do without. The crucial question, however, is what a critical theory does with this presupposition.

As Nancy Fraser (1983: 63) has pointed out, Foucault does not (and I would add, cannot) treat the characteristics of the body " 'as they really are in themselves' apart from the ways in which they are historically 'invested.' " Bodies, power, pleasures, knowledges, even one's "aesthetic" identity, are socially constituted and intersubjectively sustained. By moving to an aesthetic of existence, Foucault perhaps believed that he was articulating a grounding for resistance that was not "normalizing" or "tied to the principle of sovereignty." The problem here, however, is that this claim simply cannot be sustained. The only imaginable context in which an aesthetic of existence might avoid the problems of normalization and sovereignty would be one where we exist in a radical autonomy from others, where our existence has absolutely no impact or effect on the lives of others.

But to the extent that our identities are the creation of our histories, and to the extent that our historically constituted identities are a matter of power/knowledge constraints, Foucault's retreat to what he "calls the 'ethics,' which is the relation to oneself" (FR: 355) elides the difficult task of articulating the kind of collective action required to transform our relations with others in an emancipatory way. Such an account requires not only a conception of subjectivity, but an account of why that form of subjectivity is worthy of our rational assent, why it is a form of life that promises to enable us to reason together. But Foucault would have none of this talk:

> Shall we try reason? To my mind, nothing would be more sterile. First, because the field has nothing to do with guilt or innocence. Second, because it is senseless to refer to reason as the contrary of nonreason. Lastly, because such a trial would trap us into playing the arbitrary and boring part of either the rationalist or the irrationalist. (SP: 210)

Perhaps it is understandable that Foucault would posit such a radically autonomous—or better, skeptical—ideal of freedom given his understanding of the nature of modern discourse and power. Perhaps his call that "we have to get rid of this idea of an analytical or necessary link between ethics and other social or economic or political structures" (FR: 350) might make sense in a world where no such links exist. Foucault is right when he insists that "the questions I am trying to ask are not determined by a preestablished political outlook and do not tend toward the realization of some definite political project" (FR: 375), and that "by asking this sort of ethico-epistemologico-political question, one is not taking up a position on a chessboard" (FR: 376). Unfortunately, the world we inhabit, and will inhabit so long as we live together, does, and will continue, to have "analytical and necessary links" between ethics, social, economic and political structures. And in this, the claim that one does not take up a political position rings hollow, for the real question is whether the political position one must take, simply by virtue of living with other human beings, can contribute to the emancipation—or continued suffering—of those who are oppressed.

One lesson of this extended narrative, then, is that Foucault was never able to adequately respond to his imaginary interlocutor's question posed nearly twenty years earlier: Foucault's critique either does not reach us, or we claim it. He often seemed to prefer the first answer; and in this it should not surprise us that Foucault has been called "the enemy of man, reason, democracy, a danger to order" and "a wild irrationalist, a nihilistic misanthrope who gloated in the destruction of humanity" (Poster 1975: 334). Foucault wanted to provide us with a critical theory that would win our assent, but its acceptability is predicated upon something he is unwilling to give. John Rajchman (1986: 179) is again on the mark when he argues that Foucault's position "is not universalist: it does not appeal to people irrespective of who they are. And yet it is not *for* any one group. Foucault's philosophy was a philosophy neither of solidarity nor of objectivity." But to note this is also to note the extent to which the political implications of Foucault's critical theory had not been adequately addressed.

It may appear that my discussion might lead one to conclude that Foucault's work is without redeeming merit. But I think that for those committed to the emancipatory ideals that inform his work, a case can also be made for the interlocutor's assertion that we can lay claim to Foucault's discourse. His discourse does "reach us"; it comports with the frustrations and anger many of us feel at having been subject to unwanted domination. In this respect, Foucault makes a significant contribution to understanding what a critical theory must look like if it is going to be practically effective. As I shall argue, this contribution both recapitulates and supplements the contribution of modernist critical theory. But just as the contributions of the modernists had to be recovered from the dominant, and politically problematic, features of their critical theories, the same is true of Foucault.

BEYOND MODERNIST AND POSTMODERNIST CRITICAL THEORY

If there is any difference between Marx, the Frankfurt School, and Habermas's modernist critical theory, and the postmodernist conception offered by Foucault, it is surely to be located in the former's adherence to a "universal" concept of critical reason and the latter's principled rejection of such a concept. This difference noted, we are nonetheless left with the fact that both modernist and postmodernist critical theory are, at best, politically ambiguous. But the lessons of these critical theories are not only negative.

Surely among the most important and powerful insights established by these critical theories are those which unmasked as historically contingent those claims purporting to be timeless truths. More than this, they have also shown that critical theory must also reflect its own historical context.

I have argued that Marx, the Frankfurt School, and Habermas suggest a way out of this "impasse" of modernist critical theory by emphasizing the necessarily local, historically contingent and contextually specific character of critique. To his credit, Foucault also emphasizes this need. In a passage striking for its similarity to Habermas's appeal for localized critical theories (see chapter 2, pp. 52–53), Foucault argues that

> The role for theory today seems to me to be just this: not to formulate the global systematic theory which holds everything in place, but to analyse the specificity of mechanisms of power, to locate the connections and extensions, to build little by little a strategic knowledge. (*PK*: 145)

In this, Foucault is consistent in drawing out the reconstructive implications of what he saw as the "capillary" effects of power/knowledge: If "power" is localized in the forms it takes, so too must resistance be contextually specific. What's more, Foucault follows this insight by also providing a way of reconceptualizing the relation between critical theorist and those he or she seeks to address. He argued that where the " 'left' intellectual [once] spoke and was acknowledged the right of speaking in the capacity of master of truth and justice" (an idea "transposed from Marxism, and a faded Marxism indeed"), this notion of the "universal" intellectual had to give way to the idea of the "specific" intellectual, one who is

> used to working, not in the modality of the "universal," the "exemplary," the "just-and-true-for-all," but within specific sectors, at the precise points where their own conditions of life or work situate them (housing, the hospital, the asylum, the laboratory, the university, family and sexual relations). (*PK*: 126)

But just as the "contextualist" demands of modernist critical theory are at odds with its otherwise "universalist" tendencies, this postmodernist "contextualism" is at odds with its radical normative skepticism. If the "specific intellectual" is to make good on his or her intention to work where situated by conditions of life then that individual cannot avoid taking up a stand that is in solidarity with those who are oppressed in these contexts. To do otherwise is perhaps to fall back into another version of the transgressions of the "universal intellectual." The specific intellectual must work *through* a specific context of oppression and *with* those who share that context. In short, specific intellectuals must take a position on the political chessboard, even if that chessboard is defined in highly specific ways, for if those who suffer are to "claim" the intellectual's theory as their own, then it must be cast in a way that enables it to "reach" them.

We need not therefore fully embrace the arguments of Marx, the Frankfurt School, Habermas, or Foucault, in order to appreciate the contributions they have made toward seeing what the foundations of a practically effective critical social theory might look like. Neither a modernist universalism nor a postmodernist skepticism necessarily follows from their arguments. But if we are not going to be reduced to a politics of despair or a wistfully utopian longing for a better world that seems to recede ever farther into the future, there might be something useful to learn about critical theory as long as we seek out examples of critical theory that are more immediately related to actual struggles for empowerment. Fortunately, there are extant examples of these kinds of theories, and in the next part of this book I examine four in detail. These theories, these critical theories *in practice*, preserve the useful insights of modernist and postmodernist critical theory, but without falling prey to the philosophical—and political—problems that modernist and postmodernist critical theory entails. They show how the idea of a social theory that can be enlightening and emancipatory is realizable, and is being realized, in political practice.

PART II

Critical Theory in Political Practice

MY AIM in Part I was to show that the received view of critical theory reflected in part in the work of Marx, the Frankfurt School, Habermas, and Foucault suffers from a range of philosophical difficulties. The consequence of these is a tension between the political intentions and the political implications of their projects. But, their work provides a number of insights that promise the possibility of moving beyond these difficulties, even though these theorists do not themselves consistently pursue these insights.

The theme that informs this second part is that there are theories that vindicate the essential insights of modernist and postmodernist critical theory without also succumbing to the philosophical—and thus practical—difficulties of these approaches. In the chapters that follow I cite four extant examples of "critical theory in practice": dependency theory, Paulo Freire's critical pedagogy, liberation theology, and feminist theory. One of the characteristic features of these critical theories in practice is that they are understood by their proponents to be theoretical expressions of, and critically reflective guides for, specific political struggles. Moreover, these theories also attempt to identify in these struggles embodiments of what may be rightly called reasonable, rational, and potentially liberating political practices.

But this self-conscious association with and commitment to particular practical struggles does not necessarily qualify a social theory as a critical theory. Nor for that matter does the fact that these theories identify as "rational," aspects of the practices of which they purport to be a part. In other words, it is not enough that a theory engage in a "localized" form of critique. What is required is a metatheoretical self-understanding that can accommodate, on the one hand, the need for collective solidarity, and on the other, a respect for plurality and difference.

How these demands may be met can be approached by returning once again to the issues surrounding the relationship between theory and practice, as well as those concerning the relationship between the theorist and her/his audience. The conceptual connections here may be cast this way: The necessary relation between theory and practice is one of the central metatheoretical presuppositions established by both modernist and postmodernist critical theory, especially in their deconstructive moments. And the reconstructive import of this is that the unity of theory and practice requires the identification of those practices with which a critical theory purports to be associated. By extension, this commits the critical theorist to a form of collective solidarity with those embedded in such practices. But the historically contingent and contextually specific character of social knowledge and human identity require a recognition of the contingency of any critical claims, including, perhaps especially, those concerning the "emancipatory" potential of particular practices. Hence the need for critical theory to be open to plurality.

These are the strictures that may be gleaned from my discussion of the modernist and postmodernist projects; they are also the strictures informing the foundations of the critical theories in practice to be discussed in the following chapters. There are, however, a few general points I need to address in order to better situate these discussions.

One issue raised by the demand for solidarity is the potential for reification. Two related concerns are relevant here. First, the commitment to solidarity with particular struggles runs the risk of making a critical theory nothing more than a rationalization or ideological justification (in the pejorative senses of both terms) of those practices. Or to put the matter another way, theory may be used to do nothing more than justify the practices of which it purports to be a part. Second, failing to keep clear the contingency of all social theory, a localized critique may fall prey to yet another version of what we might call the Marxist fallacy, for it may be the case that in its partisan commitment, a critical theory will illegitimately characterize the interests and struggle of its addressees with a universal interest and promise of emancipation.[1]

Consider, first, the issue of universalism. Here, postmodernism appears to be most attentive to the potential dangers involved. Reflecting on what he calls the "problematic" of the May 1968 events in France, Foucault (1984: 385–86) offers an insightful perspective on these dangers. There was, he says,

> on the one hand, an effort that was widely asserted, to ask politics a whole series of questions that were not traditionally a part of its statutory domain (questions about women, about relations between the sexes, about medicine, about mental illness, about the environment, about minorities, about delinquency); and on the other hand, a desire to rewrite all these problems in the vocabulary of a theory that was derived more or less directly from Marxism.

[1] I am indebted to Issac Balbus and Daniel Levine for alerting me to the need to consider these issues.

As the passage suggests, there is an inherent tension between "local" issues and the desire for "universal" normative ideals. In the case of the May events, Foucault understood the "questions" asked to be part and parcel of localized, contextually specific practical problems, while the "theory" deployed to interpret them, because it appealed to a universalistic grounding, made for "a more and more manifest powerlessness on the part of Marxism to confront these problems" (Foucault 1984: 386). Thus, the universalization of particular interests, which is the consequence of a particular metatheoretical self-understanding, effectively renders the opening to plurality and difference difficult, if not impossible. We must, however, bear in mind that the postmodernist response to this, embodied in the tendency toward a radical normative skepticism, undercuts the equally important need for collective solidarity.

There still remains, however, the problem of "rationalization." For even if a critical theory can be open to plurality, it can ill afford to become nothing more than an ossified ideology of a political struggle, regardless of its normative merits. And it is here that modernist critical theory, especially that of Habermas, contains crucial insights to which any critical theorist must be attentive. As Habermas sees it, there are a number of difficulties in linking theory and practice, and these difficulties go directly to the problem of rationalization.

The relationship between a critical theory and an emancipatory practice is, he says, mediated by three particular needs (Habermas 1973a: 32). The first is "the formation and extension of critical theorems, which can stand up to scientific discourse"; the second concerns "the organization of the process of enlightenment, in which such theorems can be tested in a unique manner by the initiation of processes of reflection carried on within certain groups toward which these processes have been directed"; and the third "the solution of tactical questions" (Habermas 1973a: 32). Of these needs, a critical theory can provide insight and direction in only the first two instances. In other words, a critical theory can provide only a set of "true statements" and "authentic insights"; but, he insists, "the organization of action must be distinguished from [the] process of enlightenment" (Habermas 1973a: 33). And in this, theory "cannot have the same function" in both endeavors.

The "organization of action" seems particlarly troubling for Habermas, for it often involves a choice between "enlightenment and struggle, [and] thus between maintaining and breaking off communication" with others (Habermas 1973a: 38). There are good reasons for his discomfort; breaking off communication and taking up active confrontation may occur not only at the level of relations between oppressor(s) and the oppressed, but also at the level of relations within the empowerment struggle itself. That is, those seeking a practical over-throw of oppressive conditions may find themselves making choices of action that close off communication with others, rather than keep-ing it open. And the central problem here is that Habermas believes such choices are not compellingly justified with the aid of a reflexive theory; "Organizational questions" involving the actual process of emancipation "are not," he says, "primary things" (Habermas 1973a: 36–40).

The issue of rationalization enters here because the necessary iden-tification and solidarity of a critical theory and theorist with a partic-ular practice may imply the endorsement of practical choices that, in Habermas's view, are not "rationally" defensible. Does this, then, leave us without adequate criteria for distinguishing a truly critical from a merely rationalizing, ideological, perhaps even instrumentalist and objectifying social theory—even one which also purports to be emancipatory? To jump to this conclusion would be to ignore two-thirds of the equation here, for although it may be the case that a critical theory cannot theoretically delimit practical strategies, neither can it prescind from the requirement of providing "true statements" and "authentic insights."

Together, these supply important criteria for judging what can and cannot be called a critical theory—and they also provide a means of reducing the potential for rationalization.

On the one hand, the demand for "true statements" and "authentic insights" can authorize a retrospective characterization of the eman-cipatory potential of a particular practical struggle. "Attempts at emancipation," Habermas argues, "can, under certain circumstances be rendered plausible as practical necessities," but only by "taking into consideration the conflicts generated by the system (which have to be explained theoretically) and the avoidable repressions and sufferings" (Habermas 1973a: 37).

Whether the future practical choices made by those to whom the theory is addressed will remain emancipatory is, however, a matter that no critical theory can determine in advance. But neither are we without resources for adjudicating between choices of practical strat-egies. Indeed, the same demand that critical theory formulate "true statements" and "authentic insights" can also assist in the effort of "interpret[ing] hypothetically the constellations of the struggle" (Ha-bermas 1973a: 39). Surely any choice of action that does not promise the possibility of achieving a practical outcome that widens the possi-bility of collective self-determination, the absence of which is precisely what a critical theory is critical of, must be regarded as an illegitimate one. And in such instances, critical theory (and theorist) must retain some autonomy from practice, as Habermas's comments appear to suggest.

This takes us some distance toward understanding how a critical theory can avoid becoming the ossified ideology of a particular struggle and a particular set of interests. As I have stated it, however, the demand for collective self-determination is exceedingly ambiguous, for the crucial question now is whether collective self-determination is in fact emancipatory. The goal of a critical theory, after all, is by definition "emancipation." But it is also in terms of this question that the root differences are most evident between the critical theory of Marx, the Frankfurt School, Habermas, and Foucault, and that of the critical theories in practice I cite.

I would argue that the problems I noted in the modernist and post-modernist projects in part derive from the desire to avoid seeing critique lose its critical edge by becoming the ideology of any particular social movement. In part this was accomplished by defining the requirements of emancipation in a way that enabled critique to be autonomous from practice. But note again the conundrums of their positions.

For the modernists, the emancipatory potentials of localized struggles are legitimated only to the extent that they represent universalizable normative ideals. This may be seen in the complete passage from Habermas, part of which I quoted earlier. As he says, theory can avoid rationalization by trying to "interpret hypothetically the constellations of the struggle," but these constellations could only be characterized as truly emancipatory if they are read

> from the viewpoint that every victory sought would not merely (as is usual) lead to the assertion of one particular interest against another, but instead would be a step toward the intended goal, which would make universal enlightenment, and by virtue of it, the uninhibited discursive formation of will, possible for all participants (and thus no longer merely those affected). (Habermas 1973a: 39–40)

This is surely a laudable ideal, but it also assumes that any particularistic "emancipatory" claims are by definition illegitimate.[2] But if domination is itself particular, local, and contextually specific, as even Habermas seems to suggest, the logical conclusion is that emancipation may be so as well. The "tyranny of universalism" is, however, no less

[2] This is a point made particularly clear in the work of some feminists, especially Seyla Benhabib and Nancy Fraser. In my chapter on feminist theory, and again in my conclusion, I deploy their criticisms of Habermas to buttress my analysis of modernist critical theory.

evident in Foucault's postmodernism. While in many places he appears cognizant, perhaps excessively so, of the dangers of universalism, Foucault's normative skepticism and its concommitant derision of rationality and collective solidarity, also leads to the conclusion that every sort of struggle merely recapitulates domination, however much it may be in a new and different form.

Yet for all their difficulties, modernist and postmodernist critical theory does not leave us completely without resources for seeing beyond these issues. Habermas's description of a critical theory's relationship to practice offers a way of thinking about how theory can be simultaneously autonomous from, and in solidarity with, practice. Habermas explains that

> The theory serves primarily to enlighten those to whom it is addressed about the position they occupy in an antagonistic social system and about the interests of which they must become conscious as being objectively theirs. Only to the degree that organized enlightenment and consultation lead to those groups toward which this is directed actually recognizing themselves in the interpretations offered, do the analytically proposed interpretations actually become consciousness, and does the objectively attributed situation of interests actually become the real interest of a group capable of action. (Habermas 1973a: 32)

In other words, theory *must* be in solidarity with a particular struggle; indeed, the true "test" of a critical theory is its ability to make clear the "interests" of its addressees. This model of "confirmation," however, also points toward a relative autonomy of theory from practice. Theory posits "interests" that are immanent, but as yet not realized, by many who are involved in particular struggles. Thus, a critical theory does not embrace every aspect of a struggle, for certainly there may be features of the beliefs and practices from which struggle emerges that must be changed. This sympathetic yet critical stance cannot, however, be simply abandoned once (and if) a critical theory becomes what Habermas calls "the consciousness" of some agents. For a critical theorist must also keep central the contingency and particularity of his/her own limited horizons. To do anything less is to take the role of what Foucault calls "the universal intellectual," or, to put the matter in Habermas's terms, "there is no privileged access to truth" and "in a process of enlightenment there can be only participants" (Habermas 1973a: 33–34, 237). And what applies to the relationship between critical theorist and his or addressees applies equally to the relationships between the oppressed themselves: they, too, must keep central the contingency and particularity of their perspectives. This stance has the practical implication of giving normative priority to those choices of action that promise to widen participation in the collective determination of social and political life. All of which is to say that a critical theory worthy of the title is one that is both the expression of, and an ongoing critical guide for, a particular struggle against domination.

The upshot of this discussion is pehaps best captured by Foucault (1984: 343), who insists "the point is not that everything is bad, but rather that everything is dangerous, which is not exactly the same as bad." And "if everything is dangerous, then we always have something to do," including, not least, the need to be critically reflective of our own assumptions, and not simply those of others. Practical choices are dangerous, and sometimes tragic, but for all this we cannot avoid making them. As much as a critical theory can provide the "true statements" and "authentic insights" it must, and it can, assist those who are oppressed in making the best choices they can, given their situation.

As examples of critical theory in practice, dependency theory, Freire's critical pedagogy, liberation theology, and feminist theory, I believe, provide just this sort of assistance. Dependency theory shows that an otherwise "academic" social scientific theory can be practical-emancipatory in intent. Freire's pedagogy shows that a critical theory can, and indeed must, be educative, and that a truly emancipatory education must be critical. Liberation theology demonstrates that a religious faith cannot remain content with purely spiritual concerns, and must play a central role in assisting believers in the realization of their political emancipation. And finally, feminist theory provides important clues for understanding the foundations of self-identity and the relationships between particular forms of self-identity and oppression—or emancipation.

All of these theories share a similar metatheoretical self-understanding that preserves the demand for solidarity and the recognition of plurality and difference. Taken together, they suggest that critical theory can take different forms, each working with different theoretical and practical emphases as their context demands, each providing insights into the complexity and intricacy of the critical-theoretic project, and each attentive to the contingency and particularities of their claims. Thus, while they are informed by a particular context of application—this is one of their hallmarks—they also show that a contextualized conception of critical theory need not foreclose an openness to the plurality of emancipatory struggles. What may appear, then, as a set of theories unrelated in their concerns is in actuality a set of theories united by a concern for addressing particular forms of domination and particular relations of inequality. In this they share important features that make them more than similar; they are in fact complementary components of a larger project that seeks, as Thomas McCarthy maintains critical theory as a whole must, a form of life free from unnecessary domination in all its forms (McCarthy 1978: 273).

Before I turn to these theories, a few final comments are in order. My explications of these theories are selective, even idealized, reconstructions having metatheoretical intent. I do not assume that each and every version of these schools of thought will easily fit into my characterization. By trying to recover what I take to be the practically effective and potentially emancipatory metatheoretical underpinnings of these theories, I am also engaging in a form of immanent critique similar to that I used in my discussions of Marx, the Frankfurt School, Habermas, and Foucault. As I suggested in those earlier discussions, this tack may be justified on the basis of grounds internal to the work of the modernists and Foucault's postmodernism. In the case of the critical theories in practice I cite, this is no less true. For as we shall have occasion to see, the raising of the metatheoretical issues I attend are not only the consequence of these theories' engagement with theories and practices to which they are opposed, but are also part of debates internal to the theoretical and practical contexts of which they purport to be a part. Thus, my aim here is to contribute to the further development of these theories, and also to assist those who are involved in these specific struggles to see what they may share with those involved in other struggles—an effort, as we shall also see, that is actually called for in the writings of many of those I cite.

My metatheoretical emphasis may, however, itself be questioned on immanent grounds. For all my emphasis on practice, I say relatively little about the actual practices of which these theories purport to be a part. This is perhaps in one sense crucial, for certainly one would like to know whether, or in what ways, the practices inspired by these theories are indeed "emancipatory." In defense of my metatheoretical emphasis, and my relative lack of discussion of actual practices, I want to appeal to an intellectual division of labor. A great deal of the extant literature on the theories (and movements of which they are part) that I discuss is rich in empirical detail. But it is also thin, or in some cases (like dependency theory in particular) distorting, with respect to the sorts of metatheoretical issues I address. Given this, my emphasis on metatheory might be understood as being informed by three related aims. First, I hope to provide a complement to the existing literature rather than merely summarizing its findings. Second, I want to provide a way of understanding, and even a kind of prolegomenal framework for critically assessing the actual practices that have inspired, and have been inspired by, these theories. By reconstructing their philosophical presuppositions, I hope to give the judicious reader some way to assess the extent to which the practices in question realize their emancipatory potential. Third, I want to show that such an assessment is actually called forth by the metatheoretical foundations of any social theory worthy of the title of a critical theory. For one of the conclusions I reach is that dependency theory, Freire's critical pedagogy, liberation theology, and feminist theory both can and are committed to undertake a process of self-correction, and critical engagement with the practices they support, when changed circumstances or new insights require as much.

In short, to put the matter in terms I have introduced here, what I want to show is that a critical theory presupposes a metatheoretical foundation that mediates the relation between theory and practice in a way that authorizes practical solidarity and an openness to plurality and difference. What the received view of critical theory entails is an inability to make good these demands;[3] what these critical theories in practice show is that they may be realized.

[3] At this point it would be useful to bear in mind that critical theory after Marx never gave up the theory/practice connection. Foucault's support of "subjugated knowledges," Marcuse's (1964: 256) appeal to "the substratum of the outcasts and outsiders, the exploited and persecuted of other races and other colors, the unemployed and the unemployable," and Habermas's recent (1981a) endorsement of "new social movements" all suggest that critical theory remains committed in principle to the identification of potentially emancipatory struggles. But for all this, the gap between the practical aims and practical implications of modernist and postmodernist critical theory still remains, for the endorsement of these struggles remains tied to problematic normative ideals.

Arguments regarding the constitutive relation between theory and practice has been an identifying earmark of critical social theory in its variety of forms. The necessary relationship between social theory and political practice is the subject of an enormous literature, not the least of which has been that of Marx, the Frankfurt School, Habermas, and Foucault. A useful historical treatment of this issue can be found in Lobkowicz (1967).

In spite of all the lip service paid to this ideal, very little work has stressed how this relation is to be realized in practice. The notable exceptions in this regard are Fay's work (1975: especially 92–110; 1977; 1987) and O'Neill's (1976; 1985) articles. I take this book to be in part an extension of their efforts. (Indeed, it was Fay's and O'Neill's work that drew my attention to Freire and feminist theory.)

CHAPTER 4

Dependency Theory: Changing Latin America

> Although critical theory at no point proceeds arbitrarily and in chance fashion, it appears, to prevailing modes of thought, to be subjective and speculative, one-sided and useless. Since it runs counter to prevailing habits of thought, which contribute to the persistence of the past and carry on the business of an outdated order of things it appears to be biased and unjust.
>
> —Max Horkheimer

> There is no intention to put "arbitrary" in place of "objective" knowledge. What is intended is an approach that accepts and starts from the idea that history is movement and that structures are the result of impositions; even though these impositions may become crystallized, they contain tensions among classes and groups which always make them, at least potentially, dynamic.
>
> —Fernando Henrique Cardoso

IT IS fitting that dependency theory should serve as my first example of a critical theory in practice. Indeed, my introduction to dependency theory and my attempts to understand its philosophical foundations provided the questions and themes around which this book initially took shape. Two related issues were central. The first concerned the way dependency theory had been appropriated, interpreted, and criticized by various social scientists. What I found was that most of these efforts presupposed a methodological self-understanding that was at odds with that advanced by some of the original formulators of the dependency perspective. The second issue was raised simultaneously with the first: if dependency theory had been misunderstood, misused, or distorted by many of its advocates and critics, it was because they failed to see that dependency theory was originally intended as a *critical* theory.

These two theses will guide much of my reconstruction of dependency theory. They also bring this reconstruction into line with one of the central analytical threads of this study taken as a whole, namely, the intimate relationship between metatheory, theory, and practice. In the case of dependency theory this relationship is particularly important, for judgments regarding the viability and promise of this approach turn precisely on how one understands these otherwise abstract philosophical questions. Interestingly enough, few scholars have really been concerned with such issues in their discussions of dependency theory, and fewer still have recognized the critical metatheory subtending its original formulations.[1] And this oversight is made all the more odd in light of the fact that two of the most often cited works by Fernando Enrique Cardoso—"the grandfather of dependency theorists" (Dominguez 1978: 107)—emphasize just these matters.

One of my primary concerns in this chapter, then, is to provide something of a corrective to this oversight, by showing that dependency theory has been systematically misunderstood by many (if not most) of the social scientists who have attempted to engage it.[2] But I also aim to work on a second intellectual/disciplinary front as well, in order to show that dependency theory makes good the idea of a critical theory as it is expressed in Marx, the Frankfurt School, Habermas, and Foucault, without also succumbing to the conceptual and practical difficulties of their work. The results of pursuing these themes are that (1) much of my reconstruction of dependency theory is conducted in the form of an intellectual history, but one having a philosophical intent[3] and (2) this intent also gives this chapter a distinct flavor as a treatise on social scientific methodology that will not be found in my examinations of Freire's work, liberation theology or feminist theory. But in this respect it also serves to frame many of the themes I consider in greater depth in subsequent chapters.

My plan is as follows. First I discuss the sociopolitical context in which dependency theory was formulated. I then focus more narrowly on the practice of social scientific inquiry by examining both the "modernization" and "dependency" interpretations of development. It

---

[1] Two notable exceptions in this are Palma (1978) and Levine (1988). The former offers a sympathetic reading of dependency theory, while the latter criticizes dependency theory in part for its commitment to critical theory. Later in this chapter I shall address Levine's objections, albeit indirectly.

[2] Some methodologically and politically sensitive uses of dependency theory may be found in Becker (1983), Gereffi (1983), Hamilton (1982), and Sheahan (1987). Later in this chapter I question some of Becker's characterizations of dependency theory, but I think our differences are relatively minor.

[3] Elsewhere (with John Dryzek) I argue that there is an intimate and necessary relationship between intellectual (or disciplinary) history and theoretical justification (Dryzek and Leonard 1988). I take Cardoso's reconstruction of the development of dependency theory to represent a self-conscious attempt to articulate a rational justification for its theoretical and metatheoretical stances.

was in large part against several features of the modernization perspective that dependency theory came together, its aim being the provision of an alternative account of the trajectory and limitations of socio-political and economic change in the Third World, and particularly Latin America. After this, I consider various interpretations and criticisms of dependency theory advanced by many—particularly Western—social scientists. These interpretations and criticisms fall into two more or less distinct periods. The first I call the "consumption" period (late 1960s–late 1970s), and the second the "impasse" period (since about 1980). Using Cardoso's work as my primary foil, I argue that most of the works from both periods distort the theoretical claims and practical intentions of the "original" dependency theorists because they misconstrue how these claims are mediated by a critical-theoretic methodological framework.[4] All of this should take me some distance toward establishing the credentials of dependency theory as a critical theory, which I then take up in my concluding section.

The gist of my argument here is that dependency theory, properly understood, is unlike either the orthodoxy of the received view of development or the bastardized versions of dependency popular among so many social scientists, recent or contemporary. This difference, at root, is between a philosophically sound, theoretically rich, and potentially emancipatory self-understanding, and one that is not. Against those who now see dependency theory as anachronistic, I shall argue that such a view is simply wrong-headed. Dependency theory was, is, and will remain a critical theory—at least until those to whom it is addressed overcome the oppressive conditions in which they find themselves. And by committing themselves to this, the dependency theorists have shown that their work indeed deserves the title of "critical theory."

THE CONTEXT OF DEPENDENCY THEORY: SOCIOECONOMIC CHANGE IN LATIN AMERICA

Since the end of the Second World War, a combination of developments has led to the increasing prominence of the situation of the Third World. The end of the war signaled the close of the colonial period and the rise of new, politically sovereign nations. But political sovereignty did not, in most Third World nations, mean the attainment of independence and self-determination, for most Third World nations emerged in an era of interdependent rather than independent

---

[4] Cardoso's arguments are directed against the "consumption" of dependency theory, but the insights of these criticisms may also be applied to the "impasse" period.

nation-states. In a situation characterized by rapid communications and an increasingly complex world economy, the socioeconomic status of Third World peoples inevitably became a persistent international concern.

One crucial feature of this concern centered on the question regarding the processes by which Third World nations would "modernize" or "develop." In the postwar years, the foreign policy activity of practically every nation on the globe has been shaped by this question, and in the Third World itself, the question all but monopolized domestic policy considerations as well.

In the decades following the end of the war it became for many painfully evident that the Third World nations were in a historically unprecedented social, political and economic situation. The Third World did not "modernize" as so many academics and policy makers thought it would. As one observer has noted, "the assumption that countries in the Third World, in Asia, Africa, and Latin America, were developing was as much a wish as an empirically determined fact" (Riggs 1970: 3–4). But in spite of the policy failures of the past, there was, and in some instances continues to be, very little real change in the policy approaches in either the industrial, aid-giving states, or in the Third World itself. The general character of policies designed to promote "development" can be crudely—though not inaccurately—summarized as disciplinary. By this I mean that the aid policies pursued by both east and west, and the domestic policies pursued by the Third World governments themselves, were aimed at keeping public debate about the content of policy alternatives to a minimum. This disciplinary preoccupation, more than anything else, helps explain why the Third World was wracked by a cycle of reform, repression, and revolution. Participatory reforms give way, almost inevitably, it seems, to renewed repression, and even revolution seems to do little to change the cycle. The purpose of such policies is in the final analysis, the limitation or destruction of opposition to a chosen path of development. These are broad generalizations, but they nonetheless contain more than a kernel of truth.[5]

In Latin America, the evidence of this cycle is particularly clear. Modern Latin American history is largely a tale of authoritarian government, with an occasional foray into democratic politics. Few democratic experiments in the region succeeded in the face of military coups and destabilizing activities carried out by foreign, particularly U.S., interests, and the jury is still out on the recent "redemocratiza-

[5] For arguments along the lines I have followed, see Griffin (1971) and Griffin and James (1981).

tion" of many Latin American nations (a point to which I shall return later). But why did the cycle of reform and repression continue for so long? Why were these policies of discipline still used, even in the face of the overwhelming evidence demonstrating their ineffectiveness in bringing about "development" in Third World nations? The answers to these questions are to be found in the way that development has been interpreted and explained. For, as is so often the case, policy makers were simply filling out the practical implications of theoretical work completed in the academy.[6] To understand the continued preoccupation with disciplinary policies is thus to understand the theory that informs them.

INTERPRETING DEVELOPMENT

As a rule, social scientific interest in the societies we now know as the Third World was minimal until the period after the Second World War.[7] Although anthropological study in this area had flourished prior to the war, there was very little research into the social structures that were to emerge as the foundations of the new nations (Roxborough 1979: 13). When sociologists and political scientists, like policy makers, finally turned their attention to the Third World in response to the "emergence" of these societies after the war, they produced a massive theoretical literature. Usually identified as the school of modernization theory, this literature is characterized by a diversity of emphases, though it shares a common set of crucial assumptions.[8] These as-

[6] Valenzuela and Valenzuela (1978) provide some telling evidence of this theory-practice connection. They suggest that modernization theory "became the cornerstone of a conceptual framework which would influence the U.S. response to the third world" (p. 536), and cite the cases of Myron Weiner's *Modernization: The Dynamics of Growth* (1966) and Bert Hoselitz's *Sociological Aspects of Economic Growth* (1960). The former work "is a good collection of essays by modernization writers which were first prepared for the Voice of America"; the latter "was translated into twenty-five languages by the U.S. Department of State" (p. 553).

[7] My treatment of the literature on modernization is very selective, limited primarily to U.S. social scientists. My reason for excluding some important contemporary modernization theorists, such as the German theorist Niklas Luhmann (whose work serves as a focus of some of Habermas's criticisms of modernization theory [see McCarthy 1978: 213–32]) is that it is the Americans who have been most influential in discussions of Third World modernization.

[8] The "modernization" school is actually a rather broad way of characterizing this literature, for there are within the school significant differences between many of its members. However, it is nonetheless the case that these authors share a number of important assumptions, many of which I mention here. In itself, these shared assumptions I think warrant calling this literature a "school." For a similar view, see Valenzuela and Valenzuela (1978) and Hettne (1983).

sumptions are the theoretical foundations of the disciplinary policies favored by Third and First World regimes alike.

But modernization theory has not been without its critics. Not surprisingly, the most important criticisms of the modernization perspective have come from those who have actually experienced the repercussions of policies informed by modernization theory. These critics have helped shape what has become known as theories of dependency.[9] And the differences between the two perspectives of modernization and dependency are striking. Although both purport to explain the same reality, they originate in different contexts, make use of two almost incommensurable conceptual schemes, offer radically different explanations of the plight of the Third World nations, and have practical implications of very different sorts.

The Received (or Modernization) View

Theories of socioeconomic modernization are actually parasitic on earlier theories of socioeconomic development. Their context of origin is Western liberal society, their primary proponents are Western social scientists, and the ideal model of modernization they identified was, not surprisingly, derived from a theoretical reconstruction of the Western developmental experience. In spite of its continuities with earlier developmental theory (of which more shortly), the shift in emphasis from development to modernization turned on the attempt to answer a fundamental question: Why was there such a stark contrast between the developmental experiences of the Western countries and most of the rest of the world? (Valenzuela and Valenzuela 1978: 536).

From its intellectual antecedents, modernization theory inherited both a set of rigid conceptual categories and a kind of philosophy of history, and from these were derived specific prescriptive assumptions. As Clement Dodd noted, modernization theory was "inspired by the writings, principally, of Max Weber, Durkheim, and Talcott Parsons, with Herbert Spencer hovering in the background, and sidestepping Marxism-Leninism and the claims of political anthropology" (Dodd 1973: 367). On the one hand, modernization theory shared with its precursors a dichotomous categorization of development. A

[9] It should be recognized that dependency theory is a wide ranging tradition in the study of development, having many distinctions and variations, not the least of which are methodological. In this essay I use only the work of Cardoso and Faletto. My reasons for this selectivity are two: first, theirs is the most systematic, if still incomplete, attempt to elaborate the methodology of dependency theory; second, their criticisms of competing models of inquiry within the dependency tradition are, more often than not, on the mark. For a similar view see Palma (1978).

society, on this account, was either "modern" or "traditional," the latter usually understood as "largely a residual category, established by logical opposition to the modern end" of the dichotomy (Valenzuela and Valenzuela 1978: 538). The Western societies were seen as representing modernity, and to the extent they did not embody Western cultural norms and practices, Third World societies were cast as the contemporary equivalents of the "traditional," "*Gemeinschaft*," even "feudal" societies said to have been the historical antecedents of the Western "modernity" (Roxborough 1979: 1–26; see also Higgott 1981: 16–17).

This conceptual dichotomy was, moreover, usually accompanied by a philosophy of history that treated the so-called modernized societies as the end-point of developmental evolution (Roxborough 1979: 14–15). S. N. Eisenstadt (1966: 1) offered a characteristic definition when he claimed modernization was that

> process of change towards those types of social, economic and political systems that have developed in Western Europe and North America from the seventeenth century to the nineteenth and then have spread to other European countries and in the nineteenth and twentieth centuries to the South American, Asian, and African continents.

But there was more to the formulation of these assumptions than simply a social scientific interest in conceptual clarity and theoretical construction. For the aim of these projects was ultimately practical: providing answers to the fundamental question of why there was such a marked difference between the developmental experiences of the modernized and Third World societies was merely a necessary step in the formulation of practical strategies that would reduce, if not eliminate, this difference.

Given these assumptions, modernization theorists seemed to suggest that the modernizing societies had to follow the "evolutionary" path of the now-developed states. They also led to the identification of the "traditional" practices in the Third World as obstacles to modernization. But where moderization theory may have shared the evolutionary and dichotomous presuppositions of its intellectual forebears, it nonetheless departed from its predecessors in its practical conclusions. For the modernization theorists believed that the development process could be accelerated by the "diffusion" of Western achievements, making it possible for Third World societies to "skip stages" and "telescope time" (Valenzuela and Valenzuela 1978: 538–39). In this, modernization theory could be demarcated from its precursors by virtue of the fact that it assumed that, unlike the already modernized societies, late-modernizers could rely on external, not just internal, factors to bring about the completion of the modernization process.

> The practical implications of this perspective were obvious: Modernizing Third World elites are understood to be guided by the Western model, adopting and adapting its technology; assimilating its values and patterns of action; importing its financial, industrial, and educational institutions, and so on. Western colonialism, foreign aid, foreign educational opportunities, overseas business investments, the mass media, etc., are all important channels for the transmission of modernity. (Valenzuela and Valenzuela 1978: 539)

And in this respect, "modernization" was seen as a technical problem (Higgott 1981: 18); a matter of creating a society that is "highly organized, centralized, stratified, and controlled (penetrated) by large institutions (both public and private)" (Kesselman 1973: 154). In short, it was seen as the realization of a "rationalized" society (Valenzuela and Valenzuela 1978: 539; Higgot 1981: 18).

On this much, at least, most forms of modernization theory agree. But beyond this, there have been significant shifts and differences within the modernization perspective. The most important of these is rooted in two radically different understandings of the requirements of modernization. And these, in turn, may be related to two different conceptions of the general trajectory of development.

Historically speaking, the first form of modernization theory assumed that modernization occurred with the concommitant development of both rationalization and democratization. Particularly prominent between 1954 and 1964, this perspective was committed to the establishment of liberal democracy in the Third World (Higgott 1981: 15–18). Here the evolutionary presuppositions of modernization theory were expressed in the belief that the Western societies had been able to modernize because of a widespread consensus on basic "liberal" social, political, and economic values.

There is no doubt that the experiences of much of the Western world as well as many Third World societies in the immediate postwar period provided some empirical grounding for this commitment. Following the war, many Third World states, particularly those in Latin America, pursued policies (supported by Western aid) intended to strengthen and modernize the state apparatus and mobilize hitherto excluded groups; many even appeared to be on the verge of completing a transition toward a stable, nearly self-sufficient domestic economy (Cardoso and Faletto 1979: 1–5; Veliz 1980: 291). Such developments certainly must have appeared to many social scientists as a confirmation of the modernizing potential of the Third World, especially given their understanding of the Western societies. For in a sense the "liberalization" of these states seemed to fit well with the assumption that "the world is converging toward a uniform and standardized culture resembling that of the United States and Western Europe" (Valenzuela and Valenzuela 1978: 539).

The modernization theorists were not, of course, alone in holding to these panglossian assessments. Indeed, they seemed to be expressing a view widely held in the Western (especially the U.S.) social scientific community. This particular version of modernization theory coincided with what came to be called the "end of ideology" interpretation of Western liberal democracy.[10] In this view, it was assumed that the Western societies had finally reached "the end of ideology"; social conflict had been eliminated, and practical politics were guided by pragmatic compromise within a "consensus" on basic norms and values.

But the optimistic assessments of both the end of ideology and early modernization theorists soon ran aground in changed historical circumstances. Whatever liberalizing successes some Third World nations enjoyed, by the early 1960s many were feeling the effects of destabilizing economic difficulties, the consequence of which was an inability to maintain the kind of growth necessary for meeting the distributive demands brought on by rising popular expectations. There followed a rise in social conflict in the developing nations, and a marked turn toward authoritarian recentralization. Thus, modernization theory's optimism for the developing nations "disappeared with the growing disillusionment over the actual performance of new states in the post-independence period" (Higgot 1981: 18). Added to this was the fact that the end of ideology thesis was conceptually and theoretically ill-equipped to account for the rise of the social conflict in the Western states, which reached its height by the mid-1960s.

In a comment that applies to modernization theory as much as it does to the end of ideology assumption he criticizes, Alasdair MacIntyre says that "The 1950s were a decade of immoderate claims made on behalf of what its defenders took to be moderation" (1978: 3). MacIntyre also argued that one of the failures of the end of ideology thesis was that it tended to ignore the fact that "the costs of consensus are paid by those excluded from it" (1978: 10)—a criticism no less applicable to modernization theory. Beneath the veneer of consensus in both the developed and developing societies there still re-

---

[10] The most influential of the "end of ideology" arguments were Shils (1955), Bell (1960), and Lipset (1960; esp. chapter 13).

Collections of essays on the end of ideology thesis (pro and con) may be found in Waxman (1969) and Rejai (1971). A recent overview of this debate set in the context of the history of American political science may be found in Ricci (1984: 126–31).

mained latent conflicts between different classes and groups. In the prosperous 1950s these conflicts were smoothed over and obscured; in the tense 1960s they became highly visible. Thus "while the end of ideology thesis [and early modernization theory] was sensitive to a widespread mood in the 1950s . . . it proved to be highly discordant with the mood . . . of the 1960s" (MacIntyre 1978: 10).

While MacIntyre, among others, was arguing that the end of ideology thesis was indeed nothing more than an ideology itself (1978: 5), similar criticisms had been leveled at modernization theory (see, e.g., Bodenheimer 1971). For many of those opposed to the prevailing orthodoxies in both the developed and developing worlds, this suggested that modernization theory and the end of ideology were to some extent theoretically, practically, and methodologically bankrupt. But all of this also pointed to a still deeper problem in both accounts, particularly those aspects explicating the conditions of modernity and its trajectory of development. Not only was it assumed that rationalization and democracy went hand in hand, but that they had historically developed simultaneously. As many critics pointed out, however, the reality of the Western experience was something quite different. For example, C. B. Macpherson had argued some years earlier that "In our Western societies the democratic franchise was not installed until after the liberal society and the liberal state were firmly established. Democracy came as a top dressing" (1966: 5). And Barrington Moore, in his seminal study of modernization, turned these sorts of empirical claims against the kind of "consensus historiography" that appeared to inform the panglossian views of many Western academics (1966: 486).[11] Noting that when one turns "cultural and social continuity" into conditions that "do not require explanation," Moore argued that the resulting view "obliterates the fact that [this continuity has] to be created anew in each generation." But more than this, consensus was often achieved "with great pain and suffering":

> To maintain and transmit a value system, human beings are punched, bullied, sent to jail, thrown in concentration camps, cajoled, bribed, made into heros, encouraged to read newspapers, stood up against a wall and shot, and sometimes even taught sociology. (Moore 1966: 486)

The reality of the Western "ideal," in short, was that it not only misdescribed the forces at work in the Western societies, but also misdescribed the historical developments that created those forces.

[11] For a critique of "consensus historiography" and an attempt to bring to light the systematic political repression this school has managed to obscure, see Robert Goldstein's *Political Repression in Modern America* (1978).

This is a telling point, the implications of which are often over-looked.[12] For if the modernization theorists are right about Western political economy—that its culture is "rationalized" (Valenzuela and Valenzuela 1978: 539)—then it would seem that the Third World is merely pursuing the swiftest path that leads directly to Weber's "Iron Cage." In this sense modernization theory proposed as an ideal the same form of social organization that Marx, the Frankfurt School, Habermas, Foucault, and as we shall see, the dependency theorists, understand as a reality to be resisted and changed. By ignoring the pernicious effects of individualism, capitalism and centralized bureaucratic organization, the modernization theorists simply failed to note how the demands of these practices often clashed with the "democratic" norms they cherished so deeply. A "rationalized," "modern" society requires order and hierarchy, and democracy is a very "inefficient" means of achieving this kind of social order. Over a protracted period the political economy of rationalization may be muted or obscured, as perhaps it had been in the developed societies. But where modernization had to be compressed, rationalization must be carried out swiftly and therefore ruthlessly.

With the breakdown of peaceful liberalization in the Third World and peaceful liberalism in the First, the defenders of "order" came to the fore. In many Third World nations, the forces of reaction imposed disciplinary and exclusionary measures required for "telescoping" the development process. These policies, moreover, seemed to be supported by a newer form of modernization theory emerging from the Western academy. In numerous reformulations of the modernization problem, "democracy" was severed from "modernization," and the latter was now understood as requiring "order" as a necessary presupposition. "At least temporarily," this particular form of modernization theory seemed to suggest, "the maintenance of order requires a lowering of newly acquired expectations and levels of political activity" (Pool 1967: 26).[13]

Political repression fit easily into this schema. Where early modernization theory tended to emphasize economic and sociopsychological variables as factors in the development process, later theory emphasized institutional ones, especially governmental capacity to respond to popular demands (Higgott 1981: 17, 19). Part of this shift of emphasis was no doubt due to the fact that "order" theorists saw the modernization process as one that preceded, and was not concomitant

[12] For a similar argument, see Mark Kesselman's essay "Order or Movement? The Literature of Political Development as Ideology" (1973).

[13] For useful overviews of the shift in the modernization tradition, see Higgot (1981: 18–21), Roxborough (1979: 113), and Chilcote (1981: 280–83).

with, democratization. Thus, Samuel Huntington, one of the most influential of the "order" theorists, argued (in apparent agreement with more radical critics), that "The experience of the West, indeed, suggests that an inverse correlation may exist between the modernization of governmental institutions and the expansion of political participation" (1968: 94). But even here the evolutionary and teleological assumptions of earlier modernization theory were present, although now the "primary problem of politics" in the Third World was "the lag in the development of political institutions behind social and economic change" (Huntington 1968: 5).

Another continuity in earlier and later modernization theories was that they tended to treat the process of development as if it were contingent on more or less endogenous conditions (Valenzuela and Valenzuela 1978: 539). Even when the possibility of economic and cultural "diffusion" was tendered, the basic unit of analysis was the nation state. Undergirding all this was a kind of methodological functionalism. Whether this was expressed in the behavioralism of the early modernization theorists (Higgott 1981: 20), or the institutionalism of the later ones (Roxborough 1979: 113), these analyses assumed that the empirical evidence of the relationship between characteristic features of modernity, different as this evidence may have been cast by the various schools, implied necessary patterns in the developmental process. Finally, modernization theory in its various forms also shared a common practical perspective. Bluntly stated, it took the view of social and political elites, thereby providing theoretical justification for an elite-led developmental strategy (see Higgott 1981: 19–21; Valenzuela and Valenzuela 1978: 539).

As I have already intimated, resistance to modernization theory, and the practice of "modernization," was at both the theoretical and practical levels, in both the Western societies and the Third World. For our concerns, however, the most important expression of this resistance came in the form of a combined theoretical, methodological, and political critique advanced by some Third World, most notably Latin American, social scientists. And the analysis of Third World "development" resulting from this critique put a quite different face on the promise, possibilities and trajectory of sociopolitical and economic change in the Third World.

The Dependency View

While the received view of socioeconomic development stressed the need for Third World societies to "telescope" the developmental histories of the Western nations, in the early 1960s a number of scholars in the Third World were laying the foundations for a trenchant critique of accepted orthodoxy. This critique, which came to be known as "dependency theory," had its intellectual antecedents in traditions of discourse that had long been opposed to orthodox developmentalism, but these traditions never exercised the kind of influence that dependency theory has. Among the several reasons for this wider dissemination was that in the 1960s, criticisms of orthodox developmentalism were beginning to be heard in arenas previously closed to such thought, such as the United Nations Economic Commission on Latin America (ECLA), various Latin American universities, some government planning agencies, and even the North American academic community (Cardoso 1977: 9).

Later we shall see that this dissemination was not without problematic consequences for interpreting the nature of dependency theory, at least as some of its proponents understood it. At this point, however, it would be useful to consider the basic differences between the dependency and modernization approaches.

In the first place, the gist of dependency critique was that the disciplinary policies pursued by Third World regimes, informed in part by modernization theory, and reinforced by much Western foreign policy, had very specific unintended consequences. While orthodox developmentalism assumed that the continued difficulties of the Third World could be attributed to the fact that they remained *undeveloped*, the dependency theorists argued that the same policies designed to overcome this undeveloped status ignored the fact that historical conditions in which most Third World societies were embedded were simply different from those the "developed" societies had actually experienced, and those that modernization theory had described. In light of these differences, the critics claimed that the "replication" model of development undergirding the prevailing orthodoxy (see Roxborough 1979: 14–26) was doomed to fail by virtue of its theoretical—and practical—inadequacies.

Where the prevailing orthodoxy continued to hold to the idea that the Third World could replicate the experiences of the developed societies, the critics argued otherwise. It was not autonomous modernization that the orthodoxy produced, but a situation in which the sociopolitical and economic status of many Third World societies was one of dependence. In what might be considered a classic definition of this condition, Theotonio Dos Santos stated that "By dependence we mean a situation in which the economy of certain countries is conditioned by the development and expansion of another country to which the former is subjected" (1970: 231).

Implicit in this definition are a whole range of related theoretical presuppositions antithetical to those of modernization theory. For example, against the assumption that the Third World societies were hampered in their development by virtue of their "traditional" institutions and beliefs, the dependency theorists asserted that it was the specific character of the relationship between the First and Third Worlds that explained the failure of modernization. As a theoretical stance and practical strategy, orthodox developmentalism was blind to the conditioning effect of interdependence between societies. As Sunkel and Paz (1970: 6) argued,

> Both underdevelopment and development are aspects of the same phenomenon, both are historically simultaneous, both are linked functionally and, therefore, interact and condition each other mutually.

Thus "foreign factors are seen not as external but intrinsic" to the society under consideration (Sunkel 1972: 519). And in the context of the late twentieth century global political economy, where there is a "division of the world between industrial, advanced or 'central' countries, and underdeveloped, backward or 'peripheral' countries" (Sunkel and Paz 1970: 6), there are intimate links between "the postwar evolution of capitalism internationally [and] the discriminatory nature of the local process of development" in the Third World (Sunkel 1972: 519).

The dependency theorists, then, found the prevailing orthodoxy wanting because it did not recognize that the most important obstacle to Western-style development in the Third World was, in essence, Western-style development in the industrialized nations. That is, where modernization theory more or less ignored how the relative status of a society in the contemporary international political economy conditions its potential for development, the dependency theorists took this to be one of the most important determining factors in explaining the lack of development in the Third World. But there is a stronger claim involved than that which identifies the interdependence of the developed and less-developed societies. In their inquiries the dependency theorists also demonstrated that the logic of this situation is one in which the place of the peripheral society in the global political economy results in a transfer of resources to the central societies, while at the same time giving rise to various mechanisms which hold back or "distort" development on the periphery. The specific content of this transfer, the mechanisms by which it is carried out, and the relation between the mode of transfer and the "distorting" mechanisms may be many and varied, depending on the particular historical context of a particular society, but the general logic of the relation nonetheless holds true (Roxborough 1979: 63).

These, then, are the basic shared assumptions of what has come to be called dependency theory. But beyond these rather general characterizations of the dependent status of Third World societies there is substantial disagreement among those commonly associated with dependency theory; differences are expressed not only at the theoretical level, but the practical and metatheoretical levels as well. These differences are crucial, for on their adjudication the defensibility of dependency theory turns. This point is all the more important in light of the fact that dependency theory was able to gain wide influence among social scientists, even to the point that it was interpreted as having "challenged and then eclipsed" the modernization perspective, but also because dependency theory is now seen as being "under a mounting threat of being transcended" (Browett 1980: 145). Many of the charges against dependency theory are on the mark, at least against some of its specific, and I would argue indefensible, versions. And if my account of dependency theory as a critical theory is to be sustained, these criticisms must be addressed.

THE MISAPPROPRIATION OF DEPENDENCY THEORY

Since it was first pronounced a new "paradigm" for the study of Latin American politics and society over a decade ago (Bodenheimer 1971), dependency theory has become an important and widely read framework for the study of sociopolitical development. For many scholars, dependency theory offered insights that suggested how modernization theory was problematic, and how study of the developing nations might be better carried out. But many also found it seriously deficient on methodological grounds. Not content with the approach as its founders formulated it, some social scientists have tried to recast the theory in terms antithetical to the intentions of its originators. According to Fernando Henrique Cardoso (1977), "the grandfather of dependency theorists" (Dominguez 1978: 107), most of these attempts have failed. Lamenting the distortions dependency theory had suffered at the hands of both critics and advocates, Cardoso argued that it had been "transformed into an article for consumption" grounded in an understanding of social inquiry representing "a quite distinct intellectual universe from that which gave it birth" (Cardoso 1977: 8).

Explaining the origins of these distortions is at once an exercise in intellectual history, theoretical clarification, and metatheoretical critique. And they can be best approached by starting from what Cardoso calls the "North American consumption" of dependency theory.

In assessing the "scientific" quality of dependency theory, many North American social scientists faulted its founders for failing to formulate rigorous and testable concepts and hypotheses that would provide a means of disconfirming or validating the theses of the theory. "In the 'bad old days' " writes Robert Kaufman, "the idea was to elaborate hypotheses that could be tested across time and space," but the "holistic and historical" research program advocated by dependency theorists (among others) "rejects the very idea of hypothesis testing as a form of 'vulgar positivism' " (Kaufman 1982: 42). Viewing this as a potential weakness in the dependency approach, he goes on to ask that if hypothesis testing is "vulgar positivism" in the eyes of dependency theorists, "what is to take its place?" Similarly, James Caporaso argues that what dependency theory needs is "reproducible (i.e., noncontext-bound) measures describing the internal anatomy of dependency" (Caporaso 1978a: 12). Other, similar claims abound in the literature on dependency theory.[14] But before we can assess the philosophical differences between dependency theory and the approach implicit in the above comments, we need to consider in greater detail what underlies them.

The philosophical presuppositions that inform the criticisms proffered by Kaufman, Caporaso and many other "consumers" of dependency theory partake of the dominant, or "mainstream," Anglo-American understanding of social inquiry (Bernstein 1976: xv). This mainstream position is grounded in what we might broadly call a "naturalist" or "positivist" model of inquiry.[15] Certainly there are many social scientists, including most "consumers" of dependency theory, who would object to this characterization of their methodological orientation, especially given the fact that positivism has for many become a term of disapprobation. But these denials seem more symbolic than substantive; they speak to a desire to distance oneself from positivism in name while still adhering to positivism's metatheoretical strictures and methodological injunctions. But my aim here is not to append this label so that their claims can be dismissed out of hand as much as it is to suggest that the demands they place upon dependency theory *presuppose* a positivist metatheory, with all its attendant features.

[14] Other works on dependency theory committed to some version of methodological naturalism include Sloan (1977), Jackson et al. (1979), Bath and James (1976), Kaufman et al. (1975), though this by no means exhausts the list.

Conspicuous by their absence are a number of Marxists whose metatheoretical orientation is clearly a naturalistic one. For a representative list of this latter group, see Cardoso (1977), especially pages 22–23, notes 7–12. I shall turn to the issue of Marxist misappropriations of dependency theory shortly.

[15] Cardoso (1977: 23) also characterizes these approaches as "positivist" in orientation.

According to this mainstream model of social inquiry, a social theory that can claim to be truly scientific must be able to generate hypotheses testable "across time and space" (Kaufman 1982: 42) through the use of "reproducible (i.e., noncontext-bound) measures" (Caporaso 1978a: 12). This "covering-law" (Dray 1957), "deductive-nomological" (Hempel 1965) or "subsumption-theoretic" (von Wright 1971) model of explanation lies at the heart of positivist metatheory. While it may be true that many of the doctrines associated with this model, such as the strict separation of analytic and synthetic statements, ethical emotivism, and others, have been abandoned by many methodological naturalists (von Wright, 1971: 10–16), the covering-law model nonetheless remains the thread that runs through the mainstream view.

On the covering-law model, an adequate scientific explanation involves the construction of a causal account in which a statement describing an event or action is deduced from premises containing one or more general laws, along with statements stipulating that the boundary conditions specified by these laws have in fact been met (Hempel 1965: part iv). The laws upon which explanation depends must be, first and foremost, grounded in concepts having empirical reference; "statements of fact" that provide the basis of constructing measurements which can be used to "test" generalizations against the world-as-it-is (Brodbeck 1968: 6). Moreover, such concepts cannot be time or context bound, since the generalizations themselves must be unlimited in scope, or transhistorically applicable.

These methodological strictures also imply an attendant ontology, or theory of the nature of objects. The demand for ahistorical concepts and generalizations presupposes that the object which one is studying can in fact be described in terms of elements that are themselves ahistorical (MacIntyre 1981: 79).[16] In other words, to seek to explain human institutions and action "scientifically" assumes, as George Catlin recognized some years ago, "two constants: the recurrence of like situations and the persistence of like human impulses—in brief, a human nature" (Catlin 1930: 39).

The upshot is that the social scientist who ignores these methodological strictures has not provided a *theory* at all. And for many of its positivist "consumers," dependency theory did not qualify as a "sci-

[16] This requires, *pro tanto*, that the descriptive and explanatory concepts available to the social scientist—"party," "class," "revolution," etc.—either be transhistorical or (since this is clearly not the case) that conceptual change itself be predictable. For arguments that the latter is likewise logically impossible, see Popper (1960: xii) and MacIntyre (1973: 331). Farr (1982) illustrates the argument by taking the concept of "revolution" as a case in point.

entific theory" precisely because it did not adhere to the methodological requirements of scientific inquiry. In dependency theory, many argued, there seems to be "a pervasive ambiguity in the verbal claims that constitute the theory, and because dependency theory is not a clearly distinguishable theory per se . . . it is probably inappropriate to refer to the body of literature and its knowledge claims as a theory at all (Duvall 1978: 68).[17]

Seen in these terms, dependency theory seems afflicted by methodological deficiencies for which the correctives sought by its consumers appear to be legitimate attempts to give the theory a truly scientific grounding. Yet as we have seen, some of the dependency theorists themselves see the matter in a completely different light. In their view, the problem with a positivist reading of dependency is that "the specific contribution that . . . dependency analyses might make from a methodological point of view . . . is withdrawn" (Cardoso 1977: 15). And their failure to note these methodological distinctions led many social scientists to misread dependency theory in scientistic terms.

This is not to deny that some of the formulations by self-described dependency theorists readily lent themselves to the consumers' intentions. Indeed, as Cardoso (1977: 15) notes, both Latin Americans and North Americans were given over to the temptation to establish " 'laws of movement' of 'dependent capitalism' " and thus develop a "theory" constructed along methodological naturalist lines.[18] Thus, the differentiation between a critical dependency theory and those versions that are not extends beyond just its North American "consumption." In drawing out these distinctions, moreover, methodological differences spill over into theoretical and political concerns, a fact that further illustrates the mutually informing relationship between metatheory, theory, and politics.

One example of this is found in Cardoso's criticisms of the ways in which many scholars have conflated important philosophical and practical distinctions between various types of dependency theory. In this respect, Cardoso (1977: 8) says, "two principle currents are gen-

[17] The extent to which these sorts of criticisms of dependency theory were expected is reflected in Cardoso's reluctance "to use the expression 'theory of dependency' because I was afraid of formalizing the approach" (Cardoso 1977: 15). I think it a mistake for Cardoso to abandon calling dependency a "theory" simply because many social scientists adhere to a particularly narrow conception of the term—a conception which Cardoso himself seems to think is wrong-headed in the social sciences. Dependency theory is a theory, but of a radically different sort than the naturalist type.

[18] Cardoso (1977: 23) identifies the work of Dos Santos (1970) and Bambirra (1974) as Latin American examples of this tendency.

erally cited: ECLA [the United Nations Economic Commission on Latin America], and the Marxian and neo-Marxian North American current ([Paul] Baran, [Paul] Sweezy, and [Andre] Gunder Frank)." [19]

The influence of these other traditions or schools often led interpreters to suggest that dependency theory has a variety of "distinct intellectual hues"; for example, that there are those closer to the " 'petty bourgeois nationalism' " of ECLA, and those that "adopt a position of more authentic opposition to capitalism" like the Marxists and neo-Marxists (Cardoso 1977: 9). Such characterizations may well be "plausible" or "typologically correct," but they neither "correspond to the intellectual history of these ideas" as they were worked out by Latin American scholars, nor did they account for the fact that a critical dependency theory differs from these others on crucial methodological grounds (Cardoso 1977: 9).

The extent to which this conflation has been widely disseminated may be seen in much of the Western, particularly U.S., literature in comparative politics and international relations since the early 1970s. But the most interesting indications of the distortions involved here are best illustrated in some of the recent literature on dependency theory. Since the late 1970s, many scholars have announced that dependency theory appears to be faced with an "impasse" or "crisis," that it had been "transcended" or "surpassed," or that it has been "challenged" by the recent "democratization" of many Latin American countries.[20] In a comment that seems to capture the general tenor of 1980s assessments of the state of development study, John Browett claimed that "the dependency paradigm approaches, although not yet dead, appear to be under a mounting threat of being transcended" (1982: 145). Some of these recent assessments of dependency theory are upbeat in their conclusions about the contributions dependency theory has made to the study of development, others are not. But one of the most striking features of many of these arguments is that they tend to recapitulate some of the same misappropriations and distortions of the "consumption" period.[21]

One illuminating example is the charge that dependency theory

[19] See Baran (1957), Sweezy (1942), and Frank (1967, 1969).

[20] See for example, Booth (1985: 761), Browett (1980: 145), Browett (1985: 789), Hettne (1983: 256), Levine (1988: 387), Leys (1977: 92), Smith (1982: 334), Werker (1985: 79).

[21] Works that offer positive assessments of dependency theory are Werker (1985), Leys (1977), Jaksic (1985), Street and James (1982), Hettne (1983), Reitsma (1982). Negative assessments may be found in Smith (1981). Whether positive or negative, however, all of these works fail to adequately distinguish between a critical and other forms of dependency theory.

suffers from a theoretically suspect emphasis on exogenous (or international) constraints on development, while paying insufficient attention to endogenous (or domestic) factors. But in almost every case, the target in this attack tends to be either Marxist and/or neo-Marxist versions of dependency theory. When the charge of "wholism" or "structuralism" is tendered, or when dependency theory is, by virtue of its structuralist assumptions, said to have produced a practically impoverished analysis, these characterizations are usually directed at André Gunder Frank's work, or those inspired by it.[22] The charges here may be on the mark, and ironically enough many of them are recapitulated in the arguments against what Cardoso had earlier called "mechanistic" or "vulgar Marxist" conceptions of dependency theory. And so it may be said that much of the recent literature citing the "impasse" of dependency theory merely reiterates the difficulties with such approaches that were anticipated by a critical dependency theory perspective.

Nowhere, however, have the theoretical, methodological, and philosophical foundations of a critical dependency theory been put to the test as they have in light of "the noteworthy upsurge of democratic politics in Southern Europe and Latin America over the last dozen years" (Levine 1988: 377). The reason the democratization movement challenges dependency theory is because the specific character of democratization has often taken shape in ways that appear to be at odds with some of the central theses posited by various dependency theorists. For example, as David Becker (1983) has shown in his study of "the new bourgeoisie" in Peru, "political dependency" is not "the automatic, inevitable outcome of economic exploitation" (1983: 341). Political elites in many "dependent" nations, even if they are those "whose class situation, interests, and action place them in the corporate national bourgeoisie or affiliated middle strata," have been willing to open the political process to more democratic forms of participation (Becker 1983: 335–38). Moreover, in many of these "democratizing" societies, there has been widespread popular support for liberal democratic reforms (Levine 1988: 379, 390).

Such considerations are crucial for judging the viability of dependency theory at every level of discourse, including the level of politics itself. As Daniel Levine argues, "A purportedly critical theory is self-defeating if it cannot address the operative principles of a system" (1988: 393). If dependency theory does not "articulate concepts that

[22] The notable exception in this regard is Smith (1981), who takes Cardoso and Faletto to task for their commitment to wholism. However, such a reading distorts the conceptualization of "structural analysis" found in a critical dependency theory.

make effective action within political structures possible, even if only to change them" (Levine 1988: 393–94), including the structures of liberal democratic politics that have recently taken shape in many Latin American countries, then there may be a sense in which it is indeed at an "impasse" given its own political intentions.

In my concluding section I shall argue that in fact dependency theory can develop, and has to some extent already developed, the conceptual tools that would enable it to address the changed context of "postdependency" or "postimperialist" (Becker 1983: 13) politics of the democratization movement in Latin America. As we shall see, this may indeed entail, as Becker suggests, that we lay dependency theory to rest (Becker 1983: 342). But if my arguments here are correct, a critical dependency theory itself articulates the reasons why we should do so, and it also articulates the ways in which those committed to the emancipation of the oppressed might reorient their self-understandings in light of the changed circumstances in Latin America. As a form of critical theory, dependency theory cannot do otherwise. And so drawing the distinctions between a critical dependency theory, those "vulgar" versions advanced by some self-proclaimed dependency theorists, the versions advocated by many of its "consumers," and those types that would in fact be rendered anachronistic by recent changes in Latin America, turns on understanding the basic philosophical presuppositions of a critical dependency theory. These are considered in the following section.

THE FOUNDATIONS OF A CRITICAL DEPENDENCY THEORY

Cardoso's (1977) attack on the "consumption" of dependency theory might be characterized as an intellectual history having metatheoretical intent. Apparently, he felt that the intentions of those who were central figures in the development of what he calls "a radically critical" (1977: 16) dependency theory[23] had been misunderstood. By un-

---

[23] Cardoso (1977: 8–9) identifies the intellectual antecedents of his understanding of dependency theory this way:

Historians Sergio Bagu and Caio Prado, Jr.; sociologists Florestan Fernandes, Pablo Gonzaez Casanova, and Jorge Graciarena; and economists Armando Cordoba, Antonio Garcia, and Alonso Aguilar are examples of efforts to present alternatives both to orthodox analyses and what we might call the ECLA-Keynesian analyses. A rereading of the *Revista Brasiliense* in the 1950's—and there were journals of the same sort published in almost all of the cultural centers of the area—shows that criticism of structural-functionalism and Keynesianism occurred in Latin America at the same time as the criticism of "orthodoxy" was being elaborated. In an effort to develop a double-edged critique, a few groups of intellectuals in Santiago in the mid-1960's took

packing the metatheoretical strictures he establishes, we can begin to see how this "radically critical" perspective warrants the title of a critical theory. My project is more than a simple recapitulation of Cardoso's argument, however. For despite the fact that Cardoso has specifically addressed the problem of dependency theory's misappropriation, the metatheoretical implications of these criticisms have seldom been clearly appreciated. In the absence of a sustained methodological treatise, the metatheoretical features of dependency theory must be reconstructed in order to bring to light a more complete account of its otherwise elliptically stated philosophical foundations.[24]

Perhaps the best way of getting at these issues is by first attending one of the most important features of dependency theory: its "structural" dimension of analysis. This is a particularly crucial point of contention, for there is a sense in which every social theory situates, even if only implicitly, the relationship between agents and the social structures in which they are embedded. How social structures are conceptualized thus presupposes a particular understanding of the nature of the social scientific project, and this in turn has far-reaching implications for understanding the theory/practice relationship.

In modernization theory, social structures are for the most part conceptualized in terms of " 'dimensions,' analytically independent of one another, and together independent of the economy" (Cardoso and Faletto 1979: ix). This sort of conceptualization was, of course, a holdover from the intellectual traditions from which modernization theory appropriated its philosophical presuppositions. With its characteristic stress on the "cultural" foundations of modernization, its monological "evolutionary" theory of social change, and its call for a "diffusionist" or "order" led politics, modernization theory tended to treat development as a primarily endogenous problem. By focusing its attention at the level of individual attitudes and behavior, rather than exogenous constraints on development, modernization theory reflected a suspect metatheoretical orientation. Valenzuela and Valenzuela characterized the deficiencies of modernization theory this way:

> The problem with the [modernization] model and its behavioral level of analysis is that the explanation for underdevelopment is part of the preestablished conceptual framework. It is already "known" that in backward areas the modernity inhibiting characteristics play the dominant role, oth-

---

up the ECLA problematic and tried to redefine it radically, while seeking to avoid "vulgar Marxism."

[24] The sort of reconstruction I have in mind involves taking a theory apart and recasting it in a form that provides an adequate philosophical foundation for the goals that a theory sets for itself. On this notion of theoretical reconstruction see Habermas 1976.

erwise the areas would not be backward. As such, the test of the hypothesis involves a priori acceptance of the very hypothesis up for verification, with empirical evidence gathered solely in an illustrative manner. The focus on individuals simply does not permit consideration of a broader range of contextual variables which might lead to invalidating the assumptions. . . . Discrepancies are accounted for not by a reformulation, but by adding a new definition or a new corollary to the preexisting conceptual framework. (Valenzuela and Valenzuela 1978: 552)

By contrast, dependency theory claims that theoretically relevant "structures" are not exhausted by internal conditions of a particular national situation. For the conditions that shape individuals are also shaped by the global political economy.

But while this proved to be an important theoretical insight, it has also turned out to be the source of methodological dispute. For example, much of the recent "impasse" literature citing the crisis of dependency theory has focused on its turn toward a more "global" form of structural analysis. If modernization theory misdescribed the structural constraints under which agents in the Third World acted, dependency theory seemed to make these constraints even more distant from those agents. And the practical consequence of this line of argument seemed to be one that rendered the possibility of change by the oppressed in the Third World all but impossible, a conclusion, perhaps, no critical theory worthy of the title should draw.

It should come as no surprise, then, that the methodological reflections Cardoso offered to his North American and European readers spoke directly to these matters. Upon reviewing the literature on dependency theory ten years after the draft version of their *Dependency and Development in Latin America*, Cardoso and Faletto added a preface to the book, its stated aim being "to clarify how we perceive dependency as a practical and theoretical problem" (Cardoso and Faletto 1979: vii–viii). And the core of this discussion consisted of an attempt to elaborate upon their "historical-structural" methodology.

While averring that theirs is a kind of structural analysis, Cardoso and Faletto insist that this not be narrowly construed, and that "structures can be conceived and analysed in different ways" (1979: x). For the most part, those who have deployed "structural" analyses, like many Marxists and neo-Marxists, often give this structural emphasis "a deterministic weight" through their use of a Marxist "economic determinism" or " 'mechanistic' analysis." In this, they also have reduced dependency theory to a caricature where the priority of international structures was "determining" for internal/domestic social relations. In time, the structural component of dependency theory was redefined in such a way that the "dialectical analysis" of its founders, which reflected their conception of history "as an open-ended process," became "structural-mechanical when it was not conceived in terms of antecedent causes and inert consequences" (Cardoso 1977: 10–14).

Thus, while a critical dependency theory takes as a basic presupposition that there are more or less stable structures in social life, it nonetheless refuses to tender the kind of "faulty analyses" that "convey the impression that situations of dependency are stable and permanent" (Cardoso and Faletto 1979: ix–x). What deterministic approaches failed to grasp is that the inequalities of development are maintained by operating, in Marx's apt phrase, "behind men's backs." What we need to do, as Cardoso and Faletto suggest, is consider "the mechanisms and processes of domination through which these existing structures are maintained" (1979: x).

When cast in terms of this practical issue, structural-mechanical analyses, even when they are correct, do not necessarily reveal "the 'abstract' unreeling of forms of accumulation" or "the 'logic of capitalism' " (Cardoso 1977: 14). Instead, they may suggest that something rather different is occurring. Here is how Richard Bernstein characterized the point:

> The discovery of regularities in social and political life may *not* be an indication of even a starting point for the discovery of invariant features of human life; these regularities may only reflect the entrenchment and uncritical acceptance of dominant modes of political reality. . . . [I]t is in a society that is unanimously agreed upon its goals that a social science would work best that aims at prediction and the reduction of all questions to empirical ones. (Bernstein 1976: 62)

In other words, if there are observable regularities in social life, they do not themselves provide the basis for explanations of the way the world works, for such regularities themselve require explanation. How are they to be explained? In answering this question the differences between a critical dependency theory and other forms of dependency theory become even more obvious. For what a critical dependency theory does is identify both "the mechanisms of self-perpetuation" of social structures as well as "the possibilities for change" in those structures. Because situations of dependency are "founded on social assymetries and on exploitative types of social organization," the task of a critical dependency theory is to identify the possibilities of change embodied in the struggles of "subordinated social groups and classes, as well as dominated countries" against the "dominant interests that sustain structures of domination" (Cardoso and Faletto 1979: x, xi).

These reflections point to a metatheoretical stance that is not only antithetical to that found in those forms of dependency theory that give a preponderance to structural analysis, but antithetical to the methodological naturalism of so many other "consumers" of dependency theory. Simply stated, a critical dependency theory subscribes to a position that conceptualizes the structural characteristics of any society as what one political theorist calls "artifacts of a mutable social order" (Ball 1983a: 7). Or as Cardoso and Faletto put it, social structures are "the product of man's collective behavior . . . that can be, and in fact are, continuously transformed by social movements" (1979: x).

Now from the point of view of either methodological naturalism or a mechanistic Marxism, this may appear to be an uncontroversial claim. For surely social structures are not *self*-constituting; they result from the collective activities of human agents. But how one conceptualizes these activities is crucial. And the problem is that the basic presuppositions of a naturalist or mechanistic Marxist approach appear to close off the idea that history is "an open ended process." The mutability of social "facts" implies that dependent development is not the result of (nor can it be explained by reference to) a causally efficient "human nature," or determinative social structures. Instead, it implies that this "nature" and these structures are human artifacts—the result (not necessarily intended) of the intentional actions of reflective social agents.[25] Understood this way, the important question for dependency theory is not just the the theoretical explanation of the causes of a dependent situation, but the identification of "the classes and groups which, in the struggle for control or for the reformulation of the existing order (through parties, movements, ideologies, the state, etc.) are making a given structure of domination historically viable or are transforming it" (Cardoso 1977: 16).

Methodologically, the mutability of social "facts" also means that an adequate explanation of a situation of dependency presupposes an understanding of the intentions of the persons who make up the relevant groups and classes. And this, of course, is to some degree a matter of interpretation, not the simple description of social institutions as if they existed independently of those agents' beliefs, self-understand-

---

[25] This is not to say that intentions and beliefs cannot be causes of action. However, this understanding of causation differs from that required by the deductive-nomological model of explanation. On the topic of reasons as causes, and the differences between the kind of cause a reason can be and the (Humean) conception of causality in the account of methodological naturalism, see MacIntyre (1978), "The Antecedents of Action," pp. 191–210.

ings, interests, and goals. Structural description consequently takes a back seat to *Verstehen*, or interpretation,[26] and thus our ability even to adequately describe (much less explain) the actions of social agents presupposes our being able to understand their beliefs, aims and intentions. The same may be said for social structures themselves: our ability to describe them presupposes our prior understanding of the set of background beliefs that inform the actions of individuals who engage in particular practices within institutional settings and contexts. We cannot therefore describe the workings of "capitalism" or "dependent development" without having, at least in the background, some understanding of what those institutions mean to the agents involved in them.

The intentional, belief-constituted character of human action and social institutions makes any attempt to dispense with consideration of the motivations and beliefs of human beings inadequate as a program for social-scientific explanation (Fay and Moon 1977: 222). Thus, the desire to formulate a "behavioral and structural analysis" of dependency[27] must be viewed with some skepticism. As Cardoso and Faletto note, dependency analyses, and, indeed, social scientific theories generally, ignore the reflective capacities of social agents at the very real risk of their own theoretical and practical impoverishment (1979: xi).[28] If the social scientist chooses to ignore these features of

[26] It is interesting, and I think significant, to note that Cardoso refers to Dilthey and Weber as intellectual influences. Both were important figures in the debate over social scientific methodology in their defense of the central place of *Verstehen* in social inquiry. This may go some distance toward explaining Cardoso's antipositivist leanings.

[27] James Caporaso (1978b) advocates just such an analysis. What, exactly, he means by a "structural and behavioral analysis" is not really clear in this wide ranging discussion, but numerous passages indicate that the methodological foundations of this analysis would be grounded in a form of methodological naturalism. As Brian Fay and J. Donald Moon note, "research programs, such as certain versions of systems theory, which dispense entirely with the motivations and orientations of social actors, could be dismissed as inadequate to explain intentional phenomena"(1977: 222). I take Caporaso's intentions to be the advocacy of precisely such an approach.

[28] Two prominent figures in the movement to restructure the social sciences along methodological naturalist lines, political scientist David Easton and philosopher of science Ernest Nagel, have argued that the reflective capacities of social agents *can* be accomodated in a naturalistically conceived social science. But their arguments—and they are typical for naturalists—are problematic.

Both agree that it is important to recognize the potential threat of human reflection for social scientific predictions (Easton 1953: 25; Nagel 1961: 446). Yet both insist that such difficulties can, in principle, be overcome. In both cases, however, what we find is not a defense of how human reflection—including reflection on the theoretical choices that scientists themselves make—is to be included in social scientific theory. Rather, what we find is a defense of the logical or conceptual possiblity of law-like generalizations about social life that are not subject to reflective considerations (see Easton

social life, he or she may misdescribe or reify relations of dependence: it would be to describe as natural, inevitable or "causally determined" what are in fact historically contingent and transformable conditions brought about by intentional human actions.[29] The reality of a social existence constituted by the struggles between different groups of people trying to pursue their own interests consequently becomes a "formalized history":

> The ambiguity, the contradictions, and the more or less abrupt "breaks" in reality are reduced to "operational dimensions" which, by definition, are univocal but static. (Cardoso 1977: 15)

> [And] by excluding from the explanatory model social struggles and the particular relations (economic, social and political) that give momentum to specific dominated societies, these kinds of interpretation oversimplify history and lead to error: they do not offer accurate characterizations of social structures, nor do they grasp the dynamic aspect of history actualized by social struggles in dependent societies. (Cardoso and Faletto 1979: xv)

Thus, given the intentional character of human action and the belief-constituted character of social practices and institutions, a social scientific explanation must be, in the final analysis, interpretive and historical: interpretive because of the role that prior understandings have in the identification and description of human action and insti-

---

1953: esp. 24–31, 52–63, 225–26; Nagel 1961: esp. chapter 13). No social scientist—including a critical theorist—would deny that such a possibility exists. But that is not the point.

When I say that social science risks theoretical and practical impoverishment when it ignores the reflective capacities of social agents, I mean that naturalism elides a whole range of normative questions, not least of which is how it can account for the "rationality" of problem and theory choice. The standard naturalist move of reducing these issues to "the context of discovery" as opposed to "the context of explanation" does little to help in this regard. For it fails to address the fact that the kind of *practical* reasoning involved in problem and theory choice cannot be explained by naturalist conceptions of defensible knowledge. Here the critiques of scientism found in modernist critical theory are particularly helpful in seeing through the problems involved. For if the "context of discovery" involves the use of practical reasoning (and not "theoretical" reasoning), if scientists are social agents as much as anyone else, and if the critical theorists are right about the intersubjective constitution of social reality, then the reflective capacities of social agents is not a problem that is contingently related to social scientific explanation; it is a "problem" that is *conceptually* inseparable from social science.

[29] It is important to stress that such conditions, though brought about and maintained by intentional human action, need not be conditions intended, foreseen (or even foreseeable) by the agents themselves. See Popper (1969, vol. 2, chapter 14). Even so, in order to know that some condition or outcome is *un*intended, we must first know (a) what the agents' original intentions were and (b) that it differs from the outcome originally intended. See Ball (1981) and the reply by Popper (1982).

tutions; and historical because of the ever-changing nature of the concepts and categories expressed in the behavior of social agents.

The description of a situation of dependency is thus a complex and historically changing task. What must replace attempts "to adjust realities to methodological requirements of the 'logic of scientific investigation' " is "an effort to specify each new situation in the search for differences and diversity, and to relate them to old forms of dependency" (Cardoso and Faletto 1979: xii, xiii). This is rather reminiscent of Marx's objecting to those who "insist on transforming my historical sketch of the genesis of capitalism in Western Europe into an historico-philosophical theory of the general path of development prescribed by fate to all nations whatever the historical circumstances in which they find themselves" (Marx 1975: 293). For all of these reasons—the intentional character of action, the belief-constituted character of social practices and institutions, and the historicity of social reality—the dependency theorists insist that careful attention be paid to the specific features of each situation of dependency as a precondition to any "testing" of hypotheses about these conditions.

Even when hypotheses are put to empirical test, however, this does not entail the kinds of knowledge claims that a positivist metatheory supposes it does. "The question," Cardoso and Faletto note (1979: xii), "is not whether to measure. The question is rather what and how to measure, and also concerns the methodological status of measuring." Far from being a neutral "description" of the phenomenon in question, empirical inquiry is guided by theoretical constructs that are in turn derived from the vantage point of certain interests, purposes, or standards (Connolly 1974: 23). And one clear instance of the problematic nature of this approach may be found in so much modernization theory, where "efforts in that [methodological] direction have resulted in the isolation of 'power dimensions' involved in dependency situations from its 'economic aspects' " (Cardoso and Faletto 1979: xii).

In the social sciences the conceptual disputes arising out of the quest for operational definitions are endemic. This is so not because we are not "rigorous" enough in our conceptualizations, but because of the "essentially contested" character of many social concepts.[30] At the core of these disputes are rival beliefs about what constitutes an adequate definition and/or description of a given phenomenon. Yet to operationalize via stipulative definition is not to escape from conceptual controversy, but to participate in it. Nor can one be "objective"

[30] On the idea of essential contestability, see MacIntyre (1973) and (1966), especially chapter 1; Gray (1977); and Connolly (1974), especially chapter 1.

when proposing definitions or offering testable hypotheses since any given theory will have, as it were, "its own built-in value slope" (Taylor 1974: 29). And in a critical dependency theory, "there is no presumption of scientific "neutrality" (Cardoso 1977:16).

Here the theory/practice relationship takes on a central importance for understanding what a critical dependency theory aims to accomplish, and how it defines the achievement of these aims. Insofar as they are reflective agents, human beings can scarcely avoid taking into some account rival characterizations and explanations of their situations. Social science, conceived as a project that seeks to provide human beings with a rationally grounded account of social action, institutions and practices, presupposes the possibility that its claims may also come to be used as material for reflection. Taken together, these two claims—that social science seeks rationally defensible knowledge, and that human beings are reflective agents—offers a challenge to the mainstream understanding of the relationship between social theory and political practice. For if it is the case that social theory can help shape the beliefs and language that are themselves partially constitutive of social reality, then social theory has a doubly reflexive character. On the one hand social theory reflects upon the nature of social reality, which is in turn reflected upon by social agents, reshaping their beliefs about themselves and society and therefore reshaping society itself. "If there is to be a social science," said Durkheim, "we shall expect it not merely to paraphrase the traditional prejudices of the common man but to give us a new and different view of them; for the aim of all science is to make discoveries, and every discovery more or less disturbs accepted ideas" (Durkheim 1964: xxxvii).[31]

Social science is not, and by its very nature cannot be, objective, neutral, nonpartisan or value free. After all, social theorists are social agents as much as those whose behavior they study, and their theories help to articulate, shape and justify the beliefs, goals and language of particular practices and institutions. Social theory and political practice are related if only because "Intellectual evaluation of a given situation and ideas about what is to be done are crucial in politics" (Cardoso and Faletto 1979: xi). Thus, the reflexive character of social inquiry means that rival theoretical positions often become expressed in behavior as much as in utterance, even when this utterance occurs only at the level of theory (MacIntyre 1973: 4).

[31] This is all the more surprising given Durkheim's commitment to methodological naturalism. This combination of a commitment to "value neutrality" and the kind of reflective knowledge social science makes possible leads to what Terence Ball has called "the paradox of dangerous knowledge." For an elaboration, see Ball (1980).

On a methodological naturalist or mechanistic Marxist account, however, the reflexive character of social inquiry cannot be incorporated into the "scientific" framework, for to offer a causal explanation is to show that there are specific antecedent factors efficient in bringing about the phenomenon in question; in turn it should be possible to predict—and control—these events if we can identify those causally efficacious variables. A true science of man, as Comte recognized, would enable us to control the social world, since "From science comes prevision; from prevision comes control." In a social world in which this scientific model could apply, the reflective capacities of social agents would play no part—this, perhaps, is the insight to be gleaned from the comments of Richard Bernstein I quoted earlier. Their behavior having been "causally" determined, it would be meaningless to attribute reflective capacities to agents.[32] This is why the naturalistically inclined "consumers" and the mechanistically inclined popularizers of dependency theory presuppose, by virtue of their metatheoretical commitments, a conception of man-as-object who is subject to various instrumentalities of control.

This is not to suggest that those who do not subscribe to a critical-theoretic understanding of dependency theory seek to provide knowledge of causal generalizations that can be used to manipulate people for insidious ends. In fact, many have even praised dependency theory for making analysts aware of important ethical issues involved in the study of dependent development. Nonetheless, their methodological strictures rule out the possibility that social *science* can meaningfully consider these ethical questions since they are simply beyond the pale of 'science' proper. Against this view, a critical dependency theory is understood by its proponents to embody a

> divergence [that] is not merely methodological-formal. It is, rather, at the very heart of studies of dependency. If these studies do in fact have any power of attraction at all, it is not merely because they propose a methodology to substitute for a previously existing paradigm or because they open a new set of themes. It is principally because they do so from a *radically critical* viewpoint. (Cardoso 1977: 16)

We see, then, that the differences between the founders of dependency theory, its North American "consumers," and its various Marxist and neo-Marxist popularizers, cut to the root of conceptions of social inquiry. It is the "critical" role of social theory that the founders

---

[32] See Connolly (1981), especially chapter 2, for an elaboration of the ways in which a social theory that is "deterministic" disposes of the reflective capacities of social agents by virtue of its logical structure.

of dependency theory invoke when they argue that in the societies for which dependency theory was formulated, "structures are based neither on egalitarian relationships nor on collaborative patterns of social organization" (Cardoso and Faletto 1979: x), but are instead the result of impositions that become reified, creating a social order fraught with contradictions created by the discrepancies between the promise of development and the inegalitarian policies entailed in dependent development (Cardoso 1977: 16).

For a critical theory of dependency, development in the peripheral nations of the global capitalist system must be "revealed without disguise: one side wins or loses, one form or another of domination makes way for another, the general conditions of capitalist development are sustained or reach their limits, and other forms of social organization are foreseen as a historical possibility" (Cardoso 1977: 14). The result neither of "laws" of human behavior, nor of the immutable "laws" of development, dependent development is no more than the consequence of impositions sustained by obfuscating ideologies.

In these terms, it should be obvious that dependency theory considered as *critical* theory does not appeal to an empiricist account of knowledge as a basis for its claims to be theoretical and explanatory; it does not assume that "measurement" and "statistical information and demonstrations are the only modes of explanation, as if we were dealing with hypotheses to be accepted or rejected only after statistical tests" (Cardoso and Faletto 1979: xiii). This should not be taken to mean that dependency theory is opposed to empirical research and quantitative methods (*contra* Duvall 1978: 68). As Cardoso and Faletto note, "Certainly, evidence confirming or rejecting particular analysis oriented by a dependency approach has to be taken into account if it has been established on adequate theoretical grounds . . . [S]tatistical information and demonstrations are useful and necessary" (1979: xiii). Rather, the methodological claims of the dependency theorists should be understood as a critique of the knowledge claims that are advanced after having run "tests" of the theory; it is a criticism of an epistemology and methodology appropriate only to the positivistically oriented social sciences (Cardoso 1977: 23). A critical theory by no means denies the place of nomological knowledge; it simply does not "remain satisfied with this. It is concerned with going beyond this goal to determine when theoretical statements grasp invariant regularities of social action as such and when they express ideologically frozen relations of dependence that can in principle be transformed" (Habermas 1971: 310).

Moreover, a critical theory recognizes the intimate relationship between social theory and political practice. It is, therefore, directed toward a particular end: the emancipation and enlightenment of those enmeshed in oppressive social relations. "There are," Cardoso says, "no 'dimensions' of 'variables' at stake, but tensions between interests, values, appropriations of nature and society, all of which are unequal and in opposition" (Cardoso 1977: 16). A critical theory

> does not consist solely of hypotheses and descriptions of existing social re-
> lations which are to be verified or falsified by existing facts. It is not a theory
> which pretends to be disinterested and thereby disguises or supresses the
> interests that guide it. It is not a theory that pretends to be neutral and
> divorced from action—a theory which the social engineer or the private citi-
> zen may or may not seek to implement. Critical theory aspires to bring the
> subjects themselves to full self consciousness of the contradictions implicit
> in their material existence, to penetrate the ideological mystifications and
> forms of false consciousness that distort the meaning of existing social con-
> ditions. (Bernstein 1976: 182)

On this understanding, the critical-theoretic foundations of dependency theory should be clear. "Both in the construction of interpretation and in its practical validation, realities are at stake" (Cardoso and Faletto 1979: xiv), and "if structures delimit the range of oscillation, the actions of humans, as well as their imagination, revive and transfigure these structures and may even replace them with others that are not predetermined" (Cardoso 1977: 11).

I believe that when we understand what kind of theory dependency theory purports to be—a kind of critical theory—then we are in a better position to understand that the kinds of knowledge claims it makes are incompatible with those recognized by its various consumers, popularizers and critics. When Cardoso argues that dependency studies seek to provide social agents with theoretical and methodological tools so they may overcome a given order of domination (Cardoso 1977: 16), we should recognize the radically different understanding of social inquiry that provides their underpinning.[33] Rather than relying on an empiricist account of knowledge, a dogmatic Marxism, or any other closed, self-referential, and politically pernicious philosophical self-

[33] Cardoso notes the problems with scientistic-cum-deterministic conceptions of social inquiry: having "generated up to now a relatively impoverished political analysis . . . they emphasize the 'structural possibility' of revolution and go on to discuss the overcoming of dependency in terms of a historical horizon in which socialism appears as the result of growing crises peculiar to a stagnating capitalism, or they foresee a 'new barbarism' and display an inclination for repeating cliches that explain little" (1977: 20). In any case, these scientistic analyses are seldom directed at political practice, but rather enclose the possibility of meaningful change within a set of structural constraints. Thus they deny the "passion for the possible" (Cardoso and Faletto 1979: xi) that dependency (and critical) theory aim to instill in social agents.

understanding, the "verification" of dependency theory "depends upon the capacity of social movements to implement what are perceived as structural possibilities . . . [which depend, in turn] on real social and political struggle. So the 'demonstration' of an interpretation"—and dependency theory is just such an interpretation—"depends to some extent on its own ability to show socio-political actors the possible solutions to contradictory situations" (Cardoso and Faletto 1979: xiv).

The question that remains, of course, is whether dependency theory has been able to accomplish its aims. And it is to this question I finally turn.

DEPENDENCY THEORY, CRITICAL THEORY, AND POLITICAL PRACTICE

The thrust of my reconstruction of dependency theory has been primarily metatheoretical, and I shall maintain this emphasis in my treatment of Freire, liberation theology, and feminist theory. I included dependency theory in this book because I believe it represents a form of critical theory in practice—a claim I shall also maintain with respect to these other theories. However, as I suggested earlier, the relationship between this metatheoretical emphasis and my characterization of these theories as critical theories in practice may not be clear, or it may be misunderstood. But I believe that by attending how theory and practice *have* been related in the case of dependency theory, some further clarification of these matters can be gained.

A critical theory in practice is understood as a theory tied to a particular struggle against domination. This much is clear in the case of dependency theory. Thus does Cardoso insist that dependency theory is concerned with "the real possibilities for change, seen from the point of view of the people without power" (Cardoso, in Kahl 1976: 179). But a critical theory is also "verified" by virtue of its ability to identify the possibilities of change the marginalized might pursue if they are to realize their emancipation. That dependency theory has had practical effect cannot be denied; it has influenced the practical political action of numerous social movements and actors in Latin America and elsewhere.[34] It would be a mistake, however, to assume

[34] As we shall see in my discussion of liberation theology, dependency theory has been widely disseminated and appropriated in Latin America. Establishing the influence of dependency analyses outside of the continent is more difficult. However, I think it can be plausibly argued that many antiimperialist movements in both less-developed and industrialized states are grounded in theoretical self-understandings that reflect those of the dependency theorists. Whether or not the people involved in these movements identify dependency theory as the basis of their analysis is an interesting ques-

that because of this practical influence, the case for dependency theory as a critical theory, let alone a critical theory in practice, is thereby settled. But before my thesis can be settled, there are a few important points to consider.

There is a distinct danger in that a critical theory may become nothing more than the ideology (in the pejorative sense) of a particular political practice, and by this it may lose its critical "edge." Dogmatic forms of Marxist practice are good examples of how a critical theory's self-imposed demand that it "take up the point of view of the people without power" may be turned into a practice that blunts its equally important demand that the discourse of emancipation remain reflexive. These sorts of examples perhaps provide some justification for Habermas's claim that a critical theory must retain some autonomy from practice, if only because "it can by no means legitimize *a fortiori* the risky decisions of strategic action" (Habermas 1973: 33). But this demand that theory retain some autonomy from practice does not necessarily entail severing critical theory from practice (as it seems to have been in both modernist and postmodernist critical theory); whatever "autonomy" critical theory has should be understood as a feature of its engagement with practice, as a kind of symbiotic relationship in which practice shapes, and is shaped by, theoretical reflection.

One, and arguably the most important, way in which a critical theory can preserve this "symbiotic autonomy" is by advancing its philosophical insights as a check on dogmatism. For example, Cardoso seems to do just this when he says:

> Luckily, as much as social scientists strive to enclose the structural possibilities of history in their own constructs, history continually makes us *dupes de nous-memes*, and astonishes us with unexpected revelations. (Cardoso 1977: 21)

In other words, by emphasizing the contingency of all knowledge claims (including its own), a critical theory may be able to undermine the ossification of those claims, in theory and practice. Indeed, given the necessary relationship between theory and practice, not only in the sense that practices are theoretically informed, but that every theory presupposes a particular practical orientation, the "symbiotic autonomy" of a critical theory may be expressed as much in critiques of theories as in critiques of practice itself. But in any case, no critical

---

tion beyond the scope of my inquiry. But it is also perhaps beside the point; all I mean to suggest here is that the themes of dependency theory have become integral to much public discourse about the relations between the Third and First worlds.

theory will be a critical theory *in practice* unless it is able to keep clear its relationship with the practical context from which it arises.

It may, then, be said that the practical credentials of a critical dependency theory are in part established in its critique of developmentalism, and in its critique of the "consumption" of dependency theory itself. They are also in part established by virtue of the fact that dependency theory has been a significant influence in shaping the actions of many of those involved in Latin American politics. But (to return to my earlier point) the case for seeing dependency theory as a critical theory in practice is only in part established by these sorts of considerations. The real test of dependency theory as a critical theory is whether it is able, as Daniel Levine suggests, to "articulate concepts that make effective action within political structures possible, even if only to change them" (1988: 393–94). Yet it should also be clear by now that even this is not sufficient, for a critical theory in practice must also be able to preserve its "symbiotic autonomy" in a way that prevents it from being too readily equated with practices that are perhaps informed by it, but which do not themselves realize the kind of emancipation its philosophical and theoretical inquiries establish.

My thesis may be strengthened, then, by considering the ways in which dependency theory has addressed those practices that have been in part informed by its tenets. I begin by noting a comment by Gary Becker, who says that "Dependencista ideology has been useful to political and economic elites striving to free themselves from subjugation to neocolonialism. That goal has been largely attained" (1983: 342).

That this achievement does not realize the political aims, or for that matter, the theoretical implications, of a critical dependency theory may be seen in some comments written by Cardoso and Faletto in a postscript to their *Dependency and Development in Latin America* (1979). At the time they wrote these reflections, Cardoso and Faletto recognized that the changed conditions required "a redefinition of the 'forms of dependency,'" that some countries enjoyed "less dependency," and that in many cases "the state in these countries may be capable of exercising a greater degree of sovereignty." But the key issue for dependency theory remained—even if dependency itself had changed—the issue of "the nature of class conflicts and alliances which the dependency situation encompasses" (Cardoso and Faletto 1979: 212).

The point here is that it is this question of "class conflicts and alliances" that serves as the political thread running through a critical dependency theory. When this thread is pulled, the defining features of dependency theory may indeed be viewed as if it is nothing more than "an ideology that blames all evil in the Third World on the metropoli," and such an ideology may have in fact been useful for "political and economic elites striving to free themselves and their nations from subjugation from neocolonialism." If this is all there is to dependency theory, then Becker may be right to suggest that we "lay it to rest" (Becker 1983: 342). But it is not all there is. For as Cardoso and Faletto had argued some years earlier, the issues with which a critical dependency is concerned are understanding how "subordinated social groups and classes, *as well as dominated countries*, try to counterattack dominant interests that sustain structures of domination" (1979: xi; emphasis added). So long as the changes involved in elites "freeing themselves and their nations" do not involve a transition to a fully democratic politics, then dependency theory still has a critical role to play.

Becker's recognition that dominant elites in Latin America have been able to free themselves and their nations from neocolonialism does not, then, show that dependency theory is no longer a useful interpretive—or political—framework, however much it may show "vulgar" dependency theory to be mistaken. But if dependency theory is now to be addressed to a context in which the "global" status of the Latin American countries has changed, doesn't this in some sense mean that it is a "Paradigm Lost," as Daniel Levine (1988) suggests?

This question is an important one, particularly in light of the fact that in many of the Latin American countries, "democratization" has gone hand in hand with "less dependence." But there are, I think, good reasons to see that dependency theory remains a viable, even necessary, perspective, even in light of the recent movement toward democracy. And most of these have to do with themes with which the dependency theorists have long been concerned.

First, the fact that the situation of the Latin American democracies may be one of "less dependence" does not mean that they are not still subject to the vicissitudes of the international economy. Of course, there are few countries today that are free of international economic constraints, and there may even be a sense in which any form of national "self-determination" today may have to be articulated within these constraints. But constraints, or freedom from constraints is not really the issue; it is, rather, the relative power various nations and institutions have in shaping these constraints. And in this respect, Latin America is still in an important sense "dependent."

A critical dependency theory would have to address these changes, if only because its philosophical commitments "require an effort to specify each new situation in the search for differences and diversity, and to relate them to old forms of dependency, stressing, when necessary, even its contradictory character" (Cardoso and Faletto 1979: xii–xiii). And while it may be that those inspired by a critical conception of dependency theory have yet to produce analyses that systematically address these changes, it is clearly the case that their methodological commitments both authorize and demand such analyses.

This brings me to another reason dependency theory remains viable, and this reason is more directly political. The simple fact of the matter is that the movement toward democracy in Latin America is by no means irreversible. Just as history surprised those (like many vulgar dependency theorists) who thought that national elites could not be depended upon to lead the Latin American countries into a "less-dependent" situation, and toward democracy, so too it may surprise those who see the recent democratization movement as an inexorable change in the direction of political emancipation. As Becker argues,

> Democracy is a useful tool for peaceably reconciling conflicting interest conflicts among bourgeois functional groups, for taking readings of the level of contentment of the people so that technocratic administrators can monitor their own performance, and for legitimating the corporatist administrative state behind a facade of mass participation. The rub is that the corporate national bourgeoisie's concern with it is purely instrumental and implies no normative commitment to the concept of popular power. (1983: 336)

Not surprisingly, this sort of unstable constellation of "democratic" commitments was also anticipated by a critical dependency theory. As Cardoso and Faletto argued some years ago, the crucial question today "is not between corporativism and the democratic tradition. It is between technocratic elitism and . . . truly popular forces" (1979: 216). Thus, to equate democratization with empowerment and emancipation is to ignore the ways in which democratization may be nothing more than a partial movement in the direction of popular self-determination.

This last point brings us to a third reason a critical dependency theory is viable. For it is precisely a restricted kind of democracy that has been realized in Latin America. While not denying the progressive implications of the sort of liberal democracy that has been pursued in many Latin American nations, a critical dependency theory cannot endorse this as the best of all possible options. As Adam Przeworski (1986: 63) notes, liberal democracy tends to be almost exclusively "political," but "Democracy restricted to the political realm has historically coexisted with exploitation and oppression at the workplace, within the schools, within bureaucracies, and within families." It may in fact be the case, as Daniel Levine argues, that liberal democracy "is bound to look good after lengthy bouts of abuse and arbitrary rule" (1988: 382). For this reason dependency theory may even endorse liberal democracy as a progressive moment in the realization of emancipation from the "dependency" the Latin American countries have long suffered. Indeed, many of those sympathetic to dependency theory, including Cardoso himself, have become active in "party politics." But for all this, so long as conditions that gave rise to dependency theory persist, then it will still have to retain its "symbiotic autonomy" from political practice, even when these practices realize some of the emancipatory intentions it holds.

I have given some specific examples of why a critical dependency theory must retain some autonomy from practice given its particular context. My aim in doing so, however, has been to underscore the more general point that a critical theory in practice runs a high risk of losing its critical edge because of its commitment to its addressees. But the conclusion to be drawn is not that critical theory should be severed from practice—as is apparently the case in both modernist and postmodernist critical theory. Rather, it is that the relationship between theory and practice, and theorist and audience, requires an ongoing process of self-examination on the part of all involved. Clearly the dependency theorists have continued to engage in the critique of those practices even its addressees have embraced, thus inviting those to whom it is directed to reexamine their own interests and aims. Yet it would be a radical misunderstanding of the nature of dependency theory to assume that this critique is directed only at its addressees, and not at the theory itself. As Cardoso (1977: 21) argues, the claims of dependency theory do not

> endorse the ingenuous expectation that theories of dependency explain *everything* or that, if they do not explain everything, it is because the method has been badly applied. It is necessary to have a sense—I will not say of proportion—but of the ridiculous, and to avoid the simplistic reductionism so common among the present-day butterfly collectors who abound in the social sciences and who stroll through history classifying types of dependency, modes of production, and laws of development, with the blissful illusion that their findings can remove from history all its ambiguities, conjectures, and surprises.

Cardoso's comments reveal a sensitivity to the limitations of what Foucault called the "universal intellectual," and in doing so they also once more recapitulate the underlying metatheoretical premises of a critical dependency theory. All social theory is historically and contextually bound; it cannot foreclose the possibility that its analyses may be rendered anachronistic by changed historical circumstances. As an interpretive, historical, and critical exercise, the true "test" of a critical dependency theory rests on its ability to advance a rationally defensible account of the ways that social relations became and remain oppressive and destructive of human potential, and thus spur social agents into action on their own behalf. Being historically and contextually bound, its applicability is confined to particular places, times, and situations of inequality between and within societies. In essence, dependency theory invites its own supersession through the institution of a more egalitarian set of social relations. In this respect, it also requires a constant updating and revision as historical change takes place.

All of this, I hope to have shown, is precisely what dependency theory has been able to do—although by no means should it be assumed that its aims have been completely realized. For what makes dependency theory a critical theory *in practice* is its continued relevance in a context marked by inequalities and oppression, practices undergirded or sustained by theoretical self-understandings that distort the interests and explain away the sufferings of those on the margins of Latin American society.

What I hope to show in subsequent chapters is that this kind of metatheoretical self-understanding is not an isolated one. But this is not merely an interpretation I am imposing on this reconstruction of dependency theory. It is one anticipated by Cardoso himself. Dependency theory is indeed committed to solidarity with its particular addressees, but its "theoretical-methodological field" also unites it with other social movements. In a comment that both reflects and looks beyond the time in which it was written, Cardoso says:

> The protest of American blacks, the war in Vietnam and the movement in opposition to it, the counterculture, the student movement, the feminist movement, etc., all demanded [and some continue to demand—S.L.] paradigms that were more sensitive to the historical process, to social struggles, and to the transformation of systems of domination. In such a perspective, analyses of dependency correspond better to this search for new models of explanation, not only to comprehend what is happening in Latin America, but also what is happening in the U.S. (Cardoso 1977: 17; see also Cardoso and Faletto 1979: 202)

A critical theory worthy of the title is defined by its commitment to emancipation through solidarity, but it is also open to the plurality of struggles that are directed at the transformation of systems of domination. The diversity of oppression requires as much, and dependency theory certainly does not explain *everything*. A critical dependency theory may well share a common philosophical perspective with other critical theories in practice, but there is much to be learned by examining how this is expressed in the specific contexts from which—and for which—they are articulated.

CHAPTER 5

Paulo Freire's Critical Pedagogy

> The enlightenment of political will can become effective only
> within the communication of citizens. For the articulation of
> needs . . . can be ratified exclusively *in the consciousness of
> the political actors themselves*. Experts cannot delegate to
> themselves this act of confirmation from those who have to
> account with their life histories for the new interpretation of
> social needs and for accepted means of mastering problem-
> atic situations.
>
> —Jürgen Habermas

> The starting point for organizing the program content of edu-
> cation or political action must be the present, existential,
> concrete situation, reflecting the aspirations of the peo-
> ple. . . . We must never merely discourse on the present situ-
> ation, must never provide the people with programs which
> have little or nothing to do with their own preoccupations,
> doubts, hopes, and fears. . . . It is not our role to speak to the
> people about our own view of the world, nor attempt to im-
> pose that view on them, but rather to dialogue with the peo-
> ple about their view and ours.
>
> —Paulo Freire

A CENTRAL assumption of many critical theories is that those to whom
they are addressed understand social reality and themselves in theoretically distorted ways, and that the suffering and oppression they
experience is in part due to these distortions. This is the basis of a
critical theory's goal of providing a means of "enlightenment." By engaging these self-understandings through an ideology critique, a critical theory may provide what Habermas calls "authentic insights" and
"true statements" which serve to unmask misdescriptions of social reality. On closer consideration, however, the issues here are by no
means simple ones. For if a critical theory is to become part of the
practical consciousness of the oppressed, critical theorists must be attentive not only to how the relationship between the "knowledge" provided by critical theory and the self-understandings of its addressees

should be understood, but also to how the relationship of the critical theorist and the oppressed as "knowers" should be understood.

The import of these issues is made particularly clear in light of the practical strategies typically pursued by those who seek to bring about an end to unnecessary domination. In most cases, "critical theorists" have chosen forms of practical action that would "emancipate" the oppressed from their unwarranted suffering, rather than following a course in which the oppressed would emancipate themselves. History is of course replete with examples of this sort of choice, and the insidious uses to which Marxism has been put are not the only relevant ones here. It is no exaggeration to say that most revolutionaries, guided by their belief in the "truth" of their theories, have opted for a kind of emancipation from above. But there are dangers in this approach, and they are clearly captured in this passage from Brian Fay:

> Revolutionaries in the grip of a critical theory are convinced that they possess an enlightened attitude toward the arrangements of a social order; they have a theory which presupposes that human beings are active and therefore changeable creatures; and they believe they have discovered the correct theory which indicates the rational way a social order ought to be reorganized. Given these characteristics, it is almost inevitable that proponents of a critical theory will try to force others into a particular way of acting even if they resist. For this resistance can so easily be interpreted as a retrograde allegiance to a dying and evil social system, or as a stupid and irrational refusal to see what is in their best interests. (1987: 163)

What I hope to have suggested in previous chapters is that this kind of "critical theory" does not warrant the title. Here we can perhaps appreciate why Foucault was so critical of the idea of the "universal intellectual." For the theorist to assume that his or her claims are beyond dispute is to fall prey to the fallacy of "speaking in the capacity of the master of truth and justice" (Foucault 1980b: 126). But however accurate and defensible the theorist's knowledge claims may be, the "authentic insights" and "true statements" a critical theory advances cannot simply be secured theoretically. For a truly emancipatory political practice is possible only when these insights are embodied, as Habermas (1970: 75) suggests, *"in the consciousness of the political actors themselves."*

In this chapter I explore the work of Paulo Freire, whose attempt to articulate a "pedagogy of the oppressed" addresses these issues in a particularly rich way. Freire's arguments are perhaps most compelling precisely because they grow out of his work with illiterate peasants and workers in the Third World. This context is surely one of the most demanding environments in which the principles of enlightenment and emancipation may be put to the test. Given the fact that illiterates not only cannot read or write, but often suffer from a lack of even the most rudimentary knowledge of natural and social processes, it may be tempting to seek the quickest and most "efficient" means of relieving their suffering. But as Freire sees it, good intentions are not enough. For a critical theorist to assume that he or she possesses knowledge that can simply be "given" to the oppressed is to assume a hierarchical relationship that is antithetical to the demands of critical discourse and the process and promise of real emancipation, or so Freire argues.

Freire insists that a critical theory cannot be content with simply offering and then acting on empirically defensible knowledge claims. A critical theory must be equally concerned with the method by which any purported truths come to be accepted. To accept only the former is, as Fay (1977: 226) suggests, to accept a particularly pernicious "version of the doctrine that 'the truth shall set you free'; on this view what is ultimately important for freedom is not the reasons why people believe as they do, or how they come to adopt a particular view, but rather that what they believe is correct." It is, in other words, to treat as irrelevant the process by which beliefs come to be held. Freire's work debunks this understanding: the objective of a critical theory—emancipation informed by rational insight—cannot be separated from the process or method of a critical theory—enlightenment through critical discourse and dialogue.

The question of critical theory's process or method thus serves as the theme of this chapter. By examining Freire's "pedagogy of the oppressed," I hope to show that the ability of a critical theory to fulfill its practical intent not only requires grounding critical theory in a particular historical context, but just as importantly, addressing those embedded in that context in a way that makes it possible for them to emancipate themselves. Critical theory, if it is to make good on its practical intentions, must be at heart educative (Fay 1975: 103; 1987: 85; O'Neill 1976: 8; 1985). But as John O'Neill suggests (echoing Frantz Fanon):

> The danger is that people may be herded together in the interests of their political leaders who have community on their lips but not in their hearts. . . . Indeed this is the problematic outcome of the revolution unless, as Marx anticipated in his Third Thesis on Feuerbach, the revolution lays upon itself the task of *educating the educators*. (1976: 8)

And so the possiblity of educating the oppressed so that they may emancipate themselves is as much a matter of making sure that the educators themselves can be educated. As I shall show, Freire offers us a way of avoiding the "circle of certainty" (*PO*: 23)[1] that often plagues those who would see themselves as "educators." He shows, in other words, how a critical theory might remain critical.

THE CONTEXT OF FREIRE'S CRITICAL PEDAGOGY

In my discussion of dependency theory, I noted that one of the most important political developments of the twentieth century has been the emergence of newly sovereign nations in the Third World. It is in this context that Freire first began to develop his critical pedagogy. As with any critical theory, Freire's work is situated by an ideology-critique of belief systems that perpetuate oppression; in his case this means a critical and historical analysis of the contemporary self-understandings of both the oppressed and the oppressors in Latin America, and more specifically Brazil.[2] This ideology-critique takes as its point of departure the struggle for self-determination in Latin America. But as Freire sees it, the possibility of realizing this struggle is

---

[1] All abbreviated references in this chapter are to Freire's work, found in the following texts. Full citations are in the Bibliography.

ALP: *The Adult Literacy Process as Cultural Action for Freedom*
CAC: *Cultural Action and Conscientization*
EA: *Education for Awareness*
ECC: *Education for Critical Consciousness*
LRWW: *Literacy: Reading the Word and the World*
PE: *The Politics of Education*
PL: *A Pedagogy for Liberation*
PO: *Pedagogy of the Oppressed*
PP: *Pedagogy in Process*

[2] Of the two central texts used here, *Education for Critical Consciousness* and *Pedagogy of the Oppressed*, the former provides much of Freire's discussion of the historical context of his work while the latter provides the most systematic account of the actual content of the pedagogy. *Education for Critical Consciousness* contains two essays, the first of which, "Education as the Practice of Freedom," originally appeared in 1967; this essay constitutes Freire's account of his Brazilian experience, although the last two of the four chapters in it contain sketch outlines of the themes that were further developed in *Pedagogy of the Oppressed*, which was written in 1968. The more theoretical tone of *Pedagogy*, as Freire himself says, is the result of reflections on his experiences in Brazil and during his years of exile. The second essay in *Education*, "Extension or Communication," is Freire's examination of the problems with the model of agrarian reform used in Chile prior to the election of Salvador Allende's government in 1970. It was written in 1969.

I mention these facts only to draw out the intimate relationships between all of Freire's work and how they may be seen as constituting a theoretical whole. For an account of Freire's background and the relationship between his practical experiences and theoretical reflections, see Mackie (1981).

threatened by practices and beliefs that have their roots in the colonial period.

Broadly speaking, the contemporary struggles for self-determination had actually begun in the mid-nineteenth century when a series of liberal revolutions swept the Latin American continent. Eager to break the grip of Iberian colonialism on the continent, Latin American revolutionaries actively repudiated their Hispanic heritage. At the same time, they willingly embraced liberal ideals, particularly those coming out of France, Britain, and the United States, a tendency that had the effect of blinding Latin American revolutionaries to the imperialist interests of these liberal states. By opening the continent to liberalism in both theory and practice, Latin Americans merely exchanged one colonialism for another of a different type. The "liberal pause" in the Latin American political tradition, which lasted roughly from the early nineteenth century until the Great Depression of 1929 (Veliz 1980: 163–88) in reality constituted nothing more than a "second colonial pact" characterized by support for the economic imperialism of Britain, France and the United States, defense of the privileges of the urban classes, and support for the expansion of large landholdings through the systematic repression of the peasant classes (Comblin 1979a: 52–56). It was not until the worldwide economic crisis of 1929 that this pact would be broken by the emergence of movements advocating economic, social, cultural and political autonomy from the imperialist powers.

Since this period, a nationalistic "populism" has been a major political force in Latin America. Although enjoying widespread support among all social classes, this populism tended to be moderate and reformist rather than truly revolutionary, advocating a kind of "state capitalism" that would expand state power in order to reform and regulate both internal and external structures for the purpose of economic development (Malloy 1977: 11). But populism never really challenged the structural dominance of international capital nor the elites it established in the Latin American nations. However, because populism depended on this broad social base for its legitimacy, it also opened the door to increasing participation, and by the mid-1950s more radical political movements were beginning to take shape.[3]

Freire's call for a "pedagogy of the oppressed" picks up on these developments, and they are cast specifically in terms of the Brazilian

---

[3] Freire's criticisms of postwar politics are important not only for taking a critical attitude toward the panglossian interpretations of the period found in modernization theory; they are also useful correctives to the kind of naive endorsement of the current "redemocratization" process in Latin America. In this, Freire's analysis complements that found in dependency theory.

experience. Working back from the colonial history of Brazil, Freire argues that the central feature of the relationship between Brazil and Portugal was one of rank exploitation of the former by the latter. Portugal had no intention of creating the conditions for a stable, self-sufficient society in Brazil; she was only interested in a profitable business venture (*ECC*: 22). What is most important for Freire is that the nature of this exploitation created not only a set of oppressive social relations, but a form of consciousness conducive to this oppression. At first Brazil was attractive only to adventurers interested in quick riches, and in this she suffered a fate no different from the rest of Latin America. Those who had an interest in trade were attracted to the Eastern, and more highly developed, territories of the Portuguese empire. Latin America, by contrast, was the land of pillage. Those who came "wished only to exploit it, not to cultivate it; to be 'over' it, not to stay in it and with it" (*ECC*: 22). Unsurprisingly, then, the first colonizers of Brazil lacked any sense of identity with the colony.

Even the eventual settlement of Brazil did not alter the "predatory" character of Brazilian consciousness, for the settlement of Brazil was based primarily on the large landholdings of the plantation and the sugar mill. Most of the labor on these plantations was performed by slaves; at first natives, then blacks, and those few workers who did come from Portugal did so only against their will (*ECC*: 21, 22). The political economy of the large plantation created a set of social relations marked on the one hand by "an almost masochistic desire to submit" to the power of the *senhor* on the part of the exploited, and on the other hand by "a desire to be all powerful" on the part of the exploiting classes. With governmental authority often nothing more than a distant and all but ineffective entity, the plantation functioned according to the "law of the master." The master ruled, and those living on and working the plantation had no choice but to submit to this "law" for their own protection and security. The result was a society that was "closed, colonial, slavocratic, reflex, [and] anti-democratic" which "bred the habits of domination and dependence which still prevail . . . in the form of paternalistic approaches to problems" (*ECC*: 21–23).

In this society of "closed," "circumscribed," "introverted" communities, the majority of the population suffered from a kind of submersion in the historical process. Unable to grasp their capacity to act as sentient social agents, they tended to misunderstand and misdescribe natural processes and social relations in "magical" and "illogical" terms (*ECC*: 17, 20, 102–3). The Brazilian masses, Freire argues, suffered from what he calls a "semi-intransitive consciousness" (*ECC*: 17; *CAC*: 461) in which social relations were thought to be the effect of "some super-reality or to something within" (*CAC*: 461). Lacking the concepts that would enable them to understand the real origins of their misery, the masses inhabited a "culture of silence" which made them "mute, that is, they are prohibited from creatively taking part in the transformations of their society and therefore prohibited from *being* [fully human]" (*ALP*: 213).

These characteristic attitudes remained intact throughout much of the period of the liberal pause. Yet the experiences of liberalization also helped spur their breakdown. This process had actually begun with the abolition of slavery and the beginning of industrial growth in the late nineteenth century. It accelerated during the First World War, after the Great Depression (1929), and after the Second World War (*ECC*: 8, 29–30; *ALP*: 462). The economic changes that marked these periods effectively produced a number of "cracks" in Brazilian society (*ALP*: 462–63) that eventually led to a "split" in the social fabric (*ECC*: 9). With the structural foundations of the estate economy now under attack, a period of cultural "transition" was begun; the "closed" social relations and ideology of the estate economy now came into conflict with the social relations and ideology of the new economy of free labor based in the industrialized urban centers (*ECC*: 30). "What is important," Freire says, "is that once the cracks in the structure [of the closed society and its culture of silence] began to appear, and once societies enter the period of transition, immediately the first movements of emergence of the hitherto submerged and silent masses begin to manifest themselves" (*CAC*: 462).

It is in this context that the pedagogy of the oppressed arises, and in which it is intended to serve as a catalyst for change. For while the structural changes in Brazilian society certainly paralleled specific changes in the consciousness of most Brazilians, the more or less "automatic" relationship between these changes could not be taken as a model for the development of critical consciousness or *conscientização* (*ECC*: 19) that would enable the realization of democratic self-determination. Economic development may have been in part responsible for shaping self-understandings conducive to democracy, but in the particular situation of the Latin American nations it also presented constraints that were antithetical to democratic possibilities.

Forced to mobilize the masses for the purpose of economic modernization, many Latin American political leaders opted for "populist" political strategies. But the opening of the political process these strategies involved produced political demands that could not—and perhaps still cannot—be realized given the "dependent" status of these nations in the world economy. As a result of the programs of economic modernization, the relationship of dependency may have been called into question, but this questioning could not be translated into practice without threatening the fragile structure of power in the dependent nations (*CAC*: 459). "Populist leadership," Freire says, "thus could be said to be an adequate response to the new presence of the masses in the historical process. *But it is a manipulative leadership*—manipulative of the masses since it cannot manipulate the elites" (*CAC*: 465). As a result,

the populist approach will also end up creating serious contradictions for the power group. It will find itself obliged either to break open the culture of silence or to restore it. That is why it seems to us difficult in Latin America's present historical moment for any government to maintain even a relatively aggressive independent policy towards the metropolis while preserving the culture of silence internally. (*CAC*: 460)

Breaking the culture of silence is, then, a task that populism cannot complete, nor is it a task that elites were even willing to undertake. What was needed now was a completion of the developmental process through the "passage from one mentality to another" (*ECC*: 32); mass consciousness had to be advanced to the level of what Freire calls "critical transitivity," an "ability to perceive critically the themes of [the] time, and thus to intervene actively in reality" (*ECC*: 7). The possibility of realizing a truly democratic form of self-determination required critical consciousness, or *conscientização*, and this could be brought forth only through an educational program that would

go to the people and help them to enter the historical process critically. The prerequisite for this task was a form of education enabling the people to reflect on themselves, their responsibilities, and their role in the new cultural climate—indeed to reflect on their very *power* of reflection. The resulting development of this power would mean an increased capacity for choice. Such an education would take into the most serious account the various levels at which the Brazilian people perceived their reality, as being of the greatest importance for the process of their humanization. (*ECC*: 16–17)

Freire's reconstruction of the history of Brazil's socioeconomic development and the consciousness informing and informed by this development is, he says, part of "an archeology of consciousness" (*EA*: 58),[4]

[4] As far as I know, Freire's "archeology" and Foucault's "archaeology" were developed independently of each other. There are similarities, however, in that each tries to analyze the characteristic forms of consciousness found in their respective contexts. Beyond this, of course, there are radical differences with respect to the way these thinkers conceptualize the claims of their archeological/archaeological inquiries. Later in this chapter I will discuss these differences.

the aim of which is to "invite men and women who are at [a] naive level of their consciousness, ideologised in a concrete reality in which they cannot express themselves, they cannot express the word, they don't *know that they can know!*" (*EA*: 61), to recognize that they can recreate and remake their own reality (*EA*: 58). "Therein," Freire says, "lay my own concern to analyze these historically and culturally conditioned levels of understanding" (*ECC*: 17).

A *pedagogy of the oppressed* thus becomes one practical necessity in the development of critical consciousness. The way this pedagogy proceeds, however, is radically different from, and is indeed antithetical to, most pedagogical self-understandings. As Freire demonstrates, however, it is not so much the intention of raising consciousness that is at issue, for what differentiates a critical from a dominating pedagogy turns on a much deeper and more complex constellation of issues beyond those of intentions alone.

THE PEDAGOGY OF DOMINATION

How does one break the culture of silence? For Freire, this effort involves first and foremost "a type of education which corresponds to the specifically human mode of being, which is historical" (*ALP*: 221). Real emancipation, or the realization of one's distinctly human capacities, and by extension an emancipating pedagogy, therefore takes shape in the recognition of one's historicity.

It is precisely this historicity of being that is systematically obscured in a culture of silence. But not every pedagogical model can assist in the development of *conscientização*. In fact, as we shall see, education always embodies a potential for emancipation *or* the maintenance of domination and oppression. And in light of the need for an educational program in dependent societies like Brazil, it should come as no surprise that Freire devotes a great deal of space in his work to the criticism of pedagogical practices that constitute forms of "education as the practice of domination" (*PO*: 69).

Freire's target in this criticism is not, however, only those institutionalized educational practices we find in school settings. His focus on "education" must be understood as a vehicle for opening an examination of oppressive social practices in general—and the philosophical assumptions that inform them. In fact, for Freire, "pedagogy" serves as a metaphor for social relations in general, and the teacher-student relation thus reflects social relations "at any level, inside or outside the school" (*PO*: 57). Moreover, education and politics are seen as conceptually inseparable: "From the critical point of view, it is impossible to deny the political nature of the educational process as it is to deny the educational nature of the political act" (*LRWW*: 38).

This brings into his sights not only those who would perpetuate oppression, but also those who would seek to end it. The self-emancipation of the oppressed will not, he argues, result from "humanitarian" practices which "remain distant from the oppressed by treating them as unfortunates [while] presenting for their emulation models from among the oppressors" (*PO*: 39). Nor will it result from "assistentialist" practices "which attack symptoms, but not causes, of social ills" by proposing solutions for the oppressed which are then superimposed upon them (*ECC*: 15). Even development "aid" programs do not escape Freire's indictment; he devotes a lengthy essay to a critique of agricultural extension programs that are nothing more than forms of "cultural invasion" (*ECC*: 85–164). But his criticisms do not end with such reformist programs. Even those who lead "revolutionary" movements informed by a desire to act "on behalf" of the oppressed are indicted as subscribing to "an absurd dichotomy in which the praxis of the people is merely that of following the leaders' decisions—a dichotomy reflecting the prescriptive methods of the dominant elites" (*PO*: 121).

One may well sense a common thread in Freire's attack on all of the social practices he indicts. What all "humanitarian," "assistentialist," "extensionist," "prescriptive," and elitist "revolutionary" practices share is an attitude similar to what one finds in a "banking" concept of education. "In the banking concept of education, knowledge is a gift bestowed by those who consider themselves knowledgable upon those whom they consider to know nothing" (*PO*: 58). Through the projection of an absolute ignorance unto others (*PO*: 58, 129), "banking" education draws a distinction between teacher and student in a way that "mirrors oppressive society as whole" (*PO*: 59). With this claim Freire explicates the working assumption that informs the practice of domination in all of its forms; "banking" education in this sense is but a version of the "ideology of oppression" (*PO*: 58).

Unpacking the fundamental attitudes and practices of the banking model reveals two distinct, and contradictory, moments in the teacher's self-understanding. In the first of these, the teacher conceptualizes an object of knowledge "while he prepares his lessons in his study or his laboratory; during the second he expounds to his students about that object" (*PO*: 67–68). What is most interesting—and problematic—about this dichotomization of the teacher's self-understanding is that it is underpinned and reinforced by a whole panoply of dichotomizations involving the composition of knowledge and its relation to action. At the foundation of this dichotomization is what Freire calls the "teacher-student contradiction" (*PO*: 59). In this "contradiction," the teacher "presents himself to his students as their necessary opposite" by his assumption of the "absolute ignorance" of the student. This allows the teacher to justify his existence *as* teacher. This justification is, moreover, reinforced by the students' acceptance of their ignorance (*PO*: 58–59).

Listing a number of constitutive themes which "maintain and even stimulate" this contradiction, Freire offers insight into the range of philosophical and practical presuppositions of banking education:

> the teacher teaches and the students are taught;
> the teacher knows everything and the students know nothing;
> the teacher thinks and the students are thought about;
> the teacher talks and the students listen—meekly;
> the teacher disciplines and the students are disciplined;
> the teacher chooses and enforces his choice, and the students comply;
> the teacher acts and the students have the illusion of acting through the action of the teacher;
> the teacher chooses the program content, and the students (who were not consulted) adapt to it;
> the teacher confuses the authority of knowledge with his own professional authority;
> the teacher is the subject of the learning process, while the students are mere objects. (*PO*: 59)

It is a simple matter to exchange the nouns here, replacing "teacher/student" with "agricultural extension agent/peasant," "revolutionary leader/masses" and—perhaps most importantly—"oppressor/oppressed." In every one of these instances the social relations between the "enlightened" (whether teacher, agronomist, oppressor or revolutionary leader), and the "ignorant," are embodied in social practices that are essentially antidialogical. Regardless of whether the intended goal is to educate, maintain social "order," or bring about social change, the methodology employed seeks to inculcate a very specific world-view that itself maintains relations of inequality. On the one hand stand those who, by virtue of their "knowledge," play the role of "depositor, prescriber, domesticator" (*PO*: 62). On the other hand stand the "receptacles" of this knowledge who are conceptualized as "containers" to be "filled" with it (*PO*: 58). The inculcation of knowledge is thus best attained through the use of "communiques" which the oppressed are to "patiently receive, memorize and repeat" (*PO*: 58). The effect of this "depositing" of information, "which [the 'enlightened' teacher] considers to constitute true knowledge" (*PO*: 63), is to "prescribe" a form of consciousness that conforms to that of the prescriber (*PO*: 31) and to "domesticate" consciousness by making it nothing but a passive receptacle of predetermined "truths" (*PO*: 62).

The essential fact of the "contradiction" involved in nonreciprocal relations is, then, a kind of double-standard succinctly stated in the last theme of Freire's account of the "banking" model: the teacher is the subject of knowledge and the students are mere objects. And the reason this relationship is "contradictory" is because the "enlightened" must apply a model of human identity to the student (illiterate, peasant, masses, etc.) that they cannot apply to themselves. In many ways this parallels a contradiction that the Frankfurt School and Habermas point to in their critique of scientism. Those advocating a scientistic conception of human nature cannot objectify themselves without undermining their own belief in science; in banking education, educators cannot objectify themselves in the same way they objectify students without calling into question the "knowledge" educators believe in.

What is at stake here, then, goes beyond the interests and aims of those who would "teach," for it is the very logic of the practices in question that are at issue. As Freire says, "What distinguishes revolutionary leaders from the dominant elite is not only their objectives, *but their procedures*. If they act in the same way, the objectives become the same" (*PO*: 166). Thus, those who use the "banking" concept of education, or for that matter any antidialogical theory of cultural action, can only act to dehumanize others. The oppressors may well use the banking concept of education because their interests lie in making the oppressed adapt to the situation of oppression (*PO*: 60). But by also using this model, those who believe they are acting in the best interests of the oppressed merely serve to maintain conditions of oppression.

As Freire puts it, "certainly there are numerable well-intentioned bank-clerk teachers who do not realize that they are serving only to dehumanize" (*PO*: 61). Similarly there are agricultural extension agents who want to help the peasantry improve their lot, but because of the basic assumptions implicit in their method "nearly always end up by instigating the kind of programs in which humans are diminished in stature" (*ECC*: 129). But

> Revolutionary praxis cannot tolerate an absurd dichotomy in which the praxis of the people is merely that of following the leader's decisions—a dichotomy reflecting the prescriptive methods of the dominant elites. . . . Manipulation, sloganizing, "depositing," regimentation and prescription cannot be components of revolutionary praxis, precisely because they are components of the praxis of domination. (*PO*: 120–21)

To fail to note this means that revolutionaries "either have retained the characteristics of the dominator and are not truly revolutionary; or they are totally misguided in their conception of their role, and, prisoners of their own sectarianism, are equally nonrevolutionary. They may even reach power. But the validity of any revolution resulting from antidialogical action is thoroughly doubtful" (*PO*: 121). Here, as is so often the case, theory and practice are recapitulated in each other. Antidialogical practices reinforce nonreciprocal, hierarchical relationships that cannot possibly serve the interests of the oppressed.

Those who employ specific methods may often assume that methods are neutral tools that may be used for any particular end. Their distinction between means and ends, however, is only another example of an unworkable dichotomy, "and such a naive approach would be incapable of perceiving that technique itself as an instrument of men in their orientation in the world is not neutral" (*ALP*: 206). But when method and technique is critically examined in order to uncover "its objectives, its means, and its efficacy . . . what previously did not appear as [a] theory of action, is now revealed as such" (*ECC*: 112). To reflect on what may initially appear as rather abstract philosophical issues is, then, integral to understanding the practical features of oppression and emancipation. And if there is any lesson here, it is that "true humanists . . . cannot make use of banking educational methods in the pursuit of liberation, for they would negate that very pursuit" (*PO*: 65). Even if they may believe otherwise, "The antidialogic man, in his relations with other men, aims at conquering them—increasingly and by every means, from the toughest to the most refined, from the most repressive to the most solicitous (paternalism)" (*PO*: 133–34).

In essence, then, "banking" methods are inseparable from antidialogical action, and as such they are "a concomitant of the real, concrete situation of oppression" (*PO*: 134). For this reason, the "true humanist" cannot use these methods without simultaneously buying into the theory—and the practical consequences—inherent in them: "A man is not antidialogical . . . in the abstract, but in the world. He is not antidialogical, then oppressor; he is both, simultaneously" (*PO*: 134). To break the culture of silence is not possible using the methods of the oppressor. The pedagogy of the oppressed must find its grounding in a method that is humanizing rather than dehumanizing.

THE PEDAGOGY OF THE OPPRESSED

The central problem facing those who would seek the emancipation of the oppressed is to avoid the dehumanizing practices of antidialogical action. But this is an extremely difficult task, for the oppressed not only suffer the effects of these practices, they often internalize them. "The very structure of their thought has been conditioned by the contradictions of the concrete, existential situation by which they were shaped" (PO: 30). In effect, the oppressed may accept the "model of humanity" of their oppressors; what it means to be fully human for the oppressed is to accept the oppressors' definition of humanity. The result is that they either bind themselves to the role of the oppressed by accepting the explanations of their plight given by the oppressors, or, even when they are aware of being downtrodden, they may emulate the practices of the oppressor as a means of realizing their "humanity" (PO: 30–31 passim). The oppressor and his vision of reality and humanity is thus "housed" in the oppressed (PO: 163; ALP: 216), and in this they become "dual beings" who are "at one and the same time themselves [as oppressed] and the oppressor whose consciousness they have internalized" (PO: 32; see also PO: 47). Thus, a truly liberating pedagogy must take into account the "tragic dilemma" of the oppressed as "divided, unauthentic beings" whose choice is

> between being wholly themselves or being divided; between ejecting the oppressor within or not ejecting him; between human solidarity or alienation; between following prescriptions and having choices; between being spectators or actors; between acting or having the illusion of acting through the action of the oppressors; between speaking out or being silent, castrated in their power to create and re-create, in their power to transform the world. (PO: 33)

But this problem cannot be resolved without overcoming the internalization of the oppressor in the oppressed, nor can it be carried out by those who, seeing in the oppressed a deeply embedded false consciousness, opt for paternalistic solutions.

How, then, is the pedagogy of the oppressed to be practiced in the face of these apparently overwhelming difficulties? The question can only be answered in terms of a clear understanding of what it means to be a fully "human," "authentic," and "undivided" being. For Freire, humanization constitutes an "ontological and historical vocation" (PO: 40–41) that must be rigorously affirmed amid the distortions of historically contingent dehumanizing practices. Without such an affirmation, the struggle for emancipation becomes a meaningless activity, devoid of any clear understanding of what emancipation and human freedom entail (PO: 28). But as an "ontological vocation" humanization is not merely an abstract notion devoid of any empirical content; it is, rather affirmed in the very practices that negate it (PO: 28).

This controversial claim suggests that what constitutes real freedom for human beings, the social relations that are "humanizing," are implicit in the very practices that distort this humanity. We have already seen one reason that the model of humanity embodied in antidialogical practices cannot be maintained: those who would treat others as objects cannot without contradiction apply that understanding to themselves. Yet this objectification of others persists in all forms of antidialogical action.

According to Freire, this objectification of the oppressed is the result of a particular constellation of social practices whose origins are obscured by their systematic misdescription. In this sense, dehumanizing practices are historical, and therefore mutable, facts that are interpreted as "a given destiny" by those who are complicit in their perpetuation (*PO*: 28). Not surprisingly, the essential feature of Freire's critique of antidialogical practice involves showing how this practice is grounded in and justified by an appeal to a fundamentally flawed account of the origins of social beliefs, values and practices. Antidialogical practice assumes that the social world is a static, unchanging given, reflected in "ingenuous forms of apprehending objective reality" (*ECC*: 106) that involve "explanation(s) of a reality thought to be permanently untouchable" (*ECC*: 100).

For Freire, human consciousness and "objective reality" are ontologically distinct; they are not one and the same. But, following Marx, he recognizes that "objective reality" is always a reality for subjects— human beings (Matthews 1981: 85). Human beings are thus beings who exist *in* and *with* the world (*CAC*: 452; *ECC*: 111). Whatever difficulties one finds with antidialogical practices, even when they are pursued with an "emancipatory" intent, can be readily traced back to the systematic misdescription of social reality—and therefore of human capacities, capabilities, and possibilities—in which they are grounded. This misdescription might take a number of forms. It may take an "objectivist" form that dichotomizes human consciousness and the world, as with a banking model of education. In this view, the world (both social and natural) is conceptualized as an objective datum, and human consciousness is then nothing more than a "copy" or "replica" of existing reality (*CAC*: 454). Or if the contradiction involved in maintaining the dichotomy between human consciousness and objective reality implicit in this "mechanistic objectivism" (*CAC*: 454) is called into question, human consciousness may be conceptualized in terms of "behaviorism"; here consciousness is "merely an abstraction" in a system of thought that treats human beings as "machines" (*CAC*: 455).

The problem with either objectivist or behaviorist accounts of human consciousness is that they remain incomplete. In any of these forms, an antidialogical theory treats human beings as being "merely *in* the world, not *with* the world or with others; man is spectator, not re-creator. In this view man is not a conscious being; he is rather the possessor of *a* consciousness: an empty 'mind' [however conceptualized] passively open to the reception of deposits of reality from the world outside" (*PO*: 62). Freire indicts these models for their "mechanistic, static, naturalistic, spatialized view of consciousness" (*PO*: 64; see also *ECC*: 146, *ALP*: 208). But the primary reason they remain incomplete is that they obscure, or at best leave unexplained, the fact that "consciousness is never a mere reflection of, but a reflection upon, material reality" (*CAC*: 454).

Clearly Freire is neither an "objectivist" nor an "idealist." Both objectivism and idealism constitute erroneous understandings of what a human being is and how knowledge is constituted. Objectivism "denies the presence of human beings in the world, and subordinates them to the transformation of reality which takes place without their involvement"; it views them as "abstractions and [thereby] denies them their presence as beings of decision in historical transformations" (*ECC*: 146–47). Idealism, on the other hand, "starts by denying all concrete, objective reality and declares that the consciousness is the exclusive creator of its own concrete reality" and therefore "errs in affirming that ideas which are separate from reality govern the historical process" (*ECC*: 146). The difficulties in these positions are obvious: in the case of objectivism human consciousness cannot play a role in changing reality because it is by definition incapable of transcending its conditioning. In the case of idealism, the problem of solipsism arises; idealism cannot explain, let alone advocate, the transformation of reality "since the transformation of an imaginary reality is an absurdity" (*CAC*: 454).

Neither objectivism nor idealism (in any of their forms) serve as adequate foundations for a defensible critical pedagogy. Human beings *are* able to transform the world with their projects, their work (*ALP*: 206; *CAC*: 455; *PO*: 87). In Marx's words (quoted by Freire), such transformation is brought about by "labor in a form that stamps it as exclusively human" (*CAC*: 455). In "humanizing" the world of nature (*CAC*: 455) through their work, human beings create the world they come to know: "This world, because it is a world of history and culture, is a world of men and women—not simply of 'nature' " (*ECC*: 111–12). This uniquely human capacity for agency distinguishes human beings from other animals which, Freire says, exist only *in* the world: they are unable to set objectives or infuse their transformation of nature with any significance beyond itself (*PO*: 87). Human beings, on the other hand live both in the world—their activity is first and foremost action upon nature—and with the world. "The existent subject reflects upon his life within the very domain of existence, and questions his relationship to the world" (CAC: 453).

Human beings are thus conditioned by, and in turn condition "objective reality" through their activities as reflective subjects. In this Freire is at one with Marx:

> World and men do not exist apart from each other, they exist in constant interaction. Marx does not espouse such a dichotomy, nor does any other critical, realistic thinker. What Marx criticized and scientifically destroyed was not subjectivity, but subjectivism and psychologism. (PO: 36)

We are social creatures who socially constitute our reality, and on two levels. One is the level of what Marx called "humanized nature," in which human beings come to know themselves as active subjects as they turn nature to their chosen ends. At another level stands the reality of human "culture"—those theories, public conceptions and common understandings that constitute the life individuals experience with others (PO: 91).

Given this dialectic of objectivity and subjectivity, the constant interaction between human beings and the world, both natural and social, eliminating oppression cannot simply be understood as a matter of "changing the consciousness" of the oppressed. Nor, for that matter, can oppression be eliminated by a change in "objective reality." "Making 'real oppression more oppressive still by adding to it the realization of oppression' " (PO: 37)—that is, enlightenment about one's situation—is a necessary but not a sufficient condition for liberation (PO: 34). This critical perception of reality must be followed by action designed to change that reality. By the same token, however, a transformation of oppressive reality is also only a necessary, but hardly a sufficient condition for liberation. Without a concomitant change in the consciousness of the oppressed, "without posing men's false consciousness of reality as a problem or, through revolutionary action, developing a consciousness which is less and less false" (PO: 125), any change in the objective conditions of the oppressed is bound to fail to be truly emancipatory. Thus, Freire argues, in order to become active subjects in the constitution of their own social reality, people must act as well as reflect upon the reality to be transformed (PO: 125). Critical reflection without action slides off into mere "verbalism"; objective reality remains unchanged. And action without critical reflection is mere "activism"; it is action uninformed by a proper understanding of human capabilities and capacities.

The insistence that the oppressed engage in reflection on their concrete situation is not a call to armchair revolution. On the contrary, reflection—when it is true reflection—leads to action. On the other hand, when the situation calls for action, that action will constitute an authentic praxis only if its consequences become the object of critical reflection. In this sense, the praxis is the new *raison d'être* of the oppressed; and the revolution, which inaugurates the historical moment of this *raison d'être*, is not viable apart from their comcomitant conscious involvement. Otherwise, action is pure activism. (*PO*: 52–53)

The key to the pedagogy of the oppressed is, then, to call upon the oppressed to make their own reality. "Authentic liberation—*the process of humanization*—is a praxis: the action and reflection of men upon their world in order to transform it" (*PO*: 66, emphasis added).

Freire's debt to Marx is clear enough. Like Marx, and indeed like all critical theorists, Freire recognizes the social constitution of social reality, and that given this constitution human beings can be free only when they recognize and act on this insight by transforming their world. This seems straightforward, but we are likely to miss the import of this understanding of "praxis" unless we attend to its implications for the actual process of liberation. It is precisely Freire's contention that an authentic praxis is, and can only be, *dialogical*. And for this reason the pedagogy of the oppressed can be forged only with, and not for, the oppressed. Its goal is to "make oppression and its causes objects of reflection by the oppressed, and from that reflection will come their necessary engagement in the struggle for their liberation" (*PO*: 33). But in this the oppressed must liberate themselves; they must "be their own example in the struggle for their redemption" (*PO*: 39).

The dilemma here is real enough. On the one hand the oppressed suffer from false consciousness about their situation and their own capacities, and on the other they must free themselves. This of course places tremendous demands on those who would seek to enhance the consciousness raising of the oppressed. They must trust the oppressed's ability to understand their situation, they must act with humility and out of love for others, they must have an intense faith in humanity—"an *a priori* requirement for dialogue" (*PO*: 78–79). These are radical demands:

Those who authentically commit themselves to the people must re-examine themselves constantly. This conversion is so radical as not to allow of ambiguous behavior. To affirm this commitment but to consider oneself the proprietor of revolutionary wisdom—which must then be given to (or imposed upon) the people—is to retain the old ways. The man who proclaims devotion to the cause of liberation yet is unable to enter into *communion* with the people, whom he continues to regard as totally ignorant, is greviously self-deceived. The convert who approaches the people but feels alarm at each step they take, each doubt they express, and each suggestion they offer, and attempts to impose his "status," remains nostalgic towards his origin. (*PO*: 47)

The important point to bear in mind here is that for Freire "Dialogue is thus an existential necessity" (*PO*: 77). And in contrast to antidialogical practices, a pedagogy of the oppressed begins from a recognition that "Teachers and students (leadership and people) . . . are both Subjects, not only in the task of unveiling . . . reality, and thereby coming to know it critically, but in the task of re-creating that knowledge" (*PO*: 56). The process of liberation could not be otherwise, for if oppression is constituted by the imposition of a world view that systematically distorts the nature of social reality, then emancipation can occur only when human beings can *name their own world*, thus making social reality the object of their own reflective consideration. In Freire's words, the world of human beings is communicatively constituted, "intersubjectivity, or intercommunication is the primordial characteristic of this cultural and historical world"; "It is the 'we think' which establishes the 'I think' " (*ECC*: 136–37). To systematically exclude the oppressed from participation in this intersubjective process is thus to deny them their humanity:

> Human existence cannot be silent, nor can it be nourished by false words, but only by true words, with which men transform the world. To exist, humanly, is to *name* the world, to change it. Once named, the world in its turn reappears to the namers as a problem and requires of them a new *naming*. Men are not built in silence, but in word, in work, in action-reflection.
>
> But while to say the true word—which is work, which is praxis—is to transform the world, saying that word is not the privilege of some few men, but the right of every man. Consequently, *no one can say a true word alone—nor can he say it for another*, in a prescriptive act which robs others of their word. (*PO*: 76)

> Speaking the word is not a true act if it is not at the same time associated with the right of self-expression and world-expression, of creating and re-creating, of deciding and choosing and ultimately participating in society's historical process. (*ALP*: 212)

Any form of social organization that prevents human beings from critically reflecting on this fact is a form of violence. "The means used are not important; to alienate men from their own decision-making is to change them into objects" (*PO*: 73). And for this reason emancipation cannot take place without the oppressed's active participation as partners in the dialogue through which the world is made and remade. Dialogue cannot occur between those who deny others the right to speak their own word and those whose right to speak has been denied them. But the task at hand, first and foremost, is for those who have been denied their "primordial right to speak their word" to "reclaim this right and prevent the continuation of this dehumanizing aggression" (*PO*: 77).

The conviction that such a reclamation is necessary "is not a gift bestowed by the revolutionary leadership, but the result of the [oppressed's] own *conscientização*," or critical consciousness (*PO*: 54). In the most fundamental sense, critical consciousness involves nothing less than "historical awareness itself" (*PO*: 100). This historical awareness is more than simply the recognition of the existence of a past and a future; it is constituted by "thinking which perceives reality as process, as transformation, rather than as a static entity" (*PO*: 81) in which human beings recognize themselves to be "in a situation. Only as this situation ceases to present itself as a dense, enveloping reality or a tormenting blind alley, and men come to perceive it as an objective-problematic situation—only then can commitment [to changing this reality] exist" (*PO*: 100).

Precisely because history is a "process," the pedagogy of the oppressed must avoid what Freire calls "sectarianism," which treats history in a "proprietary fashion" (*PO*: 23). This sectarianism is not confined only to the oppressor; it can equally afflict those who want to emancipate the oppressed:

> The rightist sectarian differs from his leftist counterpart in that the former attempts to domesticate the present so that (he hopes) the future will reproduce this domesticated present, while the latter considers the future pre-established—a kind of inevitable fate, fortune or destiny. For the rightist sectarian, 'today,' linked to the past, is something given and immutable; for the leftist sectarian, 'tommorow' is decreed beforehand, is inexorably pre-ordained . . . [C]losing themselves into 'circles of certainty' from which they cannot escape, these men 'make' their own truth. It is not the truth of men who struggle to build the future, running the risks involved in this very construction. Nor is it the truth of men who fight side by side and learn together how to build this future—which is not something to be received by men, but is rather something to be created by them. (*PO*: 23)

The pedagogy of the oppressed must make history a process by posing social reality as "neither a 'well behaved' present nor a predetermined future" (*PO*: 72) but as a "limit situation" which constitutes a "fetter" to liberation rather than an "insurmountable obstacle" (*PO*: 89). It must affirm human beings as "beings in the process of becoming—as unfinished, uncompleted beings in and with a likewise unfinished reality" (*PO*: 72). In this, the pedagogy of the oppressed, as a form of problem posing theory and practice, takes human historicity as its starting point (*PO*: 71).

Now certainly there is a clear distinction between those who initiate the process of consciousness raising and those whose consciousness must be raised. The distinction is not to be ignored; at root it is a difference in awareness about the constitution of social reality. But this difference in perception does not mean that those who would seek to impart this awareness to others can fall back on antidialogical practices. Where many ostensibly emancipatory political and educational plans fail is in their neglect of the context of those to whom their program is directed (*PO*: 83). Only through dialogue with the oppressed can a critical theorist come to know both the objective situation of the oppressed as well as the oppressed's understanding of that situation. Thus, the actual program content of an emancipatory praxis "must be the present, existential, concrete situation, reflecting the aspirations of the people" (*PO*: 84–85). This is, simply put, the demand for intelligibility:

> For the act of communication to be successful, there must be accord between the reciprocally communicating Subjects. That is, the verbal expression of one of the Subjects must be perceptible within a frame of reference that is meaningful to the other Subject. If this agreement on the linguistic signs used to express the object [the *context*] signified does not exist, there can be no comprehension between the Subjects, and communication will be impossible. The truth of this can be seen in that there is no separation between comprehension (intelligibility) and communication, as if the two comprised different moments of the same process or act. On the contrary, intelligibility and communication occur simultaneously. (*ECC*: 138)

And without this intelligibility, "the risk either of 'banking' or of preaching in the desert" (*PO*: 85) runs high.

To make oneself intelligible to the oppressed does *not* mean that one merely makes the oppressed the object of inquiry. Rather, the program content of the pedagogy of the oppressed begins with "the thought-language with which men refer to reality, the levels at which they perceive that reality, and their view of the world."[5] This consti-

---

[5] Freire's comments here are perhaps a bit sloppy in terms of conceptual clarity. Freire says that a critical pedagogy begins with the "thought-language with which men *refer* to reality," but this should not be taken as suggesting that he is a nominalist of some sort. For Freire, the concept of "naming" is not meant to evoke some kind of 'word-and-object' view of language; the objects to which "thought-language" refer, he

tutes the "thematic universe" of the oppressed out of which come the "generative themes" which comprise its matrix. These are the "objects" that are to be posed as problems for critical reflection (PO: 86). This is not to discount the fact that the sociostructural conditions that shape this thematic universe must be clearly understood. As Freire says, the denunciation of a situation of oppression also requires an empirically sound understanding of that situation (ALP: 220). But this structural account cannot of itself provide the basis of critique. In the first place, such an account must be cast in terms that the oppressed themselves understand; that is, to understand the nature of oppression requires interpretation in terms of idioms and experiences of the oppressed—and it is only when they recognize an interpretation as their own that it can be "verified." A critical theory, in other words, cannot "know reality without relying on the people as well as on objective facts for the source of its knowledge" (CAC: 468). In the second place, critique must find the roots or rudiments of an emancipatory practice in the experiences of the oppressed.

This last point is crucial, for it implies that the critical theorist cannot treat the cultural traditions of its addressees as mere obstacles to their emancipation—and this is indeed what most revolutionary theories appear to assume. For it is through these traditions that human beings "are the particular sorts of people they are and have the capacities and opportunities to engender the social and personal changes they can" (Fay 1987: 164). But neither does this mean that a critical theory can conceptualize traditions as do most conservative or reactionary theories, as if they were simply oracles to be consulted for solutions to present problems. As a form of dialogue with the oppressed about their situations, a pedagogy of the oppressed treats traditional practices and beliefs as something from which change must find its grounding, and to which change must be directed at transforming. A situation of oppression is thus understood as a "limit situation" that can be overcome by engaging in "limit-acts: those directed at negating and overcoming, rather than passively accepting, the 'given' " (PO: 89). This objective can be achieved only through action upon the con-

says, "do not exist 'out there' somewhere, as static entities; *they are occurring*. They are historical as men themselves; consequently they cannot be apprehended apart from these men." Thus to understand the language with which the oppressed refer to reality is also to understand "both the men who embody them and the reality to which they refer" (PO: 98)—not by any stretch of the imagination should this be taken to be an implicit denial of the intersubjectively constituted character of social reality; in this particular passage Freire is concerned with showing how those who might hold a nominalist view might mistake their view of reality as a reflection of reality *simpliciter*. To understand the specificities of a particular context requires, quite simply, understanding the language used *in* that context.

crete, historical reality in which limit situations are found (*PO*: 89). Reality and tradition are thus posed as unfinished challenges, as a situation that can be transformed, an unfinished reality for uncompleted, unfinished beings who are constantly in the process of *becoming* (*PO*: 72). And such a dialogue can be carried out only through the practice of coinvestigation between those who are intent on changing that reality (*PO*: 56, 97).[6]

In this dialogue all participate as Subjects who not only unveil an oppressive reality by coming to know it critically, but who also engage in the task of recreating knowledge and reality itself (*PO*: 56). This is why a truly liberating pedagogy must be constantly remade in praxis; in order to *be* it must *become* (*PO*: 72), and this is why every true revolution must be pedagogical (*PO*: 131). Problem posing is hence a form of "revolutionary futurity," it is "prophetic" and "utopian" precisely because it corresponds to the historicity of being (*PO*: 72, *ALP*: 219–21).

> When we defend such a conception of education—realistic precisely to the extent that it is utopian—that is, to the extent that it denounces what in fact is, and finds therefore between denunciation and its realization the time of its praxis—we are attempting to formulate a type of education which corresponds to the specifically human mode of being, which is historical. (*ALP*: 221)

> When education is no longer utopian, *i.e.*, when it no longer embodies the dramatic unity of denunciation and annunciation, it is either because the future has no more meaning for men, or because men are afraid to risk living the future as creative overcoming of the present, which has become old. (*ALP*: 220)

As reality is thus transformed and present situations are superseded, new ones will appear, which in turn will evoke new limit-situations and the need for new limit acts (*PO*: 89–90). And it is this transformational character of reality and the unfinished character of human existence that necessitate the constant remaking of the pedagogy of the oppressed (*PO*: 72).

---

[6] A useful study of how Freire's pedagogical method is articulated through the idiom of its addressees is Brown (1974). Freire's own reflections on making literacy and consciousness-raising attentive to local idioms may be clearly seen in his *Education for Critical Consciousness* (see note 2), *Pedagogy in Process* (on his experience in Guinea Bissau), and *Literacy: Reading the Word and the World* (chapter 4 discusses the Brazilian experience; chapter 5 discusses Freire's Guinea Bissau experience; and chapter 6 contains a discussion of how the U.S. context requires a recasting of the pedagogical task).

That is why there is no genuine hope in those who intend to make the future repeat the present, nor in those who see the future as something predetermined. Both have a "domesticated" notion of history: the former because they want to stop time; the latter because they are certain about a future they already "know." Utopian hope, on the contrary, is engagement full of risk. (*ALP*: 220)

And an ongoing engagement it is, a fact nowhere more clearly seen than in the practical activities of those who have taken up a pedagogy of the oppressed.

THE PEDAGOGY OF THE OPPRESSED IN PRACTICE

What does Freire teach us about the realization of critical theory's practical-emancipatory intent? Simply stated, he maintains that the emancipatory interest of critique must be drawn from a historically situated context, and that what constitutes emancipation itself will always be defined in terms of that context. It is when theory becomes abstracted from contexts that it slides off into an empty "verbalism," incapable of constructively engaging concrete, historical situations of oppression. In a passage that should serve to remind any critical theorist of this crucial insight, Freire insists that the "witness" to oppression which the critical theorist provides "may vary, depending on the historical conditions of any society" (*PO*: 177).[7] Thus, "the content of [the] dialogue [initiated by the theorist] can and should vary in accordance with historical conditions and the level at which the oppressed perceive reality" (*PO*: 52). The act of "witness" constitutes nothing more nor less than the recognition that the struggle for liberation is a common task; that to act as "witness" is "not an abstract gesture, but an action—a confrontation with the world and with men—it is not static" (*PO*: 176, 178):

> In order to determine the *what* and *how* of that witness, it is therefore essential to have an increasingly critical knowledge of the current historical context, the view of the world held by the people, the principal contradiction of society, and the principal aspect of that contradiction. Since these dimensions of witness are historical, dialogical, and therefore dialectical, witness

[7] Freire's use of the concept of witness also is reminiscent of Horkheimer, Adorno and Marcuse's use of the term. But the similarities are insignificant compared to the differences between Freire and the critical theorists with respect to what "witness" actually entails. For the critical theorists, the only witness possible in the context of the total domination of modern society is "an imaginary witness." For Freire, on the other hand, 'witness' cannot be imaginary (or what amounts to the same thing, removed from a context). Witness for him can *only* be contextual.

cannot simply import them from other contexts without previously analysing its own. To do otherwise is to absolutize and mythologize the relative; alienation becomes unavoidable. Witness, in the dialogical theory of action, is one of the principal expressions of the cultural and educational character of the revolution. (*PO*: 177)

There may be a sense in which this understanding of the role of "witness" the critical theorist must assume helps explain why it is both modernist and postmodernist critical theory are problematic. Unwilling to "witness" oppression and struggle in their historically specific forms because of their excessive universalism or radical skepticism, modernist and postmodernist critical theory retreats, to use Freire's words, into the realm of mere "verbalism" and "preaching in the desert."[8] The absence of an adequate conception of "witness" also perhaps explains the failure of orthodox Marxism and its adherence to what Alvin Gouldner aptly called "the flawed universal class" (quoted in O'Neill 1985: 73). By failing to recognize that history is a process, and not a predetermined future, that human beings are always *becoming* and can never simply *be*, the orthodox Marxist separates the revolution into two classes: it designates its leaders as thinkers and the oppressed as mere doers (*PO*: 120).

> Denial of communion in the revolutionary process, avoidance of dialogue with the people under the pretext of organizing them, of strengthening revolutionary power, or of ensuring a united front, is really a fear of freedom. It is a fear of or lack of faith in the people. But if the people cannot be trusted, there is no reason for liberation; in this case the revolution is not even carried out *for the people*, but *by the people for the leaders*: a complete self-negation. (*PO*: 124)

Freire has no illusions about the complexity and difficulties of bringing about social change and ending dehumanizing practices. "Liberation," he says, "is a childbirth, and a painful one" (*PO*: 33). The decolonization of language and life, which requires the self-emancipatory practice of the colonized through their unseating of the oppressor within, may be in fits and starts, or it may be resisted by the oppressed precisely because they live the culture of silence. But it is only "by avoiding a naive optimism [about transformative possibilities] at the beginning [that] we prevent ourselves from falling into despair and cynicism" (*PL*: 130). Moreover, the obstacles to emancipation embodied in the attitudes of the oppressed themselves do not justify excluding them in the name of their own liberation:

[8] See the interesting article by McLaren (1986), who contrasts Freire favorably with postmodernism, particularly Foucault's work.

We can legitimately say that in the process of oppression someone oppresses someone else; we cannot say that in the process of revolution someone liberates someone else, nor yet that someone liberates himself, but rather that men in communion liberate each other. (PO: 128)

For each to participate in the naming of the world requires dialogue. And in the face of the difficulties of dialogue one can only continue the strenuous commitment to such a task. It may well demand love in the form of commitment to others,[9] the courage to continue in the face of setbacks and resistance, the humility to avoid projecting ignorance onto others, and, at base a profound faith in humanity—but it cannot be otherwise (PO:77–80). No one can say a "true word" alone, nor can the word be said for another. The pedagogy of the oppressed thus calls forth the education of oppressed and, to paraphrase Marx, the education of the educators themselves.

Like all critical theories in practice, these metatheoretical insights are not simply abstract philosophical concerns—they are directly relevant to making theory practically effective. And Freire's unique contribution to critical theory stems as much from his practice as from his insights. The achievements of his own efforts are by no means minor.[10] By most accounts, his activities in Brazil during the early 1960s and again more recently, in Chile in the late 1960s, as well as those taken up in Guinea Bissau, Tanzania, Nicaragua, and a variety of other nations through his position with the World Council of Churches, have been remarkably successful in empowering hitherto marginalized individuals and groups. So much so that in those nations where forces of reaction and elitism managed to reimpose their hegemony, Freire's programs, their participants, and (in the case of Brazil in 1964) Freire himself were attacked.[11]

There are, of course objections that have been raised to Freire's practical endeavors and his philosophical presuppositions. However,

[9] Obviously, what Freire means by "love" here is not to be understood as embodying the attitudes of self-sacrifice one usually finds in mother-child or familial relations. Such a conception of love, as Mary Dietz (1985: 32) argues, is simply not suitable for understanding the need for mutual respect that is characteristic of relations between *citizens*. (See also in the following chapter my discussion of the problematic character of identifying women's experiences solely in terms of caretaking and nurturance.) For Freire, "love" as he uses the term in his discussion "is not sentimental," as such an understanding may "serve as a pretext for manipulation"; it is, rather, a commitment to the cause of liberation, "an act of bravery" that "must generate other acts of freedom; otherwise, it is not love" (PO: 78).

[10] I have drawn the following biographical account from Mackie (1981) and Collins (1977).

[11] For more extensive discussions of Freire in Brazil, see Palmer and Newsom (1982), Barnard (1981), and Bee (1981).

most of these objections have radically misconstrued Freire's project. One type of criticism focuses on the status of the critical theorist in Freire's work. Oddly enough, some, like Peter Berger's (1972: 121–27), treat Freire's project of consciousness raising as presupposing an "elitist" account of the theorist, while others, like Jim Walker's (1981: 142–43), charge that Freire does not take seriously enough the fact that theorists—intellectuals—have been able to "acquire theoretical knowledge of a certain sort" which justifies drawing distinctions between the "revolutionary leadership" and the masses they want to lead.[12]

But Freire's position is not that critical theorists and their addressees will necessarily have the same level of critical self-understanding. (If they did, there would perhaps be no need for critical theory or critical theorists). Nowhere does he deny that there will be differences in this regard. But the issue is not either/or: to assume differences in critical understanding is not necessarily elitist—any more than assuming a kind of "epistemological equality" is necessarily egalitarian. The key issue here is what one does with the obvious fact of difference. Freire's insights demonstrate that any adequate understanding of a situation and its emancipatory possibilities requires both a "sophisticated" theoretical understanding, as well as a more specific, concrete, "existential" perspective. The upshot is that the relation between critical theory and practice, and critical theorist and audience, must be seen as mutually informing and mutually transforming. In essence, the theorist/audience relationship—however useful as an analytical construct—cannot in practice be maintained, at least if emancipation is to be realized.

Such a position also assumes that emancipation is not a specified end-state; a radical pedagogy is not "utopian" in this sense, as some critics (i.e., Griffith 1972: 77–79) seem to assume.[13] But neither does it assume that emancipation is something always out of reach. Rather, the "utopian" moment in a critical pedagogy sees emancipation as an ongoing process, or as Freire puts it, one that "corresponds to the specifically human mode of being, which is historical" (*ALP*: 221).[14] As

[12] Walker's charge is embedded in a broader critique that charges Freire with inconsistency between his theory and the nationalist revolutions he has endorsed. Walker's critique is, perhaps, skewed by its overemphasis on the international constraints on Third World development, which he believes obviate the "liberating" potential of nationalist uprisings. In Freire's defense, I think it may be said that he is not unaware of these constraints, but he does hold a more hopeful attitude toward the possibility of self-determination in Third World nations.

[13] I am indebted to McLaren (1986) for drawing my attention to this criticism.

[14] I had arrived at this conclusion some time before I came across McLaren (1986); his analysis of Freire's conception of "utopian" critique is remarkably similar to my own.

Henry Giroux notes in his introduction to Freire's *Politics of Education*,

> The *utopian* character of his analysis is concrete in nature and appeal, and takes as its starting point collective actors in their various historical settings and the particularity of their problems and forms of oppression. It is *utopian* only in the sense that it refuses to surrender to the risks and dangers that face all challenges to dominant power structures. (*PE*: xvii)

Giroux's characterization also anticipates yet another set of criticisms to which Freire's work has been subjected. One of these charges that Freire has offered a method that is applicable only to the Third World,[15] and situations of illiteracy specifically. In many of these criticisms, however, what is missed is the fact that the aquisition of literacy is, for Freire, more than simply a matter of a mechanical ability to read and write (*LRWW*: 157). A critical pedagogy must not remain satisfied with this constricted understanding of "literacy," for it presupposes an understanding of literacy that incorporates "a critical comprehension of the text, and the sociohistorical context to which it refers," and which sees "the act of learning to read and write . . . [as] a creative act that involves a critical comprehension of reality" (*LRWW*: 157).

Now given this broader understanding of literacy, a critical pedagogy may well be required even in those situations where the mechanical aspects of literacy have been achieved. Thus, as Freire so cogently demonstrates in several recent discussions (*LRWW*: 120–40; *PL*: 121–41), the key issue for a pedagogy of the oppressed is not just literacy, but critical consciousness. Nor does Freire underestimate the difficulties of a radical pedagogy in the "advanced" nations:

> In Brazil, we are on the periphery, strongly dependent on the finance centers of the North. Our dependence keeps us poor and this poverty makes the social contradictions very visible everywhere in the streets of Sao Paulo, for example. In the North, power and wealth make it easier to hide the contradictions, the inequalities and the exploitation. The process, though, is similar, one of domination. But, the living cultures surround us with the look of greatly different societies. The opaque conditions of daily life in an affluent culture can cause special confusions in the North, which only make critical illumination harder and more necessary. (*PL*: 139–40)[16]

[15] Kozol (1981) and Giroux (1987) discuss these sorts of criticisms.

[16] Kozol (1980, 1981), Giroux (1983, 1987), Farmer (1972), Brigham (1977) and many of the essays in Livingstone (1987) offer insights into how a critical pedagogy of the sort Freire envisions might be realized in a North American context. Alfred (1984) discusses how Freire's pedagogical model may be adapted to community education in Britain.

Related to the objection that Freire's is a culturally specific discourse is the claim that it is also gender-specific. Writing in the late 1970s, Denis Collins (1977: 90) noted that "Female readers of Freire frequently call attention to his discussion of human beings in an apparently chauvinstic manner by use of *man* or *men* to speak of the human race." As Collins goes on to note, however, Freire (to his credit) "acknowledged this as an oversight." A partial corrective to this was achieved in subsequent republication of two of his works, where the pronoun *s/he* was used (Collins 1977: 90). More important, however, was Freire's acknowledgment that his philosophical stance required the recognition of the specificity of womens' experiences as distinct and different than those of men. Evidence Collins (1977: 90) cites was the publication of two booklets (*Liberation of Woman: To Change the World and Reinvent Life* [1974], and *Toward a Woman's World* [1975]) by Freire's Geneva-based Institute for Cultural Action. More recently, Freire (*PL*: 165–66) has discussed the matter of sexism, its particular specificity, and its practical implications in more concrete terms. As is consistent with his position, Freire declared that he was "sure the women's struggle has to be led by them" and that they "must have the main responsibility" in that struggle. But, also consistently, he noted that he hoped women would—if they were critical—recognize that "their struggle also belongs to us, that is, to those [men] who don't accept a *machista* position in the world."

The struggles of women, then, are indicative of the complexity and difference that forms of oppression may take—a fact requiring strategies of opposition and empowerment that are specific to those forms. The same is no less true of racism. Thus while Freire argues that racism and sexism are intimately linked to capitalist modes of production, they cannot be conceptualized (*contra* many Marxists) as problems that will be overcome "automatically" in a socialist society, because they cannot be "reduced only to the question of capitalism," nor can the specificity of the kind of struggle required to overcome them be "reduced into class struggle" (*PL*: 167).[17] Furthermore, the forms of oppression and struggle defined by sexism and racism have a logic of their own, and thus any attempt to "reinvent society" must be open to the need to engage these and other forms of oppression on their own terms, and not as if they can be put off until a "revolutionary transformation" is already underway (*PL*: 167).

All of this suggests that the philosophical underpinnings of Freire's pedagogy of the oppressed may be understood as providing a theoret-

---

[17] Freire's comments anticipate the feminist critiques of Marxism I discuss in chapter 7.

ical and political space for plurality *and* solidarity. In this respect, Freire's critical theory differs significantly from those of the modernists and postmodernists. Against the modernists, a pedagogy of the oppressed refuses to truck with the excessive rationalism and universalism of the Enlightenment tradition of critical rationality. In their introduction to a recent set of essays (Livingstone 1987), Henry Giroux and Freire note "the importance of developing forms of sociality that connect rationality with power and desire and not merely with discursive structures" (p. xv). A cultural tradition, on this account, must be seen as incorporating "a politics of the body, one in which everyday experiences, interests, desires, and needs configure as part of a cultural politics attempting to broaden and deepen the notions of both emancipation and oppression." Thus does "the notion of struggle" embody "a mulitiplicity of political interventions as expressed in various social movements" (p. xvi). And a pedagogy of the oppressed recognizes that "enlightenment and emancipation" is complex, site specific, but also an ongoing challenge that must be constantly renewed as historical change takes place:

> Freire understands full well that a pedagogy of liberation has no final answers: Radical praxis must always emerge from continuous struggle within specific pedagogical sites and among competing theoretical frameworks. Truth has no necessary closure, no transcendental justification. (McLaren 1986: 400)

Now this may appear to endorse the postmodernist position, and to some extent it does. But from this it should not be concluded that a pedagogy of the oppressed thereby gives up its commitment to rationality and reason. It does not entail, as Peter McLaren (1986: 396) notes, "a nihilistic relativization of values." Rather, it remains committed to locating in struggles against domination a moment of hope "that attempts to advance the discourse of democracy by linking it to oppositional forms of knowledge both inside and outside dominant public spheres" (Giroux and Freire, in Livingstone et al. 1987: xvi).

The hope and possibility of collective emancipation does not, then, mean that one is committed to a rationalist pipe-dream, nor does it commit one to a radical normative skepticism. To subscribe to this dichotomy is to recapitulate the theoretical and practical dilemmas of modernist and postmodernist critical theory. Truth, emancipation, and what Freire calls our "ontological vocation" to be more fully human, can only be expressed historically, and that expression will take a variety of forms as particular contexts demand.

For many, particularly those seeking a "universal" standard of rationality, such a conclusion may be unsatisfactory. It will be equally unsatisfactory for those who see the absence of these absolutes as grounds for a retreat into an "aesthetic of existence." Unfortunately, the lives of the marginalized are such that they can ill afford to assume either position. And if the rest of us are to make good our collective responsibility to eliminate unnecessary domination and suffering, a pedagogy of the oppressed is a good place to begin. This is not to say that such a pedagogy will be itself sufficient; as Freire says, it is important for critical educators—and I would add, critical theorists generally—to be "clear that our work, our activities as an educator, will not be enough to change the world. This is for me the first thing, not to idealize the educational task" (*PL*: 180). Moreover, a critical pedagogy cannot determine in advance that its effects will be successful in assisting the oppressed to emancipate themselves. But while there may be no guarantees of success, and even dangers, in the struggle for empowerment, as the work of Paulo Freire shows, neither are we without hope that our fellows, sisters, future generations—and we ourselves—might find those voices that do not simply repeat the destructive history from which they must emerge.

CHAPTER 6

Liberation Theology as Critical Theory

> And ye shall know the truth, and the truth shall make you free.
>
> —John 8: 32

> The philosophers have only *interpreted* the world, in various ways; the point, however, is to *change* it.
>
> —Karl Marx

> This is a theology which does not stop with reflecting on the world, but rather tries to be part of the process through which the world is transformed. It is a theology which is open—in the protest against trampled human dignity, in the struggle against the plunder of the vast majority of people, in liberating love, and in the building of a new, just, and fraternal society—to the gift of the Kingdom of God.
>
> —Gustavo Gutierrez

MY AIM in this chapter is to argue that liberation theology, like dependency theory and Freire's critical pedagogy, serves as an example of a critical theory in practice.[1] This idea may appear initially implausible, particularly in light of the historical antagonism toward religion em-

---

[1] The liberation theology I address here is that of Latin American liberation theologians. There are many other forms of liberation theology but I have chosen Latin American liberation theology as a focus because it has provided the analytical framework within which non-Latin American liberation theologies have articulated their self-understandings. As a result of the formation of liberation theology in Latin America, we now have available a wide variety of liberation theologies, many of which reflect the same model of the theory-practice relationship one finds in the Latin Americans. In this, we can safely claim there are *many* examples of theologies that are instances of critical theories in practice. For example, in my research I have come across feminist, Jewish, black, Hispanic, native American, Asian, Asian American, and Irish forms of liberation theology/critical theory. See the essays in Anderson and Stransky (1979), Tabb (1986), and Mahan and Richesin (1981); also Lane (1977), Cone (1970), and Ferm (1986).

For a dense, but extremely rich, account of the epistemological foundations of a critical liberation theology, see Boff (1987). When I first began to work on the argument in this chapter, no such work existed in English. Boff's arguments for the most part seem to parallel my own, though his is a far more systematic account that goes beyond that which I offer here, particularly with respect to specific theological disputes.

bodied in the tradition of "critical reason" to which modernist critical theory belongs. Postmodernist critical theory offers a no less uncompromising stance toward the idea of a theology of liberation. For while such a theology presupposes a faith, and would thus initially appear at odds with the rationalism of modernist critical theory, it also presupposes an understanding of that faith as part of a search for "rationality" in social life, and is therefore also at odds with postmodernist attacks on reason.

In my view, these oppositions are not only contradictory, but unwarranted. For if modernist and postmodernist critical theory are on the mark in their claim that every form of thought, including "religion," reflects historically specific social practices, an opposition to religion must also be cast in contextually specific terms. And this is exactly the position taken by the liberation theologians. Indeed, there is a sense in which we might say that liberation theology is not a religion at all—at least on the understanding of that term which, ironically enough, informs the discourse of most critics and supporters of dominant theological accounts.[2]

Liberation theology may even be said to represent a "New Reformation."[3] It marks a radical break with, or redefinition of, the meaning of faith found in orthodox Catholic and Protestant thought. And in fact, much of my defense of liberation theology as a critical theory in practice turns in part on the conceptual issue of distinguishing between the "religion" of which most critical theorists and orthodox theologians speak, and the "critical faith" the liberation theologians articulate. But I also try to show that liberation theology, like dependency theory, Freire's critical pedagogy, and as we shall later see, feminist theory, provides a more perspicacious understanding of how the idea of a critical theory might be realized than that found in modernist and postmodernist critical theory.

In keeping with the liberation theologians' own claims that commit-

---

[2] Biskowski (1986), for example, seems to argue that Marx's critique of a specific form of Christianity can be understood as a critique of religion *tout court*. In this essay one of my objectives is to show that liberation theology cannot be considered a form of the "religion" of which Marx is critical.

I have also taken up this issue in my essay, "Marx(ism), Religion and Liberation Theology" (Leonard, 1987). There I argue that the received view, which assumes an inherent antagonism between Marxism and religion is theoretically and practically deficient.

[3] My initial formulation of this idea was buttressed by a similar—although only highly suggestive—notion I later came across in an essay by Joel Kovel (in Tabb 1986). Kovel also asks if liberation theology might not be understood as a New Reformation, in a short section of his paper "The Vatican Strikes Back." This section, not surprisingly, is entitled "A New Reformation" (pp. 182–83).

ment and practice come first, and theology second, I begin by explicating the historical background and practical context of liberation theology. This discussion is followed by an examination of the reasons the liberation theologians see the need for a different understanding of religious faith. I then turn to liberation theology's version of the "critique of religion," which they understand as involving "the liberation of theology." The "theology of liberation" that emerges out of the socioanalytic and theological critiques discussed is the focus of the fourth section of this chapter. Finally, I conclude by drawing out the implications of my discussion for understanding liberation theology in practice, and what liberation theology might teach us about the idea of a critical theory.

The Context of Liberation Theology: From Practical Demands to Theological Critique

It is of course well known that a vast majority of the population of South and Central America profess a Catholic faith. This is mostly a consequence of the unchallenged hegemony the Catholic Church enjoyed as a result of its intimate relationship with the colonial powers of Spain and Portugal. The Church has historically been a highly conservative force on the continent, and for many casual observers it may seem odd that the Church would also become an institutional breeding ground for the kind of religious radicalism one finds in liberation theology.

But the emergence of liberation theology does make sense—although it is only in retrospect that one can make such claims. No one could have predicted the changes that would culminate in the development of liberation theology, and even longtime observers of the Latin American scene did not realize that a series of apparently unrelated events would come together in the late 1960s and early 1970s in the form of such a powerful internal challenge to the Church's intellectual foundations and ecclesiastical practices. Nonetheless, there are a number of historical factors that can be identified as crucial in defining the context and conditions that gave rise to liberation theology. Three in particular stand out. These are: (1) factors specific to the pastoral demands on the Latin American Church; (2) more general socioeconomic and political conditions, particularly those related to the development crises Latin American nations have faced since the early 1960s; and (3) factors external to the Latin American Church but internal to the Catholic Church at large. None of these, taken alone, can explain the rise of liberation theology, but taken together they offer a workable understanding of the origins of the movement.

After much of Latin America had managed to win its independence from the colonial powers in the early nineteenth century, the next hundred years or so were marked by a vigorous anticlericalism. This was naturally directed against the power of the Catholic Church. Many of the ideas fanning these anticlerical flames drew their strength from ideologies promulgated in Europe and imported to Latin America, the most notable of which were emphatically juridical and political rather than religious. This gave Latin American anticlericalism a unique flavor: it was not, like much European anticlericalism, antireligious; rather, it was primarily informed by the aim of depriving the Church of those means and privileges that enabled it to exercise political influence (Veliz 1980: 191–92).[4]

By the middle of the twentieth century, the major political and juridical objectives of this anticlericalism had been more or less achieved, yet even in those countries that had experienced the full force of the movement, the Catholic Church remained the dominant religious institution. Indeed, Latin American anticlericalism had simply transformed the Church from a *de jure* to a *de facto* national religion (Veliz 1980: 194).

This change to a *de facto* status was not, however, without significant consequence for the Church. In a word, it was severely weakened. This is in part illustrated by the decline in the number of priests on the continent. Before the wars of independence there was one priest for every one thousand Catholics; by 1890 this ratio was one to every three thousand; by 1930 the difference was one to five thousand (Cleary 1985: 9). Nor has the trend of decline abated; today the ratio stands at about one to seven thousand. To give some perspective on the magnitude of this problem, in the United States today the ratio is 1 priest to every 880 Catholics (Russell 1985: 59).

Thus the Church in Latin America was faced with a pastoral problem of disturbing proportion. It was virtually impossible for the Church to adequately minister its flock. Moreover, most of the clergy was involved in serving the middle and upper classes in Catholic schools and wealthier urban churches. In this situation it was often

---

[4] Veliz (1980: 190–91) offers an interesting hypothesis on the relationship between religious uniformity and political development:

[H]ad religious uniformity been achieved in the sixteenth century the political history of England and Europe would have been completely different, so different as to resemble what actually occurred in Latin America, where religious uniformity was effectively secured and institutionalized from the sixteenth century through the regalist administration of the Indies.

the case that a rural pastor might have twenty thousand or more people under his care (Berryman 1987: 13).

Beyond the problem of numbers alone, the pastoral difficulties were further complicated by the fact that many Latin Americans, particularly those in the rural areas, practiced a form of Catholicism that differed widely from the official version (Berryman 1984: 28). In these conditions, what scholars would later call "popular Catholicism" took root (Berryman 1987: 11), and this popular religion would remain a defining feature of the Church's relationship with many of its Latin American members. Characterized by highly localized, often excessively ritualistic, forms of worship, popular Catholicism was of necessity tolerated by the Church. And while the particular ways in which popular religion was practiced may have presented difficulties for official Church representatives, over the course of decades the model of a decentralized church implicit in these practices was turned from a potential liability into an asset.

By the late 1950s and early 1960s, many priests, sisters and lay workers began to pursue this decentralized model in the form of what became known as "Christian Base Communities." These base communities were originally born out of desire on the part of the Church's official representatives to engage in a form of evangelization that would be effective in the specific conditions of the continent (Berryman 1984: 31). What was needed, as the phenomenon of popular religion had shown, was a reduction in the scale of interaction between church and people, a form of instruction that was relevant to the specific context at hand, and the formation of a stronger sense of community and belonging on the part of Catholics who were isolated from traditional Church structures. These developments were no doubt also spurred on by the growth of Protestantism on the continent beginning in the late nineteenth century. With its emphasis on accessible worship and lay pastors, Protestant practices may have provided an example and impetus for the development of base communities. There were also antecedents in the Catholic Church itself. In the 1950s, organizations like Catholic Action, the Christian Family Movement and the Young Christian Workers provided additional models that extended the influence of the Church beyond the parish walls (Berryman 1987: 64–66; 1984: 30–31).

Base communities were thus pragmatic solutions to the particular pastoral problems facing the Church in Latin America. But for many Church agents, their participation in these communities was also a profoundly unsettling experience in consciousness-raising. One reason was the wide disparity between how educated Church representatives, and how the locals themselves, understood the meanings of various religious practices. As I intimated earlier, local communities tended to practice forms of worship that were at odds with orthodox theological understandings. For example, in performing a baptism a priest might believe he was taking away original sin; for locals, however, baptism might be understood as a kind of medicine against illness or a magical shield against future harm (Berryman 1987: 69).

Many of these pastoral agents responded by trying to teach a more spiritual, interiorized form of religion; this was the orthodoxy they had come to know (Berryman 1987: 70). These efforts were in many instances successful in displacing popular religion, but in other cases they merely served to exacerbate the alienation of local communities from the Church. Others involved in these communities took a different tack. They began to ask whether popular religion couldn't be understood as an expression of needs that the practices of the established Church were unable to address. Why couldn't interpretations of Church sacraments as magical and mystical protections be understood as a logical response by individuals who were unable to grasp the real causes of hunger, infant mortality and powerlessness? Since most peasants were illiterate and ignorant of modern scientific culture, couldn't their popular religion be seen as nothing more—nor less—than an understandable cultural response that gave people hope in an otherwise hopeless situation?

For many of the Church's agents, then, the effect of their base community experiences was a recognition that the institutional practices of orthodox Catholicism did not meet the needs of the Latin American poor. As a consequence, leaders in many base communities began to shift their emphasis away from purely religious and toward secular concerns. Many of these base communities became educative and organizing centers, emphasizing literacy training and local development projects. And the educative philosophy they usually followed was by no means pacifying, for it was Paulo Freire's method of *conscientização*, or consciousness-raising, that informed their efforts (Berryman 1984: 32–38; see chapter 5 for a discussion of Freire's work).

The shift toward secular projects and political empowerment was not particularly problematic in the early sixties. In fact, many of the reformist civilian governments across the continent supported and encouraged these efforts as a means of mobilizing the population. They seemed to fit well with the prevailing mood at the time. But all of this was to soon change.

This brings me to the second important factor in understanding the context in which liberation theology emerged, and that is the set of social and political changes that have taken place in Latin America since 1960. In the early 1960s, the Alliance for Progress, the policies of the Kennedy administration, and the rise of reformist democratic movements in several countries of the continent—notably Chile, Brazil, Venezuela, Peru and Colombia—all signalled a new era of hope for peaceful but steady economic and social reform in Latin America. Unfortunately, these efforts were under siege from both the Left and the Right for having failed to produce quickly enough the benefits of modernization.

Faced with what they thought was the imminent danger of communistic tendencies among much of the populace, and indeed within many of the civilian regimes themselves, the military in a number of countries took matters into their own hands. Military coups toppled one civilian reformist regime after another, and by the end of the decade the ideology of national security, Latin American style, had become firmly entrenched across the continent.

This is all familiar enough.[5] What I want to note here is the impact these developments had on the Latin American Church.

For its part, the military believed that it was offering the Church an opportunity to play a central role in defense of what was called "Western Christian Civilization." According to the ideological tenets of this view, the main enemy threatening the nation was communism, which, because it was also atheistic, threatened to destroy the Church as well. Given these premises, this common enemy, it was often argued that the Church could protect itself only by supporting the military regimes. Moreover, the system of national security that the military offered gave the Church a privileged position it had lost at the end of the colonial era. By guaranteeing, for instance, the teaching of religious doctrine in public schools, censorship of publications contrary to the interests of the Church or its official ethics, state defense of certain canon laws, especially those concerning family or public morality, and so on, the national security state was touted as the only means of securing the interests of the Church in Latin America (Comblin 1979a: 79–81).

These offers were tempting, and many Catholics, both lay and clergy, embraced the new political situation on religious grounds. Others, including many of those who were actively involved in the grass-roots base communities, refused to accept the changed political situation.

It should come as no surprise that when the developmental process collapsed and the military installed itself in power, repression of these grass-roots communities became one of the first orders of business. After all, one of the consequences of base community emphases on

[5] See the discussions in chapters 4 and 5.

literacy and political empowerment was to increase the political agitation of the poor and raise their demands on government. But the effect of repression was often further radicalization. In many contexts grass-roots communities became training grounds for popular resistance movements. And in others, where this resistance turned into armed rebellion, it was the grass roots communities that continued to serve as a focal point of organization. In other words, there was a more or less direct line of development from the secular emphases in many of these base communities, to involvment in popular resistance organizations, to armed guerilla uprisings (Berryman 1984: 35).

In part, liberation theology drew its themes and support from the developments I have thus far discussed. From the pastoral problem facing the Church and the rise of base-communities, liberation theology took its demand that the Church must "go to the poor." From the emerging criticisms of orthodox Church practices, liberation theology took a perspective that would give rise to its call for "the liberation of theology." And from opposition to repression of the poor, it called forth a criticism of existing social and political practices, which, when linked to its other constituent themes, would demand nothing less than a political commitment on the part of Christians to become part of the struggles of the poor and the oppressed. But these themes may never have been systematically articulated in a "theology of liberation" had it not been for changes in the Church that were initiated in Rome itself.

This brings me to the third factor that contributed to the development of liberation theology. In August of 1968, the Latin American bishops held a plenary meeting at Medellin, Colombia. Its ostensible purpose was to consider how the directives that had come out of the Second Vatican Council (Vatican II) called by Pope John 23, which met from 1962 to 1965, would apply to Latin America. The agenda for Vatican II was for the most part set by European theologians, and most of the issues it dealt with were church-centered. But the overall thrust of the council was a radical shift in the way the Church's mission in the modern world was to be understood (Cleary 1985: 21–27).

Among the initiatives Vatican II had encouraged was the use of the vernacular in the performance of mass. Eliminating the requirement that Church services be performed in Latin was a relatively radical step, but it was just one example of how the council redefined the way in which the Church was to meet its contemporary challenges. Two of these redefinitions in particular were to have a profound influence on the Latin American bishops. One was Vatican II's call for a reconsideration of the method of theological reflection, which did nothing less than turn traditional theology on its head. Instead of proceeding from theological or biblical principles and then applying them to present-day situations, Vatican II encouraged theologians to begin from an analysis of the present, the so-called "signs of the times," which would then inform scriptural and theological reflection, as well as the development of pastoral strategies suitable to the particular situation at hand (Cleary 1985: 59–65). Another redefinition that influenced the Latin American bishops was a pronounced tendency to link the Church's mission with struggles for social justice. Several social encyclicals that were authorized by Vatican II were laced with an emphasis on the sanctity of human rights, condemnation of economic exploitation and inequalities, and calls for a moral economy.

The bishops at Medellin took these themes from Vatican II and—in Edward Cleary's (1985: 26) apt phrase—Latinamericanized them. No one, however, expected them to author the sort of radical document that emerged from their meeting. Indeed, their pronouncements went well beyond what was called for by Vatican II, and it has even been suggested that the bishops at Medellin penned some of the most radical claims in the history of the Church (Cleary 1985: 41–44; Berryman 1987: 22–24). But in light of the discontents on the continent, the fact that the Latin American bishops turned the initiatives opened by Vatican II toward radical ends made clear sense.

Reading the "signs of the times" in Latin America, the bishops argued that the situation of the vast majority of Latin Americans was sinful and unjust. This situation, they went on, was caused by two massive evils: the domination of Latin America by outside powers, and the internal colonialism that resulted from this domination. The bishops also agreed that theological reflection in light of these "signs" indicated that the Church had to choose sides in the struggle for social justice—and the side it had to choose was that of the poor and oppressed. And as for the form of pastoral action in which this "preferential option for the poor" was to be realized, the bishops endorsed the model of grass roots, base communities.

Much of the tone of the Medellin document can be attributed to the influence of those who would become known as liberation theologians, and in particular Gustavo Gutierrez, a Peruvian theologian. Gutierrez first coined the term "theology of liberation" in a paper presented in early 1968 at a preparatory meeting for the Medellin conference. In that document, Gutierrez articulated the discontent of many critics of the Latin American scene by boldly asserting that it was liberation, not development, that was needed on the continent. These themes are clearly evident in the Medellin document, but it is not entirely correct to say that Medellin was *the* embodiment of liberation theology. For what Medellin lacked, and what liberation theology would eventually provide, was a systematic political theology that would enable Christians to see their struggles for political empowerment as legitimate expressions of their faith.

This theology, with its roots in the base community experience, the repressive atmosphere in many Latin American countries, and the shifts in perspective authorized by Vatican II and given first airing at Medellín, is still in the process of developing. In this development it has become more than simply a Catholic, or a Latin American, phenomenon. But if we are to clearly grasp the ways in which liberation theology has been, and must be, articulated to fit different contexts, we would be well advised to keep in mind the fact that it began from and emerged out of a constellation of practical needs that demanded nothing less than a radical reconstruction of faith itself.

THE "SECOND STEP": TOWARD A PRACTICAL THEOLOGY

The theology of liberation does not begin from an unpremised reflection on the role of faith in human existence. Unlike traditional theology, liberation theology sees itself as being inextricably bound up in a particular historical situation. Rather than asking how the word of God is to be universally interpreted (a task the liberation theologians see as impossible in any case), the liberation theologians ask how the word of God is to be interpreted in terms of a specific commitment to the struggle against oppression. As "a critical reflection on Christian praxis in light of the Word" (Gutierrez 1973a: 13), it is the "reflection about facts and experience which have already evoked a response from Christians" (Bonino 1975: 61; see also Fierro 1977: 182–83). Liberation theology, in other words, aims to serve as the theological expression of struggles for empowerment. It is a practical theology having emancipatory intent.

Liberation theology is therefore historically and contextually embedded; its theological dimension is inseparable from its contextual grounding, and its aim or purpose is to assist Christians engaged in the struggle against oppression in understanding that their struggle is a legitimate expression of their faith. How might such a theology be articulated? In an interesting sense, the way the liberation theologians answer this question recapitulates the logic of liberation theology's intellectual and political development. Just as it cannot be said that liberation theology was "first developed and then people began to follow the course of action appropriate to it" (Bonino 1975: 61), neither can a practical theology "know" the appropriate course to follow independently of a clear understanding of the context from which it emerges, and to which it is directed.

What this suggests is that liberation theology seeks to be more than simply a "sanctified" version of ideologies that might inform empowerment struggles. A liberation theology cannot abandon the demand for rationally defensible, empirically hard-headed analysis or it becomes virtually indistinguishable from the kinds of theology and social theory that underwrite the oppressive practices it opposes. But this is not to say that liberation theology subscribes to a particular model of knowledge only because it fits its emancipatory intent, for in fact what distinguishes an adequate practical theology from those theological and social theoretic claims that perpetuate oppression is its recognition that "the realism of knowledge is not measured in terms of its conformity with what *is* but rather in terms of what *can be*, thanks to human action" (Fierro 1977: 91).

A sketch outline of this understanding may be reconstructed by first considering the reasons why the liberation theologians believe there is a need to "liberate theology" from its orthodox expressions. Because of its particular context of origin and application, orthodox theology has been almost exclusively concerned with meeting the "spiritual" needs of believers, as well as articulating an understanding of faith that is capable of meeting what Gustavo Gutierrez calls "the challenge of the non-believer." For Latin American theologians, such concerns are simply out of place. In the first place, Latin American Christians are faced with a context in which a concern for "spiritual" needs appears morally and ethically irresponsible, if not pernicious:

> The socioeconomic, political, and cultural situation of the Latin American peoples challenges our Christian conscience. Unemployment, malnutrition, alcoholism, infant mortality, illiteracy, prostitution, an ever-increasing inequality between the rich and the poor, racial and cultural discrimination, exploitation, and so forth are facts that define a situation of institutionalized violence in Latin America. (*Christians for Socialism* 1972: part 1, 1.1; quoted in Bonino 1975: 21–22)

Much the same can be said of orthodox theology's preoccupation with "the challenge of the non-believer." For in Latin America, these concerns are actually superfluous given the widespread acceptance of Christianity. And in light of the kinds of injustices that give rise to a theological displacement of "spiritual" concerns, it is perhaps understandable that the liberation theologians would see the need for a theological displacement of the challenge of the nonbeliever:

> In a continent like Latin America the challenge does not come in the first place from the non-believer but from the non-man. . . . The non-man does

not question so much our religious world, as our economic, social, political and cultural world. (Gutierrez 1974: 78–79)

What defines the particular demands of "faith" is, then, in part determined by the needs of a particular context in which faith is practiced. For the liberation theologians, the context of faith in Latin America is a context marked by a variety of socioeconomic, political and cultural oppressions. Because orthodox theology has been concerned with a completely different set of questions derived from a different context, its conceptual tools are inadequate for understanding, and its practices are deficient for adequately attending, the needs of many Latin American Christians.

For these reasons the liberation theologians were led to ask whether orthodox theology was conceptually and practically deficient because of deeper philosophical problems that made it systematically unable to read "the signs of the times" embodied in the life experiences of the Latin American poor. As they see it, orthodox theology suffers from a highly problematic idealism and "dogmatic positivism" (Vidales 1979: 36). On the one hand, orthodox theology subscribes to an idealism that assumes the meaning of faith can be understood independently of the historical and practical contexts in which it is embedded. On the other hand, this idealist conception of faith recapitulates a conception of theological knowledge that assumes "truth belongs . . . to a universe complete in itself, which is copied or reproduced in 'correct' propositions, in a theory (namely, a contemplation of this universe) which corresponds to this truth" (Bonino 1975: 88).

But this self-understanding flies in the face of what Jose Miguez Bonino says are three facts that undermine its presuppositions:

1. The demise of metaphysics has made reference to a transcendent reality largely irrelevant.
2. The socio-analytic sciences have demonstrated that the *meaning* of Christianity and the understanding of "faith," have always been historically bound.
3. The Bible itself undermines this conception of truth; it presupposes, rather, a different notion of "truth" understood as a "right doing," not simply a "right thinking" or "right speaking." (1975: 92–93; see also Vidales 1979: 36–39)

In subsequent sections of this chapter I shall take up these claims in more detail. For the moment, however, it is sufficient to note that for the liberation theologians, the deficiencies of orthodox theology are seen as evidence of its having virtually abandoned the classical understanding of theology as rational knowledge (Gutierrez 1973a: 6; Bonino 1975: 92).

This claim, of course, only raises the philosophical ante higher, for it begs the question of what would count as "rational knowledge." I have already intimated that the answer to this question turns in part on how well theology can read "the signs of the times." And in this respect, liberation theology may be distinguished from orthodox theology by virtue of its commitment to seeing theological reflection as a "second step." For only a theology that "presupposes the voice of the human sciences, the social sciences in particular, as its first or preliminary theological word" (Vidales 1979: 41) will be adequate to the practical demands of modern social and political life.

While generally speaking liberation theology accepts the need to ground its theological reflection in the findings of the social sciences, this acceptance is not undiscriminating. This may in part be seen in the way that the liberation theologians, like the dependency theorists and Freire, draw out distinctions between social scientific explanations of the Latin American situation. As we have seen in previous chapters, development in the "received" view is usually counterposed with the concept of underdevelopment, the former being characteristically associated with the socioeconomic features of the Western capitalist nations, the latter with the situation of the Third World nations (Gutierrez 1973a: 22–25). Among the central tenets of this understanding is the idea that all societies move through distinct stages of development, and that the "developed" nations provide the model of this process (Bonino 1975: 26; 1983: 76; Gutierrez 1973a: 24). But the theory of "developmentalism," when translated into practical strategies for guiding policy, does not in fact produce what it promises. This is particularly the case in the Third World, for the "underdevelopment" of Third World societies is not a matter of their failure to follow the model of the "developed" societies, but a function of their relationship with the developed societies:

> When we realize that development and underdevelopment are not two successive stages in an abstract and mechanical process but two dimensions of one single historical movement, it becomes evident that Latin America has to be studied as the *dependent* or dominated part in that process. (Bonino 1975: 26–27; see also Gutierrez 1973a: 84–88)

This turn from "developmentalism" to an analysis of "dependent development" is, for the liberation theologians, "a key element in the interpretation of Latin American reality" (Gutierrez 1973a: 85). Moreover, it is understood as "a major scientific achievement in Latin American sociology" (Bonino 1975: 27). But more than this is implied in the liberation theologians' appropriation of dependency theory. For the liberation theologians, as for the dependency theorists and Freire, the deficiencies of developmentalism are not just theoretical and practical; they are at root philosophical. As Bonino argues, "The theory of development which was applied to the third world rests on an unhistorical and mechanistic analysis (dependent on functionalist sociology)" (Bonino 1975: 26).

If theology is going to read "the signs of the times" correctly, then it must initially turn to the social sciences. But in doing so it must be attentive to the claims of these sciences at the theoretical and metatheoretical levels because "a practical connotation is part and parcel of science, or knowledge, or theory (and also philosophy when and if it is accorded meaningfulness at all)" (Fierro 1977: 91).

Clearly the liberation theologians, like other critical theorists, reject "the analytical and positivist ideal of science" (Fierro 1977: 88) that underwrites social theories of the type one finds in developmentalism. But what kind of alternative conception of knowledge is open? Here the liberation theologians are also at one with other critical theorists, for it is in Marxism that they find "a framework of study open to the dynamism of history and to a projective view of human activity" (Bonino 1975: 34–35).

Many interpreters have assumed that the liberation theologians' appropriation of Marxism is a mistake, and at two levels. The first we have to some extent already seen: In its appropriation of Marxism, liberation theology is simply following through to the philosophical level its commitment to taking the social sciences as its "preliminary theological word." This is why liberation theology is distinguished from orthodox theology; it is also the basis of criticisms that liberation theology has abandoned "true" theology. Of course we have already seen, and will later consider in more detail, the reasons why the liberation theologians think this sort of claim is mistaken. But there is also a second charge that is often made in criticisms of liberation theology's appropriation of Marxism: that this appropriation implicates liberation theology in a dogmatic, "materialist," metaphysical system that is antithetical to anything like a religious faith.

But it would be a mistake to assume, as so many have, that liberation theology's appropriation of Marxism is uncritical.[6] What is often "taken for granted" is that "Christianity is opposed to Marxism on account of the latter's materialism" (Bonino 1976: 94) and the former's

[6] For an excellent overview—and critique—of the way the liberation theologians' appropriation of Marxism has been greeted (and misunderstood) by the Vatican, see Kroger (1985), Berryman (1987: 185–200), and Boff and Boff (1986).

"spiritualism." For the liberation theologians, however, "where Marxism . . . is concerned, neither the profession of faith on the part of the Soviet Academy of Sciences nor the horror expressed by the Congregation of the Doctrine of the Faith has any validity" (Boff and Boff 1986: 67).

The reason for this claim is that, like other critical theorists, the liberation theologians recognize that orthodox Marxism distorts the philosophical insights and practical intentions Marx himself articulated. As they argue, "Dialectical materialism and historical materialism are conceived by some as a metaphysical theory, an absolute philosophical formulation" (Bonino 1975: 96), but "Marxism cannot be a metaphysics, without betraying itself" (Segundo 1984: 194). To assume this stance is to transform Marxism into yet another form of "positivism." It entails conceptualizing human beings not as "free beings," but as mere objects subject to "the determinism that pervades the rest of the cosmos" (Miranda 1980: 32). The problems here are familiar enough; we have seen them (and will later see them) expressed in the critiques of Marxism found in other critical theories. But it is worth noting that like these other critics, the liberation theologians recognize that "If there is no subject to engage in revolutionary activity, then materialism consists in contemplation and we are stuck with a philosophy that proposes to interpret the world rather than change it" (Miranda 1980: 29). Indeed, without some conception of the possibility of "critical subjectivity," "all one gets is the passivity of a spectator pretending to be a decisive actor" (Segundo 1984: 181). Thus, for the liberation theologians,

> a rigid Marxist orthodoxy or dogmatism is immediately rejected. Class structure, for instance, has to be studied in terms of the realities given in a dependent country. . . . The Marxist scheme cannot be taken as a dogma but rather as a method which has to be applied to our own reality in terms of this reality, and this in turn reverts to a reconsideration of the method itself. (Bonino 1975: 35)

In this respect, there is a "discontinuity" between liberation theology and Marxism insofar as the former

> now talks about concrete social classes, national income levels, sex, race, language, and all the other factors that define the real existence of human beings. It seems to be fulfilling the process that Engels prescribed for the humanism of Feuerbach: i.e., that the cult of man in the abstract had to be replaced by a scientific study of real human beings and their concrete historical development. (Fierro 1977: 106)

It should now be clear that the liberation theologians see their engagement with orthodox theology, social scientific theories of development, and Marxism, as related moments in any attempt to rethink "a new definition of the relationship between theory and praxis" (Fierro 1977: 88–89). How, then, is an emancipatory practice—and theology—to be understood? And more specifically, what contribution does a theology of liberation make to a potentially emancipatory practice? I shall take up these questions shortly, but before doing so we would be well advised to keep foremost the points thus far made.

First, the very idea of a theology of liberation has its grounding in the recognition of unnecessary suffering of the "non-man" (Gutierrez) who makes up the vast majority of the Latin American peoples. Second, an adequate account of the origins of this suffering show it to be the result of a particular kind of domination that reflects a historically contingent form of dependent development rather than the "inevitable" consequence of underdevelopment. Third, this analysis is informed by a conception of knowledge in which "the realism of knowledge is not measured in terms of its conformity with what *is* but rather in terms of its investigation of what *can be*, thanks to human action" (Fierro 1977: 91).

To put this into now-familiar terms, liberation theology recognizes the two important features of social knowledge I explicated in earlier chapters. The first is the intersubjectively constituted character of social relations; the second, the historicity of these relations. What all of this implies, moreover, is that methodology is irreducibly political. For this reason, one liberation theologian has argued that

> The only thing that can maintain the liberative character of any theology is not its content but its methodology . . . [for] it is the methodology that ensures that the existing system will continue to look like an oppressor on the horizon of theology itself; that offers the best hope for the future of theology. (Segundo 1976: 39–40)

But, to return to the question I posed earlier, in what ways does this theological appropriation of critical theory affect a radical rethinking of the role of theology and true meaning of Christianity? For one, it gives a critical Christianity a more realistic temper. As Gutierrez argues, "It has and still does cost a great deal for Christians to enter into this new outlook."

> Thanks to it, however, they are moving away from the half-truths that have been so much in circulation. One such half-truth, commonly heard in Christian circles, asserted that it did little or no good to alter social structures if the heart of human beings did not undergo any change. And this

was a half-truth because it ignored the fact that "hearts" can also be transformed by altering socio-cultural structures. Both aspects, in other words, are interdependent and complementary because they are grounded in a common unity. [But] the view that a structural transformation will automatically produce different human beings is no more and no less "mechanistic" than the view that a "personal change of heart" will automatically lead to a transformation of society. Any such mechanistic views are naive and unrealistic. (Gutierrez 1979: 11)

Moreover, it enables the possibility of seeing that "It is not the simple interpretation, but the transformation of the world, which occupies the central place of the theologian's concern" (Assmann 1975: 30–31). But if the liberation theologians are to make good their theological rendering of Marx's Eleventh Thesis, then they cannot remain strictly at the level of socioanalytic discourse, even if it must be a practical theology's "preliminary theological word." As Jose Miguez Bonino says, although the theologian must accept his location as a social agent within a particular social formation, he nonetheless intends to do *theology* (1983: 42–43). And so we return to the issue with which I began this section: the status of theology itself.

THE LIBERATION OF THEOLOGY

There can be no doubt that the appearance of liberation theology presents a real problem for ecclesiastical authorities, both Protestant and Catholic. But while the liberation theologians have come under attack for failing to abide by theological orthodoxies, their alternative is not merely a "sanctified ideology." The understanding of theology they advance may well be grounded in a recognition of the importance of nontheological, or social scientific, knowledge, but the insights they glean from these inquiries are not without implications for understanding what theology itself is and can be. These implications can be articulated by considering the ways in which orthodox theology and ecclesiastical practices are themselves integrally related to political practices that sustain oppression and domination.

Given the historical propensity of Christian churches to accommodate themselves to established—and all too often repressive—political regimes in Latin America, one central conflict between the liberation theologians and orthodox ecclesiastical authorities lies in the fact that "even the minimum content of liberation theology . . . literally constitutes a political crime today" in those countries where its development has been most notable (Segundo 1976: 4). But in trying to silence the liberation theologians, orthodox critics have merely reinforced the realization on the part of many Latin Americans committed to social justice that the idea of a church cannot be separated from the practices of a church that is clearly linked to continued suffering.

Thus, this propensity for accommodation does not occur in a theoretical/theological vacuum. In fact, it is reinforced by traditional understandings of the temporal role of the Christian believer. In recent years, the effects of Vatican II and the articulation of a "social doctrine" in the Church appeared to clear a theological space for political action, yet the Vatican has seldom been accused of mixing politics and religion. The reason is that this social doctrine represents nothing more than a continued call for Christians to exercise a moral rather than a political option.[7] For the liberation theologians, this distinction is itself a kind of "political theology," and if we are to clearly grasp its deficiencies, we need to understand its origins. I turn, then, to one crucial example of how liberation theology turns the "preliminary theological word" provided by the social sciences toward a critical examination of the foundations of theology itself.

The Critique of the Historical Church

When seen in terms of the relation between the spiritual and temporal spheres, the history of Christian orthodoxy may be understood as involving two general "political theologies," each grounded in a particular historical context that shaped it, and both of which are rejected by liberation theology. The first of these perspectives, historically speaking, is what the liberation theologians call Constantinianism; the second I shall call (for the sake of brevity) post-Constantinianism.

The political theology of Constantinianism took shape in that period of Western history marked by a close unity of faith and social life (Gutierrez 1973a: 54). Actually, "Constantinianism" is used as a shorthand term to cover roughly fifteen hundred years of Church history, from the Edict of Milan (A.D. 313) to the revolutionary upheavals of the sixteenth century (Fierro 1977: 48). We need not detain ourselves with charges that the term is "generic" and thus telescopes a variety of historical vicissitudes (see Fierro 1977: 48–49). What is important here is that, whatever its variations, orthodox theology during this period had the characteristic feature of a "Christendom mentality." This mentality, as Gutierrez argues (1973a: 53–54), assumes a particular understanding of the relation between the spiritual and temporal

---

[7] For examples of the Catholic Church's new 'social doctrine', see the documents of Vatican II as well as the encyclicals of Paul IV and John Paul II.

spheres, and a concomitant account of the temporal (or political) duties of believers.

With respect to the former, Constantinianism regards the temporal sphere as having no meaningful autonomy from the spiritual. In this, temporal realities "are not regarded by the Church as having an authentic existence," and as a result "it therefore uses them for her own ends." In light of this theological account, "the Church feels justified in considering itself as the center of the economy of salvation and therefore presenting itself as a powerful force in relation to the world." The temporal duties of the Christian thus also had a very precise meaning: "to work for the direct and immediate benefit of the Church," and " 'Christian politics,' therefore, will mean assisting the Church in its evangelizing mission and safeguarding the Church's interests" (Guttierez 1973a: 53–54).

This "Christendom mentality" should not, however, be thought of as the result of a "pure" theological reflection. "It is above all a fact, indeed the longest historical experience the Church has had" (Gutierrez 1973a: 53). Putting the temporal sphere under the spiritual authority of the Church was thus a sociological reality *and* a theological ideal. As Yves Congar has noted, "The Church did not face an autonomous world, since society was ordered toward serving the ends of eternal salvation according to rules determined by the Church" (quoted in Gutierrez 1977: 59). "Christianity," the pursuit of true faith, *was* "Christendom"—a specific social, political and religious culture that dominated Western history for centuries. Nonetheless, Constantinianism still adhered to a distinction between the temporal and spiritual realms, even while making the one subservient to the other.

This perspective would not long stand as theological orthodoxy. With the strains put on the church-state relationship during the late medieval and early modern periods, Christians were faced with the problem of deciding how to act in an increasingly secularized temporal realm. Luther provided one of the most influential new accounts. His view, according to one Protestant liberation theologian, was grounded in what Luther saw as a "fatal confusion" inherent in the model of Christendom in Constantinianism: "ecclesiastical authorities, in the name of the Church, had become earthly rulers, while secular powers were claiming authority in spiritual matters" (Bonino 1983: 23). For him, then, the "two kingdoms" and the respective authority of each had been conflated, and the result was a distortion of both.

While the immediate aim of Luther's arguments was to settle a jurisdictional dispute between temporal and spiritual authorities by delineating the spheres of life with which each was to be concerned, the historical effect of his theological reformation was to eventually call into question the meaning of the doctrine of the two kingdoms.

By drawing a clear distinction between the authority of the two realms, Luther made possible a kind of dualistic thinking that would later be used to justify an absolute separation of faith and politics, church and state. Because the theological foundation of political action cannot, on Luther's account, "be named," since to do so would subject the secular sphere to the authority of spiritual demands, "Christian" political ethics were shaped by "a fixed and rigid structure determined by the prevailing social and political institutions; thus the existing secular order determines the concrete course of Christian love." In this, "political ethics then becomes a rather formal 'mandate,' the concrete content of which is autonomously determined by 'the world' " (Bonino 1983: 25). As a result, Luther's doctrine of the two kingdoms was often deployed "to justify the absolute claims of political power and to champion an almost blind acceptance of 'the powers that be' " (Bonino 1983: 24). The doctrine of the two kingdoms, in other words, had simply been changed from one in which spiritual authority reigned supreme to one in which temporal authority did.

The Catholic version of political theology that was formulated in response to the decline of Constantinian Christendom and the rise of the Reformation also drew a clear distinction between the spiritual and temporal realms. Here, as with Protestantism, the autonomy of the temporal sphere was asserted, especially in relation to ecclesiastical authority. In this the relation of the Church to the world had been modified profoundly. Although the Church continues to be at the center of the work of salvation, a Christian political ethic no longer follows directly from the defense of Church interests, but from the need to realize conditions that are merely favorable to the temporal activities of the Church. Thus, the political theology of post-Constantinian Catholicism emphasizes "the famous distinction between acting 'as a Christian as such' and acting 'as a Christian':

> In the first case [as in Constantinianism], the Christian acts as a member of the Church, and his actions represent the ecclesial community. . . . In the second case the Christian acts under the inspiration of Christian principles but assumes exclusive personal responsibility for his actions; this gives him greater freedom in his political commitments. (Gutierrez 1973a: 56)

I have suggested that both Protestantism and post-Constantinian Catholicism represent a second perspective on political theology. By this I do not mean to suggest that they are not in many ways different. Clearly Protestant political theology involves a much more radical separation of the temporal and spiritual spheres than does Catholicism. But while these differences are important, their similarities should not be overlooked. Both share a tendency to increase the separation of spiritual and temporal authority, as well as defining the content of a specifically Christian political ethic in highly circumscribed ways.

For the liberation theologians, post-Contantinianism represents a progressive moment in the development of an adequate political theology. By eliminating any causal connection between the earthly and spiritual kingdoms, post-Constantinianism opens the possibility that Christians can maintain a skeptical attitude regarding claims advanced by temporal regimes:

> This eschatological relativization of any and every existing historical reality, this desacralization of any and every political regime, initially has a liberating impact. It disestablishes the world we know; it deabsolutizes the hallowedness that any and every political regime claims in order to perpetuate itself and deny its historical relativity. (Segundo 1976: 144)

In other words, in the face of the radical breakdown of Constantinian Christendom, in both theory and practice, post-Constantinianism preserved the ideal of "Christendom" by radically separating it from an unproblematic identification with any existing political community. This has the advantage of not only rejecting any "sacralizing" claims on the part of political regimes, but also claims to political authority on the part of ecclesiastical regimes. But in spite of these positive, progressive possibilities, post-Constantinianism has not been able to realize them, and this because of the link between its commitment to preserve "Christendom" and the conception of political ethics that followed from this commitment.

By distinguishing between the roles of Christians *qua* citizens, and the roles of Christians *qua* Christians, contemporary orthodox theology assumed "a separation between dogmatic and moral theology" (Fierro 1977: 73). As citizens, Christians were to "evangelize and to inspire the temporal order, without directly intervening" (Gutierrez 1973a: 64), while as members of the community of the faithful they were to remain committed to their belief in the timeless and absolute values of the faith. Thus, Christian ethics

> had to do with the ethico-political consequences of dogma, with Christian love and Christian action as consequences of faith; but it did not have to do with the faith itself. It was political theology insofar as it embodied a social morality based on dogma and logically flowing from it. (Fierro 1977: 72–73)

The reason this ethics has nothing to do with "faith itself" is that orthodox theology's separation of the temporal and spiritual spheres also presupposes a distinction between the identity of Christian and temporal communities. As Fierro puts it, "Needless to say, there is no direct political thesis in the theological notion that Christians mystically form one body in Christ. This notion applies to the church, to an order of spiritual communion and communication, not to civil society and political organization" (Fierro 1977: 62–63). To profess one's "faith" is to therefore profess what one shares with other Christians, not with all members of the political community.

For the liberation theologians, however, the crucial question to be asked is what the content of this shared "faith" actually entails. The Christendom mentality of the Constantinian period reflected a historical situation in which the Church was faced with the problem of securing and maintaining its dominant worldly status. Hence the emphasis on the Augustinian principle, *extra ecclesiam nulla salus*— outside the church there is no salvation—which in this context meant not only professing a particular faith, but acting out that faith by serving the political interests of the Church. Post-Constantinianism shifted the emphasis toward profession alone. This was understandable: faced with a world in which the bifurcation of the "two kingdoms" was now a reality rather than merely a threat, post-Constantinian theology has tried to preserve the unity of Christianity against the centrifugal tendencies of the modern(izing) age. In this, Protestantism and Catholicism increasingly emphasized a theological outlook in which

> the internal unity of a Christian church can be maintained . . . only by minimizing and playing down the radical historical oppositions that divide its members. In other words, one must pass over in silence such matters as color, social class, political ideology, the national situation, and the place of the country in the international market. At the same time one must stress the values that are presumably shared by all the members of the Church in question. (Segundo 1976: 42)

None of this would perhaps be particularly problematic if not for the fact Bonino noted in his discussion of Luther: post-Constantinian theology has shaped a doctrine of the two kingdoms that has been used to justify "absolute claims to political power and to champion an almost blind acceptance of 'the powers that be' " (Bonino 1983: 25). Here we arrive at the gist of the liberation theologians' critique of the historical Church. Just as Constantinianism had often been deployed as a justification for the most brutal sorts of politics, so too has post-Constantinianism. This has given rise to what Gutierrez has called "the crisis of the distinction of planes model" (1973a: 63–77). By drawing clear boundaries between the "planes," or realms, of faith and temporal reality, orthodox theology authorizes a conception of pastoral action that is at odds with the realities of the pastoral activities of practicing Christians. The limits of the vision of orthodox theology can be clearly seen in the context of the Latin American situation, where the orthodox injunction of noninterference in political affairs simply cannot be maintained. In this particular context, where people are "more keenly and painfully aware that a large part of the Church is in one way or another linked to those who wield economic and political power in today's world," we must ask if the Church is really fulfilling "a purely religious role when by its silence or friendly relationships it lends legitimacy to a dictatorial and oppressive government" (Gutierrez 1973a: 64).

Thus, whatever the promise of post-Constantinianism, the dialectic of its development has meant that this promise has not been met. And the reason is that the "distinction of planes banner has changed hands. Until a few years ago it was defended by the vanguard; now it is held aloft by power groups, many of whom are in no way involved with any commitment to the Christian faith" (Gutierrez 1973a: 65). It is therefore tragically ironic that in Latin America, where "dominant groups, who have always used the Church to defend their privileged position," these same groups now "call for a return to the purely religious and spiritual function of the Church" (Gutierrez 1973a: 65).

Why this change, and how did it come about? For the answers to these questions we must turn to a more exhaustive critique of orthodox theology. With their recognition that the distinction of planes model holds only for certain actions (those that threaten the established order) and not for others (those that support the order), the liberation theologians have been led to see that "There is no socially uncommitted theology" (Bonino 1983: 43). For all the lip-service that defenders of orthodox theology and practice have paid to the idea that faith is a "purely spiritual" matter, the facts of that faith suggest otherwise. All of which indicates the need for a critique of theology itself.

The Critique of Orthodox Theology

The differences between orthodox theology and liberation theology are profound. At their root lie radically different accounts of how faith itself is to be understood. Perhaps the most important distinction in these accounts is that orthodox theology tends to emphasize a "purely spiritual" form of faith, while the liberation theologians insist that faith entails a commitment to act for the emancipation of all human beings, in body as well as soul. For this reason, critics have charged that liberation theology is "politically partisan" and "ideological"— charges the liberation theologians would not deny since those who usually make them assume that faith is neither partisan nor ideologically loaded.

These differences, argues Juan Luis Segundo, are clearly delineated in six ecclesiological points made by Protestant theologian C. Peter Wagner. These points are purported to be both grounded in biblical authority, and antithetical to the ideals of liberation theology. They also provide, Segundo suggests, an indication of the "real bedrock outlook underlying opposition statements from the Catholic hierarchy" (1976: 134). I cite them here because they serve as a useful point of departure for examining the liberation theologians' critique of orthodox theology:

1. The function of the Church is the individual reconciliation of all human beings with God. In this respect, all statements regarding the relation of theological reflection to specific historical contexts (like "the Latin American context") gloss over the real mission of the church, "which is to persuade men and women to be reconciled individually with God and become members of the church of Christ."

2. The primary function of the church is the salvation of souls; promoting social justice, while important, is secondary. Because they "judge evangelical theology not in terms of how true it is or how it will result in the salvation of souls, but what it will do to promote social justice," the liberation theologians subsume the primary function of the church under a secondary, and indeed derivative, function.

3. The work of Christ is properly understood as his activity through the gospel message within the Church, and not "in the world creating peace and order, justice and liberty, dignity and community."

4. The unity of the Church and membership in it is more important than any socio-economic-political option, for the latter implies "the possibility of failing to make the offer of salvation available to mankind."

5. Liberation theology does not take into account the *dualism* of the Bible and, in particular, the negative supernatural forces that rule this world. Rather it "searches for natural causes of evil."

6. Finally, liberation theology does not recognize that salvation is not a collective endeavor, but a specifically individual one. By "rejecting the *urgency of saving people from hell*," liberation theology appears to believe that "the thought of a human being cast into the lake of fire no longer has as much power to move the heart as does a ragged peasant who has become disinherited by moving into a favela."

For most of those who profess a Christian faith these will appear as compelling claims, but that serves only to confirm the extent to which they are in fact "orthodox." If the liberation theologians are to make good their alternative account of faith, then they must not only show that this orthodoxy cannot account for the actual historical practices of the church, but that it is an illusion—and a politically pernicious illusion at that.

Perhaps the major difficulty in overcoming orthodox theology is that "we are used to picturing our faith as a plane of eternal certitudes which are destined to be professed on the one hand and translated into actions on the other," but as the liberation theologians see it,

> a person's faith-inspired encounter with an objective font of absolute truth takes place in and through a process of ideological searching and has immediate ideological consequences. No one links up with absolute truth except in an effort to give truth and meaning to one's life. There is [always] an *ideological* intention at work. (Segundo 1976: 107–9)

Here we see how liberation theology has appropriated the insights of "the sociology of knowledge, which makes it abundantly clear that we always think out of a definite context of relations and action, out of a given praxis" (Bonino 1975: 90). And when we consider the "ideological intention" at work in orthodox theology's conception of faith, we must recognize that it was shaped by a context in which faith was being buffeted by secularizing tendencies and a constellation of political and intellectual forces that threatened to turn Christianity into nothing more than a political tool for contending interests. Thus did orthodox theology begin to articulate the mutually reinforcing ideals of a privatized faith, and the "purely spiritual" identity of the church.

Juan Luis Segundo analyzes at length this "ideological infiltration of dogma" (1976: 40–47). Taking the concepts of sacrament, Christian unity, and God as points of reference, Segundo shows how orthodox theology, in the name of a "pure faith," actually reinforces the status quo, while at the same time showing that these themes are theologically suspect. With respect to the concept of sacrament, orthodox theology subscribes to an *ahistorical* understanding: masses are held year in and year out with very little change, regardless of what is happening in the lives of human beings. "Except in minor details, the Sunday Mass remains the same before and after a general disaster, an international crisis, and a thoroughgoing revolution" (1976: 40). The very concept of sacrament is interpreted as having a timeless character that guarantees religious efficacy. But what we are seeing is a sacramental theology in practice that has no exegetical foundation. The simple fact of the matter is that the New Testament (from which

Christianity purportedly derives its concept of sacrament) provides no support for a religious efficacy that is expressed merely in ritual. Indeed, the New Testament repeatedly emphasizes the condemnation of ritual insofar as it "is based on the assumption that the grace of God was not given once and for all [in the offering of the body of Christ] but must [rather] be won over and over again in and through such rituals."[8]

In light of this hermeneutic reflection we must ask if it is "by chance . . . that this conception and practice of the sacraments dovetails perfectly with the interests of the ruling classes and is one of the most powerful ideological factors in maintaining the status quo" (Segundo 1976: 41). The only answer to the question is that orthodox sacramental practices involve a radical misinterpretation of the Bible itself—a misinterpretation that has ideological roots.

This sort of misreading is also manifest in what Paul Ricoeur has called the "ideological screen" embodied in "the ideology of conciliation at any price" (quoted in Bonino 1975: 120). Orthodox theology grounds its emphasis on the need for maintaining the unity of the faithful by reference to the Christian's "service of reconciliation" [2 Corinthians 5:18 ff.], and the universal reconciliation that is to come about as the result of Christ's work [Colossians 1:20]. As the liberation theologians argue, however, this understanding of the meaning of reconciliation involves the systematic attempt to avoid political confrontation, and is expressed in a highly suspect account of Christian love. This conception of reconciliation and love downplays any differences in interests that Christians may have as human beings in particular sociohistorical contexts, and emphasizes instead the laying aside of these differences as a means of expressing love for one's neighbor. "In other words, one must pass over in silence such matters as color, social class, political ideology, the national situation, and the place of the country in the international market" (Segundo 1976: 42).

But here, as in the case of sacrament, there is no biblical foundation for such an interpretation. In the Bible, Jesus' love is not expressed in "tolerance, compromise, or acceptance of evil or as good-natured, easy-going bonhomie" (Bonino 1975: 121–22). If that were the case, then it is difficult to understand Christ's condemnation of the Pharisees, or his contempt for Herod, or his driving the money-changers from the temple, or his many other criticisms of those he saw practicing injustice toward their fellows and sisters. Yet Christ still loved his enemies,

[8] See especially Mark 7:1–23; Matthew 15:1–20; Hebrews 10:9–14. Similar condemnation of cultus can be found in the Old Testament; see especially Amos 5:21–25.

and his example shows us that we should *love* our enemies, but not that we should not *have* any enemies. His example, and what it means to be Christian, to be one with Christ, is to express one's love for others by condemning injustices that prevent the possibility of establishing human brotherhood. In its narrow understanding of reconciliation and love, orthodox theology "forgets that the final eschatological reconciliation mentioned in those very texts [to which it refers] is supposed to come to pass in and through the liberation of human beings" (Segundo 1976: 44). In light of this, we must conclude "Either Jesus excluded from his love a very significant number and, what is more important, whole groups of people, or love must be interpreted in such a way that may include condemnation, criticism, resistance and rejection" (Bonino 1975: 122).

Why is this conception of reconciliation and love an ideological screen? Precisely because when it becomes the guiding ideal in those contexts where there is domination of some human beings by others, refusing to choose between the oppressed and their oppressors, orthodox theology chooses the latter by default. In short, refusing to side with the oppressed is tantamount to siding with the oppressor; indeed, the very doctrine of reconciliation in orthodox theology "reflects the point of view of the dominant class" (Girardi, quoted in Gutierrez 1973a: 275). Refusing to choose is to make a choice in support of the status quo (Gutierrez 1973a: 275; Bonino 1975: 127; Segundo 1976: 43; Alves 1979: 302). Thus, not only is the purported neutrality of the orthodox conception of reconciliation and love exposed as a political stance cloaked in apolitical language, but it also represents the outcome of an exegesis that distorts the meaning and the message of the gospels.

Finally, when we turn to the understanding of *God* that underpins orthodox conceptions of sacrament, reconciliation, and Christian love, we find the real root of orthodox theology's failures. As Segundo suggests, if we find orthodoxy hermeneutically and politically deficient in terms of the ecclesiastical attitudes reflected in the practices of sacrament, reconciliation, and love, we would be well advised to mistrust orthodox theological formulations of "God" as well (1976: 42). By asking the question: *what kind of God* lies behind these attitudes? what we find is not the profession of a faith in a particular God, but rather the expression of faiths in many gods. For the liberation theologians, what this implies is nothing less than the return of idolatry in Christianity, an idolatry that is condemned throughout the Bible itself. For what the privatization of faith has entailed is a concomitant privatization of God, and thus polytheism. Segundo puts the matter this way:

> One person pictures a God who allows dehumanization whereas another rejects such a God and believes only in a God who unceasingly fights against such things. Now those two gods cannot be the same one. (1976: 43)

Orthodoxy today authorizes the belief that simply saying we profess a faith in God has become sufficient "to avoid all confusion in our mailings to heaven," in spite of the fact that the word "refer[s] to any and every type of religious experience, even to experiences that are quite contrary to one another" (Segundo 1976: 45). But if this is the case, then formal orthodoxy cannot be seen as a sufficient guarantee against idolatry. Thus, "If we wanted to stand literally, then we would have to go back to the bygone days of *polytheism* and idolatry" (Segundo 1976: 45–47 passim).

This understanding of God is idolatrous insofar as it presupposes, at root, what was once a specifically *Greek* and now a *Western*, rather than a specifically *biblical* understanding of God (Miranda 1974: 44, 60; Segundo 1976: 46–47). What orthodox theology assumes is that God has a transcendental ontological status; that he is a "being" who can be *objectively* known. But if we take seriously what is involved in biblical prohibitions of making images of God, the condemnation of ritual as a means of "knowing God," and the exhortations that to know God is to do justice, then we must recognize that the mere acceptance of monotheism is not a sufficient guarantee that one is acting in true faith:

> If we are able to prescind from the cry of the poor who seek justice by objectifying God and believing that, because he is being, he is there as always, since being is objective and does not depend on any considerations of our minds nor on what we can or cannot do, at that very moment he is no longer God but an idol. And this is what happened to Christianity from the time it fell into the hands of Greek philosophy. (Miranda 1974: 58)

By "ontologizing" God, by giving him an existence that is outside of human history, orthodox theology simultaneously recapitulated a particular conception of knowledge understood as a contemplative appropriation of an objective reality:

> Truth belongs, for this view, to a world of truth, a universe complete in itself, which is copied or reproduced in "correct" propositions, in a theory (namely, a contemplation of this universe) which corresponds to this truth. . . . Truth is therefore preexistent to and independent of its historical effectiveness. Its legitimacy has to be tested in relation to this abstract "heaven of truth," quite apart from its historicization. (Bonino 1975: 88)

[Thus,] If by "to speak of God" we mean "to speak about God," it means absolutely nothing; it would suppose placing oneself outside that which is spoken about, in which case it would no longer be God. [For] the meaning of propositions of universal validity consists precisely in that they prescind from the concrete situation which is spoken of. But to situate myself outside the demand which God makes on my concrete existence is to speak of something else, not of God. (Miranda 1974: 43)

Here we arrive once again at the issue of the relationship between theory and practice, this time in a decidedly theological way. As Bonino suggests, what we find is that "It seems that both Scripture and social analysis yield the same answer: there is no . . . neutral knowledge" (1975: 90; see also Gutierrez 1973a: 275). Every practice, whether political or religious, is informed by a particular constellation of philosophical presuppositions, whether scientific or theological.

The real issue at the heart of liberation theology is, then, the articulation of a conception of truth that can "liberate the church from false theologies" (Comblin 1979b: 63) which have served as "a justifying ideology for a profound disorder, a device for the few to keep living off the poverty of the many" (Gutierrez 1973a: 48). What is required is a theology that would "necessarily be a criticism of society and the Church insofar as they are called and addressed by the Word of God; it would be a critical theory, worked out in the light of the Word accepted in faith and inspired by a practical purpose—and therefore indissolubly linked to historical praxis" (Gutierrez 1973a: 11). And this would be a theology of liberation because it is able to make good the insights of the liberation of theology.

THE THEOLOGY OF LIBERATION

The ultimate aim or goal of the theology of liberation is, of course, liberation. But this liberation is understood in a very specific way. It is a liberation of the oppressed of Latin America from the suffering wrought by the effects of their place on the global socioeconomic periphery, effects in part sustained by a particular understanding of the faith common to orthodox theology. It is also a liberation understood as realized not just in structural change, nor simply in a liberation of the "heart"; it is, rather, achieved through a struggle in which the oppressed free themselves. What this means for a *theology* of liberation is that "in the last analysis we will not have an authentic theology unless and until the oppressed are able to express themselves freely and creatively in society and within the people of God" (Gutierrez 1979: 24; see also Bonino 1983: 108).

Clearly what we have here is a conception of "truth" that is akin to that we find in other critical theories. But this conception of truth is complicated in the case of liberation theology, if for no other reason than the fact that as theology, liberation theology has a unique "double historical reference" (Bonino 1975: 144). On the one hand it is grounded in the particular historical context of oppression in Latin America, and in this respect it seeks out the "truth" of this context. On the other hand, it also seeks the "truth" of Christian faith. This double historical context is aptly reflected in Gutierrez's characterization of liberation theology as a critical reflection on historical practice in the light of the faith (Gutierrez 1973a: 6).

How, then, is the relationship between these two contexts, these two "truths," to be understood? Perhaps the best way to get at what is involved in this question is to ask what a specifically Christian faith tells us about what is the right, reasonable and rational action we should take in the particular contexts we find ourselves. But how we understand liberation theology's answers to these questions is first and foremost dependent on an appreciation of the insights that emerge from the critiques of developmentalism, orthodox theology, and orthodox Marxism I discussed earlier.

In one sense, all of these critiques are developed along the same lines, for what emerges from them is the recognition that politics and method share a common ground. At first sight this suggestion appears to conflate important differences between "science" and "religion," but for the liberation theologians this conflation is perhaps defensible if we consider the practical implications of these two types of discourse in terms of the Latin American context. What we find in developmentalism, orthodox theology, and orthodox Marxism is a clear gap between their respective promises and that which they can in fact produce. All promise to provide practical programs that would reduce the suffering of those who live on the margins of Latin American society, yet, as we have seen, all underwrite programs of political action that have, or would, perpetuate relations of domination. Thus, the critiques of the politics of developmentalism, orthodox theology, and orthodox Marxism find their common ground in terms of these practical considerations. And we should note that although the practical recommendations they involve are not the same, if we take the perspective of the oppressed, these differences do not amount to much more than the replacement of one form of domination with another.

But the similarities are not limited to the practical level alone. Indeed, these practical similarities reflect common methodological presuppositions. This is not to suggest that the "scientific positivism" of developmentalism and orthodox Marxism, and the "theological positivism" of orthodox theology can be readily reduced to being one and the same. But we may completely miss the radical, root similarities the two discourses share if we remain strictly at the level of their theoretical differences. Certainly a positivistic science denounces the "other worldly" character of religious faith, and clearly orthodox theology finds the affirmation of "death of God" that results from the rise of positivistic science an affront to its faith in a timeless God.

But on closer examination, each discourse may be seen as presupposing the other historically and conceptually. Moreover, their apparent mutual exclusivity is in a sense made possible because both share the same mistaken metatheoretical foundations. While the one deals with the "nature" of God, and the other the "nature" of society, both believe that these natures are objective realities, the essence of which consists in timeless, ahistorical truths. Simply stated, orthodox theology and positivist science presuppose a "reality" independent of the interpretive schemes of those who "observe" it, and that this reality is knowable "objectively." In other words, the "reality" of God and society have the same ontological status in the respective discourses, and knowledge of these realities is conceived in the same ways. Again, we should not lose sight of the fact that both discourses differ with respect to their understandings of what is known (God, the natural laws of development), but at the same time we should not forget that both share a common understanding of the way one "knows" these realities.

This gives rise to the ironic conclusion that "science" and "religion" are compatible at the practical level in their support for domination and oppression, and incompatible at the level of their respective knowledge claims, about the "reality" each refers to, *because they presuppose the same way of understanding the respective realities they purport to describe.* By assuming that the reality of human nature and social development, and the reality of God, are intelligible in terms of "objective" truths, orthodox theology, developmentalism, and orthodox Marxism, converge in their inability to provide an adequate foundation for any truly liberating political ethic. In the case of orthodox theology, what we have is the assumption of a God whose timelessness is identified with adherence to particular, historically contingent, ecclesiastical practices; in the case of developmentalism and orthodox Marxism, what we have is the assumption of "laws of development" that are identified with the political-economic institutions of bureaucratic, industrialized societies.

We can now return to the question I posed regarding the relationship between the "truth" of faith and the "truth" of the analysis of the Latin American context. What the foregoing comments suggest is that an adequate conception of truth for the liberation theologians is not a purely "theoretical" function; it is just as much a question of the practice in which one is involved. Practices that perpetuate oppression embody untruths; they are oppressive because they misdescribe the social world and God. By the same token, to know the truth about the social world and God is not to merely describe it as it is; it is not just a theoretical discovery, but points instead to a way of living one's life with and among others. A new theory does not embody truth, for this only a liberating (though theoretically informed) praxis can do. The liberation theologians' conception of the relationship between the truth of God and the truth about Latin America is, then, that *the theological and social location of the Christian are one, unified in the specific commitment to the poor* (Bonino 1983: 44).

In this we can see the reasons that liberation theologians insist that "Theology is reflection, a critical attitude" and that, as such, "Theology *follows*; it is the second step"—it is a critical reflection on practice in light of the faith (Gutierrez 1973a: 11). Theology is related to practice not as if the latter is merely the application of the former, but in the sense that practice is theology's originating foundation. When the liberation theologians speak of the method of their inquiry as the rejection of "any *logos* that is not the *logos* of a *praxis* (Assmann 1971: 87), or the "epistemological split" (Gutierrez 1973b: 16) between liberation theology and orthodox theology, or the primacy of "*orthopraxis*" over orthodoxy as "the criterion for theology" (Bonino 1975: 81), they are making clear reference to their claim that theological truth is *transformative*.

But if theological truth is to be transformative, it cannot ignore its social scientific debts. As Charles Davis argues

> Those for whom Christian faith is a form of critique as well as tradition, subversive of forms of life as well as constructive, urge the need for a critical theology alongside the usual historical and hermeneutic varieties. Such a critical theology will have two tasks: the formation and development of a critical theory of society and history, so as to provide a causal explanation of the present situation; and the initiating and fostering of critical self-reflection within the Christian community. If a critical theory of society and history produced by theology is to have an emancipatory function and provide the causal explanation self-reflection needs in order to offer an explanatory interpretation of people's actual situation in the unfree society of the present, it must arise from an investigation of the empirical data, past and present. In that sense, it must be an empirically falsifiable theory. (Davis 1980: 73)

Hence we see why the liberation theologians believe that theology must presuppose "the voice of the social sciences," and also why it appropriates a model of social science that is distinct from the kind of positivism one finds in developmentalism and orthodox Marxism. But at the same time, it would again be a mistake to reduce liberation theology to a mere "sanctified ideology," although now we must consider more closely the tension in liberation theology's "double location"; for as *theology*, liberation theology cannot dispense with its grounding in a specifically Christian tradition.

The problem here, as Juan Segundo notes, is probably the major methodological difficulty facing liberation theology: how can the relation between the two contexts of liberation theology, now seen as the social scientific and the theological, be understood as both different and complementary (1976: 154)? For the purposes of this discussion, I am going to assume that the defensibility of the social scientific self-understanding in liberation theology is adequate, and that this understanding provides good reasons for accepting liberation theology's claim that its "social location" presumes the "epistemological privilege of the poor" (Bonino 1983: 43). The question now, then, is how this social location is "unified" with the theological location, as Bonino suggests it is.

This is a complicated issue, for it cuts to the heart of the meaning of the Christian faith itself. It is (as I suggested earlier) the problem of a specifically Christian contribution to emancipation. As the liberation theologians see it, the implication of their appropriation of a critical theoretic model of social science means that, negatively, "theology cannot claim to have some 'pure kerygmatic [preached, religious— S.L.] truths or events,' unengaged, or uncompromised in a historical praxis, from where we can judge the concrete Christian obedience of a person or a community" (Bonino 1975: 99). Or, put another way, "we [end] up with the conclusion that there is no such thing as Christian theology or a Christian interpretation of the gospel message in the absence of a prior political commitment" (Segundo 1976: 94–95). This way of stating the problem obviously coincides with the critique of orthodox theology, but it also seems to preclude the possibility of saying that the "theological location of the poor" is itself anything but an arbitrary stance, chosen because of the particular location of the liberation theologians. However, the liberation theologians also see the appropriation of critical social science as having a positive consequence, for it allows us to see social scientific analysis of a particular situation as "the *unavoidable historical mediation* of Christian obedience" (Bonino 1975: 98). Still, we seem to be left with the idea that faith itself provides no basis for a particular course of action.

The simple fact of the matter is that for liberation theology faith does not provide us with any ready-made answers, and we lose sight of the truly radical nature of liberation theology if we demand that it articulate a "specifically Christian contribution" prior to a commitment that is made in light of the demands of a particular practical context. The reason is that the church cannot *know the context of her action* since obviously this type of knowledge *cannot be deduced entirely from revelation*" (Segundo 1976: 75). Indeed, as Segundo goes on to note, only on the basis of the option chosen in light of a sociological understanding of a present context "does theology have any meaning at all; and it retains meaning only insofar as it remains in touch with the real-life context" (1976: 76).

The point here is that liberation theology is truly radical insofar as it qualifies the question "What is a Christian contribution?" by asking what *kind* of action is emancipatory *today*. Without the latter, there is a sense in which the former cannot even be articulated. One's faith and one's political options have essentially the same foundation in the particular context in which one lives.

It is here that we can begin to see how liberation theology holds together the tension between its claim that faith provides no ready answers and its concurrent demand that we choose the "theological location of the poor." I will offer a preliminary account of how this tension is mediated, and then show how liberation theology grounds this mediation in its hermeneutic inquiry.

The key insight of liberation theology with respect to the question of the meaning of faith is that faith is not timeless, but radically historical. This historicity demands that we remain open to the possibility that definitions of faith will change. It also means a refusal to accept those claims of faith that are purported to be timeless, with the specific content of that refusal to be determined by the particular forms of oppression such claims support. Thus, in the context of Latin America, this "historized faith" means a commitment to the emancipation of the poor since it is they who suffer the oppression authorized by the (false) conception of faith in orthodox theology.

The denial of a "specifically Christian contribution" to political action is not, then, a denial of a "contribution, specifically Christian." My inversion of the terms is meant to convey an essential distinction. A way of life is not derived *from* faith, rather faith is the *expression* of a way of life. Indeed, it is not the expression of a faith that makes one a Christian, but a way of life that expresses whether one has a truly historical faith. A practice that supports oppression is a false faith, and that which opposes it affirms the radically historical meaning of faith.

We have seen the sociological reasons for this understanding of faith. But the liberation theologians see this as more than simply a sociological necessity. For them it is also necessary for the preservation of the true transcendence of God and his kingdom. A transcendence the meaning of which is immanent in the Word of God—the Bible—itself.

According to the liberation theologians, not only is the conception of truth in orthodox theology *phenomenologically* wrong, it also involves a conception of truth that has no support in the Bible itself (Bonino 1975: 90). Rather than positing a model of truth as orthodoxy, a contemplative activity aimed at understanding absolute truths, the Bible suggests that truth is a way of living, of acting, that one *does* or "walks" in truth (Bonino 1975: 89–90; Kirk 1979: 35; Gutierrez 1973a: 198). The difference here is between a "Greek" conception of truth and a Hebraic/biblical conception of truth (see Bonino 1975: 74; Miranda 1974: 57–58). In other words, what it means to know God and to know his love is to enact his truth. The doing and the knowing are inseparable.

The importance of this understanding and its difference with orthodox theology cannot be overstated. Orthodoxy treats doctrine, not practice, as the final norm; orthopraxis takes practice, not doctrine, as the final norm for truth. The distinction is not just a subtle play on words, for as the Bible itself shows, right practice reflects right knowledge. And it is in this sense that one must interpret the meaning of the claim that if you know the truth, the truth shall set you free. Orthodoxy presumes that right practice presupposes right knowledge, that right practice comes only after one knows God. *But the fact of the matter is that by definition one does not "know" God in this sense.* This mistaken way of "knowing" God can be seen as the result of a radically deficient interpretation of the relation between God and man and how this relation carries into the relations between human beings.

In the first place, we must recognize that in the Bible, the relation between God and man is one in which God is "encountered in history"; "The Biblical God is close to man; he is a God of communion with and commitment to man" (Gutierrez 1973a: 190). What this means is that the Bible's references are always bound by both time and place. It speaks of events that took place, take place and will take place in human history. At the same time, however, God was not similarly bound by time and place; hence the prophets' harsh criticism of idolatry and cultus (Gutierrez 1973a: 192). But does this necessarily imply that one's relation with God is purely spiritual, and in no way "material"?

For the liberation theologians, the distinction between the spirituality of God and the materiality of this world is a dualism that simply cannot be supported. From the fact that God does not dwell in "places of stone," and that the submission of faith is not embodied in religious ritual, it does not follow that God dwells *nowhere*. Indeed, what we see in the Bible is a twofold process by which God's presence moves from a localized link with particular peoples to a gradual extension to *all* people; at the same time there is an integration of his presence, moving from his dwelling in places of worship to his dwelling in human history itself. Christ is the point of convergence of the two processes, when "the Word became flesh; he came to dwell [pitch his tent] among us" [John 1:14] (Gutierrez 1973a: 193). Thus, for the liberation theologians, *to know God is to know Him through our encounter with other men, as they are the temple of the Lord.* To know God directly is impossible, not because there are inherent limitations to human understanding, but because when we try to do so we turn our backs on his real temple, humanity itself. We worship idols when we turn God into an object that is outside of humanity. The reason Yahweh of the Old Testament prohibits the making of images is because he is not objectifiable, and to objectify him is to also objectify that which is made in his image, humanity. As Miranda argues, the prohibition of images is aimed at preventing the loss of God's transcendent character—transcendent not in the sense of being of a different ontological status than man, but rather in the sense of nonbeing. "Yahweh is not among the entities nor the existings nor in univocal being nor in analogous being, but rather in the implacable moral imperative of justice" (Miranda 1974: 49). Yahweh prohibits images, the prophets and Jesus condemn cultus, and all for the same reason: *"The question is not whether one is seeking God or not, but whether he is seeking him where God himself said that he is"* (Miranda 1974: 57). In this sense God is not to be found in prayer or ritual, but in *justice*. Even this way of putting it is problematic; God *is* justice, to "know" him is to *do* justice, and to do justice is to know him. Here, then, is the essence of God's transcendence: so long as there is injustice God cannot be known, and to accept injustice is to deny God.

A true theology is thus one that seeks temporal justice. It is necessarily ethical, a "walking" of the truth of God-as-moral-imperative. In this respect, to charge liberation theology with reducing the word of God to an ethical demand depends upon a radical misreading of the Bible.

This understanding of God's transcendence is also an important part of the response to the objection that liberation theology reduces the Bible to a "human word." For the liberation theologians, this objection implies an interpretation of the Bible that views it as the Word of God independently of its historical dimension. But as they argue, there are not two dimensions of the Word, one of God and one of humanity. There is only one dimension to the Bible—and that is its historical dimension. We may interpret this "historicity" in a fairly straightforward way: the Bible is "historical" in the sense that references are always time- and place-bound. In this respect the Bible tells stories of God's relation to particular historically situated people. But there is a more complex notion of historicity here as well. If we recognize that the Biblical conception of knowledge, of knowing God, is "walking" his truth, then the Bible does not merely explain God's intervention at particular points in time. Rather, it shows that God's action "takes place in history and as history" (Bonino 1975: 134). For this reason the liberation theologians emphasize that "History is One"; "The one history in which God acts is the history of men; it is in this history that we find God" (Gutierrez 1973a: 153; Bonino 1975: 71).

This is not, however, to suggest that there is an "equation between God's sovereignty and history, as if the former would justify or sacralize everything that happens," nor does it mean that the Kingdom of God is "the natural denouement of history" (Bonino 1975: 134, 142). At the same time, this understanding also implies that "The Kingdom is not the denial of history," nor is it "merely adumbrated, reflected, foreshadowed, or analogically hinted at in the individual or collective realizations of love in history, but actually present, operative, authentically—however imperfectly and partially—realized" (Bonino 1975: 142 passim).

It is only when we realize that the Kingdom "is not an object to be known through adumbrations and signs that must be discovered, but a call, a convocation, a pressure that impels" (Bonino 1975: 143) that we will also realize that one does not ask where the Kingdom is visible or present, but rather how one can participate in it. We need not look for it, it is always there in the struggle against inhuman practices. How shall we participate? That will depend entirely on the context in which one finds oneself. As the liberation theologians assert, there is in this choice no "Christian" politics, but only a politics that can be called Christian. This is nowhere more clearly seen than in the life of Jesus, who himself clearly rejected the messianic role in terms of political power. He did not identify himself by using the divine power at his disposal in order to end injustice—instead he identified himself on the side of the poor and the oppressed in order that men would see that there is no divine substitute for acting justly toward their fellows and sisters:

God in Christ identifies himself utterly with man oppressed, destituted, and abandoned. He dies the death of the blasphemer, the subversive, the God-forgotten man. His cross therefore marks the bankruptcy of political and religious power, indeed of God conceived as a protective assurance against destitution and death. Here we meet the powerless, suffering, Godforsaken man as the last reality of God himself. Therefore all false optimism, all utopian hope is definitively shattered. But at the same time, we are called [as Christians] to this same identity in the double identification with the crucified Christ, and therefore with those with whom he himself was identified: the outcast, the oppressed, the poor, the forsaken, the sinners, the lost. This is the cradle of the Christian's identity and relevance. To be crucified together with Christ means to stand with those for whose sake God himself died the death of the sacrilege, the subversive, the Godforsaken one. (Bonino 1975: 145–46)

What the life and death of Christ shows is that there is no question of a divine war, a crusade, a specifically *Christian* struggle. Christians assume, and participate in, *human* struggles by identifying with the oppressed. We must understand our participation in these struggles as Christian in the sense that Christ understood his: not as the imposition of the will of God, but rather as the expression of that will as a call for men to "resolutely use the best *human* politics and economics at our disposal" (Bonino 1975: 149).

The hermeneutic circle (or as they call it, circulation) of the liberation theologians can now be fully understood. In their hermeneutic inquiry, the liberation theologians move from practice, to theory, to method, and back. Segundo describes this circulation as one in which liberation theology seeks out a method of interpretation that can embody the interest in *"being liberative"* rather than simply *"talking about liberation."* This hermeneutic method in liberation theology may be seen as reflected in the logic of its inquiry:

Firstly there is our way of experiencing reality, which leads us to ideological suspicion. *Secondly* there is the application of our ideological suspicion to the whole ideological superstructure in general and to theology in particular. *Thirdly* there comes a new way of experiencing theological reality that leads us to exegetical suspicion, that is, to the suspicion that the prevailing interpretation of the Bible has not taken important pieces of data into account. *Fourthly* we have our new hermeneutic, that is, our new way of interpreting the fountainhead of our faith (i.e., Scripture) with the new elements at our disposal. (Segundo 1976: 9)

At the heart of this "circulation" there emerges a clear relationship between the "truth" of social scientific and theological inquiry. What both find is that we are essentially historical and contextual beings, and that true emancipation occurs only when we free ourselves from the belief in "timeless truth." But this emancipation can occur only within the idiom of the oppressed, in terms of their own self-understandings and experiences. Without this contextual grounding, social science and theology lose their potentially liberating force. Without this grounding, critique becomes either hardened into a new form of "timeless truth," which must then itself be combatted, or it becomes a vacuous truth, unable to bridge the gap between what it promises and what is possible. In this, critical social theory and critical theology must preserve their utopian dimension by refusing to become ossified or vacuous. That this utopia is "not of this world" does not mean that it is something beyond reach from this world; it is not the belief in the possibility of a perfect society, but the belief in the non-necessity of *this* imperfect order. In the preservation of the utopian moment both science and faith have their specific roles to play, drawn together in an emancipatory praxis.

Critical social science provides the tools that open up the past and explain the present. It provides the foundation for the political, social, and economic liberation of human beings through its "denunciation" of the present. Faith provides the "annunciation" of a hopeful future which gives denunciation an eschatological significance. The two are not merely contingently related. As Gutierrez argues,

> The denunciation is to a large extent made with regard to the annunciation. But the annunciation, in its turn, presupposes this rejection, which clearly delimits it retrospectively. It defines what is not desired. (1973a: 233)

One therefore experiences a mature faith only when that hope is tempered by a recognition that what can be is first and foremost defined by the negation of what is. For "Utopia is deceiving when it is not concretely related to the possibilities offered to each era" (Ricoeur, quoted in Gutierrez 1973a: 234).

Clearly theology needs critical social theory, but does this also mean that critical social theory also requires a specifically Christian faith? From what has been said, I think we can safely conclude that it does not.[9] The reason why a theology of liberation "comes after," that it is not "concerned with the nonbeliever," that there is "no specifically Christian contribution," is that such a theology is conceived as a *service to Christians*, a means of showing *them* that their faith requires

[9] For a contrasting view, see Peukert (1984), who argues that Critical Theory needs a "fundamental" theology. I believe that the liberation theologians provide the analytical tools that could be employed to critique this claim, although it is beyond the scope of this discussion to explore this issue. See note 10.

their active participation in an emancipatory politics. The enemies of God are not those who are nonbelievers, but those who have a *false* faith, those who worship idols, whether secular or religious (Comblin 1979a: 25). The function of a theology of liberation is not the conversion of the faithless to a faith, but rather "the conversion to the neighbor, the oppressed person, the exploited social class, the despised race, the dominated country" (Gutierrez 1973a: 204–5). Theology is, or should be, aimed at the conversion of faith itself. That many non-Christians are similarly committed to the liberation of the poor is not a "problem" that requires explanation. It is, quite simply, evidence of the mystery of Grace (Bonino 1975: 100).

Liberation theology seeks to avoid the practices that gave rise to the remark: " 'God does not choose the same men to keep his word as to fulfill it' " (Gutierrez 1973a: 10–11). Human history is full of instances where the authoritative preservation and protection of "the faith" has resulted in damaged lives; it is also full of examples where resistance to damaging practices has often taken the form of religious "heresy." By unmasking the arrogance of the "keepers of the Word," and remembering the struggles of those who have in their actions tried to fulfill it, a theology of liberation denounces the former and tries to identify in current struggles for empowerment a faith that is "lived."

LIBERATION THEOLOGY, CRITICAL THEORY, POLITICAL PRACTICE

Liberation theology is a theology for the marginalized. But the model of theology it articulates transcends the Latin American context from which it emerged, for it suggests that a theology of liberation must take many forms, each specific to the context and life stories of those to whom it is addressed.

This demand for contextual specificity is, I think, one of the greatest contributions liberation theology has to offer to those committed to the idea of a critical theory, and it is one that liberation theology shares with other critical theories in practice I discuss in this book. On the one hand, it offers the possibility of seeing how critical theory can be articulated in a way that embraces a commitment to solidarity with the oppressed. On the other hand, it opens a philosophical self-understanding that can accommodate the need for a plurality of perspectives on the task of human emancipation, not only among Christians themselves, but with those who do not profess a specifically Christian faith:

> It is not for us to say whether a Christian is in a better position to exercise in . . . engaged criticism. This will be seen concretely in experience, or not

at all. But it is possible to say, I think, that a Christian is called to do it . . . [given] the nature of the Christian kerygma . . . [and the fact that as a Christian he] can offer his praxis to the fire of criticism totally and unreservedly on the trust of free grace. (Bonino 1975: 100)

The distinctive merit of this conception of critical theory may be further fleshed out by contrasting it with modernist and postmodernist critical theory.[10] As I noted in earlier chapters, perhaps the most useful insights offered by Marx, the Frankfurt School, Habermas, and Foucault, emerge from their deconstructive critiques of various social theories. These critiques show that social relations are intersubjectively constituted and historically contingent. The critical theorists use these findings to criticize a wide variety of knowledge claims that purport to be "purely theoretical," that is, independent of the practices of which they are expression. And on this point, at least, liberation theology, modernist and postmodernist critical theory are of the same mind.

The crucial problem, however, is this: how can one come to possess knowledge that is emancipating from the oppressive practices authorized, or at least conserved, by these "purely theoretical" theories? It would seem that the fact that our knowledge is shaped by our contexts would favor the adoption of a conception of knowledge that refuses to separate the grounding that practice provides for theory. It would, in other words, see that practice is not only the goal, but the very precondition of any theory. But here, modernist and postmodernist critical theory parts ways with liberation theology.

What differentiates liberation theology from modernist and post-

---

[10] I shortly discuss how liberation theology differs from both modernist and postmodernist critical theory; at this point I would like to mention that these same sorts of differences have also been contested among theologians themselves. Some American and European theologians have noted the similarities and differences between the aims of contemporary political theology and critical theory, particularly its modernist versions (see Schillebeeckx 1974; Fierro 1977: 91–94; Siebert 1979; Davis 1980; Lamb 1982; Lane 1984; Peukert 1984; Kroger 1985). Some are more or less sympathetic to liberation theology (for example, Davis, Lamb, Lane, and Kroger), but others belong to a tradition of political theology (Siebert, Schillebeeckx, Peukert) which many liberation theologians criticize for being "idealist," a position that undermines their practical-emancipatory commitment (see Gutierrez [1973a: 45, 220–25]; Bonino [1975: 144–50]; Segundo [1976: 98–99, 147–49]; and the excellent summation of the differences between Latin American liberation theology and European political theology in Davis [1980: 16–27], and Lamb [1982: 65–99]).

What is most interesting about these criticisms is that they are directed against theologians who have appropriated modernist critical theory into their theological self-understandings; thus there is a kind of indirect criticism of critical theory in liberation theology *via* the liberation theologians' attacks on much contemporary European political theology.

modernist critical theory is in one sense what separates it from orthodox theology. Modernist and postmodernist critical theory seem to
share with orthodox theology a kind of "negative utopianism." Certainly this takes different forms. For Marx, emancipation meant the
emancipation of the proletariat, the effect of which was to close Marxism off to the plurality of forms in which emancipation might take
shape. For the Frankfurt School and Habermas, emancipation is defined in terms so abstract that it is difficult to see how critical theory
might be in solidarity with the oppressed, wherever they are found.
For Foucault, emancipation is so thoroughly individualized that it, too,
precludes solidarity. And for orthodox theology, emancipation is cast
in spiritual and eschatological terms that make it impossible to realize
the "worldly" needs of the marginalized. In other words, modernist
and postmodernist critical theory, and orthodox theology, define
emancipation in a way that presupposes either the equation of particular practices with "universal" emancipation, or they completely sun-
der the possibilities of emancipation from extant practices.

But we need not choose between either the total identification or
total nonidentification of emancipation with a given historical practice. And this the liberation theologians try to make clear. By insisting
that the question, What political choices must we make? can be answered only by reference to the particular contexts in which they
must be made, the liberation theologians show that the essence of
nonidentity between what is and what can be, between emancipation
and unfreedom *can be found only in the nonidentity between what
the oppressed are told they are, and what they are in reality.* A critical
theory, even one in theological guise, must be capable of commiting
itself to solidarity with the oppressed, wherever they may be found. It
must also be capable of recognizing that oppression—and emancipation—may take a variety of forms, and in this it must be open to the
plurality of ways in which liberation might be realized.

However acceptable or controversial these themes may be, the true
test of liberation theology is its ability to assist those to whom it is
addressed in taking up the tasks of empowering themselves. The
"preferential option for the poor" is, after all, a vacuous claim if it is
not an option embodied in practice. And it has been. In Latin America
"you can find it any weekend in any slum, shantytown, or rural parish," where "liberation theologians" of various sorts have acted as
"pastors, analysts, interpreters, advocates, brothers or sisters in faith,
and fellow pilgrims" (Boff and Boff 1987: 19). It may even be found
at another level of practice: "in retreats, in diocesan planning meet-
ings, in discussions of rural pastoral problems or discrimination

against women, in debates on the problems of ethnic minority groups and culture" (Boff and Boff 1987: 20).

Have these efforts been effective in bringing about the self-emancipation of the oppressed? That depends on one's assessment of whether those practical activities inspired in part by liberation theology, such as "Christian base communities, Bible societies, groups for popular evangelization, movements for the promotion and defense of human rights, particularly those of the poor, agencies involved in questions of land tenure, indigenous peoples, slums, marginalized groups, and the like," have been the "powerful factors for mobilization and dynamos of liberating action" (Boff and Boff 1987: 7) that so many liberation theologians and observers believe they are.[11] Certainly the reaction to both liberation theology *and* the struggles with which it is identified on the part of Church authorities, political authorities, and other defenders of the status quo would seem to lend some credence to the effectiveness of this kind of critical theology in practice.

But however one judges, it should not be thought that liberation theology is exhausted by these practices. It cannot be. One reason is that it remains committed to "the *little utopia* of at least one meal for everyone every day, the *great utopia* of a society free from exploitation and organized around the participation of all, and finally the *absolute utopia* of communion with God in a totally redeemed creation" (Boff and Boff 1987: 94–95). In this commitment, liberation theology preserves its utopian moment, which is to say that it cannot identify with liberating practices without also retaining an ongoing critical examination of these practices. But this demand applies no more, or less, to a theology of liberation than it does to the self-understandings of those who are engaged in struggles for self-empowerment.

Another reason that liberation theology (and now we can include the theoretical self-understandings of the oppressed themselves) cannot be exhausted by a particular political practice is because all such practices are themselves contingent and contextually defined. As much as a liberation theology does not "claim to be an absolute, everlasting, or perennial theology," and remains committed to viewing itself as a "historical theology" (Boff and Boff 1987: 91), it must view the practices with which it is identified in the same light. The identity and oppression of "the poor," after all, may be constituted in a plurality of ways. For this reason, a theology of liberation is always open to the plurality of struggles, and perspectives, taken up by the oppressed in light of the particular forms of oppression they suffer.

[11] See, for example, Berryman (1987: especially chapter 4).

Whether a theology of liberation, or better, theologies of liberation, will help bring about the "great utopia" or "absolute utopia" of which the Boff brothers speak is an open question. But as examples of critical theory in practice, such theologies recognize that if the utopian hopes of the marginalized are to be realized, they must first be heard. What other meaning could possibly be given to the idea that a critical theory is both enlightening and emancipatory?

CHAPTER 7

Feminist Theory and Critique

The splinter in your eye is the best magnifying glass.
— Theodor Adorno

To say that feminist consciousness is the experience in a certain way of certain specific contradictions in the social order is to say that the feminist apprehends certain features of social reality *as* intolerable, as to be rejected in behalf of a transforming project for the future.
— Sandra Lee Bartky

MY AIM in this chapter is to argue that feminist theory can be understood as a form of critical theory. Unlike my discussions of dependency theory, Freire's critical pedagogy and liberation theology, however, reconstructing a critical feminist theory requires a greater degree of interpretive latitude than I have exercised in earlier chapters. For feminism is not a coherent whole. It is, rather, a patchwork of arguments, texts, and practices marked as much by discontinuity and difference as by common threads. In this chapter I draw on only a small set of the myriad works constituting "feminist theory," focusing specifically on those that might contribute to a feminist critical theory. There are many forms of feminism I do not consider, and others I treat only briefly.[1] What follows here, then, is a selective reading of a particular body of literature informed by the desire to build conceptual and practical bridges between feminist theory and other forms of critical theory in practice.

Stated this way, it may appear that I am engaging in what one feminist has called "grand theorizing" (Tronto 1985: 23). Many feminists are justifiably suspicious of attempts to provide definitive and exhaustive political theories, particularly since such attempts are characteristic of sexist, racist and/or Eurocentric perspectives (Tronto 1985: 23). Given this, it may well appear that my metatheoretical emphasis

---

[1] However, it should become clear by the end of this chapter that there is an implicit critique of those forms of feminism that appeal to some questionable aspects of dominant discourse for their presuppositions. I have in mind here liberal, Marxist, maternalist, and various other versions of feminism.

and the related aim of revealing a defensible model of critical theory in practice may confirm the suspicions of many feminists. Moreover, this suspicion also stems from the recognition by feminists themselves that there is no abstract "woman" for whom a single theory can suffice. Women are diverse; they experience domination in different forms and different ways depending upon the particular context in which they find themselves.

These possible objections noted, I want to suggest that whatever "grand theorizing" one may find here is not intended to ignore these problems. Indeed, the model of critical theory I articulate here actually embraces the kinds of suspicions some feminists have expressed. What I seek to show is that a critical feminist theory, like other critical theories in practice, can accommodate the plurality of life experiences and the particular forms of domination and struggle reflecting this plurality. If my reading of feminist theory is on the mark, the relevance of metatheory to theory and practice is not merely contingent, but conceptual. The possibility of a political practice that can be enlightening and emancipatory in a variety of contexts means, in the last instance, having a conception of critique that clears a philosophical or metatheoretical space for a political practice that allows—indeed requires—that the oppressed emancipate themselves, and this in a way that embodies a commitment to both solidarity and plurality.

As I see it, feminists have contributed much to understanding this metatheoretical-cum-political space. By closely attending those conceptions of self, knowledge, and practice that characterize many dominant discourses, conceptions that purport to be objective, neutral and free from the narrow, and presumably "parochial," interests of everyday life, feminists have developed an insightful and rich ideology critique. But this is not the only contribution feminists have made. By drawing out the reconstructive implications of their ideology critique, feminists have also sketched an alternative conception of self, knowledge and practice that fills out in greater detail the model of critical social theory I have been trying to develop.

A critical feminist theory may have more in common with other critical theories in practice than might be apparent at first sight. I believe a critical feminist theory offers yet another way of viewing the shortcomings of both modernist and postmodernist critical theory. Briefly, what feminists have shown is that critique cannot be grounded in an ahistorical, transcendental or abstract understanding of knowledge and self that is separated from a particular, historically contingent context. Nor can it simply assume that the contingency of knowledge and identity reduces critique to nothing more than a radical skepticism. The modernist and postmodernist critical theorists, as we have seen, recognize this themselves, yet they remain captives of a discourse that subverts the possibility of acting on that recognition.

Many feminists, by contrast, have refused to succumb to the politically debilitating debate between a normative universalism and a normative skepticism. Rather than asking how an emancipatory political practice can be theoretically defined and defended—a preoccupation that appears to account for critical theory's inability to meet its practical aims—feminists ask instead what theory must look like if it is to speak to practical concerns. The issue for feminists is, in short, less one of realizing theory in practice than it is of realizing the practical demands theory must meet. It is to begin from one's life experiences, working back to theory and taking this beginning and this theorizing for what they are—real, concrete struggles against domination—with the express intent of transforming those experiences in less destructive and oppressive directions. Reconstructing this conception of critique, one that requires and reflects its grounding in the immediacy and plurality of life experiences, is thus my central aim in this chapter.

Gender Oppression and the Task of Feminist Theory

The adage that "history is written by the winners" suggests that how we understand the past is selective, and that this selection serves the particular interests of those who are its greatest beneficiaries. In the commonly received view, however, history is not usually understood as a kind of self-serving narrative written from a particular point of view; it is, rather, usually treated as if neutral, unsituated and objective. The consequence of this view is that received history "domesticates" in a double sense: it domesticates the past by systematically ignoring or interpreting as marginal the lives of those by whose oppression the present has been established and by whose continued oppression the status quo is maintained, and in doing so domesticates the present by denying the oppressed a past and a language with which they might make sense of their present plight.

The past and the present are, however, notoriously resistant to this sort of domestication, for submerged within the dominant discourse are those whose lives do not neatly fit its concepts and categories, those whose lives constitute a reality that clearly contradicts the smooth metaphors of evolution or triumph that characterize accepted wisdom. When written from the perspective of those who live on history's margins and who *see* themselves as marginalized, the past and the present appear to us in a new and previously unexamined light. History written from the margins forces us to reconsider who we really are, what we know about ourselves, and how our institutions and practices have been—and might be—constituted.

Feminist theory has its roots in history from the margin. It is, however, a unique margin, cutting across almost the entirety of written history and cultural context.[2] Its subject is the reality of women's lives, past and present, captured in artifacts and documents or known only by inference, experienced as oppression in association with men who dominate women, men who are often themselves dominated by other men (Keohane and Gelpi 1981: vii).

But as many feminists have suggested, engaging in history from the margin implies the task of rethinking not only those practices and theories that have confined women to the margin, but the activity of theorizing itself. To begin to question what the historical experiences of women have meant, to make sense of them as the foundation of present oppression, required a recognition of the apparent tension between the accumulation of evidence about the historical experiences of women and the desire to understand those experiences more fully:

> Only recently has the nature of this tension become clear. Within the theories, concepts, methods and goals of inquiry we inherited from the domi-

---

[2] I say *almost* universal because although feminists have for the most part treated the domination of women by men as a universal social feature, in doing so they have overlooked those instances where the roles have been reversed. There is at least one culture that I am aware of in which women are the oppressors, and men the oppressed. This is the Kanhabeque culture of Guinea Bissau.

The extent to which the "traditional" roles of men and women are reversed among the Kanhabeque is astounding. Kanhabeque women consider themselves to be superior in every way to men, and they characterize the differences between themselves and men in much the same ways that men do in patriarchal societies. Men are considered (and consider themselves) less than fully rational, submissive—"feminine" as the term is usually used in our culture, and women are considered smarter, stronger—or "masculine" (even "macho"). In interviews with members of both sexes it was quite clear that women saw themselves and were seen by men as possessing a *natural* right to dominate, and men were seen as naturally subordinate.

Even though the Kanhabeque provide a example that negates feminist claims regarding the "universal" character of male domination, this does not, I believe diminish the validity of feminist criticisms of those cultures in which men actually do dominate. Furthermore, there is a sense in which a feminist critique could be turned against the Kanhabeque matriarchy, for Kanhabeque women display all of those self-understandings feminists have attacked in male dominated cultures. (In the Kanhabeque culture this would have to be a masculinist critique!)

I became aware of this society while (of all things) watching *National Geographic Explorer* with my son. Library research and inquiries to local sources and to the National Geographic Society for more information on the Kanhabeque have been fruitless; apparently the television documentary is the only study currently available. I have been continuing this search for more information as I believe that the Kanhabeque provides us with an example of the dangers and destructiveness of sexism, regardless of which gender is dominant.

nant discourses we have generated an impressive collection of "facts" about women and their lives, cross-culturally and historically—and we can produce many, many more. But these do not, and cannot, add up to more than a partial and distorted understanding of the patterns of women's lives. (Harding and Hintikka 1983: ix)

If feminist theory is to be a viable, critical and self-critical activity, women must continue to remember their past, for without this remembrance women may well suffer "from a collective amnesia, which makes [them] vulnerable to the impositions of dubious stereotypes, as well as limiting prejudices about what is right and proper . . . to do or not to do" (Johansson 1976: 427). But this remembrance must also be informed by "*re*thinking, an examination of the way that certain assumptions about women and the female character enter into the fundamental assumptions that organize all our thinking" (Jehlen 1981: 189).

Clearly the lives of women cannot be adequately understood within inherited frameworks of thought and inquiry. (Moreover, if this is the case, then neither can these frameworks adequately account for the lives of men [Harding and Hintikka 1983: ix].) For if women are oppressed by practices that rely upon systematic misdescriptions of social reality, these misdescriptions must be seen as having their origins in fundamentally flawed philosophical foundations. Thus, feminists have moved beyond the criticism of existing practices in order to demonstrate the link between the practices that oppress women and the theories and philosophical presuppositions that mirror and support these practices. But this deconstructive effort forms only part of the feminist project; like all critical theories it must also engage in a reconstructive effort by offering a sketch of an alternative conception of theory and practice that avoids the deficiencies of dominant discourse. To the extent that feminist theory *is* a form of critical theory, it cannot merely exchange one form of domination for another. And to articulate the outlines of an emancipatory political practice also involves grounding this practice in an understanding of knowledge and the self that is both empirically and normatively defensible. Like any critical theory, however, such a discourse does not begin from scratch; rather, it develops its insights out of an ideology critique of domination in both theory and practice. Or so we shall see.

The Feminist Deconstruction of "Male" Discourse

A critical feminist theory opens most fundamentally with recognition of the fact that the life experiences on which the claims of most dominant discourses have been founded have been the experiences of men, and not those of women. The exclusion and domination of women by men, and the purported neutrality and objectivity of male experience cannot, then, be treated as if they are merely contingently related. They are, rather, constitutive of the fact that "patriarchy—like many another dictatorship—controls the information available in order to ensure the perpetuation of its own power. . . . It practices censorship and engages in propaganda on a massive scale, so that its version of sense, and reality, can be unquestioningly accepted" (Spender 1983: 369). As Catherine MacKinnon argues, "men *create* the world from their own point of view, which then *becomes* the truth to be described," and in this the neutrality and purported objectivity of male discourse "is revealed as a strategy of male hegemony" (1981: 23).

For feminists, then, the social and political practices that issue in the domination of women by men are systematically linked with both received social theories and the metatheoretical assumptions that undergird these theories. This is not to say that the character of male domination, social theory, and metatheory has been monolithic or univocal. Yet in one respect these differences may be understood as merely formal, and not substantive. For whatever differences one may find in practice, theory, and competing conceptions of knowledge throughout history, they are nonetheless similar in that they fail to provide adequate philosophical models that can accommodate the practical task of women's self-emancipation.

This criticism suggests nothing less than the presence of a specific political agenda at every level of social life. Simply put, this agenda involves the systematic exclusion of women from full participation in the constitution of that life. In the contemporary context, this exclusionary politics is reflected in the philosophical presuppositions of scientistic discourse as well as in the moral and ethical discourse embodied in various forms of liberalism and Marxism. In their interrogation of these, feminists have brought to light a number of shared themes in what otherwise appear to be diverse, and often competing, modes of thought and action. What unites scientistic, liberal, and Marxist discourse is that which one finds in pervasive form throughout the history of Western thought: a belief in the objectivity, and hence universal applicability of its theoretical claims. And this objectivism, as we shall see, supports and is supported by particular conceptions of self-identity that are gender specific. To reveal the exclusionary politics explicit in these contemporary discourses is thus also to reveal the deficiencies of the themes of self and knowledge on which they are founded.

A feminist approach to social inquiry, as Catherine MacKinnon argues, turns interpretive questions of the sort we are discussing into a *political* hermeneutics; feminist inquiry is grounded in a self-understanding that sees itself "as an answer to the question, What does it mean? that would comprehend that the first question to address is, To whom? within a context that comprehends gender as a social division of power" (MacKinnon 1981: 24). And in terms of these questions, many feminists have come to realize that much of modern discourse means "objectivity" from the standpoint of a "disinterested" observer who in reality is being neither objective nor disinterested, but rather distinctively male.

The Feminist Critique of Scientism

Nowhere is the evidence of this gap between appearance and reality clearer than in the understanding of science that pervades much modern thought. In some respects, the feminist critique of scientism provides a clear example of how feminist theory complements the work of both modernist and postmodernist critical theory. This complementarity, moreover, links feminist theory with dependency theory, Freire's critical pedagogy, and liberation theology, in that it, like them, strives to bridge the gap between an otherwise abstract metatheoretical concern and immediate practical and political concerns.

The feminist critique of scientism is akin to that found in the modernist critical theory insofar as it also takes advocates of scientism to task for their dependence on a radically mistaken understanding of the social foundations of science (see Westkott 1979: 425). Like the modernists, feminists have argued that in failing to recognize that supposedly "objective" knowledge is actually an intersubjectively and communicatively constituted form of knowledge, those committed to scientistic thinking fail to see that "Science is made by people who live at a specific time in a specific place and whose thought patterns reflect the truths that are accepted by the wider society" (Hubbard 1983: 45). But feminist criticism of scientism does not merely recapitulate the critique of the sort offered by the critical theorists and other contemporary philosophers of science. What these critical insights fail to address, according to feminists, is the relation between the scientistic commitment to objectivism and *androcentrism* (Keller 1981: 118; Keller 1983: 187).

Thus, while the assertion that scientific inquiry is in part shaped by wider sociological influences is by no means an insight unique to feminists, the fact that these influences reflect a gender bias *is* unique. This "gender turn" in the critique of scientism is reflected even in the way feminists have posed the problem of scientism. Note, for example, how Evelyn Fox Keller turns the scientistic preoccupation with methodology into a deeper question about the gender-specific presuppositions of that discourse:

> As long as the course of scientific thought was judged to be exclusively determined by it own logical and empirical necessities, there could be no place for any signature, male or otherwise, in that system of knowledge. (Keller 1981: 117)

The critical question many feminists have used to open the examination of scientism has been to ask how women fit within the scientistic world-view. On one level, the gender bias of scientism is evident in the fact that women have been systematically written out of (potential) membership in the community of scientists. With respect to traditional scientific understandings of women, feminists have tried to show that the ideal of scientific objectivity—indeed, rationality itself—has been "genderized." In this view, the capacity for objectivity, which requires the faculty of rationality, has historically been conceptualized from an exclusively male point of view. From this perspective women by definition have been considered incapable of rational thought, and therefore objectivity.

> In the history of Western thought, sex has been considered a variable in the *distribution* of rationality. . . . From antiquity to the present day, women have been claimed less capable of developing a mature sense of justice than men, more ruled by the emotions, the passions, and the appetites than men, and more inclined toward subjective assessments and less toward objective ones than men. (Harding 1983: 43)

Thus, the ability to "think scientifically" has been one version of the tendency to differentiate between the innate capabilities of men and women to engage in "objective" or "rational" thinking. This criticism links the received view of rationality and objectivity with the politics of exclusion, for the conjunction of objectivity and androcentrism must be understood as serving sexist political practices. Rationality and objectivity are thought to be intellectual capacities available only to males, or, at best, also to those women who "think like men." And while the reasons for the exclusion of women from the realm of rational discourse have been different in different historical epochs and between different scientific theories, a "defective" rationality has nonetheless been consistently attributed to women (Harding 1983: 43).

Now the initial response to this critique of the ways science has been used to underpin and justify the exclusion of women from the community of (potentially) "rational" actors might well be to argue that we need only expand the definition of this community to include women. However, this response assumes that the *cognitive* trait of rationality and the *gender* trait of masculinity stand in a relation that is merely historically contingent; that objectivity and rationality can be thought of as gender neutral once we have purged our epistemological self-understandings of their unwarranted gender assumptions. But this strategy cannot but fail given the constitutive connections between the philosophical and sociological dimensions of scientific inquiry. Dorothy Smith makes this point clear:

> The conceptual practices, methodologies, instrumentalities, and so on, which in the concrete instance organize the cognitive domain of the particular science in which the subject is practitioner, are not merely tools to be picked up and laid down at will. They are together those practices which organize and bring into being the phenomena *as such* in the knower's relation to the known object. . . . The methods of inquiry and of thinking are integral not only to the relation among knowers in a discourse but constitute also a determinate social relation among knowers and the human objects of their knowledge. . . . Anonymity, impersonality, detachment, impartiality, objectivity itself, are accomplished by socially organized practices that bring into being a relation of a definite form between knowers and known. (Smith 1979: 158)

Initially, then, we have good reason to ask whether in fact the genderization of rationality is merely a contingent or epiphenomenal feature of scientism. We must, therefore, question whether the genderization of rationality is the result of a deeper problem that implicates the epistemological presuppositions of "objectivity" and "rationality." We must ask if the " 'canons of science' [are] themselves [so] socially biased that their gender distortions are invisible" (Harding 1983: 46). And it would be naive, Evelyn Fox Keller asserts, to believe that the genderization of science affects only its findings, leaving the very structure of science itself untouched (Keller 1983: 190).

On closer inspection, an objectivist/androcentric nexus is revealed not only at the level of how science has traditionally conceptualized women, but also at the level of the purported relation of the scientist to the object of scientific inquiry (Keller 1983: 190). When we attend to the understanding of the relation between the subject of knowledge (the knower) and the object of knowledge (that which is known) that is implicit in scientistic discourse, what emerges is a view that presupposes a relation of distance and separation (Keller 1983: 191; Smith 1979: 158; Westkott 1979: 425). That is, subject and object of knowledge stand in a relation that is "radically divided, which is to say no worldly relation" (Keller 1983: 191). This relation is dictated by the methodological injunction requiring the subject of knowledge to assume an " 'Archimedean' point—that is, a point external to any particular position in society" (Smith 1979: 156) thereby guaranteeing its autonomy by setting apart its mode of knowledge from those "subjective" modes of knowing in which the dichotomy is threatened (Keller 1983: 191).

The extent to which this conception of objectivity is pervaded by sexist presuppositions has been well documented in the groundbreaking work of Dinnerstein (1976), Chodorow (1978), and Gilligan (1982). What these feminists have shown is that at the heart of an objectivist ideal is a concept of the self that reflects patterns of socialization in which autonomy, detachment, and "objectivity" itself, are traits associated with culturally prescribed understandings of male gender identity. On this account, the "abstract knower" is revealed as a member of that "definite social category" that is the male gender. As a result, what we see is "a network of interactions between gender development, a belief system that equates objectivity with masculinity, and a set of cultural values which simultaneously elevates what is defined as scientific and what is defined as masculine." And "the structure of this network is such as to perpetuate and exacerbate distortions in *any* of its parts—including the acquisition of gender identity" (Keller 1983: 199–200).

The point I have been driving at here is that it is the ideal of detachment and objectivity itself that is problematic, not just the fact that women have historically been treated as if they cannot think in these terms. As feminists have tried to show, this ideal is itself an illusion, and a politically conservative illusion at that. There are no "brute facts" about the world (natural and social) that can be "objectively" known; the "facts" are communicatively constituted, reflecting theoretical presuppositions that "bring into being the phenomena *as such*" (Smith 1979: 158). And this implicates the status of the subject of knowledge as well; "the knower turns out after all not [to] be [an] 'abstract knower' perched on an Archimedean point but a member of a definite social category occupying definite positions in the society" (Smith 1979: 160).

The conservative political character of the ideal of objectivity is thus manifested in two ways. In the realm of social inquiry, even when the ideal of objectivism is linked to a commitment to social change, on the epistemological level it denies the possibility of such change. The scientistic assumption of a world of unvarnished facts, especially in the context of social inquiry, "recognizes as valid only the factual recording of what is [and] allows no justification for attending to alternatives to present conditions. The effect of this approach is to justify the present," ethical commitments to the contrary notwithstanding (Westkott

1979: 427–28). And when women are the objects of this inquiry, "women's devaluation and the consequences of this devaluation are reinforced by a social science which records these conditions while systematically ignoring alternative possibilities" (Westkott 1979: 428).

The second way in which the scientistic ideal is politically conservative is related to the status of the inquirer, and has repercussions that extend to natural scientific as well as social inquiry. For the scientistic understanding of knowledge as impersonal, abstract, universal, and absolute, must also be seen as parasitic on male gender identity. The objectivist methodology of science is thus to be understood not as a neutral method, but rather as a reflection of a particular socially organized practice. In this, social practice, epistemology and ontology recapitulate and reinforce each other: the way we organize our social relations, the way we think about the nature of knowledge, and the way we understand ourselves (our self-identity) are logically and conceptually linked. Our practices and conceptions of knowledge and self constitute mutually supportive aspects of a discourse. And for feminists, this discourse is gender biased, no less at the metatheoretical than at the practical level.

Now none of this should be taken to mean that feminists believe that science, and particularly natural science, have been devoid of achievement. Sandra Harding makes this clear:

> A final caution: it is important to understand that scientific theories whose conceptual schemes contain oppressive political metaphors can nevertheless extend our understanding of the regularities of nature and their underlying causal tendencies . . . modern science did not throw away recognition of the regularities of nature charted by earlier investigators. (1986: 239)

There is, in this, a recognition of crucial differences between the natural and social sciences, and in my concluding chapter I shall return to these differences. For the moment, however, I simply want to emphasize that the feminist critique of scientism, while it does not deny that natural science has produced useful and viable knowledge claims, shows that whatever knowledge of nature science has produced must be evaluated from the perspective of the social costs involved in these accomplishments. And it is precisely the philosophical presuppositions of scientism that have served "as a way of consolidating and maintaining men's gender identities":

> Science affirms the unique contributions to culture to be made by transhistorical egos that reflect a reality only of abstract entities; by the administrative mode of interacting with nature and other inquirers; by impersonal and universal forms of communication; and by an ethic of elaborating rules for

absolute adjudications of competing rights between socially autonomous—
that is, value-free—pieces of evidence. These are exactly the social characteristics necessary to become gendered as a man in our society. (Harding
1986: 238)

But it is not just in scientistic discourse that one finds this commitment to epistemological objectivity and ontological abstractionism;
much of modern moral and political theory also seems to reflect this
commitment—and the androcentric bias it presupposes.

The Feminist Critique of Liberalism

At the heart of liberal thought one finds yet another version of the two
crucial presuppositions of scientism: an objectivist epistemology and
an ontology of the person that is grounded in the belief in a prepolitical
or asocial human "nature."[3] The conceptual relationship between
these presuppositions is best captured in Hobbes's claim that we must
think of ourselves "as if but even now sprung out of the earth, and
suddenly, like mushrooms, come to full maturity, without all kinds of
engagement with each other" (quoted in Benhabib 1982: 47). Liberal
ontology recapitulates liberal epistemology. Subscribing as it does to
an objectivist epistemology, liberal theory assumes human nature to
be comprised of a set of psychological dispositions that attach to us
qua individual human beings. And it also assumes that it is only if we
treat human beings as individual entities having these psychological
features prior to and/or independent of our social relations that this
"nature" can be understood. Thus, "our liberal view of persons as separate individuals would seem to require, or at least fit most naturally
with, a view of psychological objects as existing brutely in us" (Scheman 1983: 234).

This "methodological individualism" is not, however, limited only to
the level of metatheory, for liberalism also uses "the individual as a

---

[3] My initial characterization of the liberal tradition rests on an understanding of liberalism as a coherent philosophical/methodological tradition rather than a consistent
political one. I believe that any attempt to characterize liberalism as having a more or
less consistent political agenda is an interpretive mistake because it tends to conflate
important political distinctions between thinkers who nonetheless share (what I call) a
"normative methodology." The political differences between "liberals" can be explained
by the fact that the normative methodology they share is problematic. Thus, Hobbes is
as much part of the liberal tradition as Locke, Kant, the Utilitarians, Mill, Rawls, Nozick, etc. For while each has been called a liberal, the political programs they advocate
are not the same. To understand this is thus to appreciate that what makes them the
same at the level of normative methodology helps us understand why they are so different at the level of politics.

foundation on which to justify both scientific and political theories" (Scheman 1983: 232).

> Thus, it is supposed to be a natural fact about human beings, and hence a constraint on any possible social theory, that, no matter how social our development may be, we exist essentially as separate individuals—with wants, preferences, needs, abilities, pleasures, and pains—and any social order has to begin by respecting these as attaching to us determinately and singly, as a way of respecting *us*. (Scheman 1983: 231)

In this we see how liberalism posits the methodological withdrawal from the actual world of politics to be a precondition for future political emancipation, for liberalism is grounded in the assumption that it is only by treating the psychological states of individuals "in abstraction from their social setting [that] we can expect to appeal to them to justify forms of social organization" (Scheman 1983: 232).

The extent to which this methodological-cum-political individualism is pervasive in liberal thought is obvious. To take but a few examples, we can see its influence in a range of theorists. For Kant, "moral concepts have their seat and origin completely *a priori* in the reason," and "Since moral laws ought to hold true for every rational creature we must derive them from the general concept of a rational being" and not from "any merely contingent knowledge" (Kant 1949: 159–60). For J. S. Mill, "men . . . in a state of society are still men; their actions and passions are obedient to the laws of individual human nature" (Mill 1947: 573). For John Rawls, the theoretical foundations of justice are to be found only when one assumes a hypothetical "original position . . . which corresponds to the state of nature in the traditional theory of the social contract" (Rawls 1971: 12). For Robert Nozick, the principles governing moral and ethical action can be drawn only from a "focus upon a fundamental abstract description that would encompass all situations of interest" (Nozick 1974: 4), a counterfactual state of nature that "begins with fundamental general descriptions of morally permissible and impermissible actions . . . and goes on to describe how a state would arise from that state of nature . . . *even if no actual state ever arose that way*" (Nozick 1974: 8). Even staunch critics of liberalism like Robert Paul Wolff appeal to the methodology of abstraction. While questioning the efforts of liberals like Rawls, Wolff nonetheless believes that "as Kant correctly insisted, in the realm of moral philosophy nothing but apriori proof has any value whatsoever" (Wolff 1973: 225).

Now while Kant, Mill, Rawls, Nozick and Wolff are committed to an individualism of method, they are not similarly committed to an individualism of substance.[4] For while they hold that moral and ethical principles must be derived from a prepolitical or asocial conception of human nature and rationality, they arrive at radically different conclusions regarding the specific principles derived from the counterfactual characterization of that nature. Kant arrives at the categorical imperative, Mill at an inviolate sphere of self-regarding actions, Rawls at a politics of distributive justice, Nozick at a libertarian state, and Wolff at anarchism.

What this suggests, I think, is that the *methodology* of abstraction is itself problematic. This methodology is supposed to be a formal procedure yielding substantive conclusions. As a kind of "normative metatheory," it is conceptualized as a neutral method that justifies normative principles. In this sense, the methodology of abstraction is to liberal moral and political theory what scientific methodology is to scientific theory: it is supposed to yield replicable findings. That is, it is supposed to yield the same moral and ethical norms regardless of who employs it, for the crucial presupposition here is that such norms are—and can only be—universally binding because they derive from a point of view shorn of particular historically situated subjects having specifically situated interests. But even a cursory examination of the history of liberal political thought suggests that what theorists who employ this methodology say they are doing, and what they actually are doing, are in fact rather different things. For this "universal" method has yet to produce anything like universally agreed upon normative principles.

As one feminist has said, liberal metatheory "purports to be a statement about how things naturally are [but] is instead an expression of a historically specific way of structuring some set of social interactions" (Scheman 1983: 229–30). What appears, then, as a formal procedure for justifying universally binding norms in actuality presupposes a particular understanding of "human nature" for which those norms would be "rationally binding"—a "nature" whose psychological characteristics are historically contingent rather than timeless. But if this is in fact the case, then it constitutes a real dilemma for liberal theory and metatheory, for the more this account moves in the direction of a minimal and general characterization of human identity, the more unlikely it is that it will yield defensible normative principles (Benhabib 1982: 51). Thus, "The problem for the liberal," says Naomi Scheman, "is this: if individuals, their identities and life plans are to be identifiable independently of forms of social organization (and the liberal needs them to be), then we are hard pressed to come up with

---

[4] I have purloined this distinction from Scheman (1983), who uses it in much the same way.

anything that could make this identification non-arbitrary" (Scheman 1983: 233). We do not, in other words, arrive at "universally binding" norms from the perspective of an asocial, historically unsituated point of view; rather, we reason from a particular context. Again, the project of developing an "Archimedean point," whether in scientific or moral and political theory, is revealed as a methodological chimera.

Moreover, liberal theory and metatheory can be indicted as sexist for much the same set of reasons as scientistic discourse. The methodological individualism of liberal moral and political metatheory can be seen as part and parcel of a particular conception of self-identity that is male gender specific in its presuppositions.

> The norms of personhood, which liberals would strive to make as genuinely universal as they now only pretend to be, depend in fact on their not being so—just what one would expect from an ideology. (Scheman 1983: 240)

On this liberal account, personhood is characterized by an autonomous individuality, normative principles as impersonal, abstract, universal and absolute, and "just" moral and political practice as action informed by elaborated rules for the adjudication of competing and absolute rights between disembodied persons (Ferguson 1984: 160). And again, it is precisely these assumptions that the work of Gilligan, Chodorow and Dinnerstein have shown to be specific to the social construction of male gender identity.

Seen in these terms, the gender specific character of modern discourse is not simply a function of the commitment to a scientific and/or moral and political methodology of abstractionism. Clearly scientism and liberal individualism are deficient in the sense that they subscribe to questionable methodological presuppositions. Again, these are insights that are by no means unique to feminist theory. What feminists have demonstrated, however, is that this methodology is both philosophically deficient *and* politically sexist. As such, it cannot provide an adequate grounding for a political practice that can emancipate women precisely because it authorizes the continuation of those modes of thought that have been the source of women's oppression.

But if both scientism and liberalism are problematic with respect to the emancipatory interests of feminists, Marxism fares no better—and, not surprisingly, for many of the same reasons.

The Feminist Critique of Marxism

It might initially appear that grouping scientism, liberalism and Marxism together would be highly problematic. From the point of view of one who subscribes to any one of these ways of thinking this would indeed be true; from a feminist perspective it may not be. This is not to say that differences between proponents of any one of these frameworks do not exist. Defenders of scientism, after all, have expressed skepticism regarding the "value-ladeness" and "subjective" character of moral and political theorizing. Nor have moral and political theorists, of almost every imaginable stripe, been reticent to attack the "objectivist" pretensions of those committed to scientism (especially in the social sciences). And certainly liberals and Marxists have been mutual critics of each other for some time.

It is also true that the criticisms and arguments made by proponents of these various perspectives have been influential in feminist thought. But, again, the differences between them are of only secondary importance for feminists, for whom the "women question" is "seen as *the* question, calling for an analysis on its own terms" (MacKinnon 1981: 13).

In this respect, feminists see Marxism as deficient to the extent that it, too, remains blind to the particular experiences and needs of women. And this blindness takes a number of different forms, occurring at both the methodological and theoretical levels.

At the level of methodology, feminists have emphasized the now familiar distinction between scientistic and what we might call "critical" versions of Marxist metatheory. It is the scientistic version that feminists have targeted, and for the same reasons that they have criticized other kinds of objectivist metatheoretical stances. As the "dominant tradition" in Marxist inquiry, scientistic Marxism has been characterized by "an epistemology . . . that claims to portray a reality outside itself" (MacKinnon 1981: 13–14). Scientistic Marxism thus shares an objectivist commitment with scientism and liberalism, even while it criticizes the ideological content of "bourgeois science":

> [Scientific Marxist] theory is acontextual to the extent that it is correct. . . .
> Theory as a form of thought is methodologically set apart both from the illusions endemic to social reality—ideology—and from reality itself, a world defined as thinglike, independent of both ideology and theory. Ideology here means thought that is socially determined without being conscious of its determinations. Situated thought is as likely to produce "false consciousness" as access to the truth. Theory, by definition, is, on the contrary, nonideological. Since ideology is interested, theory must be disinterested in order to penetrate myths that justify and legitimate the status quo. (MacKinnon 1981: 13)

Whose interests are served by this discourse? For feminists, the answer is clear: scientistic Marxism does not speak for women precisely because it fails to provide a metatheoretical ground from which the interests of women can be addressed. Indeed, we must recognize this form of Marxism as yet another example of the fact that "the relation between content and method is often not accidental," and it should come as no surprise that there is a clear connection between "the positivistic aspects of Marxism and the disappearance of women" in Marxist theory (Flax 1983: 270).

It would of course be wrong to say that all Marxists subscribe to this scientific view. And, in fact, many feminists have themselves appealed to a "critical" version of Marxist metatheory as a useful analytical tool (see, for example, Hartsock, 1983a, 1983b; Smith, 1974, 1977, 1979). Rather than seeing Marxist metatheory as objectivist and disinterested, they stress that a critical Marxist metatheory "embraces its own historicity" (MacKinnon 1983: 13), thereby constituting "[a] standpoint [that] is not simply an interested position (interpreted as bias) but interested in the sense of being engaged" (Hartsock 1983a: 285). Thus, this metatheoretical perspective "emphasizes ... the idea that social knowledge is always interpreted within historical contexts, and that truths are, therefore, historical rather than abstract, and contingent rather than categorical" (Westkott 1979: 426). I shall later discuss the implications of this metatheoretical perspective in greater detail, but for now we should note that even when feminists have interpreted Marxist metatheory in these terms, they still distance themselves from the specific theoretical content of Marxism. Nancy Hartsock's claim that "[b]y setting off from the Marxian meta-theory I am explicitly suggesting that this, rather than his critique of capitalism, can be most helpful to feminists" (Hartsock 1983a: 284) exemplifies this sort of stance.

The implication here is that even when the "interested" character of a critical Marxist metatheory is recognized, Marxist rules of inquiry nonetheless prescribe that one can adequately understand social life only if one takes the "interested" perspective of those dominated by the division of labor by class, that is, the proletariat (Harding 1983: 320). Marxist class analysis thus reduces the problem of domination generally to the specific domination of the working class in the sphere of relations of production; the proletariat's specific interest in emancipation is treated as if it constitutes a universal interest in emancipation, and, by extension, the (immanent) emancipation of the proletariat is seen as the realization of universal emancipation. From a feminist perspective—and here again feminist theory shows its similarities to other critical theories in practice I have addressed—the use of class analysis and the purportedly privileged position of the proletariat as a basis for understanding the ideological distortions of class-based ideology creates a theoretical outlook in which "women as a 'sex-class' do not exist and sex/gender cannot be an organic social variable" (Harding 1983: 320; see also Jaggar 1983: 27–31).

To focus on class analysis and the historically particular, though purportedly "universal," interests of the proletariat ignores three crucial insights of feminist inquiry. First, Marxism overlooks the fact that male domination of women has existed, and continues to exist, in cultures that are clearly "pre-class" societies (Harding 1983: 321). Second, it ignores the extent to which this form of domination persists even today in societies that have undergone significant economic/social/political change, particularly those that now call themselves 'socialist' (Harding 1983: 321; Jaggar 1983: 30; MacKinnon 1981: 8; Markovic 1976: 145–52). Third, and perhaps most important, the concepts and categories of Marxist analysis systematically preclude the possibility of detecting the sources of male domination in the sphere of human reproduction (Harding 1983: 321; Jaggar 1983: 30; Markovic 1976: 158–59; MacKinnon 1981: 1–2). Thus,

> From the Marxist perspective, the special needs and interests of women are invisible. And, by concealing those special needs and interests, traditional Marxist theory mystifies social reality and therefore constitutes yet another ideology of male domination. (Jaggar 1983: 31)

This sort of feminist criticism of Marxism has led to a number of attempts to resituate the relationship between Marxism and feminism, many of which have been criticized as deficient by feminists. Some Marxists have attempted to simply dismiss the concerns of feminists as

> bourgeois in theory and practice, meaning that it works in the interest of the ruling class. They argue that to analyze society in terms of sex ignores class divisions among women, dividing the proletariat. Feminist demands, it is argued, could be fully satisfied within capitalism, so their pursuit undercuts and deflects the effort for basic change. (MacKinnon 1981: 3)

Other Marxists have been more sympathetic to feminist concerns, although they have attempted to conceptualize sexism and gender inequalities as "an ideological consequence—an epiphenomenon—of attempts to maintain the division of labor by class" (Harding 1983: 320). Still others, most notably some "socialist feminists," have attempted a reconciliation of Marxism and feminism, "as if nothing essential to either theory fundamentally opposes their wedding" (MacKinnon 1981: 13).

Each of these approaches fails to adequately accommodate feminist concerns to the extent that they also fail to recognize the theoretical implications of feminist inquiry that have been sketched out here. Simply put, the attempt to characterize the feminism/Marxism relationship in dismissive, subsumptive, or reconciliatory terms is "politically disastrous for women and theoretically disastrous for Marxism" (Jaggar 1983: 30). To dismiss or subsume feminist theory from a Marxist perspective means committing oneself to an analytical framework that obscures the interests that women share with women, and those that men share with men, irrespective of the particular class to which they may belong. For feminists, class differences between women may well help to explain why women of different classes have not yet united against male domination, but it does not explain that domination itself (MacKinnon 1981: 7). Thus, Marxists have systematically ignored the evidence demonstrating that male domination is common to preclass, class, and even (so-called) classless societies; their concepts and categories do not enable them to explain the origins and persistence of women's subordination precisely because they begin by assuming a sexual division of labor that remains unexplained (Jaggar 1983: 31). Even attempts by some socialist feminists to reconcile the two theories does not accomplish its intended purpose. "Adding" women to traditional Marxist class analysis does not give rise to an adequate *feminist* theory. Iris Young has pointed out the shortcomings of this reconciliation, which she calls "dual systems theory":

> The dual systems approach to socialist feminist theorizing accepts the traditional Marxian theory of production relations, historical change, and analysis of the structure of capitalism in basically unchanged form. It rightly criticizes that theory for being essentially gender blind, and hence seeks to supplement Marxist theory of capitalism with feminist theory of a system of male domination. Taking this route, however, tacitly endorses the traditional Marxian position that "the woman question" is auxiliary to the central questions of a Marxian theory of society. (Young 1980: 180)

And as for the political implications of this theoretical perspective, consider the comments of MacKinnon and Jaggar:

> For Marxist political economy, the market is the main stage of history, and class struggle its main action. (Jaggar 1983: 30)

> The failure to contain both theories on equal terms derives from the failure to confront each on its own ground: at the level of method. Method shapes each theory's vision of social reality. It identifies its central problem, group, and process, and creates as a consequence its distinctive conception of politics as such. (MacKinnon 1981: 13)

At this point, it should be sufficiently clear that the kinds of philosophical pretensions, theoretical presuppositions, and practical implications characteristic of scientism, liberalism and Marxism cannot serve to ground a feminist critical theory. When we frame the question regarding the adequacy of these forms of discourse in terms of their ability to shed light on the status and needs of women, then we can see why feminists would characterize much of modern thought as either implicitly or explicitly sexist. And in light of this fact, it is clear that women cannot repeat these forms of discourse—or better, this form of discourse—lest they undermine the possibility of defending their practical intentions.

I turn, then, from feminist deconstruction of modern discourse to the reconstruction of the foundations of a *feminist* critical theory. This is nothing less than a perspective that articulates an understanding of knowledge, self-identity, and practice, that can be the basis for the emancipation of women, but at the same time avoids the deficiencies of those perspectives that have contributed to the continued persistence of male domination.

Feminism as Critique: Rethinking Emancipation in Theory and Practice

When the truth status or philosophical defensibility of social theory is assumed to be a function of its ability to articulate forms of knowledge or normative principles to which all "rational" persons would assent, the result is an "epistemological imperative" (Marcil-Lacoste 1983: 128). This methodological injunction precludes from consideration women's particular experiences. Because particular, these experiences must, in the received view, be irrelevant in the formulation of "rationally binding" moral and ethical norms. This is tantamount to saying that conceptions of the good life women hold (whatever they may be), and the forms of oppression against which these conceptions of the good take shape, are in some sense trivial, or unimportant, or simply wrong.

For feminists, to rethink these issues is to also rethink the meaning and means of emancipation. Consequently, a feminist critical theory must begin by taking seriously the insights gained from the critique of the objectivist, abstractionist and universalistic claims of dominant discourses. Perhaps the most important of these insights is, again, the recognition that we reason *from* our history, and not *to* it from some abstract, disembodied point of view. These perspectives arise from our experiences as members of particular cultures, classes, groups—and genders.

A feminist perspective thus involves no claim to be timeless, nor universal in its applicability to all human beings. It cannot be, and to assume otherwise is to assume that "feminist writings are ways of repeating men, or else what they say is of no primary importance" (Marcil-Lacoste 1983: 121–22). It would be to say that "somehow feminist writings are on a par with any other writing, that they are allowed to share whatever *uninteresting* features our [accepted] ways of practicing knowledge may have" (Marcil-Lacoste 1983: 122). And precisely because feminist discourse does not simply repeat men, or settle for sharing only the "uninteresting"—and potentially oppressive—features of male discourse, women's knowledge about themselves and the world is dismissed as at worst naive, and at best low-ranking or secondary to the "timeless" truths to which the dominant discourse aspires (Ferguson 1984: 157–58).[5]

Such charges, Louise Marcil-Lacoste argues, are nothing less than the feminist "epistemological 'repos de guerrier' " (1983: 122). This means that feminist theory must craft a discourse that "seeks historical, structural and linguistic grounding for an emancipated self-understanding that provides a base for political opposition and struggle" (Ferguson 1984: 158). Thus, feminist theory attempts to provide a conception of self, knowledge, and practice, that is better able to address the experiences of women, while at the same time providing a rudimentary sketch of an emancipated future. "By locating and giving voice to the continuing creation and expression of women's subjugated knowledge, feminist discourse calls upon the newly disinterred past and the newly revealed present to move toward a freshly imagined future" that is "distinguished from the world of men by different

[5] This aspiration is pervasive in a wide variety of disciplines. For example, Elizabeth Meese sees the same sort of aspiration at play in literary criticism:

The "phallic" critics have produced extremely narrow views of what great literature is and how to interpret it, not so much because they enjoy seeing reflections of themselves and their values in what they praise (though this is partially true), but because they close ranks—through pretenses to equality, objectivity and universality—in the service of maintaining masculinist values. (Meese 1986: 12)

Meese goes on to argue that feminist literary criticism must avoid this aspiration if it is also to avoid its deficiencies. Thus, "feminist criticism remains a monumental undertaking which involves changing the very structure/sex of knowledge" (Meese 1986: 13).

Similarly, in her book on semiotics, Kaja Silverman argues that "sexual difference [is] an organizing principle not only of the symbolic order and its 'contents' (signification, discourse, subjectivity), but of the semiotic account of these things" (Silverman 1983: viii). Moreover, this account is represented by "theoretical systems. . . [which] present themselves as relevant to any cultural situation" but whose "categories are culturally fabricated and . . . function to seal off criticism and change" (Silverman 1983: 192).

notions of individual identity, by different standards of morals and by different approaches to the problems of politics" (Ferguson 1984: 159).

At the base of this reconstructive project is the articulation of a conception of self-identity that results from an "ontological shock" (Bartky 1977: 29), stemming from the realization that what human beings are *supposed* to be by "nature" is something that women are assuredly not. While divided by their experiences as members of certain classes, races, ethnic and cultural groups, women "nonetheless encounter a characteristic set of linguistic and institutional practices constitutive of the second sex" (Ferguson 1984: 158–59). And the concept of the self that arises out of these practices "is forthrightly and consistently defined in terms of the contexts of social relationships" (Ferguson 1984: 159).

What is this "relational" self, and how do its characteristic features bear on social knowledge and political practice? As feminists believe it is difficult, if not impossible, to detach or uncouple and examine elements of a discourse in isolation from a particular set of interests that inform them, we must see feminist discourse in the same light. Thus, Catherine MacKinnon's suggestion that "feminism is the first theory to emerge from those whose interests it affirms," and whose "method recapitulates as theory the reality it seeks to capture" (MacKinnon 1981: 29) serves to alert us to the intimate relationship between the emancipatory interests of feminist discourse and the character or content of that discourse at every level.

But this is not to say that feminist discourse serves as a mere rationalization of the struggle for women's emancipation. On the one hand, feminist metatheory seeks a better, and more accurate, description of the constitution of the self, knowledge and practice; on the other, it seeks to exploit this description as a basis for the projection of what an emancipated existence can be. The normative ideal of emancipation is thus in part parasitic on the descriptive accuracy of the metatheoretical account, and the goal of seeking descriptive accuracy is driven by the interest in the emancipation of women.

This is *not*, however, to say that a defensible metatheory leads to an interest in emancipation any more than an interest in emancipation leads to a defensible metatheory. But clearly the possibility of either requires the other. Indeed, as Kathy Ferguson has pointed out, "one can certainly choose to avoid defining one's own situation and instead embrace the definition of the situation that others apply. People can choose to deny freedom and affirm subordination" (Ferguson 1980: 114). But an interest in emancipation can lead to real emancipation only if it is grounded in an accurate understanding of how social and political practices, knowledge and self-identity come to be structured. As Bartky notes:

> Feminists are not aware of different things than other people; they are aware of the same things differently. Feminist consciousness, it might be ventured, turns a "fact" into a "contradiction;" often, features of social reality are only apprehended *as* contradictory from the vantage point of a radical project of transformation.
>
> Thus, we understand what we are and where we are in the light of what we are not yet. But the perspective from which I understand the world must be rooted in the world, too. That is, my comprehension of what I and my world can become must take account of what they *are*. (Bartky 1977: 29)

When we reconsider the general tenor of feminist critiques of dominant discourse, what we see is an attack on the incoherence of the various dualisms presupposed in this discourse: mind/body, ideal/material, social/natural, knower/known, theory/practice, public/private, self/other, etc. And if feminists (and others) are right in their claim that all such distinctions are relative to a social framework or institutionalized set of norms, then our practices, knowledge and self-identities likewise must be understood in this light. That is, what we do, what we know, and who we are is the result of the intersubjectively constituted character of social reality as much as anything else.

Thus, to return to the question of self-identity, feminists have shown that those forms of discourse that would take our identity as something already given, existing outside of, or prior to, our social relations are radically mistaken. Rather, we should recognize that one's "relationships to other people are fundamental to being a person, and one cannot become a person without relationships to other people. A person is a historical being whose history is fundamentally a history of relationships to other people" (Whitbeck 1983: 77; see also Ferguson 1980: 24).

From this preliminary characterization of the relational self, it seems to follow that we are nothing more than "identities" determined by the historical contexts in which we find ourselves. But feminist theory does not simply oppose a "socially determined self" to a "naturally determined self." To some extent we see in these two stances a replication of the nature-nurture debate: either we have an identity that is independent of social conditioning (and indeed, liberalism employs this claim as a critical lever against "unnatural" social impositions), or our identities are exhausted by the roles that are imposed upon us. This is not the place to rehash this debate except to note that it, too, can be understood as yet another example of dualistic (male) thinking.[6] Depending upon which side one opts for, such thinking overlooks the way in which the self is socially constituted, or it emphasizes the context-dependent character of our self-identity while ignoring the ways in which those contexts are shaped *by conscious human action*—action that can, in principle, aim at changing the context in which it takes place.[7] The feminist conception of a relational self must be distinguished from dualistic thought of every sort. For feminists, the self is indeed socially constituted, but at the same time it may be socially constitutive. Identity is "dialectical" (O'Brien 1981: 105; Ferguson 1980: 24), "wholistic," "organic" (Davaney 1981: 3), or "transformative" (MacKinnon 1981: 29). Although the terms used by feminists are varied, they all point to a conception of self-identity that is the result of a process "in which the individual and the social group interact with one another and are selectively and causally determinative of both each other and the environment" (Ferguson 1980: 24). The self is not something given prior to social relations, nor is it something that need be exhaustively determined by those relations; it is not static, but always (potentially) a condition of *becoming* rather than *being*.[8]

To take this relational or processual conception of the self as basically accurate, indeed as a "universal condition" in which the self is viewed "not as a thing that develops but as the very process of development itself" (Ferguson 1980: 65, 114), is to abandon those philosophical arguments that conceptualize the self in terms that lend themselves to dualistic thinking. Moreover, the implication of this claim is that we must also abandon conceptions of knowledge and practice that fall prey to dualistic thinking, for it is not only the self that is relational. In this we can discern the connection between the descriptive and normative aspects of feminist discourse—indeed we can see the extent to which even this dualism is incoherent. To ask "what is the self?" is thus to ask by what process identity is created. To ask "what is an adequate form of knowledge?" is to ask whether knowledge claims acknowledge their processual character. And to ask "what kind of practice is rational?" is to ask to what extent practice is

---

[6] For feminists, both the nondeterminist and the determinist fail to provide models of the self that can inform truly emancipatory political practices. This struggle can be informed only by a conception of subjectivity that recognizes that women have been "determined" only because of theories that distort reality, and that freedom is not a matter of seeing oneself as "self-made," but rather as "self-making *with* others." This conception of subjectivity should become clear shortly.

[7] The criticism here was a central focus in my treatment of Foucault. See chapter 3.

[8] The affinities between critical feminist theory and Freire on this matter are particularly evident. See chapter 5.

the result of "an ongoing interaction with others, with nature, and with the world in which the individual both creates herself and is created through these connections" (Ferguson 1984: 178).

To the extent that dominant discourse acknowledges none of these things it remains a *dominating* discourse. To see that one is victimized as a woman is to recognize that "interpretations of reality emerge from and reflect their social contexts," *and* that "unlike most men, women have been denied significant participation in this meaning process" (Davaney 1981: 3).

> To be dominated is to be in a situation that has been defined by another person or group and to be forced to operate within this situation without being able to effect one's own definition of it. [Consequently,] The first condition for liberation requires that one be able to define one's own situation in order to insure that this definition is not encroached upon by others. (Ferguson 1980: 105)

But while realizing that "the conditions for liberation correspond to sociality and process" (Ferguson 1980: 105), "the mere apprehension of some state of affairs as intolerable does not, of course, transform it. This only power can do" (Bartky 1977: 26–27 passim).

Clearly the first condition of liberation is possible only when one has the power to be self-defining. This struggle for autonomy cannot, however, be understood as asserting one's self-definition at the expense of the autonomy of others, for as we have seen, it is precisely that form of *"power to create the world from one's point of view [that] is power in its male form"* (MacKinnon 1981: 23). What this means is that there is a second condition for liberation as well, and that is "the ability to take the role of other in order to appreciate the perspective of the other":

> To take the role of the other is to affirm the other as a unique durational being and at the same time to affirm oneself as a social being. This second condition might well be called compassion, for it involves taking the perspective of the other in order to understand and appreciate him. (Ferguson 1980: 106)

In what sense does this constitute the outlines of a uniquely *feminist* critical theory? Before answering this question we must note that there is more implied here than what is at first apparent. Feminists have shown that dominant discourses have distorted reality, that a better account of knowledge and the self shows us to be historically and relationally defined and defining beings, and that recognizing this gives us a better understanding of those conditions necessary for true emancipation. But what makes this the foundation of a truly *feminist* critical theory is the claim that a more adequate understanding of self and knowledge is reflected in, and reflective of, women's self understandings, and, therefore, *that the kinds of practices that would bring about real emancipation are immanent in the actual practices of women.*

The relation between the descriptive and normative character of feminist metatheory thus extends to the embracing of women's self-understandings and practices as aspects of a model of an emancipatory discourse. "The articulation of a feminist standpoint based on women's relational self-definition and activity exposes the world men have constructed and the self-understanding which manifests these relations as partial and perverse" (Hartsock 1983a: 305). At the same time, this perspective demonstrates that those practices that aim at "the (mutual) realization of people" are manifest "in a variety of particular forms, most, if not all, of which are regarded as women's work and are therefore largely ignored by the dominant culture" (Whitbeck 1983: 65).

In this respect, feminist "theory" seeks to identify as feminist "practice" those experiences of women that embody a relational self, knowledge and practice. But the articulation of this experience must proceed carefully. One cannot simply embrace all aspects of women's experiences equally, any more than Marx thought one could embrace all aspects of the proletariat's conditions equally. To do so would make the idea of a critical theory superfluous, for any such critical theory tries to identify which aspects of life can be embraced as potentially emancipating, and which aspects are destructive and conducive to continued subordination. This discourse

> will not be discovered full blown and whole, to be laid down in place of the established regimes of thought; rather [it] will be articulated through an ongoing process of self-discovery and self-creation, an emergent process involving the crafting and recrafting of particular insights into unfolding and ever-shifting unities of explanation and action. (Ferguson 1984: 157)

Nonetheless, as a critical theory, feminist theory must be developed by articulating the experience of women's lives, and it must take as its practical grounding the ways these lives provide models of emancipation in practice.

FEMINIST THEORY IN PRACTICE: THE POLITICS OF EMANCIPATION

If we take as established fact the almost universal subordination of women, then we must acknowledge the risk that feminist discourse may well reflect a kind of "subordinate self," hardly the sort of self-understanding that would be conducive to self-emancipation. Among feminists, this particular question has become an important issue, for there has been a tendency to uncritically cast womens' experiences as necessarily emancipating, thus avoiding the need to parse those experiences for their potentially destructive features.

The most common version of this tendency has involved an uncritical appropriation of women's experiences as "nurturers" or "caretakers." This is usually understood as a kind of practice and form of self-identity coextensive with the activity of mothering (see, for example, Ruddick 1980; Elshtain 1979, 1982). The problems with this particular characterization of women's experience are multiple. For one, this understanding "has often been used to evoke a sentimental picture of a woman doing a variety of mindless tasks in response to the demands of others" (Whitbeck 1983: 65). Caretaking is thus "all too easily romanticized and sentimentalized, reduced to terminal cheerfulness or to a masochistic need for self-sacrifice" (Ferguson 1984: 170).

Nonetheless, most feminists have embraced caretaking as an important example of the kind of practice that can be considered potentially emancipating. But while most have emphasized the compassionate character of "mother-child relationships and the practice of mothering and/or family living" as well as those of "nursing and caring for the sick, disabled, and elderly, teaching, psychotherapy and counseling, and various forms of spiritual practice" (Whitbeck 1983: 75), some have been wary of overly simplistic accounts of these practices.

A critical feminist theory would, then, also entail a critique of "maternal thinking." This critique would try to show that there is a danger in reducing women's caretaking practices to those of maternal self-sacrifice and altruism. It would anticipate the problems resulting from an uncritical linking of traditional female roles with a set of moral, ethical and political prescriptions. The danger here, as many feminists have argued, is that such prescriptions may perpetuate the oppression of women precisely because the attitudes they prescribe reflect the ways women are usually socialized and those actual conditions, institutions and roles in which they typically function (Blum et al. 1976: 223; Tormey 1976: 218). But pointing out such problems does not thereby mean that women can ignore their traditional experiences. It does, however, mean they cannot appropriate them without reconceptualizing their meanings.

One way of doing so is to point out that what these maternal practices lack is "a positive conception of 'caring-with-autonomy' " (Blum et al. 1976: 224). This deficiency is in part due to the fact that "to the extent that these relationships have been represented in the dominant culture, they have been misrepresented" (Whitbeck 1983: 75). By re-interpreting these practices in terms of a relational ontology, however, we can appreciate that it is only by a " 'pathological twist of social memory' [that] is the predictable consequence of [a dualist] ontology" that we forget the mutually supportive character of the relations with which women are traditionally associated (Whitbeck 1983: 78). Thus, feminists have argued that the attitude of self-sacrifice or altruism associated with such practices need not take the form of "giving up what one has a right to have, i.e., one's fair share":

> If self-sacrifice takes the form of giving up one's share, then the refusal to be self-sacrificing can take the form of accepting (or insisting upon) those things that one has a right to have. But this is compatible with taking the interests of others into account, indeed, it requires that their interests be given consideration and the weight they deserve. (Tormey 1976: 220)

To reconceptualize traditional women's roles in this way is to see that each person's moral integrity is contingent on the achievement of the moral integrity of others, and that self interest is not something that can be neatly separated from the interests of others (Whitbeck 1983: 80).

Moreover, there is a sense in which the appeal to "caretaking" experiences of women *qua* mothers also involves a serious distortion of the different kinds of experiences women have had. After all, women have been shaped not only by their experiences as mothers, but equally as daughters, factory workers, secretaries, nurses, painters, poets, novelists, lawyers, doctors, academics, etc.

> Locating women's experience as a place to work from . . . does not, if we follow this line of analysis, land us in a determinate type of position or identify a category of persons from whose various and typical positions in the world we must take as our starting point. Women are variously located in society. Their situations are much more various than the topics we recognize somewhat stereotypically as women's topics would suggest. Their position also differs very greatly by class. Even among housewives, who appear to share a universal fate, there are rather wider differences in the conditions, practices, and organization of housework and the social relations in which it is embedded than our studies and the ways in which they have been framed would allow. (Smith 1979: 170)

The values of care and connection that are characteristic of mothering are therefore but an aspect of, and not the whole, of women's experience (Ferguson 1984: 173). And if we look beyond the caretaking-of-mothering, we would see that a more politically relevant form of caretaking is also manifest in other practices that are exemplary for their "intense, reciprocal, face-to-face ties" and by their "voluntary and egalitarian quality." Practices such as "consciousness-raising groups, housekeeping 'pools,' collective/communal living arrangements, and co-parenting," all of which "have drawn on support networks based upon the ties of friendships" (Ferguson 1984: 173).

Finally, an emphasis on maternal caretaking as exemplary of women's experiences leads to a problematic conception of feminist politics, and, as such, potentially undermines the emancipatory intent of feminist discourse (see, especially, Dietz 1985). A political practice that regards maternal caretaking as its central organizational strategy can be paternalistic—or maternalistic—as much as anything else. In fact, maternal caretaking presupposes relations of inequality embodied in the mother-child relation, and even though it is only a temporary inequality, it nonetheless serves as a poor model for larger relations between equals, which must be based on mutual respect, not familial love (Dietz 1985: 31; Ferguson 1984: 171). The stability of relationships among people who accepted this model "could as easily be nurtured by a benevolent despotism, in which rulers do what is best for us" (Ferguson 1984: 172), and the self-sacrifice engendered by an uncritical commitment to caretaking "ultimately contributes to the perpetuation of practices and relationships of domination and competition" (Whitbeck 1983: 81). Instead, a critical feminist theory must seek "in its own territory" models of political identity that are "participatory and democratic" (Dietz 1987: 18, 14).

A number of relevant lessons for a feminist critical theory may be drawn from the feminist critique of caretaking/nurturance. First, while acknowledging the potentially emancipatory features of a caretaking ethos, feminist discourse must be clear about those aspects of this attitude that may prove destructive. A second concern is that this conception of the self must be adequate to the range of differences in the experiences of women. Third, this self-understanding must be adequate to the task of political struggle; that is, it must be emancipatory *for women* without at the same time implicating itself in a conception of political practice that merely exchanges one form of domination for another. It must, in other words, seek womens' practices that

> entail a struggle for individual autonomy that is *with others* and for community that *embraces diversity*—that is, for an integration of the individual and the collective in an ongoing process of authentic individuation and genuine connectedness. (Ferguson 1984: 157)

In this respect, even the activity of feminist theorizing itself has been seen as an exemplary practice that reflects a relational conception of self and knowledge. For example, Marcia Westkott argues that feminist approaches to social science are not intended to be just about women, but are rather constituted for women by women:

> A social science for women does not exclude information about women, but informs the knowledge it seeks with an intention for the future rather than a resignation to the present. The intention is not an historical inevitability but a vision, an imaginative alternative that stands in opposition to the present conditions of the cultural domination of women and is indeed rooted in these conditions. (Westkott 1979: 428)

Furthermore, while feminist criticisms of social science content, method and purpose are not yet "tightly integrated into an academic discipline," in emphasizing "the dialectics of self and other, person and society, past and future, knowledge and practice," they embody an "approach to social knowledge as open, contingent, and humanly compelling, as opposed to that which is closed, categorical, and human controlling" (Westkott 1979: 430).

In all of these practices, we see a common thread: a commitment to a form of human relationship that exemplifies the need to think of oneself as self-defining with others, as embodying a form of knowledge that is constituted with others, as entailing a political practice that is self-emancipatory because it is *with others*. The understanding of self, knowledge and practice they embody should not, however, be taken as a model for the structuring of all relationships irrespective of context. In fact, this ideal must be seen as a call to struggle against those discourses, past, present, and future, that would deny the possibility of a continuous process in which we mutually make and remake ourselves and our world. The "utopian moment" of feminist theory does not involve separating what can be from what actually is; feminist theory does not posit an unbridgable gap between the ideal and the actual. Feminist theory does not seek to define and defend a conception of emancipation *a priori*; on the contrary, it seeks to articulate just those kinds of practices here and now that can be considered emancipating. And the difference between the attempt to define an *emancipated* and an *emancipating* practice should not be lost to us. It constitutes nothing less than the difference between the idea of a critical theory and a critical theory in practice.

FEMINISM AND CRITICAL THEORY

My intention has been to show how feminist theory represents the realization of the idea of a critical theory in practice. In this, I have attempted to bring to light the ways in which feminist theory is informed by a recognition of the oppression of women, how this oppression gives rise to the "emancipatory interest" of feminist theory, how feminist theory brings the real foundations of this oppression to light through a critique of the distortions and misdescriptions in dominant discourse, and how feminist theory both originates and anticipates its application *in its addressees' practices*. In this respect, feminist theory can be seen as having the characteristic goal, logical structure, and conception of verification that Raymond Geuss suggests are constitutive of a critical theory (see the introduction to Part II). But more than this, feminist theory also offers important lessons for critical theory. In my concluding chapter I shall expand these lessons and relate them to those gleaned from dependency theory, Freire's critical pedagogy and liberation theology, but a preliminary sketch involves pointing out the most important differences between a feminist conception of critical theory and that found in both modernist and postmodernist critical theory. The clearest difference is that feminists make central the historicity and contextuality of their own interests and horizons:

> Feminism does not begin with the premise that it is unpremised. It does not aspire to persuade an unpremised audience because there is no such audience. Its project is to uncover and claim as valid the experience of women, the major content of which is the devaluation of women's experiences. (MacKinnon 1981: 4)

We have seen that both modernist and postmodernist critical theory also posit the need to be contextually sensitive in one's analysis. But the predominant thrust of modernist and postmodernist critical theory is toward a radical separation of theory and practice, a separation feminist theory does not endorse.

Consider, for example, the character of feminist critiques of modernist critical theory. While the Frankfurt School and Habermas identify their work as a kind of of philosophically transformed Marxism, and in this find a common ground with feminist critiques of Marxism, there are aspects of their work that are at odds with feminist concerns. As we have seen, the modernists tend to retreat, in David Held's (1980: 371) words, to "a concept of critique which they, themselves, in other contexts, had rejected: an ahistorical essence becomes the criterion for the evaluation of the present" (Held 1980: 371). The problem with this retreat, at least from a feminist perspective, should be clear: it is but another example of an argument that seeks universal normative grounding for concrete practical problems. The exclusion of womens' interests may not be as explicit in modernist critical theory as it is in the case of traditional Marxism. In fact, as I noted in earlier chapters, modernist critical theory founders in part because its attitude toward *any* historically situated struggle is ambiguous. But implicit or explicit, it is nonetheless an exclusion.

We should not, however, lose sight of the differences between the modernists. Clearly the politics of despair that characterized the later work of the Frankfurt School members is insufficient for the practical tasks of women's emancipation, but is this equally true of Habermas, who has been unwilling to fall into despair as did his intellectual predecessors? For some feminists it is not, and they have latched on to Habermas's model of the ideal speech situation as one that has "salience" for feminist concerns in that it "provides intimations of a future in which human speech and discursive reflection is undominated, uncoerced, [and] unmanipulated" (Elshtain 1981: 143–44). But however attractive the ideal, I believe that a critical feminist theory must see Habermas's work as problematic for the specific needs of a women's struggle.

In the first place, Habermas assumes a particular conception of human identity, a particular personality type, *for* whom the conditions of the ideal speech situation would appear as the correct procedural context for arriving at justifiable norms. This "personality" embodies a "post-conventional ego-identity" (Benhabib 1982: 62). This understanding would be controversial enough, I think, for feminists to view Habermas's arguments with some skepticism, for the "post-conventional ego-identity" which Habermas (following Lawrence Kohlberg) assumes to be necessary for rational discourse is none other than the personality type that Carol Gilligan (1982) has shown to be constitutive of male gender identity. And feminists would be right to criticize Habermas's use of this conception of self-identity for its gender-specific features.

In this sense, Habermas's counterfactual construction of the ideal speech situation is flawed because it is circular: whether we accept the ideal speech situation as an adequate arrangement for the "legitimate" determination of norms depends upon whether we accept the particular conception of self-identity presupposed by it (Benhabib 1982: 63). But even if we leave aside the difficulties feminists might have with Habermas's theory at this level, other problems still remain.

Unlike liberal theorists, Habermas does not preclude the appeal to any relevant social knowledge and places no restrictions on the kind of social information that individuals may use in their normative deliberations (Benhabib 1982: 69). Thus, the findings of feminist inquiry would be, it seems, admissible in passing judgement on the legitimacy of any particular social order. However, it must be noted that the function of the ideal speech situation is to act as a procedure of discursive will formation on generalizable interests (Habermas 1975: 111–17).

And the problems here, as Seyla Benhabib (1982: 70–71) argues, are threefold.

First, the notion that generalizable interests can be articulated only in the ideal speech situation means that we are unable to judge any such claims outside of that ideal context since, as Habermas himself admits, the conditions in which we find ourselves rarely, if ever, resemble that condition. Bluntly stated, it would be impossible to determine which particular interests genuinely qualify as general, given that we speak *only* from our particular historical contexts. In this, Benhabib says, "The gulf between the ideal and the actual, the normative and the empirical is unbridgable."

Second, the ideal speech situation does not guarantee that arguments advanced for particular interest claims *will* be "rational"; it only guarantees the equal rights of participants to advance claims. What Habermas's description of the ideal speech situation fails to recognize is that the "intelligent exercise of these rights . . . depends on the nature of the arguments advanced, on their quality, and rationality." Moreover, what "we have to know beforehand is whether these claims are true and rational." Because the ideal speech situation is supposed to define what is "rationally acceptable" *a priori*, it closes off the possibility of articulating a conception of rationality that would allow us to make such judgements on the basis of historically contingent knowledge claims.

Finally, given that we lack those universal standards necessary to distinguish "distorted" and "undistorted" communication, and that the ideal speech situation is itself inadequate to define the conditions of rational consensus, can we actually compare "normative structures existing at a given time with the hypothetical state of a system of norms formed, *ceteris paribus*, discursively" (Habermas 1975: 113)? In light of these difficulties, Benhabib (1982: 71) says, "Do we know in the name of which or what we are to criticize?"

By treating only universalizable need interpretations as legitimate, Habermas effectively interprets all diversity of interests that lead to conflict as illegitimate particularisms (Benhabib 1982: 71). But, as Benhabib sees it,

This is a transcendental illusion, for, although the very project of an emancipated society means eliminating *certain structural* sources of interest conflict in present societies, a human society freed from all sources of conflict and diversity of interests cannot be conceived of without eliminating the radical plurality of ways of life, of cultural traditions and individual biographies which differentiate humans from one another. Such a society of reconciled intersubjectivity would be a self-identical collectivity, but not a

human community. When the critique of the false universalism of particularistic interests is conceived as the desubjectivization of all interests, then
those interests that are rooted in the pluralisms of autonomous life forms,
living communities and self-conceptions are excluded from political discourse. (1982: 72)

What Benhabib's critique of Habermas shows is that Agnes Heller
is indeed right in saying that Habermas cannot answer the question
"of whether, and, if so, how, distortion of communication is motivated
. . . nor can he answer the question of what would motivate us to get
rid of this distortion" (Heller 1982: 25). The reason is that Habermas
seems to be unable to conceptualize contextually defined struggles in
any terms that do not appeal to a universal grounding. While he points
toward "a dialogic conception of normative reason [which] promises a
critique of the assumption that normative reason is impartial and universal," he nonetheless "reneges on this promise . . . because he retains a commitment to the ideal of normative reason as expressing an
impartial point of view" (Young 1986: 391, 392).

Perhaps none of these objections would mean much were it not for
the fact that they are integral to issues of practice. The attempt to
conceptualize reason as impartial is, after all, not only illusory, but
oppressive (Young 1986: 383). As Benhabib notes, Habermas understands emancipation not only as the elimination of those structural
obstacles that create relations of domination and subordination, but as
a form of human society freed from *all* sources of conflict and diversity; he posits as an emancipated existence a "society of reconciled
intersubjectivity" that is also a "self-identical collectivity." But the
problem with this, Benhabib continues, is that such a society "is not
a human community" and that, furthermore, "not only is the project
of such a transparent and self-identical collectivity impossible, it is not
even desirable" (Benhabib 1982: 72).[9]

The feminist aim of preserving plurality and difference is of course
grounded in the desire to see that the self-empowerment of women is
always kept open against the impositions of authoritarian discourses.
Yet this should not be taken to mean that a critical feminist theory is
indifferent regarding the normative worth of different self-understandings, traditions, and practices. Or to put the matter another way,
by respecting plurality and difference a feminist critical theory does
not endorse a kind of postmodernist normative skepticism. A critical
feminist discourse is after all a discourse of practical solidarity as well,
a fact which requires feminism to distinguish between potentially

[9] For a more concrete application of this criticism to issues of particular concern to
feminists, see Fraser (1985b: 128–29).

emancipating and oppressive theories and practices. This should be obvious in light of the several critiques feminists have leveled not only at androcentric discourses, but at many purportedly "feminist" discourses. And it is in feminist critiques of Foucault that the need for plurality *and solidarity* is further clarified.

One way in which feminists have criticized Foucault dovetails with my own critique (see chapter 3). What Foucault lacks—and what a critical feminist theory requires—is an adequate conception of subjectivity (see for example, Ferguson 1984). But there is also a deepening of this critique on the part of other feminists. For Foucault's inadequate conception of subjectivity is merely indicative of a whole range of philosophical difficulties in his work, all of which point toward problems his theory has for conceptualizing both the sources and promise of a specifically feminist struggle.

The major sources of trouble in Foucault's work are at once conceptual and practical. But there is more. For these criticisms also suggest that the deficiencies in his theory can be linked to the fact that his discourse is androcentric. Focusing on Foucault's criticisms of the disciplinary character of "continuous history," critical "reason," and the notion of a "founding subject," Issac Balbus (1986) suggests that Foucault simply goes too far, and the result is that "Foucault's deconstruction of disciplinary discourse/practice betrays all the signs of its masculine origin" (Balbus 1986: 475).

In his efforts to dismiss "continuous histories" as providing "a privileged shelter for the sovereignty of consciousness" (Foucault 1972), Foucault would seem to "make it impossible for women even to speak of the historically universal misogyny from which they have suffered and against which they have struggled" (Balbus 1986: 475).[10] While a critical feminist theory must be aware of the various ways in which androcentric discourse has attempted to privilege a "male" consciousness, its critical edge in part derives precisely from the recognition of the historically and cross-culturally pervasive character of women's oppression. "Continuous histories," in other words, may be put to critical or conservative ends. And Foucault seems to leave us rudderless in our attempts to parse them for their adequacy by virtue of his sweeping philosophical condemnation of all such histories.

Furthermore, Foucault's opposition to critical reason would seem to "condemn as totalitarian the very awareness of the pervasiveness of male domination women have so painfully achieved" (Balbus 1986:

[10] While I agree with much of what Balbus says *against* Foucault, I have more difficulty with his emphasis on "mothering" attitudes as the basis of reconstructive moral and political norms. This should be obvious from my earlier deployment of feminist critiques of "maternal thinking."

475). Here again Foucault seems to leave us rudderless. By dismissing all attempts to give a rational grounding to critique, Foucault cannot distinguish between those that appeal to a kind of "totalizing" logic of identity and those that do not. A critical feminist theory is (like Foucault's critical theory) opposed to "totalizing" identity claims. In its emphasis on plurality and difference, as well as its attempts to recover the "rational core" of women's experiences, a critical feminist theory steers a course between the totalitarian logic of identity of which Foucault is justifiably wary, and the radical dismissal of rationality and reason his position seems to imply.

Finally, Foucault's attack on subjectivity appears to make it correlative with subjugation—a conclusion no critical feminist can accept. Recapitulating my earlier criticism of Foucault, I quote Balbus (1986: 477), who notes that

> the one subject who cannot be gotten rid of is the theorist him/herself. The very intention to identify knowledge/power complexes as objects for deconstruction presupposes a subjectivity that is . . . an animating source of the deconstructive discourse.

The trick here is not to simply posit "a subject," but rather to articulate those forms of subjectivity that are viable sources of both deconstruction *and* reconstruction. Where a critical feminist theory differs from a postmodernist one is that the former tries to take up this task while the latter refuses to do so. Thus does Nancy Fraser (1985a: 182) argue that "the feminist interrogation of autonomy is the theoretical edge of a movement that is literally remaking the social identities and historical self-interpretations of large numbers of women and of some men."

The irony in all these criticisms is that Foucault himself appeared to finally recognize the fact that his sweeping philosophical condemnations would not wash. However, even while his later appeals to "the insurrection of subjugated knowledges," "new forms of subjectivity" and, finally, to "bodies and pleasures" and an "aesthetic" subjectivity seem to lend themselves to an endorsement of feminist theory and practice, Foucault nonetheless offered (in John Rajchman's [1986: 179] apt description) "a philosophy neither of solidarity nor of objectivity."

Certainly a critical feminist theory does not appeal to a philosophy of objectivity, for no such philosophy is possible—at least when understood in terms of the kind of objectivity one finds in scientistic, liberal, Marxist, and perhaps modernist critical theoretic discourse. But neither does a feminist critical theory prescind from the task of articulating a discourse of solidarity. And in this it distinguishes itself from the kind of postmodernism Foucault's work represents.

A critical feminist theory, I submit, offers a metatheoretical self-understanding that provides a way of moving beyond the modernist/postmodernist impasse. Against the modernists, feminists show that neither the self, nor knowledge, nor theory, nor emancipation itself can be apprehended *a priori*. To take seriously the fact that we are historical beings, that human life is a continuous process of making and remaking social life, is to recognize that the purported goal of critical theory, "a form of life free of domination in all of its forms," cannot be interpreted as a form of life that is free of all conflict of interests. To take seriously our historicity is to see that it is neither possible nor desirable for critical theory to treat emancipation in universal terms. And the relational perspective on self, knowledge and practice characteristic of feminist theory avoids this problem, precisely because it does take our historicity seriously. In a passage I believe dovetails neatly with Benhabib's criticism of Habermas's universalist vision, and that also taps into the conception of emancipation implicit in that criticism, Kathy Ferguson offers this account of the "emancipated form of life" which follows from a specifically feminist critical theory:

> Feminist discourse does not envision some underlying unanimity in political life, but it does envision a polity in which modes of conflict and definitions of interests are worked out within a context of general concern for the humanness of others. This vision is not based on some abstract idea of human nature or on pie-in-the-sky hopes for a promised land. . . . Presumably there would still be conflict in a feminist society, but there would be a public space available for the ongoing process of conflict resolution. All interested individuals would have access to this space. . . . Conflict would not be either eliminated or suppressed; rather, individuals would be drawn into an interactional process in which adaptation and reconciliation are encouraged by a feminist understanding of the relation between the individual and the collective. (Ferguson 1984: 198)

Such a politics would respect the kind of plurality and difference that is our lot as human beings. But from this it does not follow that a feminist critical theory will be indifferent toward difference and plurality—a position that appears to follow from a postmodernist normative skepticism. In Nancy Hartsock's words, "Feminism as a mode of analysis leads us to respect experience and difference, to respect people enough to believe that they are in the best position to make their own revolution" (Hartsock 1981a: 40). All of which is to say that a critical feminist theory must remain committed to solidarity with others who struggle to find their own voices.

Which of these voices should feminists embrace, and which should they reject? That will depend on the character of the arguments advanced and the practices they presuppose. But feminism does not leave us without some direction here. Ironically enough, one of the clearest statements of how a specifically feminist critical theory might address the need to respect plurality and difference while also being vigilant in its commitment to solidarity comes from Theodor Adorno:

> Hope cannot aim at making the mutilated social character of women identical to the mutilated social character of men; rather its goal must be a state . . . in which all that survives the disgrace of the differences between the sexes is the happiness that difference makes possible. (Quoted in Cornell and Thurschwell 1986: 484)

PART III

Rethinking Critical Theory

CRITICAL THEORY is meant to be a form of knowledge that can enlighten us about the roots of social and political oppression, and help us collectively transform our relations in ways that might overcome the damaging and destructive legacies we have inherited from the past. Indeed, it might be argued that critical theory is about the way human emancipation and social progress might be achieved. Those who have been central figures in the articulation of the idea of a critical theory—Marx, the Frankfurt School, Habermas, and Foucault—as well as some of those who have been engaged in trying to realize its aims—the dependency theorists, Freire, liberation theologians, and feminists—provide compelling arguments in support of the need for critical theory, as well as useful insights into how it might be carried out.

There are, of course, differences between the various critical theories I have discussed about what emancipation and progress would entail. Some of these understandings we might view with skepticism; others may prove more attractive and coherent. But one point I have been trying to make is that the standards we might use in accepting or rejecting the arguments involved can be developed out of a critical engagement with critical theory itself.

When the useful insights of critical theory are turned toward an interrogation of its own claims, what emerges is a model of intellectual reflection and practical reasoning that both embodies and demands that we recognize the historical contingency and contextual specificity of our self-understandings. Critical theory thus takes—and compels us to see—the specific traditions of discourse and practice in which we are embedded as the source of our frustrations *and* aspirations, and it invites us to critically engage our own and others' self-understandings and lives for those transformative possibilities worthy of rational assent.

This model will no doubt sit uncomfortably with many. It challenges us to rethink some of the most deeply held beliefs we may have. I will address this discomfort in my concluding chapter, in order to show it to be unwarranted. When we appreciate the shortcomings and potential strengths of critical theory, whether in its "received" or less well-known versions, we will be in a better position to understand what emancipation and progress requires. Critical theory is a form of knowledge we ignore at our peril, for it facilitates the sorts of activities, intellectual and practical, that promise to give human rationality its greatest due. These are perhaps bold claims, but I think they are also plausible ones.

CHAPTER 8

In Defense of Critical Theory

> All social life is essentially *practical*. All mysteries which
> mislead theory into mysticism find their rational solution in
> human practice and the comprehension of this practice.
>   —Karl Marx

THIS EPIGRAPH, which is the eighth of Marx's famous Theses on Feuerbach, is the kernel of an adequate foundation for critical social theory. It is also the kernel of an adequate understanding of how human progress, both intellectual and practical, may be secured. In this final chapter I will explain how critical theory articulates these two related claims.

First I review the reasons for my belief that the received view of critical theory, that which is found in both modernist and postmodernist critical theory, points toward a defensible articulation of these claims, even while it demonstrates the sorts of difficulties and limitations this articulation may involve. I then attend the reasons why "critical theory in practice" makes good the insights of modernist and postmodernist critical theory, and opens them up in a way that demonstrates the potential of critical theory. This discussion is followed by a more systematic examination of what I call the metatheoretical mediation of theory and practice. All of this brings us to a consideration of the role of critical theory in social progress, and of the implications of my arguments for the future of critical social theory—and social and political life.

This terse plan abstracts a series of systematically related theses the richness and density of which I cannot hope to do justice to here. However, I hope that what follows, even if it is only suggestive, indicates how, against the historical closure that dominant—and dominating—discourses and practices embody, critical theory offers a future open to be made and re-made. There are certainly less desirable legacies we can leave to our children.

THE LIMITATIONS OF CRITICAL THEORY: MODERNIST AND POSTMODERNIST CRITIQUE

The idea of a critical theory is a worthy one. This much, I think, the work of Marx, the Frankfurt School, Habermas, and Foucault, establishes. But modernist and postmodernist critical theory also shows that critical theory may suffer limitations and constraints that restrict its ability to realize its emancipatory aims. These limitations are perhaps best understood as issuing from modernist and postmodernist critical theory's preoccupation with the status of "modernity."

In its concern with "realizing" the promise of modernity, modernist critical theory has not, of course, been uncritical of much that characterizes modern thought and practice. In this, it has been joined by postmodernism, although the critique of modernity that postmodernism offers seeks a radical break with modernity. But while these two discourses are united in their opposition to the predominant forms of theory and practice in modern life, and opposed in their judgments about the potential for human emancipation and historical progress implicit in these theories and practices, their preoccupation with modernity itself seems to have blinded them both to the possibilities for transformation that do not easily fit into the concepts and categories of "the metacritique of modernity." These possibilities are certainly "modern" in a temporal sense, but they are not "modern" in the sense that either modernist or postmodernist critical theory assumes. Perhaps "contemporary" would be a more suitable category for conceptualizing these resources. At any rate, the point is that these conceptual issues are not unrelated to how we judge the emancipatory potential of contemporary empowerment struggles, nor for that matter are they unrelated to either modernist or postmodernist critical theory's ability to identify and facilitate these empowerment movements. In short, "critical theory"—at least as it is usually understood—is deficient in terms of the practical, emancipatory goals its proponents have set for their work.

This deficiency may be revealed by attending the question: Why have both modernist and postmodernist critical theory continued to subscribe to a conception of normative "truth" that is clearly subverted by its deconstructions of so much modern discourse? Raymond Geuss (1981: 94) has given one answer to this question in his study of the Frankfurt School and Habermas, but it is an answer equally applicable to Marx: "Critical theories must be 'true' because the legitimating ideologies of the society claim to be 'true.'" In the case of Foucault's postmodernism the issue might be recast this way: Critical theory must be radically skeptical of all claims to "truth" because the legitimating ideologies of the society claim to be true. But neither the "normative universalism" of modernist critical theory, nor the "normative skepticism" of postmodernism, necessarily follow from their criticisms of the kind of "truth" that the legitimating ideologies of modern societies claim.

In Marx's case, the discourse of normative universalism is expressed in terms of a substantive thesis that identifies the particular interests of the proletariat as the embodiment of the emancipatory interest of "mankind as such." This claim rests on two related assumptions, which, when fully articulated, are undermined by Marx's own attacks on Hegelian idealism and the bourgeois political economists.

First, Marx assumed that there are interests that may unproblematically be cast as "universal." At one level of understanding, this may not be a problematic claim. It might be argued, for example, that all human beings share an interest in being free from domination. But this claim does not carry us very far, for the fact of the matter is that it is vacuous; it gives us no purchase on what kind of freedom we should seek, or even what kind of domination we suffer. This Marx knew. The idea of "emancipation" required substantive practical content, and Marx provided it with content when he identified his critical theory with the interests of the proletariat. But in expressing the unity of these two assumptions, Marx cast the particular, substantive interests of the proletariat as those which would realize a universal interest in emancipation.

These claims are problematic because (in Marx's own words) "Consciousness is . . . from the very beginning a social product, and remains so as long as men exist at all" (Marx 1978: 158), which is in effect to say that the ideals, aspirations, and interests that may be attributed to human beings—even when qualified by the appellations "real" and "enlightened"—cannot be laid down once and for all "so long as men exist." Moreover, these assumptions appear to conflict with the claim (again, in Marx's own words) that "categories are no more eternal than the relations they express. They are historical and transitory products" (Marx 1978: 140).

Now if consciousness—indeed social reality itself—is a "social product," and its categories—and social reality—are historically contingent, then this applies no less to Marxism's claims than to the theories and practices Marx criticizes. Thus, Marx recapitulates the ideal of "truth" found in the theories he opposes.

Where idealism and crude materialism posited their own historically contingent and contextually specific knowledge claims as natural, necessary, universal truths, Marx does so as well. Of course Marx believed that his version of the truth was justified on the grounds that it represented the practical interests of the *real* universal class, as opposed to those of the partial and particular interests of the ruling classes which other social theories advanced. We might even commend Marx for having put the interests of the working class on the theoretical and political agenda. But we should also be wary of the dangers of equating emancipation from domination with the particular emancipatory interests of the working class. For if universalism is the metatheoretical foundation of those practices that have historically entailed the exclusion and manipulation of some persons by others, the history of those societies in which Marx's universalistic assumptions have been acted upon provides little comfort for those who would continue to hold to such assumptions while simultaneously hoping that emancipation might be realized.

But the gap between the deconstructive and reconstructive moments in modernist critical theory is not, as I have argued, limited to Marx's work alone. For even while the critiques of scientism and instrumental reason in the Frankfurt School and Habermas seem to agree with the metatheoretical insights established by Marx's attacks on idealism and crude materialism, these thinkers are also like Marx in their inability to break through the discourse of normative universalism. And the political consequences of their positions are no more promising than those of Marx.

In the case of the Frankfurt School, this lack of promise is manifested in what I have called a politics of despair. Because they continued to accept Marx's universalist assumptions as basically correct, even when they denied that the proletariat is the bearer of a universal interest, the members of the Frankfurt School caught themselves in a self-imposed dilemma. Unable to fully endorse any particular empowerment struggles because each seemed to fall short of expressing a "universal" interest, critical theory was now cast as thought without a movement; hence Lukács' charge that the members of the Frankfurt School had "taken up residence in the 'Grand Hotel Abyss' " (quoted in Jay 1984: 18).

Habermas, by contrast, is not so pessimistic regarding the potential of some social movements to realize an emancipatory politics. But his project of reconstructing historical materialism, which (currently) culminates in the theory of communicative ethics, is so closely tied to the desire to identify the "universalizable" features of these struggles that it effectively ignores the ways in which the substantive social norms that emerge from them are necessarily culturally and historically specific. The unfortunate effect of this, as one feminist has argued (Fraser 1985b: 129), is that Habermas is too easily led to dismissing such norms "as particularistic lapses from universalism." As a result, Habermas seems to preclude from "rational" discourse a consideration of the historically contingent and contextually specific self-understandings (and emancipatory ideals) of the same social movements he purports to endorse. Moreover, even where Habermas is able to identify what he takes to be the universalizable thrust of particular oppositional discourses, the lessons of failed revolutions, imposing on future generations the "universal" interests they identify in the present, should be sufficient to disabuse anyone of the naive belief that what is seen as "emancipating" today will not turn out to be the basis of a suffocating political straightjacket tommorrow.

Modernist critical theory, then, seems unable to close the gap between its practical-emancipatory intentions and its political implications because of its commitment to normative universalism. It is at this point that Foucault's postmodernism re-enters the discussion. For he is no better able to close this gap than are the modernists.

Foucault's failure is that he essentially recapitulates the same discourse of normative universalism he opposes because he advances its obverse as a normative standard of judgement. Where the modernists assume that norms must be universal, Foucault assumes the failure of such arguments implies that all norms are merely arbitrary, personal preferences. This turning of the normative coin, however, is unwarranted and indefensible. And it is here that the issue of the tension between the deconstructive and reconstructive moments in his critical theory may be brought into play.

Like the modernists, Foucault aptly demonstrates the historical and contextual contingency of all forms of social thought. This is the clear message of his deconstructions of the "will to truth" and the "will to power." Foucault can even be commended for having made a significant contribution to recognizing the limits and dangers of the sort of universalist project modernist critical theory embodies. Now in light of this, it might be argued that in a sense there is no tension between the deconstructive and reconstructive moments of his work, for the failure of universalism is the confirmation of Foucault's theses regarding the arbitrary and disciplinary character of all claims to truth. Foucault even seems to often approach a characterization of his own thought in these terms, especially when he claims that his is a discourse that does not seek to find its own "rational" grounding. But in spite of his steadfast commitment to a historicity of knowledge and identity, his commitment to an emancipatory politics and his increasing willingness to address the normative standards of such a politics belies the attempt to characterize *all* knowledge claims as merely arbitrary and all attempts to articulate intersubjectively secured norms as equally insidious.

The tension between the deconstructive and reconstructive moments in Foucault's work is instructive in a way that complements the lessons we can glean from that tension in modernist critical theory. Where the latter demonstrates the practical bankruptcy of normative universalism, the former demonstrates the practical bankruptcy of its opposite, normative skepticism. Or to put the matter in terms I used earlier in this book, universalism closes off the possibility of recognizing the plurality of ways in which emancipation might be realized, while skepticism closes off the possibility of taking up solidarity with those who are oppressed. How, then, does Foucault's work reflect a tension between the two moments of his discourse? It does so by showing that in spite of the facts of contingency, skepticism does not follow. Clearly all knowledge claims are going to be historically and contextually specific, but such specificity does not mean that all such claims are going to be equally defensible, or that it is impossible to rationally adjudicate between them. Were we to take Foucault's normative theses at their face value, the political implication would be exactly what he opposes: arbitrariness and, perhaps, more of the insidious discipline he abhors.

These are obviously nothing more than brief sketches of the ground I covered in the first three chapters. But they do provide a way of getting at the notion that in spite of their apparent differences, there is a sense in which modernist and postmodernist critical theory are more alike than their proponents would perhaps care to admit. Failing to follow their own deconstructive insights through to an adequate reconstruction of a practically effective, potentially emancipating conception of critical theory, modernist and postmodernist critical theory seem unable to bridge the gap between the promise and the realization of their own ideals.

To be sure, the work of Foucault and the modernists appears antithetical, one confirming, one rejecting "reason." But both the confirmation and the rejection are, practically speaking, not altogether unalike. In this respect, Foucault's work is not the antithesis of modernist critical theory or a real challenge to it. This, it seems to me, is the only adequate reading of the fact that the modernists hold out a model of normative truth that no struggles against domination seem to have been able to meet, even while they insist that such norms are indeed realizable. And it is also the only adequate reading of the fact that Foucault confidently condemns all practices as "disciplinary" while at the same time holding out the hope that emancipation is indeed possible.

The common ground both share might be best understood in terms of what I have called the "tyranny of universalism." By seeking a form of practical reason that tends toward establishing normative standards that are not subject to the vicissitudes of human history and contingency, modernist and postmodernist critical theory make it appear that emancipation in practice and theoretical reflections on emancipatory ideals have little, if anything, to do with each other. But theory is not politically innocent, and the failures of modernist and postmodernist critical theory merely drive home the point.

When a critical theory that purports to be the expression of an emancipatory struggle equates that struggle with the realization of universal human emancipation, it lends itself to a kind of political dogmatism that is dictatorial and destructive. This is the tragedy of Marx and the politics of orthodox Marxism. When critical theory takes the form of obstinate insistence on the radical nonidentity between the truth of reason and any existing practice, it justifies political paralysis. This is the tragedy of the Frankfurt School and the politics of despair. When critical theory makes reason immanent in the very structures of human life, so that every practice embodying those ideals that are not "universal"—which the theory alone apprehends—is dismissed as particularistic and distorted, it projects a political vision that recedes into a future when the real task is to make that future a reality today. This is the tragedy of Habermas and the politics of transcendental reflection. And when critical theory takes the form of a totalized critique of thought itself, in which case theory is committed to refusing to name the ground on which it stands, it plays into a politics of evasion. And this is the tragedy of Foucault and the politics of radical skepticism.

But whatever its form, the refusal to see contingent practices as the ground of theory opens a practical and political wound that is difficult to heal. It may of course be objected that modernist and postmodernist critical theory is not unsituated; that it does presuppose specific, historically contingent practices as its own grounding. Nothing in what I have said, however, is meant to deny this claim. Indeed, if these critical theorists are right about the necessary relationship between theory and practice, then it would be absurd to deny that such a relationship exists in their own work. Perhaps a better way of putting my criticisms is to say that the tyranny of universalism is politically stunting. Perhaps it might be argued that the kind of politics that follows from modernist and postmodernist critical theory is best suited to those who do not, in Habermas's words, "have to account with their life histories for the new interpretations of social needs and for accepted means of mastering problematic situations." But this is not the situation of those who are most marginalized by dominant practices.

I do not want to push this characterization too far. It is enough to recognize that modernist and postmodernist critical theory at once points toward, but does not realize, a model of critical theory and practical reason that is suited to the daunting task of taking up solidarity with those who most need it, wherever they may be found.

TRANGRESSING THE LIMITS: CRITICAL THEORY IN PRACTICE

For all of the critical theories in practice I discuss in this book, one crucial question that must be asked of any social theory—critical or not—is: Whose interests are being served by the claims theory provides? How this question is answered is perhaps the first issue on which any judgment of critical theory must turn. No theory is politically neutral; this is a clear lesson that critical theory in practice teaches, and it is one all too often lost on those who seek a truth innocent of its own practical foundations.

The correlative demand that theory clearly address a specific context of oppression and provide the theoretical tools that could issue in an emancipating practice implies a demand for the sublation of theory to practice. This demand is an interested one. It requires nothing less than a commitment to social change. But insofar as a critical theory in practice seeks a change in social life that is liberating, the demands for theoretical coherence, adequacy, and hard-headed verification of truth claims are not minimized, but intensified. In this regard, these critical theories in practice represent a commitment to the advancement of reason and rationality in the structuring of social life without falling prey to the equally treacherous illusions of universalism or skepticism. In the model of the theory-practice relationship that is articulated in these critical theories in practice, the theorist is always driven back to actual practices as the ground on which knowledge claims are to be verified. As we have seen, this verification is both empirical and normative, both retrospective and prospective. Retrospectively, it is empirical in its aim of understanding the reality of particular practices, and normative in its suspicion of the adequacy of dominant discourses as well as its own adequacy. Prospectively, it is empirical in its attempts to critically and constantly reassess the practices of which it aims to be a part, and normative in its insistence that its truth claims must be verified in practical discourse of its addressees. The sublation of theory to practice thus makes practice both the foundation and the goal of theory. I think the term used by the liberation theologians—orthopraxis—is probably the best label available for this model. And it signals, quite simply, the articulation of a model of social theory that is trying to bring an end to the age of innocent criticism, of criticism innocent of its own presuppositions. If there is one thing I hope to have made clear in my treatment of dependency theory, Freire's pedagogy of the oppressed, liberation theology, and feminist critical theory, it is that this model of orthopraxis is not just a reflection on theory, nor even just a reflection on method, but rather a reflection on the politics of social theory and method with the aim of producing a method, theory and practice that is politically emancipating.

Critical theory in practice shows how both the deconstructive and reconstructive moments of critique can be mutually constitutive. These theories dovetail with modernist and postmodernist critical theory insofar as they, too, recognize the contingency of all knowledge, every practice, each understanding of self-identity. But they depart from modernist and postmodernist critical theory by turning these philosophical insights into the foundation of an emancipatory critique. By recognizing the facts that norms, beliefs, identity and practices are intersubjectively constituted and historically and contextually contingent, they posit an ethic of solidarity and plurality as the political presuppositions of their critiques. Mindful of the dangers of normative skepticism for those whose lives are most damaged, they are committed to a kind of theory that is able to justify its solidarity with the victims of oppression. And equally mindful of the dangers of normative universalism, they are committed to a kind of theory that is open to difference and plurality. To be committed to solidarity *and* plurality is no mean task, but to be anything less runs the risk of repeating the same mistakes that gave rise to the need for critical theory.

Such a conclusion is not simply the achievement of taking seriously the arguments of dependency theory, liberation theology, Freire, and feminists. It is what necessarily follows from recognizing that Marx was more or less on the mark when he asserted that all social life is essentially practical, and that it is only when theory comprehends its practical foundations that it will find rational solutions to the challenges and mysteries social life presents to all of us.

METATHEORY AND THE RATIONAL COMPREHENSION OF PRACTICE

We have seen how the commitment to emancipation persistently drives critical social theory back to metatheory. A number of related questions are raised by these philosophical concerns, not the least of which attend the most basic issues of knowledge and being. These questions, the ontological and epistemological, can be treated as analytically distinct, but the achievement of critical theory is that it shows them to be both mutually informing and integrally related to social and political practice. My recurring arguments that what we see in every social theory is the mutual recapitulation of conceptions of knowledge, human identity, and practice, were meant to convey just this point.

I have already addressed in detail how critical theory begins to answer these questions. The metatheoretical presuppositions of critical theory are that human identity and social relations are intersubjectively constituted, historically and contextually contingent; from this it follows that all social knowledge will be similarly constituted and contingent. Any adequate critical theory will embrace these claims.

Some readers who have come this far with me may find such claims suggestive, but abstract, perhaps even vacuous, in terms of the substantive guidance they provide for assessing the claims of critical theories, let alone the practices of which they purport to be expressions. They are, after all, *meta*theoretical claims; they are about what theory can be, and do not specifically attend the questions of whether the substantive analyses and practical activities endorsed by critical theories are "rational." In one sense such objections are on the mark, for the assertion that critical theory must necessarily embrace certain metatheoretical presuppositions is to abstract principles of inquiry from inquiry itself. To engage in metacritique is not to do critique; metatheory is not theory; the "rational comprehension" of practice is not practice. Or so it may seem.

I bring up this objection because the questions it raises cut to the root of the project I have undertaken in this book. And the challenge of the objection is to show that the model of critical theory I have been developing offers a workable response to it. This task may be approached by further unpacking a number of related themes, from which a more or less adequate model of critical theory emerges. With this we can then return to the issue of judging critical theory and political practices.

Human Nature and Human Agency

On this much, at least, all the critical theorists I have discussed here agree: Domination is characteristically underwritten by theoretical self-understandings (or beliefs) that are systematically distorting, and these self-understandings are characteristically grounded in ontological theses that are neither defensible nor coherent. In most instances, these distortions are the consequence of an assumption that human nature is unchanging, or perhaps changing in a way that points toward a stable, universal identity, and that the social relations in which we are embedded are the consequence of a progressive realization of arrangements best suited to that nature or that telos.

The achievement of critical theory is to have shown that these sorts of arguments cannot be sustained. Human nature and society itself are in large part constituted by the beliefs we hold, and these beliefs change over time. If we have a "nature," then, it is a "historical" one.

This is why critical theory must understand its own claims as historically and contextually contingent.

From this it does not, however, follow that critical theory has no
conception of human nature it may deploy in criticizing existing social
arrangements. Every social theory presupposes some kind of ontological stance. But it might be better to understand that the ontology to
which critical theory subscribes is one that identifies our nature not
as fixed and unchanging, but a matter of the potentialities and capacities we have as self-transforming agents. Human nature, for critical
theory, is human agency.

The crucial question for critical theory is, then, whether this agency
is being realized. When our contingent beliefs are reified as natural,
necessary, or inevitable, our agency is denied. Of course this (still)
begs the question of which practices, which social arrangements,
would best realize the potential and capacity for human agency. Here
we must turn to epistemological issues, for the "rationality" of social
and political practices cannot be judged independently of the knowledge claims that support them.

Objectivism and Objectivity

Critical theory is characteristically cast in terms that contrast "dominating" and "emancipatory" practices, "distorted" and "undistorted"
theoretical self-understandings, and "indefensible/incoherent" and
"defensible/coherent" metatheory. On what grounds may these distinctions be drawn?

This is a question for which critical theory provides no ready, hard
and fast answers, and it is one for which I cannot claim to have provided unassailable solutions either. For many, this may seem a rather
unsatisfactory way of addressing such a crucial concern. For some it
may even appear to call this entire project into question. But critical
theory (and my book as a whole) does not leave us without epistemological resources for addressing the issue of normative adjudication of
practices, theories and metatheories.

One important implication of an adequate understanding of critical
theory is that it is precisely the desire to seek ready, hard and fast,
unassailable—"objectively secured"—answers that is one source of
our inability to achieve the kinds of social and political arrangements
that merit our collective assent. This last point is drawn from what the
critical theorists say in their deconstructive critiques of so much extant social theory, past and present; it is also drawn from my criticisms
of modernist and postmodernist critical theory. For the upshot of these
criticisms is that it is a mistake of the most pernicious sort to assume

that what counts as rational practice, theory and metatheory can be laid down *a priori*—or that the failure of such attempts renders the concept of "objectivity" vacuous.

Simply stated, critical theory—and what counts as "objective truth"—takes shape in a critical confrontation between and within traditions of discourse. Or as Marx once suggested, critique does "not attempt dogmatically to prefigure the future," rather, it attempts to "find the new world through criticism of the old" (Marx 1978: 13). In this sense, the characteristic structure of a critical theoretic argument *reflects the model of rational inquiry it is trying to articulate*. Put another way, it may be said that critical theory proceeds by probing the gap between what many extant theories purport to do (e.g., describe timeless or objective truths) and what they actually do, namely, advance theoretical and practical self-understandings informed by historically contingent and contextually specific relations of power, and it is out of these criticisms that critical theory's conception of truth emerges.

In short, the reason critical theory does not provide any hard and fast standards for distinguishing between "dominating" and "emancipatory" practices, "distorted" and "undistorted" theoretical claims, and "indefensible" and "defensible" metatheoretical arguments, is because these distinctions are the consequence of a critical confrontation between competing practices, theories, and metatheories. Rationality, then, will be historically and contextually contingent, if only because the way in which claims of rationality emerge is in confrontations between contextually situated practices and arguments. This is the achievement of the deconstructive criticisms of (for example) idealism and bourgeois political economy, scientism and instrumental reason, the will to truth and power, orthodox modernization theory, banking models of education, orthodox theology, and androcentric discourse. In unmasking these forms of theory, the critical theorists show that each suffers from a systematically distorted view of its own origins and philosophical foundations, but this criticism is established through a critical confrontation with those accounts—not by trying to "attempt dogmatically to prefigure the future."

The implications of the criticisms of theories of domination offered by the critical theorists, and those of modernist and postmodernist critical theory I have offered, may be (again) brought together this way: Social and political theory reflects its historical context, and its claims will be contingent ones. But from this contingency it does not follow that these claims cannot be rationally adjudicated, for it is only in the process of critical engagement within and between the traditions of which they are the expression that standards of judgment can be articulated. To be "objective" in one's claims does not require "objectivism," for the obstacle to achieving an adequate understanding of what we should do here and now is not our inability to withdraw from the practical demands before us, but our inability to see that it is these practical demands that shape the theoretical perspectives from which we speak.

With this we return to the theme of this section, metatheory and the rational comprehension of practice. For now it should be clear that the distinction between a potentially emancipating critical theory, and a form of theory that closes off this potential, is the distinction between a theory that recognizes its own contingency, and one that does not. All of which brings us to the role that critical theory plays in human progress.

CRITICAL THEORY AND HUMAN PROGRESS

Any discussion of human progress is likely to immediately become bogged down in questions about whether progress has, or has not, taken place in history; indeed, the very meaning of progress itself may be dragged into the mire of debate. I suggest that critical theory, when properly understood, endorses neither a whiggish nor a skeptical attitude toward the question of progress, such as those that seem to be embodied in modernist and postmodernist critical theory.[1] Against those whigs who assume that human history has been moving inexorably in the direction of a progressive unfolding of a human *telos*, critical theory shows that such arguments are conceptually incoherent and politically suspect. And against those skeptics who see human history as just one damned thing after another, critical theory shows that human beings have been able to achieve progressively rational insights and politically progressive practical arrangements. In fact, one may view the existence of critical theory itself as a testament to both the achievements and limitations of human progress. For it presupposes both a continued need to engage in the improvement of human understanding and existence, thus overcoming the failures and deficiencies of past attempts to do so, and the successes, however limited and partial they may be, of past struggles to realize a clarity of self-understanding and forms of life worth defending.

Critical theory is thus a kind of historically situated discourse, fully cognizant of its own achievements and limitations. And in this I believe Raymond Geuss (1981: 94) is right to suggest that "rational ar-

---

[1] For a discussion of the character and failures of "whiggish" and "skeptical" histories as they are used in disputes over the status of political science, see Dryzek and Leonard (1988).

gumentation can lead to the conclusion that a critical theory [at least when it is, again, properly understood—S.L.] represents the most advanced position of consciousness available to us in our historical situation." Although I have already gone some distance toward establishing this claim, I will develop this thesis further by briefly considering the ways in which critical theory embraces the kind of self-understanding that promises to secure its potential for human progress, both intellectual and practical.

Emancipation and Historicity, Solidarity and Plurality

If there is any lesson at all in critical theory, it is that emancipation is not so much an end-state to be achieved as it is a demand to put an end to practices that can be shown to be unwarranted. Recognizing this also makes it possible to once again situate my distinction between the modernist and postmodernist critical theory, and critical theories in practice. In the former instances, the "tyranny of universalism" raises the philosophical ante so high that modernist and postmodernist critical theory is led to conceptualize emancipation in terms that no contingent political struggle could possibly meet. In each of the latter we have seen that the emancipation they seek is not envisioned as something that will put an end to all forms of domination. It is, rather, a contingent emancipation, the projection of a way of life in which particular forms of domination have been overcome. This is why dependency theory, in Cardoso's words, is not intended to "explain everything." It is why Freire sees the pedagogy of the oppressed as an activity that must be constantly renewed as new "limit situations" emerge. It is why the liberation theologians see liberation theology as a "historical theology" of "annunciation and denunciation." And it is why a critical feminist theory "is not based on some abstract idea of human nature or on pie-in-the-sky hopes for a promised land."

None of this is to suggest that critical theory, whatever its form, does not have a vision of what a better life would be. Indeed, if the metatheoretical theses regarding our capacity for self-transformation and the historicity of our identity and knowledge is followed, and if I am right in concluding that the form critical theory takes provides a model for understanding how rationally warranted knowledge claims are secured—through a hard-headed critical confrontation between and within traditions of discourse and practice—then the political consequence is a demand to clear a public space in which such confrontations may occur. The realization of such a space requires, in Nancy Fraser's words (1986: 425), the recognition that "we owe each other behavior such that each is confirmed as a being with specific collective identifications and solidarities" and the kind of autonomy in which individuals may express themselves as

> a member of a group or groups which have achieved a degree of collective control over the means of interpretation and communication sufficient to enable one to participate on par with members of other groups in moral and political deliberation; that is, to speak and be heard, to tell one's own life story, to press one's claims and point of view in one's own voice.

This does not mean that such a space will guarantee the rationality of these claims, and these voices. This will depend upon their quality, their coherence, their defensibility. Such judgments, however, cannot be subject to normative standards laid down in advance, for such standards will emerge, if at all, in the context of examining the various arguments made. This is precisely why critical theory must be inextricably linked and committed to a historically contingent and contextually specific way of life—a fact nowhere more clearly demonstrated than in the activity of critical theorizing itself. And it is also why critical theory must remain committed to respecting the plurality of ways in which human beings find their "own voice" while also being committed to solidarity with those who are struggling, against the impositions of others, to find that voice.

The Historical Role of Critical Theory

By providing examples of how we might remake our social relations by avoiding the mistakes of the past, critical theory shows us how we can perhaps realize Marx's claim that "*Every* emancipation is a *restoration* of the human world and of human relationships to *man himself*." In this respect, critical theory undermines the all-too-common tendency today to treat practical, political issues as if they could be answered in purely technocratic, instrumental terms. It also provides good reasons for seeing that it is moral and political argument that should guide our instrumental interests, and not the reverse. This thesis, as Sandra Harding (1986: 250) notes, derives its prescriptive force from its adequacy as a descriptive account of how the sciences, social and natural, are actually related. In Harding's words:

> It has been and should be moral and political beliefs that direct the development of both the intellectual and social structures of science. The problematics, concepts, theories, methodologies, interpretations of experiments, and uses have been and should be selected with moral and political goals in mind, not merely cognitive ones. (1986: 250)

Given this fact, which critical theory in large part has helped us to recognize, the task that lies before us is to articulate the best arguments we can in light of our historical situations and contextual constraints. And insofar as critical theory both shows us how this can be done, and actually *does* so, it merits Geuss's characterization as "the most advanced position of consciousness available to us in our historical situation." This does not of course mean that critical theory will always be the most advanced form of consciousness available to us, for there may be a time when critical theory is no longer necessary, or there may be a time when critical theory is shown to have been wrong about the kinds of creatures we are—self-defining and self-transforming ones—and the kind of knowledge we are capable of attaining about ourselves—historically contingent and contextually specific knowledge. But if the arguments I have made here are correct, and if critical theory is correct, there is no contradiction in holding that critical theory is both the most advanced form of knowledge available to us and a historically and contextually limited form of knowledge.

There is, however, more to be considered. Critical theory not only shows how we might rationally adjudicate between beliefs and desires, it also suggests that there are better and worse perspectives from which this adjudication is best pursued. And understanding what this entails brings this study to a close.

CRITICAL THEORY AND THE END OF THEORETICAL INNOCENCE

The critical theories I have discussed seek to assist us in acting responsibly in the face of our historicity.[2] Success in this task is, in the last analysis, the judgment of a critical theory's worth. Without it, a critical theory is, in Paulo Freire's words, "preaching in the desert." A critical theory without an audience to whom it is addressed and for whom it is intended to be enlightening and emancipatory cannot help us to act responsibly toward each other and the future. It is seldom heard by those who most need it. On the other hand, a critical theory in practice may well help us to act responsibly, but the price of responsibility may be high: it often requires us to act to change circumstances and relations we find intolerable, sometimes forcing us to make enemies when we would prefer to have peace. Moreover, the very fact of our historicity means that we can never be certain that our attempts to act responsibly will not result in tragedy for some of us. But we need not take this as a reason for inaction or despair. The real

[2] The title of this section is purloined from Matthew Lamb (1982), whose discussion of "the end of theoretical innocence" has been influential in shaping my closing comments.

question is whether we will allow ourselves to recognize our own roles in the perpetuation of unredeemed suffering, or retreat from the world of that suffering by seeing ourselves as merely innocent bystanders. In either case, we are not now innocent, nor can we ever really be innocent—as social agents or social theorists.

To act responsibly is to do the best one can in light of the available evidence about the beliefs and practices that perpetuate suffering and oppression. What critical theory, and in particular critical theory in practice, shows is that it is when we take the perspective of those whose lives are most damaged, most distorted, most deformed, we are in a better position to understand what is required for us to act responsibly and rationally. This position is fully consistent with the need to recognize that we always speak from a particular historical context. But it is also consistent with the need to recognize that it is those interests, those perspectives, undergirding coercion, domination, and the marginalization of vast numbers of our fellows and sisters that distort and mystify our understandings of ourselves and our relations. Domination and oppression take a variety of forms, and because of this, enlightenment and emancipation will also take a variety of forms. From this it should be clear that any adequate account of critical theory must be cognizant of the need to be sensitive to the plurality and difference that defines our identities and characterizes our lives, and it must also be attentive to the need to open a philosophical and political space in which individuals can find their own voices, however plural and different those may be. At the same time, a critical theory cannot ignore the harsh reality of those who are the victims of history; it must be in solidarity with those victims, or it risks seeing its aims and conclusions transformed into idle posturing and hopeless despair. Plurality and solidarity: these must be the watchwords of critical theory.

This is an ideal that is made possible only by *living* it; it is not simply an end we should seek, but also the only means by which we can do so. Such an ideal does not assume that we can or will live in harmony and agreement, but it does assume that we can perhaps live with our differences without resorting to coercion. Neither, however, does it mean that we must be tolerant to the point of indifference. Every voice cannot be realized, and not every voice *should* be realized. Does this, then, imply a contradiction at the heart of critical theory, a contradiction between the plurality it needs to respect and the solidarity it must pursue? Taken in the abstract, it may. But if this study of critical theory demonstrates anything at all, it is that questions about when we should act, and how we should act, cannot be answered only in the abstract. Rather, they must be answered in terms acceptable to those who must pay with their own lives the consequences of these choices—which is but another way of saying that at this point in history they must be answered, ultimately, in the discourse of the oppressed themselves. Whether the oppressed, and those of us who live lives of privilege and comfort, can act here and now in ways that might forge a future that avoids the mistakes of the past remains an open question. But however limited we are in our abilities to see what that future might be, however uncertain we are about the practical choices we make, make them we must. Fortunately, we are not without resources for doing so; and critical theory is surely foremost among those resources.

Bibliography

To FACILITATE the reader's access to the texts, wherever possible I have used widely available English translations and anthologies of works originally published in other languages and at earlier dates. Two issues may be raised regarding this practice, one having to do with the use of translations, the other concerning periodization of the texts.

Regarding the problem of periodization: I have provided dates of original publication and/or references to standard sources of translations in cases where the date of the cited work is significantly later than the original. This should assist some readers who may be confused about the periodization of the texts. Where periodization is not a problem, enterprising readers may find references to original texts in the sources I have cited. The sole justification for not providing references to the original editions of all English translations of the texts I cite is that it keeps the bibliography from becoming excessively cumbersome. This leaves the problem of using translations.

It may, of course, be objected that translations do not always reflect the meaning of the original texts. This is a complicated issue, and one beyond the scope of consideration here. The rough rule of thumb I have used is that in the absence of controversies regarding the translations cited in this bibliography, I have deferred to the judgment of the translators (whose work, in many cases, has been authorized by the authors). Where translations are not available, or are controversial, I have provided my own translations. These instances should be obvious.

Adorno, T. 1976. "Sociology and Empirical Research." In P. Connerton, ed., *Critical Sociology*. New York: Penguin.
———. 1973. *Negative Dialectics*. New York: Seabury.
———. 1969. "On the Logic of the Social Sciences." In Adorno et al., *The Positivist Dispute in German Sociology*. London: Heineman.
Alfred, D. 1984. "The Relevance of the Work of Paulo Freire to Radical Community Education in Britain." *International Journal of Lifelong Education* 3(2):105–13.
Alves, R. 1979. "From Paradise to the Desert: Autobiographical Musings." In R. Gibellini, ed., *Frontiers of Theology in Latin America*. Maryknoll, N.Y.: Orbis.
Anderson, G. H., and T. F. Stransky, eds. 1979. *Mission Trends*. No. 4, *Liberation Theologies*. New York: Paulist Press.
Apel, K. O. 1972. "The A Priori of Communication and the Foundation of the Humanities." *Man and World* 5:3–37.
Arato, A., and P. Breines. 1979. *The Young Lukács and the Origins of Western Marxism*. New York: Seabury.
Assmann, H. 1975. *Practical Theology of Liberation*. London: Search.

Assmann, H. 1971. *Opresión—Liberación: Desafío a los cristanos*. Montevideo: Editorial Tierra Nueva.

Balbus, I. 1986. "Disciplining Women: Michel Foucault and the Power of Feminist Discourse." *Praxis International* 5(4):466–83.

Ball, T. 1984. "Marxian Science and Positivist Politics." In T. Ball and J. Farr, eds., *After Marx*. Cambridge: Cambridge University Press.

———. 1983a. "The Ontological Presuppositions and Political Consequences of a Social Science." In J. Wallulis and D. Sabia, eds., *Changing Social Science*. Albany: SUNY Press.

———. 1983b. "Contradiction and Critique in Political Theory." In J. S. Nelson, ed., *What Should Political Theory Be Now?* Albany: SUNY Press.

———. 1981. "Popper's Psychologism." *Philosophy of the Social Sciences* 11:65–68.

———. 1980. "Dangerous Knowledge? The Self-subversion of Social Deviance Theory." *Inquiry* 23:377–95.

Bambirra, V. 1974. *El capitalismo dependente latinoamericano*. Mexico: Vientiuno Editores.

Baran, P. 1957. *The Political Economy of Growth*. New York: Monthly Review Press.

Barnard, C. 1981. "Imperialism, Underdevelopment and Education." In R. Mackie, ed., *Literacy and Revolution*. New York: Continuum.

Bartky, S. L. 1977. "Toward a Phenomenology of Feminist Consciousness." In M. Vetterling-Braggin et al., eds., *Feminism and Philosophy*. Totowa, N.J.: Littlefield, Adams and Co.

Bath, R. C. and D. D. James. 1976. "Dependency Analysis of Latin America: Some Criticisms, Some Suggestions." *Latin American Research Review* 11(3):3–54.

Becker, D. G. 1983. *The New Bourgeoisie and the Limits of Dependency*. Princeton, N.J.: Princeton University Press.

Bee, B. 1981. "The Politics of Literacy." In R. Mackie, ed., *Literacy and Revolution*. New York: Continuum.

Bell, D. 1960. *The End of Ideology: On the Exhaustion of Political Ideas in the Fifties*. New York: Free Press.

Benhabib, S. 1986. *Critique, Norm and Utopia*. New York: Columbia University Press.

———. 1985. "The Utopian Dimension in Communicative Ethics." *New German Critique* 35 (Spring/Summer):83–96.

———. 1982. "The Methodological Illusions of Modern Political Theory: The Case of Rawls and Habermas." *Neue hefte fur philosophie* 21 (Spring):47–74.

Berger, P. 1972. *Pyramids of Sacrifice*. New York: Basic Books.

Berghof, G., and L. Dekoster. 1984. *Liberation Theology: The Church's Future Shock*. Grand Rapids, Mich.: Christian's Library Press.

Berlin, I. 1981. *Concepts and Categories*. New York: Penguin.

Berryman, P. 1987. *Liberation Theology*. New York: Pantheon.

————. 1984. "Basic Christian Communities and the Future of Latin America." *Monthly Review* 36(3):27–40.

Bernstein, R. 1983. *Beyond Objectivism and Relativism*. Philadelphia: University of Pennsylvania Press.

————. 1976. *The Restructuring of Social and Political Theory*. Philadelphia: University of Pennsylvania Press.

————. 1971a. *Praxis and Action*. Philadelphia: University of Pennsylvania Press.

————. 1971b. "Herbert Marcuse: An Immanent Critique." *Social Theory and Practice* 1(4):97–111.

Biskowski, L. 1986. "Marxism and Christianity." Unpublished manuscript, University of Minnesota.

————. 1984. "Critical Praxis and Sandanismo." Unpublished manuscript, University of Minnesota.

Blum, L. et al. 1976. "Altruism and Women's Oppression." In C. Gould and M. Wartofsky, eds., *Women and Philosophy*. New York: Capricorn.

Bodenheimer, S. J. 1971. *The Ideology of Development: The American Paradigm-Surrogate for Latin American Studies*. Beverly Hills, Calif.: Sage.

Boff, C. 1987. *Theology and Praxis: Epistemological Foundations*. Maryknoll, N.Y.: Orbis.

Boff, L. and C. Boff. 1987. *Introducing Liberation Theology*. Maryknoll, N.Y.: Orbis.

————. 1986. *Liberation Theolology: From Confrontation to Dialogue*. New York: Harper and Row.

Bonino, J. M. 1983. *Toward a Christian Political Ethic*. Philadelphia: Fortress Press.

————. 1976. *Christians and Marxists*. Grand Rapids, Mich.: Eerdmans.

————. 1975. *Doing Theology in a Revolutionary Situation*. Philadelphia: Fortress Press.

Booth, D. 1985. "Marxism and Development Sociology: Interpreting the Impasse." *World Development* 13(7):761–87.

Bowers, C. A. 1986. "Review: *The Politics of Education*." *Educational Studies* 17(1):147–54.

Brigham, T. M. 1977. "Liberation in Social Work Education: Applications from Paulo Freire." *Journal of Education for Social Work* 13(3):5–11.

Brodbeck, M. 1968. *Readings in the Philosophy of the Social Sciences*. Toronto: Macmillan.

Browett, J. 1985. "The Newly Industrializing Countries and Radical Theories of Development." *World Development* 13(7):789–803.

————. 1980. "Out of the Dependency Perspectives." *Journal of Contemporary Asia* 12(2):145–57.

Brown, C. 1974. "Literacy in Thirty Hours: Paulo Freire's Process." *Urban Review* 7(3).

Brown, R. M. 1980. *Gustavo Gutierrez*. Atlanta: John Knox Press.

Buck-Morss, S. 1977. *The Origin of Negative Dialectics*. New York: Free Press.

Caporaso, J. A. 1978a. "Introduction: Dependence and Dependency in the Global System." *International Organization* 32(1):1–12.

———. 1978b. "Dependence, Dependency, and Power in the Global System: A Structural and Behavioral Analysis." *International Organization* 32(1):13–44.

Cardoso, F. H. 1977. "The Consumption of Dependency Theory in the United States." *Latin American Research Review* 12(3):7–23.

———, and E. Faletto. 1979. *Dependency and Development in Latin America.* Berkeley: University of California Press.

Catlin, G.E.G. 1930. *Principles of Politics.* London: Allen and Unwin.

Chilcote, R. H. 1981. *Theories of Comparative Politics.* Boulder, Colo.: Westview.

———. 1974. "Dependency: A Critical Synthesis of the Literature." *Latin American Perspectives* 1(1):4–29.

Chodorow, N. 1978. *The Reproduction of Mothering.* Berkeley: University of California Press.

Cleary, E. L. 1985. *Crisis and Change: The Church in Latin America Today.* Maryknoll, N.Y.: Orbis.

Collins, D. 1977. *Paulo Freire: His Life, Works and Thought.* New York: Paulist Press.

Comblin, J. 1979a. *The Church and the National Security State.* Maryknoll, N.Y.: Orbis.

———. 1979b. "What Sort of Service Might Theology Render?" In R. Gibellini, ed., *Frontiers of Theology in Latin America.* Maryknoll, N.Y.: Orbis.

Cone, J. 1970. *A Black Theology of Liberation.* New York: Lippincott.

Connolly, W. E. 1985. "Taylor, Foucault,and Otherness." *Political Theory* 13(3):365–76.

———. 1983. "The Dilemma of Legitimacy." In J. S. Nelson, ed., *What Should Political Theory Be Now?* Albany: SUNY Press.

———. 1981. *Appearance and Reality in Politics.* Cambridge: Cambridge University Press.

———. 1974. *The Terms of Political Discourse.* Lexington, Mass.: D. C. Heath.

Cornell, D. and A. Thurshwell. 1986. "Feminism, Negativity, Intersubjectivity." *Praxis International* 5(4):484–504.

Cousins, M., and A. Hussain. 1984. *Michel Foucault.* New York: St. Martin's Press.

Crittenden, P. J. 1980. "Neutrality in Education." *Educational Philosophy and Theory* 12:1–18.

Dallmayr, F. 1984. *Polis and Praxis.* Cambridge, Mass.: MIT Press.

Davaney, S. G. 1981. "Introduction" In S. G. Davaney, ed., *Feminism and Process Thought.* Lewiston: Edwin Mellen Press.

Davis, C. 1980. *Theology and Political Society.* Cambridge: Cambridge University Press.

Descartes, R. 1958. *Descartes: Philosophical Writings.* N. K. Smith, ed. New York: Modern Library. Original of cited text, *Regulae ad directionem in-*

genii: Règles pour la direction de l'esprit, written sometime between 1619 and 1629. Latin and French translation on adjacent pages in the text revised and translated by G. Le Roy, Paris, 1933.

Descombes, V. 1980. *Modern French Philosophy*. Cambridge: Cambridge University Press.

Dietz, J. L. 1980. "Dependency Theory: A Review Article." *Journal of Economic Issues* 14(3):751–58.

Dietz, M. 1987. "Context Is All: Feminism and Theories of Citizenship." *Daedalus* 116(4):1–24.

———. 1985. "Citizenship with a Feminist Face: The Problem with Maternal Thinking." *Political Theory* 13(1):19–37.

———. 1983. "Citizenship with a Feminist Face: The Problem with Maternal Thinking." Paper presented at the 1983 Western Political Science Association meeting.

Dinnerstein, D. 1976. *The Mermaid and the Minotaur*. New York: Harper and Row.

Dodd, C. 1973. "Political Development: The End of an Era?" *Government and Opposition* 8 (Summer):367–74.

Dominguez, J. I. 1978. "Consensus and Divergence: The State of the Literature on Inter-American Relations in the 1970's." *Latin American Research Review* 13(1):87–126.

Dos Santos, T. 1970. "The Structure of Dependence." *The American Economic Review* 60(2):231–36.

Dray, W. 1957. *Laws and Explanation in History*. Oxford: Oxford University Press.

Dreyfus, H. L., and P. Rabinow. 1982. *Michel Foucault: Beyond Structuralism and Hermeneutics*. Chicago: University of Chicago Press.

Dryzek, J., and S. Leonard. 1988. "History and Discipline in Political Science." *American Political Science Review* 82(4):1245–60.

Durkheim, E. 1964. *The Rules of Sociological Method*. New York: Free Press. Originally: 1895. *Les règles de la méthod sociologique*. Paris: Felix Alcan.

Duvall, R. D. 1978. "Dependence and Dependencia Theory: Notes Toward Precision of Concept and Argument." *International Organization* 32(1):51–78.

Easton, D. 1953. *The Political System*. New York: Alfred A. Knopf.

Eisenstadt, S. N. 1966. *Modernization: Protest and Change*. Englewood Cliffs, N.J.: Prentice-Hall.

Elshtain, J. B. 1982. "Feminism, Family and Community." *Dissent* (Fall):442–49.

———. 1981. "Feminist Discourse and Its Discontents: Language, Power, and Meaning." In N. Keohane et al., eds., *Feminist Theory*. Chicago: University of Chicago Press.

———. 1979. "Feminists against the Family." *The Nation*, November 15, 497–500.

Evans, P. 1979. *Dependent Development*. Princeton, N.J.: Princeton University Press.

Farmer, J. A. 1972. "Adult Education for Transiting." In S. M. Grabowski, ed., *Paulo Freire: A Revolutionary Dilemma for the Adult Educator*. Syracuse, N.Y.: ERIC Clearinghouse on Adult Education.

Farr, J. F. 1982. "Historical Concepts in Political Science: The Case of 'Revolution.' " *American Journal of Political Science* 26(4):688–708.

Fay, B. 1987. *Critical Social Science*. Ithaca, N.Y.: Cornell University Press.

———. 1977. "How People Change Themselves: The Relationship between Critical Theory and Its Audience." In T. Ball, ed., *Political Theory and Praxis: New Perspectives*. Minneapolis: University of Minnesota Press.

———. 1975. *Social Theory and Political Practice*. London: Allen and Unwin.

———, and J. D. Moon. 1977. "What Would an Adequate Philosophy of Social Science Look Like?" *Philosophy of the Social Sciences* 7:209–27.

Ferm, D. W. 1986. *Third World Liberation Theologies*. Maryknoll, N.Y.: Orbis.

Ferguson, K. 1984. *The Feminist Case against Bureaucracy*. Philadelphia: Temple University Press.

———. 1980. *Self, Society, and Womankind*. Westport, Conn.: Greenwood.

Fierro, A. 1977. *The Militant Gospel*. Maryknoll, N.Y.: Orbis.

Fiorenza, F. P. 1975. "Political Theology and Liberation Theology." In T. M. McFadden, ed., *Liberation, Revolution, and Freedom*. New York: Seabury.

Flax, J. 1983. "Political Philosophy and the Patriarchal Unconscious: A Psychoanalytical Perspective on Epistemology and Metaphysics." In S. Harding and M. B. Hintikka, eds., *Discovering Reality*. Boston: D. Reidel.

Foucault, M. 1984. *The Foucault Reader* = FR. (P. Rabinow, ed.). New York: Pantheon.

———. 1983. "Michel Foucault: Is It Really Important to Think?" *Philosophy and Social Criticism* 9(11):29–46.

———. 1982. "The Subject and Power" = SP. In H. L. Dreyfus and P. Rabinow, *Michel Foucault: Beyond Structuralism and Hermeneutics*. Chicago: University of Chicago Press.

———. 1980a. *The History of Sexuality, Volume I: An Introduction* = HS. New York: Vintage Books.

———. 1980b. *Power/Knowledge: Selected Interviews and Other Writings, 1972–1977* = PK. New York: Pantheon.

———. 1979. *Discipline and Punish: The Birth of the Prison* = DP. New York: Vintage.

———. 1977. *Language, Counter-memory, Practice: Selected Essays and Interviews* = LCP. Ithaca, N.Y.: Cornell University Press.

———, ed. 1975. *I, Pierre Riviere. . . .* New York: Random House.

———. 1973. *The Birth of the Clinic* = BC. New York: Tavistock.

———. 1972. *The Archaeology of Knowledge* = AK. New York: Tavistock.

———. 1970. *The Order of Things* = OT. New York: Vintage.

———. 1965. *Madness and Civilization* = MC. New York: Random House.

Frank, A. G. 1969. *Latin America: Underdevelopment or Revolution*. New York: Monthly Review Press.

———. 1967. *Capitalism and Underdevelopment in Latin America*. New York: Monthly Review Press.

Fraser, N. 1986. "Toward a Discourse Ethic of Solidarity." *Praxis International* 5(4):425–29.

———. 1985a. "Michel Foucault: A Young Conservative?" *Ethics* 96 (October):165–84.

———. 1985b. "What's Critical about Critical Theory? The Case of Habermas and Gender." *New German Critique* 35 (Spring/Summer):97–131.

———. 1983. "Foucault's Body Language." *Salmagundi* 63:55–70.

———. 1981. "Foucault on Modern Power: Empirical Insights and Normative Confusions." *Praxis International* 1(3):272–87.

Freire, P. 1985. *The Politics of Education* = *PE*. South Hadley, Mass.: Bergin and Garvey.

———. 1983a. *Pedagogy of the Oppressed* = *PO*. New York: Continuum.

———. 1983b. *Pedagogy in Process: The Letters from Guinea Bissau* = *PP*. New York: Continuum.

———. 1982. *Education for Critical Consciousness* = *ECC*. New York: Continuum.

———. 1981. "Education for Awareness: A Talk with Paulo Freire" = *EA*. In R. Mackie, ed., *Literacy and Revolution*. New York: Continuum.

———. 1970. "Cultural Action and Conscientization" = *CAC*. *Harvard Educational Review* 40:452–77.

———. 1970. "The Adult Literacy Process as Cultural Action for Freedom" = *ALP*. *Harvard Educational Review* 40:205–25.

Freire, P., and D. Macedo. 1987. *Literacy: Reading the Word and the World* = *LRWW*. South Hadley, Mass.: Bergin and Garvey.

Freire, P., and I. Shor. 1987. *A Pedagogy for Liberation* = *PL*. South Hadley, Mass.: Bergin and Garvey.

Gardner H. 1981. *The Quest for Mind*. Chicago: University of Chicago Press.

Gereffi, G. 1983. *The Pharmaceutical Industry and Dependency in the Third World*. Princeton, N.J.: Princeton University Press.

Geuss, R. 1981. *The Idea of a Critical Theory*. Cambridge: Cambridge University Press.

Gilligan, C. 1982. *In a Different Voice*. Cambridge, Mass.: Harvard University Press.

Giroux, H. 1987. "Introduction." In P. Freire and D. Macedo, *Literacy: Reading the Word and the World*. South Hadley, Mass.: Bergin and Garvey.

———. 1983. *Theory and Resistance in Education*. South Hadley, Mass.: Bergin and Garvey.

Goldstein, R. 1978. *Political Repression in Modern America*. New York: Schenckman.

Gorz, A. 1981. *The French New Left*. Boston: South End Press.

Gray, J. 1977. "On the Contestability of Social and Political Concepts." *Political Theory* 5(3):331–48.

Griffin, K. B. 1971. *Underdevelopment in Spanish America*. 2d ed. London: Allen and Unwin.

Griffin, K. B. and J. James. 1981. *The Transition to Egalitarian Democracy.* New York: St. Martins Press.

Griffith, W. S. 1972. "Paulo Freire: Utopian Perspective on Literacy Education for Revolution." In S. M. Grabowski, ed., *Paulo Freire: A Revolutionary Dilemma for the Adult Educator.* Syracuse, N.Y.: ERIC Clearinghouse on Adult Education.

Gutierrez, G. 1983. *The Power of the Poor in History.* Maryknoll, N.Y.: Orbis.

———. 1979. "Liberation Praxis and Christian Faith." In R. Gibellini, ed., *Frontiers of Theology in Latin America.* Maryknoll, N.Y.: Orbis.

———. 1974. "Praxis de liberación, teología y evangelización." In *Liberación: diálogos en el CELAM.* Bogota: CELAM.

———. 1973a. *A Theology of Liberation.* Maryknoll, N.Y.: Orbis.

———. 1973b. *Praxis de liberación y fe cristiana.* Lima: Centro de Documentacion MIEI–JECI.

Hacking, I. 1984. "Five Parables." In R. Rorty et al., eds., *Philosophy in History.* Cambridge: Cambridge University Press.

Habermas, J. 1987. *The Philosophical Discourse of Modernity.* Cambridge, Mass.: MIT Press.

———. 1984. *The Theory of Communicative Action, Vol. 1: Reason and the Rationalization of Society.* Boston: Beacon.

———. 1982. "A Reply to My Critics." In J. B. Thompson and D. Held, eds., *Habermas: Critical Debates.* Cambridge, Mass.: MIT Press.

———. 1981a. "New Social Movements." *Telos* 49:33–37.

———. 1981b. "Modernity versus Postmodernity." *New German Critique* 22:3–14.

———. 1979. *Communication and the Evolution of Society.* Boston: Beacon.

———. 1976. *Zur Rekonstruction des Historischen Materialismus.* Frankfurt: Suhrkamp.

———. 1975. *Legitimation Crisis.* Boston: Beacon.

———. 1973a. *Theory and Practice.* Boston: Beacon.

———. 1973b. "A Postcript to *Knowledge and Human Interests.*" *Philosophy of the Social Sciences* 3:157–89.

———. 1971. *Knowledge and Human Interests.* Boston: Beacon.

———. 1970. *Toward a Rational Society.* Boston: Beacon.

Hamilton, N. 1982. *The Limits of State Autonomy: Post-Revolutionary Mexico.* Princeton, N.J.: Princeton University Press.

Harding, S. 1986. *The Science Question in Feminism.* Ithaca, N.Y.: Cornell University Press.

———. 1983. "Is Gender a Variable in Conceptions of Rationality?: A Survey of Issues." In C. Gould, ed., *Beyond Domination.* Totowa, N.J.: Rowman and Allenheld.

———, and M. B. Hintikka. 1983. "Introduction." In S. Harding and M. B. Hintikka, eds., *Discovering Reality.* Boston: D. Reidel.

Hartsock, N. 1983a. "The Feminist Standpoint: Developing the Ground for a Specifically Feminist Historical Materialism." In S. Harding and M. B. Hintikka, eds., *Discovering Reality.* Boston: D. Reidel.

————. 1983b. *Money, Sex, and Power: Toward a Feminist Historical Materialism.* New York: Longman.

————. 1981. "Political Change: Two Perspectives on Power." In Quest Staff, eds., *Building Feminist Theory.* New York: Longman.

Held, D. 1980. *Introduction to Critical Theory.* Berkeley: University of California Press.

Heller, A. 1982. "Habermas and Marxism." In J. B. Thompson and D. Held, eds., *Habermas: Critical Debates.* Cambridge, Mass.: MIT Press.

Hempel, C. 1965. *Aspects of Scientific Explanation.* New York: Free Press.

Henning, E. M. 1982. "Archeology, Deconstruction and Intellectual History." In D. LaCapra and S. L. Kaplan, eds., *Modern European Intellectual History.* Ithaca, N.Y.: Cornell University Press.

Hettne, B. 1983. "The Development of Development Theory." *Acta Sociologica* 26(3/4):247–66.

Higgot, R. A. 1981. *Political Development Theory.* London: Croom Helm.

Hirsh, A. 1981. *The French New Left: An Intellectual History from Sartre to Gorz.* Boston: South End Press.

Horkheimer, M. 1982. *Critical Theory: Selected Essays.* New York: Herder and Herder.

————. 1974. *Critique of Instrumental Reason.* New York: Seabury.

————, and T. Adorno. 1972. *Dialectic of Enlightenment.* New York: Herder and Herder.

————. 1968. *Kritische Theorie II.* Frankfurt-Maim: Fischer.

————. 1947. *The Eclipse of Reason.* New York: Oxford University Press.

Hoselitz, B. 1960. *Sociological Aspects of Economic Growth.* New York: Free Press.

Hoy, D. C. 1979. "Taking History Seriously: Foucault, Gadamer, Habermas." *Union Seminary Quarterly Review* 34(2):85–95.

Hubbard, R. 1983. "Have Only Men Evolved?" In S. Harding and M. B. Hintikka, eds., *Discovering Reality.* Boston: D. Reidel.

Huntington, S. 1968. *Political Order in Changing Societies.* New Haven, Conn.: Yale University Press.

Ions, E. 1977. *Against Behavioralism.* London: Basil Blackwell.

Jacoby, R. 1987. *The Last Intellectuals.* New York: Basic Books.

Jackson, S. et al. 1979. "An Assessment of Empirical Research on Dependencia." *Latin American Research Review* 14(3):7–28.

Jaggar, A. 1983. "Human Biology in Feminist Theory: Sexual Equality Reconsidered." In C. Gould, ed., *Beyond Domination.* Totowa, N.J.: Rowman and Allenheld.

Jaksic, M. 1985. "The Theory of Modes of Production and Changes in International Economic Relations." *Journal of Contemporary Asia* 15(3):361–74.

Jay, M. 1984. *Adorno.* Cambridge, Mass.: Harvard University Press.

————. 1973. *The Dialectical Imagination. A History of the Frankfurt School and the Institute for Social Research, 1923–1950.* Boston: Little, Brown.

Jehlen, M. 1981. "Archimedes and the Paradox of Feminist Criticism." In

N. O. Keohane et al., eds., *Feminist Theory*. Chicago: University of Chicago Press.

Johansson, S. R. 1976. "Herstory as History: A New Field or Another Fad?" In B. A. Carroll, ed., *Liberating Women's History*. Chicago: University of Illinois Press.

Kant, I. 1949. *The Philosophy of Kant*, C. J. Friedrich, ed., New York: Modern Library. Originally published 1785 as *Grundlegung zur Metaphysik der Sitten*. The standard source is: E. Cassirer, ed. 1912–22. *Kants Werke*, vol. 4. Berlin: Bruno Cassirer.

Kahl, J. A. 1976. *Modernization, Exploitation and Dependency in Latin America*. New Brunswick, N.J.: Transaction Books.

Kaufman, R.R. 1982. "Trends and Priorities for Political Research on Latin America." Unpublished. Princeton, N.J.: Institute for Advanced Study.

———— et al. 1975. "A Preliminary Test of the Theory of Dependency." *Comparative Politics* 7(3):303–30.

Keller, E. F. 1983. "Gender and Science." In S. Harding and M. B. Hintikka, eds., *Discovering Reality*. Boston: D. Reidel.

————. 1981. "Feminism and Science." In N. Keohane et al., eds. *Feminist Theory*. Chicago: University of Chicago Press.

Kennedy, D. 1979. "Michel Foucault: The Archeology and Sociology of Knowledge." *Theory and Society* 8:269–90.

Keohane, N., and B. C. Gelpi. 1981. "Foreword." In N. Keohane et al., eds. *Feminist Theory*. Chicago: University of Chicago Press.

Kesselman, M. 1973. "Order or Movement?: The Literature of Political Development as Ideology." *World Politics* 26 (October):139–54.

Kirk, J. A. 1979. *Liberation Theology*. Atlanta: John Knox Press.

Kortian, G. 1980. *Metacritique: The Philosophical Argument of Jürgen Habermas*. Cambridge: Cambridge University Press.

Kozol, J. 1981. "Foreword." In R. Mackie, ed., *Literacy and Revolution*. New York: Continuum.

————. 1980. "Literacy and the Underdeveloped Nations." *Journal of Education* 162(3):27–39.

Kroger, J. 1985. "Prophetic-Critical and Strategic Tasks of Theology: Habermas and Liberation Theology." *Theological Studies* 46:3–20.

Kuhn, T. 1962. *The Structure of Scientific Revolutions*. Chicago: University of Chicago Press.

Lamb, M. L. 1982. *Solidarity with Victims*. New York: Crossroads.

————. 1981. "Generalized Empirical Method and Praxis." In M. L. Lamb, ed., *Creativity and Method: Essays in Honor of Bernard Lonergan, S.J.* Milwaukee, Wisc.: Marquette University Press.

————. 1980. "The Challenge of Critical Theory." In G. Baum, ed., *Sociology and Human Destiny*. New York: Seabury.

Lane, D.A. 1984. *Foundations for a Social Theology*. Dublin: Gill and Macmillan.

————. 1977. *Liberation Theology: An Irish Dialogue*. Dublin: Gill and Macmillan.

Lange, L. 1983. "Women Is Not a Rational Animal: On Aristotle's Biology of Reproduction." In S. Harding and M. B. Hintikka, eds., *Discovering Reality*. Boston: D. Reidel.

Lash, N. 1981. *A Matter of Hope*. London: Darton, Longman and Todd.

Lemert, C. C., and G. Gillan. 1982. *Michel Foucault: Social Theory and Transgression*. New York: Columbia University Press.

Leonard, S. 1987. "Marx(ism), Religion and Liberation Theology." Paper presented at the 1987 Midwest Political Science Association meeting.

Levine, D. H. 1988. "Paradigm Lost: Dependence to Dependency." *World Politics* 40(3):377–94.

———. 1981. *Religion and Politics in Latin America*. Princeton, N.J.: Princeton University Press.

Leys, C. 1977. "Underdevelopment and Dependency: Critical Notes." *Journal of Contemporary Asia* 7(1):92–107.

Lipset, S. M. 1960. *Political Man: The Social Basis of Politics*. Garden City, N.Y.: Doubleday.

Livingstone, D. W., ed. 1987. *Critical Pedagogy and Cultural Power*. South Hadley, Mass.: Bergin and Garvey.

Lobkowicz, N. 1967. *Theory and Practice*. Notre Dame, Ind.: Notre Dame University Press.

Lukes, S. 1977. *Essays in Social Theory*. London: Macmillan.

MacIntyre, A. 1984. "The Relationship of Philosophy to Its Past." In R. Rorty et al., eds., *Philosophy in History*. Cambridge: Cambridge University Press.

———. 1981. *After Virtue*. Notre Dame, Ind.: Notre Dame University Press.

———. 1978. *Against the Self-Images of the Age*. Notre Dame, Ind.: Notre Dame University Press.

———. 1977. "Epistemological Crises, Dramatic Narrative and the Philosophy of Science." *Monist* 60(4):453–72.

———. 1973. "The Essential Contestability of Some Social Concepts." *Ethics* 84 (October):1–9.

———. 1973. "Ideology, Science and Revolution." *Comparative Politics* 5:321–42.

———. 1970. *Marcuse*. New York: Viking.

———. 1966. *A Short History of Ethics*. New York: Macmillan.

Mackie, R. 1981. "Introduction." In R. Mackie, ed., *Literacy and Revolution*. New York: Continuum.

MacKinnon, C. 1981. "Feminism, Marxism, Method and the State: An Agenda for Theory." In N. Keohane et al., eds., *Feminist Theory*. Chicago: University of Chicago Press.

Macpherson, C. B. 1966. *The Real World of Democracy*. Oxford: Oxford University Press.

Mahan, B., and L. D. Richesin. 1981. *The Challenge of Liberation Theology*. Maryknoll, N.Y.: Orbis.

Major-Poetzl, P. 1983. *Michel Foucault's Archaeology of Western Culture*. Chapel Hill: University of North Carolina Press.

Malloy, J. 1977. "Authoritarianism and Corporatism in Latin America." In

J. Malloy, ed., *Authoritarianism and Corporatism in Latin America*. Pittsburgh, Pa.: University of Pittsburgh Press.

Manicas, P. 1987. *A History and Philosophy of the Social Sciences*. Oxford: Basil Blackwell.

Marcil-Lacoste, L. 1983. "The Trivialization of the Notion of Equality." In S. Harding and M. B. Hintikka, eds., *Discovering Reality*. Boston: D. Reidel.

Marcuse, H. 1976. "On the Problem of the Dialectic." *Telos* 27:12–39.

———. 1974. "On Science and Phenomenology." In A. Giddens, ed., *Positivism and Sociology*. London: Heinemann.

———. 1969. "Contribution to a Phenomenology of Historical Materialism." *Telos* 4:3–34.

———. 1968. *Negations: Essays in Critical Theory*. Boston: Beacon.

———. 1964. *One Dimensional Man*. Boston: Beacon.

———. 1958. *Soviet Marxism*. New York: Columbia University Press.

———. 1955. *Eros and Civilization*. Boston: Beacon.

Markovic, M. 1976. "Women's Liberation and Human Emancipation." In C. Gould and M. Wartofsky, eds., *Women and Philosophy*. New York: Capricorn.

Marx, K. 1978. *The Marx-Engels Reader = MER*. R. Tucker, ed. New York: Norton. Note: All cited texts for Marx were originally written between 1837 and 1895 (Marx died 1883; Engels 1895). The standard source is: Marx and Engels. 1957–68. *Werke*. Berlin: Dietz Verlag.

———. 1975. *Selected Correspondence = SC*. Moscow: Progress Publishers.

———. 1970. *German Ideology = GI*. New York: International.

———. 1959. *Economic and Philosophical Manuscripts = EPM*. Moscow: Progress.

———. 1955. *The Poverty of Philosophy = PP*. Moscow: Progress.

Matthews, M. 1981. "Knowledge, Action and Power." In R. Mackie, ed., *Literacy and Revolution*. New York: Continuum.

McCarthy, T. 1978. *The Critical Theory of Jürgen Habermas*. Cambridge, Mass.: MIT Press.

McLaren, P. 1986. "Review Article—Postmodernity and the Death of Politics: A Brazilian Reprieve." *Educational Theory* 36(4):389–401.

McLellan, D. 1979. *Marxism after Marx*. London: Macmillan.

Meese, E. A. 1986. *Crossing the Double-Cross: The Practice of Feminist Criticism*. Chapel Hill: University of North Carolina Press.

Metz, J. 1973. *Theology of the World*. New York: Seabury.

Mill, J. S. 1947. *A System of Logic*. New York: Longmans, Green and Company. Originally: 1843. The standard source is: J. M. Robson, ed. 1973. *The Collected Works of John Stuart Mill*. Toronto: University of Toronto Press.

Milliband, R. 1977. *Marxism and Politics*. Oxford: Oxford University Press.

Miranda, J. 1980. *Marx against the Marxists*. Maryknoll, N.Y.: Orbis.

———. 1974. *Marx and the Bible*. Maryknoll, N.Y.: Orbis.

Moon, J. D. 1975. "The Logic of Political Inquiry." In F. I. Greenstein and

N. W. Polsby, eds., *The Handbook of Political Science*. Reading, Pa.: Addison-Wesley.

Moore, B. 1966. *Social Origins of Dictatorship and Democracy*. Boston: Beacon Press.

Nagel, E. 1961. *The Structure of Science*. New York: Harcourt, Brace, and World.

Nozick, R. 1974. *Anarchy, State, and Utopia*. New York: Basic Books.

O'Brien, M. 1981. "Feminist Theory and Dialectical Logic." In N. Keohane et al., eds., *Feminist Theory*. Chicago: University of Chicago Press.

O'Brien, P. J. 1975. "A Critique of Latin American Theories of Dependency." In I. Oxall et al., eds., *Beyond the Sociology of Development*. London: Routledge and Kegan Paul.

O'Neill, J. 1985. "Decolonization and the Ideal Speech Community: Some Issues in the Theory and Practice of Communicative Competence." In J. Forester, ed., *Critical Theory and Public Life*. Cambridge, Mass.: MIT Press.

———. 1976. "Critique and Remembrance." In J. O'Neill, ed., *On Critical Theory*. New York: Seabury.

———. 1972. *Sociology as a Skin Trade*. London: Heinemann.

Palma, G. 1978. "Dependency: A Formal Theory of Underdevelopment or a Methodology for the Analysis of Concrete Situations of Dependency?" *World Politics* 6:881–924.

Palmer, M. R., and R. Newsom. 1982. "Paulo Freire's Consciousness Raising: Politics, Education and Revolution in Brazil." *Educational Studies* 13(2):183–89.

Peukert, H. 1984. *Science, Action and Fundamental Theology*. Cambridge, Mass.: MIT Press.

Phillip, M. 1983. "Foucault on Power: A Problem in Radical Translation." *Political Theory* 11:29–52.

Pitkin, H. F. 1972. *Wittgenstein and Justice*. Berkeley: University of California Press.

Pool, I. de Sola, ed. 1967. *Contemporary Political Science: Towards Empirical Theory*. New York: McGraw Hill.

Popper, K. 1982. "Popper's Psychologism: A Reply to Ball." *Philosophy of the Social Sciences* 12:69.

———. 1969. *The Open Society and Its Enemies*. London: Routledge and Kegan Paul.

———. 1960. *The Poverty of Historicism*. New York: Harper and Row.

Poster, M. 1982. "The Future According to Foucault: The Archaeology of Knowledge and Intellectual History." In D. LaCapra and S. L. Kaplan, eds., *Modern European Intellectual History*. Ithaca, N.Y.: Cornell University Press.

———. 1975. *Existential Marxism in Post-War France*. Princeton, N.J.: Princeton University Press.

Przeworski, A. 1986. "Some Problems in the Study of the Transition to Democracy." In G. O'Donnell et al., eds., *Transitions from Authoritarian Rule*. Baltimore, Md.: Johns Hopkins University Press.

Putnam, H. 1981. *Reason, Truth and History*. Cambridge: Cambridge University Press.

Rajchman, J. 1986. "Ethics after Foucault." *Social Text* 5(1 and 2):165–83.

———. 1985. *Michel Foucault: The Freedom of Philosophy*. New York: Columbia University Press.

Rawls, J. 1971. *A Theory of Justice*. Cambridge, Mass.: Harvard University Press.

Reitsma, H-J. A. 1982. "Development Geography, Dependency Relations, and the Capitalist Scapegoat." *The Professional Geographer* 34(2):125–30.

Rejai, M., ed. 1971. *Decline of Ideology?* Chicago: Aldine-Atherton.

Ricci, D. 1984. *The Tragedy of Political Science*. New Haven, Conn.: Yale University Press.

Riggs, F. 1970. *Frontiers of Development Administration*. Durham, N.C.: Duke University Press.

Rose, G. 1978. *The Melancholy Science: An Introduction to the Thought of Theodor W. Adorno*. London: Macmillan.

Roxborough, I. 1979. *Theories of Underdevelopment*. London: Macmillan.

Ruddick, S. 1980. "Maternal Thinking." *Feminist Studies* 6(2):342–67.

Russell, G. 1985. "Taming the Liberation Theologians." *Time*, February 4, 56–59.

Schillebeeckx, E. 1974. *The Understanding of Faith*. London: Sheed and Ward.

Said, E. W. 1984. "French Philosopher Foucault: Death at an Early Age." *In These Times*, September 5–11.

Sartre, J. P. 1963. *Search for a Method*. New York: Alfred Knopf.

Scheman, N. 1983. "Individualism and the Objects of Psychology." In S. Harding and M. B. Hintikka, eds., *Discovering Reality*. Boston: D. Reidel.

Schoolman, M. 1980. *The Imaginary Witness: The Critical Theory of Herbert Marcuse*. New York: Free Press.

Schroyer, T. 1973. *The Critique of Domination*. New York: George Braziller.

Segundo, J. L. 1984. *Faith and Ideologies*. Maryknoll, N.Y.: Orbis.

———. 1976. *The Liberation of Theology*. Maryknoll, N.Y.: Orbis.

Sheahan, J. 1987. *Patterns of Development in Latin America*. Princeton, N.J.: Princeton University Press.

Sheridan, A. 1980. *Michel Foucault: The Will to Truth*. London: Tavistock.

Shils, E. 1955. "The End of Ideology?" *Encounter* 5 (November):52–58.

Siebert, R. N. 1979. *From Critical Theory of Society to Theology of Communicative Praxis*. Washington, D.C.: University Press of America.

Silverman, K. 1983. *The Subject of Semiotics*. Oxford: Oxford University Press.

Simon, J. 1971. "A Conversation with Michel Foucault." *Partisan Review* 2:192–201.

Sloan, J. W. 1977. "Dependency Theory and Latin American Development: Another Key Fails to Open the Door." *Inter-American Economic Affairs* 31(3):21–40.

Smart, B. 1983. "Foucault, Sociology and the Problem of Human Agency." *Theory and Society* 9:121–42

Smith, D. E. 1979. "A Sociology for Women." In J. A. Sherman and E. T. Beck, eds., *The Prism of Sex*. Madison: University of Wisconsin Press.

———. 1977. "Some Implications of a Sociology for Women." In N. Glazer and H. Y. Waehrer, eds., *Woman in a Man-Made World*. 2d ed. Chicago: Rand McNally.

———. 1974. "Women's Perspective as a Radical Critique of Sociology." *Sociological Inquiry* 44:7–13.

Smith, N. 1982."Theories of Underdevelopment: A Response to Reitsma." *Professional Geographer* 34(3):332–37.

Smith, T. 1981. "The Logic of Dependency Theory Revisited." *International Organization* 35(4):755–61.

———. 1979. "The Development of Underdevelopment Literature: The Case of Dependency Theory." *World Politics* 31(2):247–88.

Spelman, E. V. 1983. "Aristotle and the Politicization of the Soul." In S. Harding and M. B. Hintikka, eds., *Discovering Reality*. Boston: D. Reidel.

Spender, D. 1983. "Modern Feminist Theorists: Reinventing Rebellion." In D. Spender, ed., *Feminist Theorists*. London: The Women's Press.

Street, J. H., and D. D. James. 1982. "Institutionalism, Structuralism, and Dependency in Latin America." *Journal of Economic Issues* 16(3):673–89.

Sunkel, O. 1972. "Big Business and Dependencia." *Foreign Affairs* 50 (April):517–31.

———, and P. Paz. 1970. *El subdesarrollo latinoamericano y la teoría del desarrollo*. Mexico: Siglo Veintiuno.

Sweezy, P. 1942. *The Theory of Capitalist Development*. New York: Monthly Review Press.

Tabb, W. K. 1986. *Churches in Struggle*. New York: Monthly Review Press.

Taylor, C. 1985. "Connolly, Foucault, and Truth." *Political Theory* 13(3):377–85.

———. 1984. "Foucault on Freedom and Truth." *Political Theory* 12(2):152–83.

———. 1977. "Interpretation and the Sciences of Man." In F. R. Dallmayr and T. A. McCarthy, eds., *Understanding and Social Inquiry*, 101–31. Notre Dame, Ind.: Notre Dame University Press.

———. 1975. *Hegel*. Cambridge: Cambridge University Press.

———. 1974. "Neutrality in Political Science." In W. Connolly and G. Gordon, eds., *Social Structure and Political Theory*. Lexington, Mass.: D.C. Heath.

Thompson, J. B., and D. Held, eds. 1982. *Habermas: Critical Debates*. Cambridge, Mass.: MIT Press.

Tormey, J. 1976. "Exploitation, Oppression and Self-sacrifice." In C. Gould and M. Wartofsky, eds., *Women and Philosophy*. New York: Capricorn.

Tracy, D. 1981. "Theologies of Praxis." In M. L. Lamb, ed., *Creativity and Method: Essays in Honor of Bernard Lonergan*. Milwaukee, Wisc.: Marquette University Press.

Tronto, J. 1985. "Women's Morality: Beyond Gender Differences to a Theory of Care." Unpublished manuscript. New York: Hunter College.

Tucker, R. C., ed. 1978. *The Marx-Engels Reader*. New York: W. W. Norton.

Valenzuela, J. S. and A. Valenzuela. 1978. "Modernization and Dependency." *Comparative Politics* 10(4):535–57.

Valle, L. G. del. 1979. "Toward a Theological Outlook Starting from Concrete Events." In R. Gibellini, ed., *Frontiers of Theology in Latin America*. Maryknoll, N.Y.: Orbis.

Veliz, C. 1980. *The Centralist Tradition of Latin America*. Princeton, N.J.: Princeton University Press.

Vidales, R. 1979. "Methodological Issues in Liberation Theology." In R. Gibellini, ed., *Frontiers of Theology in Latin America*. Maryknoll, N.Y.: Orbis.

von Wright, G. H. 1971. *Explanation and Understanding*. Ithaca, N.Y.: Cornell University Press.

Walker, J. 1981. "The End of Dialogue: Paulo Freire on Politics and Education." In R. Mackie, ed., *Literacy and Revolution*. New York: Continuum.

Walzer, M. 1983. "The Politics of Michel Foucault." *Dissent* (Fall):481–90.

Waxman, C. L., ed. 1969. *The End of Ideology Debate*. New York: Simon and Schuster.

Weber, M. 1949. *The Methodology of the Social Sciences*. E. Shils, ed. New York: Free Press. The three essays in this collection were originally published in 1904 and 1905, *Archiv für Sozialwissenschaft und Sozialpolitik*, and 1913, *Logos*.

Weffort, F. 1989. "Why Democracy?" In A. Stepan, ed., *Democratizing Brazil: Problems of Transition and Consolidation*. Oxford: Oxford University Press.

Weiner, M. 1966. *Modernization: The Dynamics of Growth*. New York: Basic Books.

Wellmer, A. 1971. *The Critical Theory of Society*. New York: Seabury.

Werker, S. 1985. "Beyond the Dependency Paradigm." *Journal of Contemporary Asia* 15(1):79–95.

Westkott, M. 1979. "Feminist Criticism of the Social Sciences." *Harvard Educational Review* 49(4):422–30.

Whitbeck, C. 1983. "A Different Reality: Feminist Ontology." In C. Gould, ed., *Beyond Domination*. Totowa, N.J.: Rowman and Allenheld.

———. 1976. "Theories of Sex Difference." In C. Gould and M. Wartofsky, eds., *Women and Philosophy*. New York: Capricorn.

White, H. 1973. "Foucault Decoded: Notes from Underground." *History and Theory* 1:23–54.

White, S. 1986. "Foucault's Challenge to Critical Theory." *American Political Science Review* 80(2):419–32.

Wolff, R. P. 1973. *The Autonomy of Reason*. New York: Harper and Row.

Wolin, S. 1983. "On Reading Marx Politically." *Nomos* 26:79–112.

Yeatman, A. 1984. "Introduction: Gender and Social Life." *Social Analysis* 15:3–10.

Young, I. 1986. "Impartiality and the Civic Public: Some Implications of Feminist Critiques of Moral and Political Theory." *Praxis International* 5(4):381–401.

———. 1980. "Socialist Feminism and the Limits of Dual Systems Theory." *Socialist Review* 10(2/3):169–88.

Index